DATE DUE

Demco, Inc. 38-293

Dictionary of
Food Science and Nutrition

A & C Black • London

www.acblack.com

First published in Great Britain in 2006, reprinted 2010

A & C Black Publishers Ltd
36 Soho Square, London W1D 3QY

A CIP record for this book is available from the British Library

ISBN-10: 0 7136 7784 8
ISBN-13: 978 0 7136 7784 3

Text Production and Proofreading
Heather Bateman, Howard Sargeant, Katy McAdam

This book is produced using paper that is made from wood grown in managed,
sustainable forests. It is natural, renewable and recyclable. The logging and
manufacturing processes conform to the environmental regulations of the country
of origin.

Text typeset by A & C Black
Printed in Croatia by Zrinski d. d.

Preface

This dictionary provides a basic vocabulary of terms used in food science and nutrition. It is ideal for all students of food technology and related subjects, as well as those working for the first time in jobs such as catering, dietetics and public or environmental health.

Each headword is explained in clear, straightforward English. There are also supplements including nutrient RDAs and sources, a body mass index calculator, conversion tables for cooking and a guide to food hygiene procedure, as well as a list of key contacts in the fields of nutrition, health and food production.

Thanks are due to Emma Parker, Assoc. Nutr., for her valuable help and advice during the production of this book.

A

AA *abbreviation* **1.** Alcoholics Anonymous **2.** arachidonic acid

abattoir *noun* a place where animals are slaughtered for their meat

abdomen *noun* a space inside the body that contains the stomach, intestines, liver and other vital organs

abdominal cavity *noun* the space in the body below the chest

ABIM *abbreviation* Association of Bakery Ingredients Manufacturers

aboyeur *noun* same as **kitchen clerk**

abrosia *noun* abstinence from eating (*technical*)

absolute alcohol *noun* alcohol that contains no water

absorption *noun* the process of taking into the body substances such as proteins or fats that have been digested from food and enter the bloodstream from the stomach and intestines

absorption method *noun* a method of cooking rice in which it is removed from the heat after a while and allowed to soak up any remaining water (NOTE: Rice cooked in this way is also known as steamed rice.)

abstemious *adjective* tending not to eat or drink very much

ABV *abbreviation* alcohol by volume

a.c. *abbreviation* ante cibos

acacia gum *noun* same as **gum arabic**

açaí *noun* a berry with very high concentrations of essential fatty acids and anthocyanins, considered a superfood

acarbose *noun* a drug used for treating type 2 diabetes

accelase *noun* a mixture of enzymes used for maturing cheese

accelerated freeze-drying *noun* a method of preserving food by heating it for a short time, then freezing it rapidly and drying it in a vacuum. Abbreviation **AFD**

Acceptable Daily Intake *noun* the amount of an additive that can be eaten without risk. Abbreviation **ADI**

accompaniment *noun* a small helping of food served with a dish, e.g. croutons served with fish soup or grated Parmesan cheese served with minestrone

ACE *abbreviation* angiotensin-converting enzyme

ACE inhibitor *noun* same as **angiotensin-converting enzyme inhibitor**

acesulphame K *noun* a type of sweetener

acetate *noun* a salt or ester of acetic acid

acetic acid *noun* an acid that turns wine into vinegar (NOTE: Acetic acid is also used as a preservative in food such as pickles.)

acetoacetate *noun* a ketone substance secreted by the liver which indicates a failure of metabolism

acetoglyceride *noun* a fat with a relatively low melting point, used for compounding shortening

acetoin *noun* a compound in butter

acetone *noun* a colourless volatile substance formed in the body after vomiting or during diabetes. ◊ **ketone**

acetonuria *noun* excessive excretion of acetone in the urine, an indicator of diabetic acidosis

acetylcholine *noun* a substance that is released from the ends of some nerve fibres to transmit impulses to other nerve cells or to muscles

acetylcholinesterase *noun* an enzyme, present in blood and some nerve endings, that aids the breakdown of acetylcholine and suppresses its stimulatory effect on nerves

acetyl CoA *abbreviation* acetyl coenzyme A

acetyl coenzyme A *noun* a coenzyme produced during the metabolism of carbohydrates, fatty acids, and amino acids. Abbreviation **acetyl CoA**

ACFM *abbreviation* Association of Cereal Food Manufacturers

achalasia *noun* difficulty in swallowing

achlorhydria *noun* an acid deficiency in the digestive system

acholia *noun* a bile deficiency in the digestive system

acid *noun* a chemical substance that is able to dissolve metals

acidaminuria *noun* an excessive excretion of amino acids in urine

acid brilliant green BS *noun* ♦ **E142**

acid calcium phosphate *noun* the acid ingredient in some types of baking powder

acid food *noun* any food that leaves an acid residue after being metabolised. Compare **basic food**

acidic *adjective* referring to acids

acidic salts corrosion *noun* the rusting of a can

acidification *noun* the process of adding an acid to a food in order to preserve it (NOTE: The usual acids are acetic, citric and lactic, although benzoic acid is sometimes used.)

acidify *verb* to make a substance more acid, or to become more acid

acidimeter *noun* a device for measuring the acidity of a liquid

acidity *noun* the concentration of acid in a substance, of which pH is a measure

acidity regulator *noun* an additive used for controlling the pH of food

acidogenic *adjective* producing acids, or promoting the production of acids

acidophilus milk *noun* a cultured milk made from fresh milk that is allowed to go sour in a controlled way, of which yoghurt is a type

acidosis *noun* **1.** a medical condition in which there are more acid waste products than usual in the blood because of a lack of alkali **2.** same as **acidity**

acid protease *noun* a protein-digesting enzyme activated in stomach acid

acid reflux *noun* the regurgitation of gastric juices into the oesophagus, where the acid causes irritation and the burning sensation commonly referred to as heartburn

acid salt *noun* a chemical salt in which some of the acidic hydrogen atoms of the original acid have been replaced

acid-sensitive *adjective* used for describing bacteria that are made inactive by acidic conditions

acidulant *noun* an additive such as phosphoric acid which is added to food to lower its pH

acidulate *verb* to make a substance slightly acid, or to become slightly acid

ACMSF *abbreviation* Advisory Committee on Microbiological Safety of Food

acne *noun* an inflammation of the sebaceous glands during puberty which makes black-heads appear on the skin, which often then become infected and produce red raised spots

ACNFP *abbreviation* Advisory Committee on Novel Foods and Processes

acrid *adjective* having a strong bitter smell or taste

acrodermatitis enteropathica *noun* zinc deficiency

acrolein *noun* the acrid-smelling chemical produced by overheated fat, which causes eye and throat irritation

acrylamide *noun* a chemical found in baked and fried foods, thought to increase the risk of cancer in humans

activated dough development *noun* a method of speeding up the first rising of dough by adding small quantities of other substances, e.g. ascorbic acid or cysteine (NOTE: These substances modify the properties of the gluten in the dough.)

activator *noun* any compound that stimulates enzymes

active oxygen method *noun* a method of measuring the susceptibility of fats to damage by oxidation

active packaging *noun* food packaging that interacts chemically or biologically with its contents to extend shelf-life or to modify the product during storage

active site *noun* the region of an enzyme molecule where a substance (**substrate**) is bound and acted upon by the enzyme

active transport *noun* a transfer of substances across a cell membrane for which energy is required

activity level *noun* a measurement of the number and function of enzymes in the digestive tract

acute *adjective* used for describing pain that is sharp and intense

acute benign hydrocephalus *noun* a short-lived reaction to a large overdose of vitamins A and D in small infants, causing extreme bulging of the fontanelle

acute cholecystitis *noun* inflammation of the gallbladder caused by a gallstone blocking the biliary duct

acute intermittent porphyria *noun* a type of porphyria that causes abdominal pain and nausea, treated with a high-glucose diet. Abbreviation **AIP**

acute toxicity *noun* a concentration of a toxic substance that is high enough to make people seriously ill

ADA *abbreviation* adenosine deaminase

ADA deficiency *noun* a genetic disease resulting from the deficiency of the metabolic enzyme adenosine deaminase, causing increased susceptibility to lymphomas and chronic infections

adaptation *noun* the process by which the senses become less sensitive to particular odours or flavours with repeated contact, which accounts for the tolerance of high levels of spices in some cultures

adaptogen *noun* a set of active ingredients in homeopathic remedies

ADD *abbreviation* attention deficit disorder

added water *noun* extra moisture added to a food product such as ham to increase its weight and bulk

addict *noun* a person who is addicted to a harmful drug

addiction *noun* a state of physiological or psychological dependence on a potentially harmful drug

additive *noun* a chemical substance that is added to food to improve its appearance, smell or taste, or to prevent it from going bad

adenine *noun* one of the four basic components of DNA

adenosine *noun* a compound, consisting of the base adenine and the sugar ribose, found in DNA, RNA and energy-carrying molecules such as ATP

adenosine deaminase *noun* an enzyme involved in the breakdown of adenosine in the body. Abbreviation **ADA**

adenosine triphosphatase *noun* full form of **ATPase**

adenosine triphosphate *noun* a chemical that occurs in all cells, but mainly in muscle, where it forms the energy reserve. Abbreviation **ATP**

adenylate cyclase *noun* an enzyme involved in the formation of cAMP from ATP

adephagy *noun* excessive eating (*technical*)

ADHD *abbreviation* attention deficit hyperactivity disorder

ADI *abbreviation* Acceptable Daily Intake

adipectomy *noun* a surgical operation to remove subcutaneous fat

adipolysis *noun* hydrolysis of fats during digestion by the action of enzymes

adiponectin *noun* a hormone that affects energy homeostasis

adipose *noun* fatty

adipose tissue *noun* tissue in which the cells contain fat

adipsia *noun* the absence of thirst (*technical*)

adoucir *verb* to make food less strong or salty

adrenal glands *plural noun* two endocrine glands at the top of the kidneys which secrete cortisone, adrenaline and other hormones

adrenaline *noun* a hormone secreted by the medulla of the adrenal glands that has an effect similar to the stimulation of the sympathetic nervous system. Also called **epinephrine**

adrenocortical *adjective* relating to the cortex of the adrenal glands

adulterant *noun* a cheaper substance added to food in order to increase its weight without changing its appearance (NOTE: Some are added legally, as is water in chicken.)

adulterate *verb* to make something less pure by adding inferior or unsuitable substances to it

adulterated *adjective* made less pure by the addition of inferior or unsuitable substances

adulteration *noun* the act of making something less pure by adding an inferior or unsuitable substance

Advisory Committee on Microbiological Safety of Food *noun* a statutory committee that provides advice to the government on matters of food safety. Abbreviation **ACMSF**

Advisory Committee on Novel Foods and Processes *noun* an independent body that advises the Food Standards Agency on matters relating to new foodstuffs and processes. Abbreviation **ACNFP**

adzuki bean, azuki bean *noun* a small, slightly sweet, reddish-brown bean from Japan and China, used as a pulse or ground into flour (NOTE: Its botanical name is *Phaseolus angularis*.)

-aemia *suffix* blood

aerate *verb* to allow air to enter a substance, especially soil or water

aerated bread *noun* bread made from dough that has been mechanically mixed with carbon dioxide without using yeast

aerating agent *noun* a substance that allows small bubbles of gas to be dispersed evenly in a liquid or solid foodstuff

aeration *noun* the process of adding air or oxygen to a liquid

aerobacter *noun* a genus of bacteria normally found in the intestine

aerobe *noun* a living thing, particularly a microorganism, that needs oxygen for metabolism. Compare **anaerobe**

aerobic *adjective* involving or requiring oxygen

aerobic exercise *noun* exercise such as walking, jogging, cycling and swimming that increase respiration and heart rates

aerobic metabolism *noun* the breakdown of carbon and fats into energy using oxygen

aerobic respiration *noun* the process in which oxygen that is breathed in is used to conserve energy as ATP

aerogastria *noun* a medical condition in which the stomach is distended by gas

Aeromonas *noun* a microorganism that causes food poisoning

aerophagy *noun* the swallowing of air while eating (*technical*)

aerosol *noun* a canister that contains liquid under pressure, usually one that releases the liquid as a fine spray

aetiology *noun* the causes of a disease

AFD *abbreviation* accelerated freeze-drying

affinage *noun* the process of ripening cheese

aflatoxin *noun* a toxin produced by a species of the fungus *Aspergillus*, especially *Aspergillus flavus*, which grows on seeds and nuts and affects stored grain

aftertaste *noun* a taste left in the mouth by food or drink after it has been swallowed

agar-agar *noun* a natural gelling agent made from seaweed, sometimes used instead of gelatine. Also called **seaweed gelatine** (NOTE: As it is plant-based, it is suitable for vegetarians.)

agastric *adjective* used for describing an animal that has no alimentary canal

age *verb* to store food or a wine for a period of time to enable it to develop a desired flavour or become more tender

aged *adjective* allowed to mature to develop flavour

ageing *noun* the process of improving a food by leaving it to age, as when game is hung, or by artificially ageing it using chemicals, as when oxidising agents are added to flour

ageusia *noun* loss of the sense of taste (*technical*)

agglomerate *verb* to treat something such as flour so that it forms larger, more dispersible particles

agglomerated flour *noun* flour in the form of large dispersible particles, easily wetted and dust-free

agitate *verb* to cause something to move vigorously or violently, e.g. by shaking or stirring it

Agricultural Industries Confederation *noun* a trade association for suppliers of feed, fertilisers, seeds and grain to the agricultural sector. Abbreviation **AIC**

agriculture *noun* the cultivation of land, including horticulture, fruit growing, crop and seed growing, dairy farming and livestock breeding

agri-food *adjective* used for describing industries that are involved in the mass-production, processing and inspection of food made from agricultural products

agrochemical *noun* any chemical used in farming, e.g. a fertiliser or pesticide

agroecology *noun* the study of the relationship between food production and the environment

agroindustry *noun* any industry dealing with the supply, processing and distribution of farm products

agronomy *noun* the scientific study of the cultivation of crops

agrophilous *adjective* used for describing pests, mould and bacteria that affect crops

AHP *abbreviation* Alliance for Health Professionals

AIC *abbreviation* Agricultural Industries Confederation

aioli *noun* mayonnaise flavoured with garlic, used especially to garnish fish and vegetables

AIP *abbreviation* acute intermittent porphyria

air-chilled *adjective* cooled using a blast chiller

air-conditioning *noun* a system for cooling and controlling the humidity and purity of the air circulating in a space

air-dry *verb* to remove moisture from something by placing it in a current of air

air entrainment *noun* the generation of small air bubbles to make food light, as by the action of yeast in bread

airtight *adjective* not allowing air to get in or out

ALA *abbreviation* alpha-lipoic acid

à la carte *adjective* used for describing a meal in which dishes are ordered separately from a menu

alactasia *noun* a deficiency of lactase in the small intestine

à la mode *adjective* served with ice cream

alanine *noun* an amino acid

albinuria *noun* a condition in which the urine is pale or white

albumen *noun* the white of an egg, containing albumin

albumen index *noun* a measure of egg quality which compares the ratio of the height of a mass of egg white to its diameter as it sits on a flat surface, with a higher index indicating higher quality

albumin *noun* a common water-soluble protein coagulated by heat, found in egg white, blood plasma and milk. ◊ **ovalbumin**

albumin index *noun* a measure of the freshness of an egg

alcohol *noun* **1.** a pure colourless liquid that is formed by the action of yeast on sugar solutions and forms the intoxicating part of drinks such as wine and whisky. Symbol C_2H_5OH **2.** any drink made from fermented or distilled liquid

alcoholaemia *noun* the presence of ethanol in the blood

alcohol by volume *noun* the amount of alcohol in a drink, shown on the label. Abbreviation **ABV**

alcohol content *noun* the presence or concentration of pure ethanol in an alcoholic liquid

alcohol dehydrogenase *noun* an enzyme found in the liver and stomach that promotes the conversion of alcohols to aldehydes

alcoholic *adjective* containing alcohol ∎ *noun* a person who is addicted to drinking alcohol and shows changes in behaviour and personality as a result of this addiction

Alcoholics Anonymous *noun* an organisation of former alcoholics that helps people to overcome their dependence on alcohol by encouraging them to talk about their problems in group therapy. Abbreviation **AA**

alcohol intake *noun* the amount of alcohol consumed by a person during a given period such as a week

alcoholise *verb* to infuse something such as fruit with alcohol

alcoholism *noun* the excessive drinking of alcohol to an addictive degree

alcohol unit *noun* a measure of alcohol consumption, consisting of 10ml or 8g of absolute alcohol

alcoholuria *noun* the presence of alcohol in the urine

alcopop *noun* a drink, manufactured and sold commercially, that is a mixture of alcohol and a soft drink such as lemonade

aldehyde *noun* one of the main groups of organic compound hydrocarbons

al dente *adjective* used for describing pasta that is still firm when bitten, said to be perfectly cooked

aldolase *noun* an enzyme that aids the breakdown of fructose

aldosterone *noun* a hormone, secreted by the adrenal gland, that regulates the balance of sodium and potassium in the body and the amount of body fluid

ale *noun* a bitter beer brewed using barley and usually hops, especially one brewed and stored using traditional methods

aleurone layer *noun* a layer of cells under the bran coat on cereal grains

alfacalcidol *noun* a substance related to vitamin D, used by the body to maintain the right levels of calcium and phosphate, and also as a drug to help people who do not have enough vitamin D

algae *plural noun* tiny plants that live in water or in moist conditions, contain chlorophyll and have no stems, roots or leaves

algal bloom *noun* a rapid increase in the population of algae in an area of water

algin *noun* a compound extracted from algae, used for bulking out ice cream and puddings

alginate *noun* a salt of alginic acid

alginic acid *noun* an insoluble powdery acid obtained from brown seaweed and used as a thickener in foods

alible *adjective* nourishing or providing nutrients

alimentary *adjective* providing food, or relating to food or nutrition

alimentary canal *noun* a tube in the body going from the mouth to the anus and including the throat, stomach and intestines, through which food passes and is digested

alimentary system *noun* same as **digestive system**

alimentation *noun* the act of taking in food (*technical*)

alipogenic *adjective* not forming fat

alkali *noun* a substance that neutralises acids and forms salts

alkaline phosphatase *noun* an enzyme that controls hydrolysis, used in the clinical diagnosis of many illnesses

alkaline tide *noun* an increase in blood pH caused by the secretion of gastric acid

alkalinity *noun* the concentration of alkali in a solution, measured in terms of pH

alkaloid *noun* a naturally occurring alkali in food, especially one that has an effect on the consumer

allantoin *noun* the oxidation of uric acid

allergen *noun* a compound that reacts with the proteins of the skin and mucous membranes of some people to cause rashes, irritation, asthma and other unpleasant symptoms (NOTE: Typical food allergies occur with strawberries, eggs, milk, cereal, fish, peas and nuts.)

allergenic *adjective* producing or triggering an allergy

allergenic potential *noun* an assessment of the potential of a GM food to produce an allergic reaction

allergy *noun* a sensitivity to particular substances that causes an unpleasant physical reaction

Alliance for Health Professionals *noun* a trade union federation with members that include the British Dietetic Association. Abbreviation **AHP**

allicin *noun* the chemical compound in garlic that gives it its characteristic smell and taste

Allium *noun* the Latin name for a family of plants including the onion, leek, garlic and chives

allogotrophia *noun* growth in one organ that occurs when nutrients from another organ leach into it

allosteric *adjective* used for describing a binding site on an enzyme at which interaction induces altered activity at another site

allotriogeusia *noun* a distorted sense of taste

allotriophagy *noun* a desire for unusual foods

allspice *noun* the ground dried berries of a tropical evergreen tree, used as a spice

almond *noun* a sweet nut from the almond tree

almond essence *noun* an alcoholic extract of fermented bitter almonds, used for giving an almond flavour to cakes and other foods (NOTE: Some almond essences are made from apricot kernels.)

almond flavouring *noun* a synthetic chemical product with an almond flavour and smell, much cheaper than almond essence and commonly used as a substitute

almond oil *noun* a delicate oil derived from bitter almonds, used in confectionery and for oiling dessert moulds

almond paste *noun* same as **marzipan**

aloe vera, aloe *noun* a soothing, moisturising extract made from the leaves of a species of aloe plant, used in drugs and cosmetics

alpha amylase *noun* an enzyme present in wheat seed, which changes some starch to sugar. Excessive amounts can result in loaves of bread with sticky texture.

alphafoetoprotein *noun* a blood protein produced in the liver, yolk sac and gastrointestinal tract of a foetus, used as an indicator of cancer and other diseases in adults

alpha-linolenic acid *noun* a fatty acid found in high proportion in walnut oil, soya oil and the leaf vegetable purslane (NOTE: It is said to be the reason why Cretans and Japanese have a low incidence of heart attacks.)

alpha-lipoic acid *noun* a sports supplement that maintains insulin sensitivity. Abbreviation **ALA**

alphatocopherol *noun* same as **vitamin E**

Alpine scurvy *noun* same as **pellagra**

aluminium *noun* a metallic element extracted from the ore bauxite. Symbol **Al**

aluminium calcium silicate *noun* ♦ **E556**

aluminium foil *noun* very thin, flexible aluminium used for wrapping for food and for cooking. Also called **cooking foil**, **tin foil**

aluminium sodium silicate *noun* ♦ **E554**

alveograph *noun* an instrument that uses a jet of air to measure the strength of dough prior to baking (NOTE: It works by injecting air into the dough at a fixed depth and flow rate and recording the pressure at which the resulting bubble bursts.)

Alzhelmer's disease *noun* a disease in which a person experiences progressive dementia owing to nerve cell loss in specific brain areas, resulting in loss of mental faculties including memory

amaranth *noun* **1.** a plant grown for ornament and sometimes as a grain crop or leafy vegetable **2.** ♦ **E123**

amaretti *plural noun* small crisp Italian biscuits flavoured with almonds

ambient temperature *noun* the temperature of the air in which you live or work

ambient yoghurt *noun* yoghurt that may be stored at room temperature, without chilling

American Association of Analytical Chemists *noun* an association for scientists who analyse the compositions of foodstuffs, beverages and drugs. Abbreviation **AOAC**

American service *noun* a method of serving food in a restaurant by dividing it among individual plates in the kitchen rather than serving it from a platter at the table

American Society for Nutrition *noun* a professional research body that publishes a monthly journal on nutrition. Abbreviation **ASN**

Ames test *noun* a test of the capacity of a food additive to cause genetic mutation

amine *noun* any organic derivative of ammonia in which one or more hydrogen atoms is replaced with an alkyl group

amino acid *noun* a chemical compound that is broken down from proteins in the digestive system and then used by the body to form its own protein. ◊ **essential amino acids**

aminoaciduria *noun* the presence of abnormal levels of an amino acid in the urine

aminogram *noun* a diagram of the composition of an amino acid

amino group *noun* a group of substances that consists of amino acids and amines

aminopeptidase *noun* an enzyme that removes amino acids from a peptide or protein

ammonia *noun* a strong-smelling gas that is a compound of nitrogen and hydrogen and is used to make artificial fertilisers, or in liquid form as a refrigerant. Symbol NH_3

ammonium alginate *noun* a food additive used as an emulsifier, thickener and stabiliser

ammonium bicarbonate *noun* a raising agent

ammonium chloride *noun* a white crystalline material used in cough medicines

ammonium ferric citrate *noun* ♦ E381

ammonium hydroxide *noun* a solution of ammonia in water

ammonium phosphatide *noun* a food additive used as an emulsifier and stabiliser for cocoa and chocolate products

ammonium polyphosphate *noun* ♦ E545

amoeba *noun* an organism that consists of a single cell (NOTE: The plural form is **amoebae**.)

amoebiasis *noun* an infection caused by an amoeba, which, in the large intestine, can cause dysentery

amphetamine *noun* a drug that stimulates the central nervous system, formerly used to treat depression and as an appetite suppressant

amuse-bouche, amuse-gueule *noun* a small appetiser served before a meal or while the customer is looking at the menu

amydated pectin *noun* a synthetic derivative of pectin that is more stable than the parent product. Also called **E440**

amylaemia *noun* an excess of starch in the blood

amylase *noun* an enzyme that converts starch into maltose

amylodyspepsia *noun* the inability to digest starch

amyloid *noun* a non-nitrogenous food consisting mostly of starch

amyloidosis *noun* any disease in which amyloid plaque is deposited in an organ or in tissue

amyloid plaque *noun* a build-up of amyloids in bodily tissues, causing organ failure

amylolysis *noun* the conversion of starch into sugars by the action of enzymes

amylopectin *noun* a polysaccharide substance that is an insoluble component of starch

amylopeptic *adjective* used for describing enzymes that are capable of making starch soluble

amylophagia *noun* a morbid desire to eat starch

amylopsin *noun* an enzyme that converts starch into maltose

amylose *noun* a carbohydrate of starch

amyxorrhoea *noun* the presence of undigested starch in stools, indicating amylase deficiency

anabolic *adjective* building up muscle or tissue

anabolism *noun* the part of metabolism that builds up muscle or tissue

anacidity *noun* the abnormal lack of hydrochloric acid in gastric juices

anaemia *noun* a medical condition in which an unusually low level of red blood cells or haemoglobin makes it more difficult for the blood to carry oxygen, producing symptoms of tiredness and paleness of lips, nails and the inside of the eyelids

anaemic *adjective* having anaemia

anaemotrophy *noun* insufficient nourishment of the blood

anaerobe *noun* a microorganism that lives without oxygen, e.g. the tetanus bacillus

anaerobic *adjective* able to function without oxygen

anaerobic exercise *noun* exercise that involves the exchange of energy in the muscles without the use of oxygen

anaerobic metabolism *noun* the breakdown of carbon and fats into energy without the presence of oxygen

anaphylactic *adjective* relating to or caused by extreme sensitivity to a substance

anaphylactic shock *noun* a sudden severe, sometimes fatal reaction to something such as an ingested substance or a bee sting

anaphylaxis *noun* **1.** extreme sensitivity to a substance introduced into the body **2.** same as **anaphylactic shock**

anchovy *noun* a small fish with a strong, salty taste, used, e.g., on pizzas and in salade niçoise

anchovy essence *noun* a liquid extract of cured and salted anchovies used as a flavouring

ancylostomiasis *noun* a disease caused by a hookworm, with symptoms of weakness and anaemia. Also called **hookworm disease**

andrographis *noun* a herbal remedy said to boost the body's immune system

androstenedione *noun* a dietary supplement that increases testosterone production, energy, strength and muscle development (NOTE: Unwanted side effects include disruption of hormonal balance, leading to aggressive behaviour, mood swings and hair loss.)

anencephaly *noun* a severe birth defect that can be prevented by the mother taking folic acid before and during pregnancy

angel hair *noun* pasta in the form of long, very fine strands

angelica *noun* a plant with dark green stems that are crystallised with sugar and used in confectionery

angina *noun* a medical condition in which lack of blood to the heart causes severe chest pains

angiotensin *noun* a hormone that causes blood pressure to rise, formed in the blood by a series of processes that can be influenced by drugs

angiotensin-converting enzyme *noun* same as **ACE**

angiotensin-converting enzyme inhibitor *noun* a drug that counters the effect of an enzyme that causes high blood pressure

Angostura bitters a trade name for a bitter-tasting flavouring for alcoholic drinks, made from herbs and spices

angular stomatitis *noun* inflammation at the corners of the mouth caused by vitamin B2 deficiency

animal fat *noun* fat rendered from animal sources, e.g. lard and ghee

animal heat *noun* same as **diet-induced thermogenesis**

animal nutrition *noun* the study of how to feed animals for maximum productivity

animal product *noun* any foodstuff or non-food product that comes from an animal, e.g. meat, eggs, leather and wool

animal testing *noun* the development of a drug or cosmetic product using animals as early testers, to determine the possible effects on humans

animal welfare *noun* the idea that animals raised on farms should be treated humanely and protected from unnecessary pain or distress

anisakiasis *noun* same as **herringworm disease**

anise *noun* a herb that produces a small aromatic fruit called aniseed that is used for flavouring

aniseed *noun* the seed of the anise plant

ankylostomiasis *noun* infection of the intestines by hookworms

annatto *noun* a yellowish-red dye made from the pulp around the seeds of a tropical tree, used as a food colouring

anorectic *adjective* suppressing the appetite

anorexia athletica *noun* compulsive overexercising, often a feature of eating disorders other than anorexia nervosa

anorexia nervosa *noun* a psychological condition, usually found in girls and young women, in which a person refuses to eat because of a fear of becoming fat

anorexigenic *adjective* same as **anorectic**

anosmia *noun* loss of the sense of smell

anoxia *noun* a complete absence of oxygen from the blood and bodily tissues

antacid *adjective* controlling the amount of acid that forms in the stomach and therefore preventing or easing heartburn ■ *noun* an antacid substance

ante cibos *adverb* marked on a prescription medicine to show that it should be taken before food. Abbreviation **a.c.**

antemetic *adjective* used for describing a medicine that relieves nausea

anthelmintic *noun* a substance that removes worms from the intestine ■ *adjective* removing worms from the intestine

anthocyanin *noun* a water-soluble plant pigment responsible for blue, violet and red colours

anthropometry *noun* the gathering of physical data from people for the purposes of statistical analysis

anti-adhesion *adjective* preventing bacteria from adhering to the walls of the digestive tract and developing further

antibacterial *adjective* destroying bacteria

antibiotic *adjective* stopping the spread of bacteria ■ *noun* a drug such as penicillin that is developed from living substances and stops the spread of microorganisms

antibiotic resistance *noun* the ability of a strain of bacteria over time to develop a resistance to the usual treatments

antibody *noun* a protein that is stimulated by the body to produce foreign substances such as bacteria, as part of an immune reaction

anticaking additive *noun* an additive that prevents food from becoming solid

anticholinesterase *noun* a substance that blocks nerve impulses by reducing the activity of the enzyme cholinesterase

anticoagulant *noun* a natural or synthetic agent that prevents the formation of blood clots

antidiarrhoeal *noun* a drug that treats diarrhoea

antidiuretic *noun* a drug that stops urine being formed

antiemetic *noun* a medicine that relieves feelings of nausea

antifoaming agent *noun* a substance that prevents excessive foaming in a food product

antigen *noun* a substance that stimulates the production of antibodies, e.g. a protein on the surface of a cell or microorganism

antihistamine *noun* a drug used to control the effects of an allergy that releases histamine

antimetabolite *noun* a compound that affects normal metabolism

antimicrobial *adjective* preventing the growth of microbes for hygienic purposes

antimotility agent *noun* a drug that relieves diarrhoea

antimycotic *noun* a substance that inhibits the growth of mould

antiobesic *noun* a drug that reduces or prevents obesity

antioxidant *noun* a substance that makes oxygen less damaging, e.g. in the body or in foods or plastics

antipasto *noun* a food served at the beginning of an Italian meal or as a snack

antiperistalsis *noun* a movement in the oesophagus or intestine that leads to vomiting

antisialagogue *noun* a drug that reduces the flow of saliva

antispattering agent *noun* an additive that stops oils from spattering when heated

antistaling agent *noun* a substance that makes bread and cakes stay fresh for longer

antivitamin *noun* a substance that interferes with the normal action of a vitamin

anuria *noun* a failure to produce urine

anus *noun* a short passage after the rectum at the end of the alimentary canal, leading outside the body between the buttocks and through which faeces are passed

AOAC *abbreviation* American Association of Analytical Chemists

AOC *abbreviation* Appellation d'Origine Controlée

aorta *noun* the main artery in the body, which sends blood containing oxygen from the heart to other blood vessels around the body

apastia *noun* a refusal to take food

aperient *noun* a laxative (*technical*)

aperitif *noun* an alcoholic beverage drunk before a meal

aphagia *noun* the refusal to eat or swallow

aphagosis *noun* an inability to eat

APM *abbreviation* aspartame

apoenzyme *noun* the protein part of an enzyme that only becomes catalytically active after it combines with a non-protein-supporting molecule (**coenzyme**)

apoprotein *noun* the protein part of a protein molecule that also contains a non-protein component

aposia *noun* same as **adipsia**

apositia *noun* aversion to food

Appellation d'Origine Controlée *noun* a certification for French wine that guarantees its origin and verifies that it meets production regulations in that region. Abbreviation **AOC**

appendix *noun* a small tube attached to the caecum that serves no function but can become infected, causing the dangerous condition appendicitis

appertisation *noun* the process of making food sterile

appertise *verb* to heat a substance to a high temperature, either by retorting or using the high temperature short time method of processing

appetiser, appetizer *noun* a snack taken with drinks before a meal

appetising *adjective* looking, smelling or tasting good

appetite suppressant *noun* a drug such as amphetamine that makes the user feel less hungry

apple *noun* the common hard, edible fruit of the apple tree *Malus domestica*

apple corer *noun* a tube-shaped implement used for removing the core from apples

apricot *noun* the small yellow fruit from the deciduous tree *Prunus armeniaca*, similar to a small peach, but not as juicy

apyrase *noun* an enzyme that aids the breakdown of ATP, producing energy

aquaculture *noun* the farming of sea and freshwater plants and animals for human consumption

arachidonic acid *noun* an essential fatty acid. Abbreviation **AA**

arborio *noun* a short-grained rice used for making risotto and other Italian dishes

arginase *noun* a liver enzyme involved in the production of urea

argininaemia *noun* a genetic disease that affects the body's metabolisation of arginine

arginine *noun* an amino acid that helps the liver form urea

argininosuccinic aciduria *noun* a genetic disease that affects the formation of urea

ariboflavinosis *noun* a deficiency of vitamin B2

Armagnac *noun* a brandy made in southwestern France

aroma *noun* the pleasant smell of something you can eat or drink

aroma chemical *noun* a chemical that can be either naturally or artificially manufactured, detected by the nose as an odour

aromatic *adjective* having a strong pleasant smell ■ *noun* a substance, plant or chemical that has a pleasant smell

aromatic hydrocarbon *noun* a compound such as benzene, with a ring of carbon atoms held by single and double bonds

aromatise *verb* to use herbs and spices to add flavours and aromas to a liquid (NOTE: For water-based liquids, the herbs or spices are boiled in it, whereas for oil-based liquids they are fried.)

arrhythmia *noun* a variation in the rhythm of the heartbeat

arrowroot *noun* a thickening agent in the form of a white powder made from the root of a West Indian plant

arteriosclerosis *noun* a medical condition in which calcium deposits in the arteries cause them to harden

artery *noun* a blood vessel that takes blood from the heart to the tissues of the body

arthritis *noun* a painful inflammation of a joint. ◊ **osteoarthritis, rheumatoid arthritis, reactive arthritis**

artichoke *noun* any of three types of vegetable, the **globe artichoke** with a thistle-like head and edible fleshy leaves, the **Jerusalem artichoke** with edible tubers and the Chinese artichoke with edible tubers

artichoke heart *noun* a young globe artichoke eaten as a vegetable

artificial additive *noun* a substance added to food to improve its appearance, flavour, texture or shelf-life

artificial colour *noun* a colorant substance added to food to improve its appearance

artificial flavour *noun* a substance added to food to improve its flavour

artificial sweetener *noun* a synthetic substance used in place of sugar to sweeten food

artisanal food *noun* any food that has been made individually by hand

asafoetida *noun* a powdered resin from an Asian plant, used sparingly in Indian cookery to give a truffle-like flavour and improve digestion. Also called **hing** (NOTE: The resin is obtained from the root or stem latex of the plants *Ferula asafoetida* and *Ferula narthex*, found in Afghanistan and Iran.)

ascariasis *noun* a disease of the intestine and sometimes the lungs, caused by infestation with *Ascaris lumbricoides*

ascorbate *noun* a salt or ester of L-ascorbic acid used as an antioxidant

ascorbic acid *noun* vitamin C, found in fresh fruit

ascorbin stearite *noun* a form of vitamin C used as an antioxidant

-ase *suffix* enzyme

asepsis *noun* the process or methods of bringing about a condition in which no disease-causing microorganisms are present

aseptic *adjective* sterilised, or involving sterilisation, and therefore without infection

aseptic canning *noun* the canning of food in a sterile environment in which all containers have been separately sterilised as well as the food

aseptic packaging *noun* methods of food packaging designed to kill off germs (NOTE: The two methods are packaging in unsterilised containers at 124°C, closing and leaving at temperature until all contaminants are inactivated, or packaging in sterilised containers inside an apparatus that is itself sterilised.)

ashwagandha *noun* a plant used in ayurvedic medicine and as a rennet substitute for cheese-making

asitia *noun* an extreme dislike of food

ASN *abbreviation* American Society for Nutrition

asparaginase *noun* an enzyme that catalyses the breakdown of asparagine

asparagine *noun* an amino acid

asparagus *noun* a cultivated plant the new shoots of which are eaten as a vegetable

aspartame *noun* a protein produced from aspartic acid, used for making substances sweeter. Abbreviation **APM**

aspartic acid *noun* an amino acid

Aspergillus *noun* a genus of moulds, one of which produces aflatoxins

aspic *noun* 1. jelly made from the cooked juices of meat, poultry or fish 2. a form of salad, with small pieces of cold meat, poultry, eggs or vegetables set in firm aspic jelly in a mould

aspiration *noun* the action of breathing food particles into the lungs when eating

assiette *noun* a plate of cold meats

assimilate *verb* to take into the body's tissues substances that have been absorbed into the blood from digested food

assimilation *noun* the action of assimilating food substances

Association of Bakery Ingredients Manufacturers *noun* a trade organisation representing manufacturers and suppliers of goods to the bakery industry. Abbreviation **ABIM**

Association of Cereal Food Manufacturers *noun* a trade organisation representing manufacturers and suppliers of breakfast cereals. Abbreviation **ACFM**

astaxanthin *noun* the pink colouring in a small shrimp-like creature that gives the pink colour to the flesh of salmon (NOTE: Now fed to farmed salmon, which are generally pinker than wild salmon.)

astragalus *noun* a plant extract said to boost the body's immune system

astringency *noun* the ability of some foods to make the mouth feel dry and tight

-ate *suffix* a chemical compound derived from a particular element or compound

atheroma *noun* a fatty deposit that causes atherosclerosis

atherosclerosis *noun* a condition in which deposits of fats and minerals form on the walls of an artery, especially the aorta or one of the coronary or cerebral arteries, and prevent blood from flowing easily

athrepsy *noun* malnourishment

Atkins diet *noun* a plan to help people lose weight that suggests that they should eat a lot of protein and fat but little carbohydrate

atmit *noun* an enriched porridge that is highly nutritious, distributed by humanitarian agencies during times of famine

atmospheric steamer *noun* a device used for cooking foods in steam at atmospheric pressure, making use of the fact that condensation of steam on the surface of the food or its container gives a very high rate of heat transfer

atom *noun* a fundamental unit of a chemical element and the smallest part of an element that can exist independently

atonic non-functioning colon *noun* a lack of muscle tone in the bowel leading to constipation and intestinal obstruction

ATP *abbreviation* adenosine triphosphate

ATPase *noun* an enzyme that aids the breakdown of ATP into ADP with a release of energy. Also called **adenosine triphosphatase**

atrophy *noun* the process of wasting away because of a lack of nutrients

attention deficit disorder *noun* a condition in which a person is unable to concentrate, does things without considering their actions properly and has little confidence. It occurs mainly in children. Abbreviation **ADD**

attention deficit hyperactivity disorder *noun* a condition in which a child has an inability to concentrate and shows disruptive behaviour. Abbreviation **ADHD**

aubergine *noun* a shiny purple-black vegetable that is the fruit of plant *Solanum melongena*. Also called **eggplant**

audit *noun* an official investigation into whether procedures are being followed

audition *noun* in sensory analysis, the sense of sound

au gratin *adjective* ♦ gratin

AutismMedical *noun* a charitable body that researches links between diet and autism

autoclave *noun* a strong steel vessel in which pressure can be raised artificially, used for steam sterilisation and for creating chemical reactions at high temperature

autoimmune *adjective* used to describe an immune reaction in a person against antigens in his or her own cells

autolysate *noun* a product of the process autolysis, by which cells are broken down by enzymes produced in the cells themselves

autolysin *noun* an enzyme that causes autolysis

autolysis *noun* the partial digestion of food by enzymes already present in it, as occurs e.g. when meat is hung

automated *adjective* worked automatically by machines

automation *noun* the use of machinery to save manual labour

auxology *noun* the study of human physical growth and development

available nutrients *plural noun* nutrients in food that can be digested and absorbed in the body (NOTE: Some nutrients are unavailable when bound to another compound, but cooking often frees them.)

avena sativa *noun* a stimulant and nutritive supplement

avidin *noun* a protein found in egg white that makes the vitamin biotin inactive

avitaminosis *noun* vitamin deficiency

avocado *noun* a pear-shaped green fruit with a rather savoury flavour and pulpy yellowish-green flesh, often used in salads

axial load *noun* the amount of pressure that food packaging can withstand when stacked before it is crushed

azodicarbonamide *noun* ♦ E927

azo dye *noun* a substance extracted from coal tar and added to food to give it colour

azorubine *noun* ♦ E122

azyme *noun* bread that has not undergone fermentation

B

baby food *noun* food that has been prepared or manufactured in such a way that it can be fed to a baby

baby milk *noun* a preparation that imitates the composition of human breast milk and that may be used for feeding babies

bacalao *noun* dried cod, salt cod, cod or ling

Baccillus cereus *noun* a pathogen found in cress sprouts

Bacillus cereus *noun* a bacterium that grows on rice and can cause food poisoning (NOTE: It is usually found in temperate countries in the form of spores. Symptoms are nausea and vomiting and occasionally diarrhoea.)

Bacillus thuringiensis *noun* the bacteria used in thuricide

back bacon *noun* a cut of bacon that provides very lean rashers, from the back of the pig in front of the rear haunches

back fat *noun* hard fat from the back of the pig, usually used in high-quality sausages

bacon *noun* salt meat from a pig, sliced into thin strips and cooked before serving (NOTE: There is no plural form: *some bacon*; *a pound of bacon*; for a single piece say **a rasher**.)

baconer *noun* a pig reared to produce bacon

bacon rasher *noun* a thin slice of bacon cut at right angles to the backbone. Also called **rasher**

bacteria *plural noun* submicroscopic organisms that help in the decomposition of organic matter, some of which are permanently present in the intestines of animals and can break down food tissue, and some of which cause disease (NOTE: The singular form is **bacterium**.)

bacterial contamination *noun* the state of something such as water or food that has been contaminated by bacteria

bacterial count *noun* the number of bacteria per unit weight or volume of a foodstuff, sometimes used as an indicator of food quality

bacterial flora *plural noun* ♦ **intestinal flora**

bactericide *noun* a substance or agent that destroys bacteria

bacteriocin *noun* a substance produced by bacteria that is toxic to other bacteria, preventing them from growing

bacteriophage *noun* a virus that affects bacteria

bacteriostatic *adjective* causing bacteria to become inactive

bacteroid *noun* a rod-shaped or branched bacterium

bactometer *noun* a device for measuring bacteria levels in food

bad *adjective* deteriorated in quality to the point of being unfit to eat or drink

bad cholesterol *noun* cholesterol that is transported towards cells and tissue by low density lipoprotein (*informal*)

BADS *abbreviation* biologically active dietary supplement

bagel *noun* a ring-shaped bread roll with a slightly chewy texture

bagged salad *noun* pre-packaged salad in modified-atmosphere packaging

bagged snacks *plural noun* crisps and crisp-like products in foil packets

bagna cauda *noun* a warm sauce of olive oil, garlic and anchovies, served as a dip for raw vegetables

baguette *noun* a long loaf of French bread

bain-marie *noun* a pan holding hot water into which another vessel containing food to be cooked or heated is placed (NOTE: The plural form is **bains-marie**.)

bake *verb* to cook food, especially bread and cakes, in an oven

bake blind *verb* to bake pastry without the filling for a short time

baked beans *plural noun* haricot beans, cooked in a tomato sauce, traditionally baked in the oven with pieces of pork and molasses but now more generally available in tins

baked potato *noun* a potato baked in an oven without being peeled, then served cut open, with butter or various fillings, commonly cheese, chopped ham, baked beans and chilli. Also called **jacket potato**

baker *noun* a person whose job is to make bread and cakes

baker's yeast *noun* a strain of yeast used fresh in breadmaking (NOTE: It is a strain of the yeast *Saccharomyces cerevisiae.*)

bakery *noun* a shop or part of a shop where items of baked food, especially bread and cakes, are sold

bakeware *noun* trays and dishes used for baking food in the oven

baking *noun* a method of cooking by placing something such as a bread or cake mixture in an oven

baking apple *noun* same as **cooking apple**

baking chocolate *noun* same as **bitter chocolate**

baking parchment *noun* same as **silicone paper**

baking powder *noun* a mixture containing sodium bicarbonate, starch and acids that is used for making cakes rise when they are cooked

baking sheet *noun* a heavy steel sheet on which biscuits, rolls and similar foods can be baked in an oven. ◊ **baking tray**

baking soda *noun* sodium bicarbonate, especially when used as a raising agent in cookery

baking tray *noun* a flat metal tray used for baking food in an oven

balanced diet *noun* a diet that contains the right quantities of basic nutrients

Balance of Good Health *noun* a piechart representation of the proportions in which food groups should be consumed for health

balantidiasis *noun* a bacterial infection of the large intestine, causing diarrhoea and ulceration

Bali belly *noun* diarrhoea associated with travel in South East Asia or with eating South East Asian food (*informal*)

baller *noun* a kitchen implement used for cutting ball-shaped pieces from soft foods such as melons and cucumbers, consisting of half a hollow sphere with sharp edges on the end of a handle

balloon whisk *noun* a hand-held whisk made of stiff wires that form a loop at one end and are gathered into a covered handle at the other

balsamic vinegar *noun* thick rich Italian vinegar from unfermented grape juice, stored for years in wooden barrels

balti *noun* a spicy dish originally from Pakistan that is traditionally served in the bowl-shaped pan it is cooked in

bamboo *noun* a plant with long woody, often hollow stems that grows in dense clumps, native to tropical and semitropical areas

bamboo shoots *plural noun* young shoots from the bamboo plant, used in Chinese and Malaysian cooking

banana *noun* the long yellow curved fruit of a large tropical plant

BANT *abbreviation* British Association for Nutritional Therapy

barbecue *noun* **1.** food cooked in the open air, over a charcoal fire **2.** a meal or party where the food is cooked on a barbecue **3.** a metal holder for charcoal over which food is cooked in the open air ■ *verb* to cook food over a barbecue

barbiturate *noun* a drug with sedative and hypnotic properties, belonging to a group of derivatives of barbituric acid

bar code *noun* a sequence of numbers and vertical lines identifying an item and often its price when interpreted by an optical scanner

bard *verb* to put a strip of fat or fatty meat over a joint of meat to prevent it from drying out when cooking

barding *noun* the practice of covering meat with strips of lard to prevent drying

barium *noun* a metal used in x-rays of the stomach and digestive tract. ◊ **barium meal**

barium meal *noun* a suspension containing a salt of the metal barium, given by mouth before X-raying the oesophagus, stomach, and upper intestine to help produce a clear image

barley *noun* a common cereal crop grown in temperate areas (NOTE: Its botanical name is *Hordeum sativum.*)

Barlow's disease *noun* a disease in children caused by a vitamin C deficiency, analogous to scurvy in adults

barn egg *noun* an egg from chickens that are allowed the freedom to roam in barns

Barrett's Oesophagus Foundation *noun* a charitable research body

basal metabolic rate *noun* the amount of energy used by the body in exchanging oxygen and carbon dioxide when at rest, formerly used as a way of testing thyroid gland activity. Abbreviation **BMR**

basal metabolism *noun* the chemical processes that convert food into energy which take place in the human body when it is at rest

base *noun* a substance that reacts with an acid to form a salt

basic food *noun* a type of food that leaves an alkaline residue after being metabolised. Compare **acid food**

basil *noun* a herb with strongly scented leaves, used especially in Italian cuisine. ◊ **holy basil** (NOTE: Its botanical name is *Ocimum basilicum.*)

basket meal *noun* a simple meal, usually of fried chicken, sausage or scampi, served in a basket with chips

basmati *noun* a type of aromatic long-grained rice widely used in Asian cooking

Basra belly *noun* diarrhoea associated with travel in the Middle East or with eating Middle Eastern food food (*informal*)

bass *noun* a name shared by various fish of the perch family found in rivers, lakes and seas and caught for food

baste *verb* to pour melted fat and juices over meat as it is cooking

baster *noun* a cooking utensil, consisting of a long tube with a rubber bulb attached at one end, with which to draw up cooking juices from the pot and release them over the food

batch code, batch mark *noun* a reference number indicating the batch in which a food product was manufactured, a required element in food labelling in the UK

batch production *noun* the production of food in batches

bat out *verb* to flatten a piece of raw meat with a cutlet bat so that it will cook faster

batter *noun* a thin liquid mixture of flour, eggs and milk, used for making foods such as pancakes or toad-in-the-hole, or for coating food before frying

battery farming *noun* a system of keeping very large numbers of chickens in a series of small cages

bay *noun* a small evergreen tree of the laurel family with stiff dark green aromatic leaves, used as a flavouring in cooking. Also called **sweet bay**, **laurel** (NOTE: Its botanical name is *Laurus nobilis*.)

bay leaf *noun* an aromatic leaf of a bay tree, used in cooking

BBQ *abbreviation* barbecue

BCA *abbreviation* body composition analysis

BCAA *abbreviation* branched-chain amino acid

BCB *abbreviation* British Cheese Board

BCCCA *abbreviation* Biscuit, Cake, Chocolate and Confectionery Alliance

bdelygmia *noun* an extreme aversion to food

beading *noun* ripples stamped onto a tin that expand slightly during heat processing, stopping the tin from bursting or deforming

bean *noun* **1.** a seed or the long thin pod of various different plants, cooked and eaten **2.** a dried seed that is ground and is used in cooking or to make drinks

bean curd *noun* same as **tofu**

bean sprouts *plural noun* shoots of beans, eaten especially in Chinese cooking

beard *noun* the fibrous threads by which mussels attach themselves to rocks

béarnaise sauce *noun* a savoury sauce for meat, thickened with egg yolk and flavoured with tarragon

beat *verb* to mix something fast, e.g. to combine ingredients or to incorporate air into a mixture

beater *noun* an implement for beating mixtures, e.g. a whisk

béchamel sauce *noun* a rich sauce made from milk thickened with butter and flour and served hot

bed *noun* a layer of food on which other foods are served

bee balm *noun* same as **bergamot**

beef *noun* meat from a cow or a bull

beefburger *noun* same as **burger**

beef dripping *noun* the fat collected from roasting beef or rendered from beef suet

beef protein *noun* isolated meat protein from beef, used as a bodybuilding supplement, to provide iron and to enrich other meats

beefsteak *noun* a slice of lean beef that can be grilled or fried

beefsteak tomato *noun* a large fleshy variety of tomato suitable for stuffing

beef stroganoff *noun* a dish consisting of thin strips of beef cooked with onions and mushrooms in a sour cream sauce

beef tea *noun* a drink made by boiling beef to extract the juices, formerly given to hospital patients as a digestible form of nourishment

beef Wellington *noun* a dish consisting of a fillet of beef covered in pâté de foie gras, wrapped in pastry, and baked

beer *noun* **1.** an alcoholic drink made by fermenting malted grain, usually barley. ◊ **ale**, **lager 2.** a glass of beer

beeswax *noun* the dark yellow substance secreted by honeybees and used for building honeycombs

beet *noun* a genus of plants that includes the sugarbeet and the beetroot (NOTE: Genus *Beta*.)

beetroot *noun* a vegetable with a dark red root, often eaten cooked as salad, or pickled with vinegar

beetroot red *noun* a red food colouring extracted from beetroot. Also called **betanin**, **E162**

beet sugar *noun* sugar that has been extracted from sugar beet

beeturia *noun* the red colouring of urine after eating beetroot

behavioural approach *noun* a formal method of changing somebody's habits and long-term behavioural patterns through education and guidance

BEIS *abbreviation* British Egg Information Service

belch *noun* a noise made through the mouth when air is suddenly forced up through the oesophagus from the stomach ■ *verb* to make a noise through the mouth when air is suddenly forced up through the oesophagus from the stomach

belly *noun* **1.** the abdomen or the stomach (*informal*) **2.** the fatter central part of a muscle

belly pork *noun* same as **pork belly**

bench scraper *noun* a kitchen utensil used in the preparation of dough

benign *adjective* generally harmless

bentonite *noun* ♦ **E558**

benzalkonium chloride *noun* a colourless or pale yellow toxic liquid mixture, used as a biocide in the food industry

benzene *noun* a simple aromatic hydrocarbon produced from coal tar that is very carcinogenic

benzoate *noun* a salt of benzoic acid used as a food preservative (NOTE: Types are sodium benzoate, E211, potassium benzoate, E212 and calcium benzoate, E213.)

benzoic acid *noun* the simplest aromatic carboxylic acid, a white crystalline solid found in some natural resins (NOTE: It is used as a food preservative and in pharmaceuticals and cosmetics manufacture.)

bergamot *noun* **1.** a hybrid citrus fruit, probably of Seville orange and sweet lime, used only for its highly perfumed rind oil that is sprayed on tea to produce Earl Grey (NOTE: Its botanical name is *Citrus bergamia*.) **2.** a perennial lemon-scented herb used in salads and summer drinks. Also called **bee balm** (NOTE: Its botanical name is *Monarda didyma*.)

beri-beri *noun* a degenerative disease of the nerves caused by a deficiency of the vitamin thiamine and marked by pain, inability to move, and swelling

berry *noun* a small fleshy seed-bearing fruit of a bush, usually with many seeds in the same fruit, and the seeds enclosed in a pulp. ◊ **blackberry, blueberry, raspberry, strawberry** (NOTE: The plural form is **berries**.)

best-before date *noun* an indication of when a food product will start to degrade from its optimum quality, a required element in food labelling in the UK. ◊ **display-until date, use-by date**

best end *noun* a cut of meat, especially lamb, taken from the neck and formed of a series of chops joined together. ◊ **crown roast, rack of lamb**

beta-apo-8'-carotenal (C30) *noun* an orange carotene compound extracted from fruit and vegetables, used as a food colouring. Also called **E160(e)** (NOTE: The more fat soluble ethyl ester, E160(f), is also available.)

beta-carotene *noun* same as **carotene**

beta glucan *noun* a soluble fibre present in oats that reduces blood cholesterol

beta-hydroxy beta-methylbutyrate *noun* a metabolite of leucine, used by body-builders to increase muscle gain. Abbreviation **HMB**

beta-hydroxybutyrate *noun* a ketone substance secreted by the liver that indicates a failure of metabolism

betanin *noun* same as **beetroot red**

beta-oxidation *noun* the breakdown of fatty acids during cellular metabolism to produce acetyl coenzyme A

Better Hospital Food Programme *noun* a campaign supporting quality food provision at NHS facilities

beurre manié *noun* a mixture of butter and flour, added at the last minute to soups or stews to make them thicken (NOTE: **beurre manié** comes from the French and means 'kneaded butter'.)

beverage *noun* any drink, whether alcoholic or non-alcoholic

bezoar *noun* a hard ball of undigested food that causes an obstruction in the stomach

BFFF *abbreviation* British Frozen Food Federation

BFJ *abbreviation* British Food Journal

BFS *abbreviation* blow fill seal

BHA *abbreviation* **1.** British Hospitality Association **2.** butylated hydroxyanisole

bhaji *noun* an Indian food consisting of chopped vegetables in a spicy batter, deep-fried

BHT *abbreviation* butylated hydroxytoluene

BIA *abbreviation* bioelectrical impedance analysis

bicarbonate of potash *noun* ♦ E501

bicarbonate of soda *noun* same as **sodium bicarbonate**

Bifidobacterium *noun* a type of naturally-occurring probiotic

bilberry *noun* a wild berry that is blue when ripe, eaten raw with sugar and cream or cooked in pies and jams

bile *noun* a yellowish-green fluid produced in the liver, stored in the gallbladder, and passed through ducts to the small intestine, where it plays an essential role in emulsifying fats

bile duct *noun* a tube that links the cystic duct and the hepatic duct to the duodenum

biliary calculus *noun* a gallstone (*technical*)

biliary colic *noun* a condition in which the duct that drains from the gallbladder is intermittently blocked by a gallstone

biliary duct *noun* the bodily tube that drains fluid from the gallbladder

bilirubin *noun* a red pigment in bile

bind *verb* to stick together, or cause things to stick together, so as to form a solid mass

binding agent *noun* an additive that makes prepared food keep its shape and texture

binding site *noun* a cavity on the surface of a protein that contains a pattern of amino acids arranged so that they can form a chemical bond only with a specific molecule

binge drinking *noun* the consumption of an excessive amount of alcohol in a short period of time for the purpose of becoming drunk

binge eating *noun* uncontrolled eating, especially when caused by bulimia

binge eating disorder *noun* a psychiatric disorder in which the person has a compulsion to overeat, but does not purge afterwards

binge-purge syndrome *noun* any disorder in which bingeing is followed by purging, e.g. bulimia

bioaccumulation *noun* the accumulation of substances such as toxic chemicals in increasing amounts up the food chain

bioactive *adjective* producing an effect in living tissue or in a living organism

bioavailability *noun* the extent to which a nutrient or medicine can be taken up by the body

bioavailable *adjective* used for describing the extent to which a nutrient or medicine can be taken up by the body

biochemistry *noun* the chemistry of living tissues

biocide *noun* a chemical designed to kill organisms, especially microorganisms

biodiversity, biological diversity *noun* the range of species, subspecies or communities in a specific habitat such as a rainforest or a meadow

bioelectrical impedance analysis *noun* an accurate method of measuring body fat using an electrical current. Abbreviation **BIA**

bioflavonoid *noun* any of various complex chemicals that are widely found in fresh raw fruits and vegetables, thought to protect the body's stores of vitamin C

biofortification *noun* plant breeding or modification designed to give the food higher nutrient levels

biologically active dietary supplement *noun* a substance used for enriching food that contains nature-identical compounds in a concentrated form. Abbreviation **BADS**

biological preservation *noun* the preservation of food such as cheese by the presence of beneficial bacteria already in the food, which prevent others from settling

biological value *noun* a measure of protein quality, expressed as the amount of it that is absorbed and retained in the body. Abbreviation **BV**

biology *noun* the study of living organisms

biomarker *noun* a distinctive indicator of a biological or biochemical process, e.g. a chemical whose occurrence shows the presence of a disease

biopreservation *noun* the preservation of food using natural antimicrobial agents

bioproduct *noun* a consumer product made using biotechnology

biosurface *noun* the region on the surface of a protein, enzyme or receptor that acts as a binding site for molecules

biotech *noun* biotechnology (*informal*)

biotechnology *noun* the use of technology to manipulate and combine different genetic materials to produce living organisms with particular characteristics

biotin *noun* a type of vitamin B found in egg yolks, liver and yeast

bio yoghurt *noun* yoghurt containing naturally occurring probiotic bacteria

biphenyl *noun* a white or colourless crystalline substance used as a fungicide and applied as a preservative to the skins of citrus fruit. ◊ **diphenyl** (NOTE: The preservative has E number E230.)

birth defect *noun* same as **congenital anomaly** (NOTE: The word 'defect' is now avoided as it can be offensive.)

biryani *noun* in South Asian cooking, a dish containing spicy coloured rice mixed with meat, fish or vegetables

biscotta *noun* **1.** an Italian biscuit, especially of the kind often served with coffee in Italian restaurants **2.** an Italian rusk

biscuit *noun* a small hard cake, usually sweet

Biscuit, Cake, Chocolate and Confectionery Alliance *noun* a trade organisation representing manufacturers in the biscuit, cake and confectionary industries. Abbreviation **BCCCA**

bisque *noun* a cream soup made with shellfish

bitter *adjective* not sweet ■ *noun* beer made bitter by the addition of hops

bitter almond *noun* an almond containing hydrogen cyanide, used as a flavouring

bitter chocolate *noun* chocolate containing 5% to 20% sugar, used for baking and confectionery rather than for eating. Also called **baking chocolate**

bitterness *noun* a bitter taste

bitter orange *noun* same as **Seville orange**

bitters *noun* same as **Angostura bitters**

bittersweet *adjective* smelling or tasting both bitter and sweet at the same time

bivalve *noun* any saltwater or freshwater invertebrate animal that has its body contained within two shells joined by a hinge, e.g. an oysters, mussel or clam

bixin *noun* a golden-yellow food colouring obtained from the seeds of achiote. ◊ **annatto**

black bean *noun* a black-seeded soya bean that is fermented for use in East Asian cookery

blackberry *noun* a small soft black berry, growing on plants with long spines, eaten in jams and pies. Also called **bramble**

black cohosh *noun* a herbal supplement used for treating menstrual and menopausal symptoms

blackcurrant *noun* a small round cultivated black berry, eaten cooked in jams and pies, used also in making soft drinks and liqueurs

black-eyed bean *noun* a small beige bean with a black spot

black grouse *noun* a large grouse with a lyre-shaped tail, the male of which is black with white patches on its wings, native to Europe and western Asia. Also called **black game, blackcock, greyhen** (NOTE: Its scientific name is *Lyrurus tetrix.*)

black pepper *noun* a dark brown seasoning made by grinding pepper seeds that have not had their black outer covering removed

black PN *noun* ♦ E151

black pudding *noun* a dark sausage of varying thickness made with blood and fat, sometimes fried in slices and eaten for breakfast

black treacle *noun* same as **treacle**

blade *noun* **1.** the sharp cutting part of a knife **2.** a long thin flat part of some tools or machines, e.g. of a food mixer

blanch *verb* to cook vegetables for a short time in boiling water

blancmange *noun* a cold dessert similar to jelly, made with milk, sugar, flavourings and cornflour

bland *adjective* used for describing food that is not spicy, irritating or acid

blanquette *noun* a dish consisting of white meat such as veal cooked in a white sauce

blast chiller *noun* a machine for chilling food in a blast of freezing air

blast freezing *noun* a method of quick-freezing oddly-shaped food by subjecting it to a blast of freezing air

bleach *verb* to make something whiter or lighter in colour, or to become whiter or lighter in colour

bleach figure *noun* a measure of how bleached flour is

bleaching agent *noun* a compound such as chlorine or chlorine dioxide used for whitening flour and other foodstuffs

bleeding bread *noun* a bacterial infection of bread that stains it red

blend *noun* a mixture of different types ■ *verb* to mix things together

blender *noun* a kitchen appliance used for mixing different food items together thoroughly

blind baking *noun* the practice of baking a pastry case without its filling for a short time, often using dried beans to prevent warping

blind testing *noun* a way of testing the efficacy of supplements using a test group and a control group for the purposes of comparison

blini *noun* a small pancake made with yeast and buckwheat flour, traditional in Russia and other parts of Eastern Europe

blood *noun* a red liquid moved around the body by the pumping action of the heart

blood alcohol level *noun* the concentration of alcohol in a person's blood, expressed as millilitres of alcohol per litre of blood

blood cholesterol *noun* the concentration of cholesterol in the bloodstream, which increase the risk of coronary heart disease if too high

blood clotting *noun* the process by which blood changes from being liquid to being semi-solid and so stops flowing

blood group *noun* same as **blood type**

blood homocysteine *noun* the concentration of homocysteine amino acids in the blood stream

blood lipid profile *noun* a test which assesses the levels of LDL and HDL cholesterol and triglycerides in the blood, used to identify patients at risk of cardiovascular heart disease

blood pressure *noun* the pressure, measured in millimetres of mercury, at which the blood is pumped round the body by the heart

bloodstream *noun* the blood flowing round the body

blood sugar *noun* the amount of glucose in blood, regulated by insulin

blood sugar level *noun* the amount of glucose in the blood, which is higher after meals and in people with diabetes

blood type *noun* one of the different groups into which human blood is classified. Also called **blood group**

blood type diet *noun* a slimming plan based on the premise that different blood types respond best to different diets

bloom *noun* a white deposit on chocolate caused by fat diffusing to the surface

blow fill seal *noun* a fully automated method of packaging in which the package is formed, filled and sealed in a sterile enclosure without human intervention. Abbreviation **BFS**

blown can *noun* same as **swell**

blow torch *noun* a handheld device that produces a gas flame, used for heating the surface of dishes such as crème brûlée

BLT *noun* a bacon, lettuce and tomato sandwich

blue *adjective* used for describing meat cooked with the surface just seared brown and the inside still raw

blueberry *noun* a wild berry that is dark blue when ripe, eaten raw with sugar and cream, or cooked in pies and jams

blue cheese *noun* any cheese with a blue fungus growth in it, e.g. Stilton or Roquefort

blue-veined *adjective* used for describing cheese that is ripened by blue mould, causing a striped appearance

BMES *abbreviation* British Meat Education Service

BMI *abbreviation* body mass index

BMNES *abbreviation* British Meat Nutrition Education Service

BMR *abbreviation* basal metabolic rate

BMS *abbreviation* burning mouth syndrome

BNF *abbreviation* British Nutrition Foundation

boar *noun* a species of wild pig still hunted in parts of Europe and Asia. Also called **wild boar** (NOTE: Various species of the genus *Sus*.)

bodybuilding *noun* the practice of developing the muscles of the body through weight-lifting and diet

body composition analysis *noun* a method of testing the proportions of different fat and lean tissues that make up a person's body. Abbreviation **BCA**

body fat composition *noun* the proportion of fat to lean tissues that makes up a person's body, determined using body composition analysis. Abbreviation **BCA**

body fluid *noun* a liquid in the body, e.g. water, blood or semen

body image *noun* the mental image that a person has of their own body. Also called **body schema**

body mass index *noun* an index that expresses adult weight in relation to height. It is calculated as weight in kilograms divided by height in metres squared. A body mass index of less than 25 is considered normal, and one of over 30 implies obesity.

body water content *noun* the amount of water in body tissues

body weight *noun* a measure of how heavy a person is

boeuf bourgignon *noun* a dish of beef braised in red wine and brandy, served with button mushrooms and onions, fried diced bacon and often with croûtons

BOGOF *abbreviation* buy one get one free

boil *verb* **1.** to heat water until it reaches 100°C **2.** to cook something by putting it in boiling water

boiled egg *noun* an egg that has been cooked by boiling in water

boiling pan *noun* a large container used in a kitchen for boiling food and making soup

boil-in-the-bag *adjective* stored in a sealed plastic bag and cooked by placing the bag in boiling water

bok choy *noun* same as **pak choi**

boletus *noun* a type of mushroom that has a rounded cap with pores rather than gills on the underside, of which cep mushrooms are a variety

bolognese *adjective* used for describing a pasta dish served with a sauce made with minced meat and tomatoes

bolus *noun* **1.** a mass of food that has been chewed and is ready to be swallowed **2.** a mass of food passing along the intestine

bomb calorimeter *noun* a device for measuring the amount of heat released during chemical combustion

bond *verb* to stick together, or make two surfaces stick together ■ *noun* a fundamental attractive force that binds atoms and ions in a molecule

bone *noun* any of the numerous solid structures in the body that make up the skeleton ■ *verb* to take the bones out of something such as a chicken (NOTE: For fish, it is more usual to say 'to fillet' before the fish is cooked, or 'to debone' at table.)

boned and rolled *adjective* used for describing a joint of meat with the bones removed and the flesh flattened, rolled up and tied for roasting

bone density *noun* the amount of strong mineralised fibres present in a bone, which prevent it being weak or brittle

bone formation *noun* the creation of new bone fibres within the body from calcium carbonate and calcium phosphate

boneless *adjective* used for describing meat and fish from which the bones have been removed in preparation for cooking or eating

bone loss *noun* the weakening of bone fibres caused by ageing or disease, causing conditions such as osteoporosis

bone mass *noun* the concentration of fibres in bone

bonemeal *noun* a fertiliser made of ground bones or horns, reduced to a fine powder

bone mineralisation *noun* the absorption of essential minerals into bone fibres

boner *noun* a kitchen implement designed for boning meat or fish

bone resorption *noun* the breakdown of the calcium in bone that is then reabsorbed into the bloodstream

bone strength *noun* the ability of bone to withstand pressure and shock without damage

bone structure *noun* **1.** the system of jointed bones that forms the skeleton **2.** the shape of a bone or set of bones

boning knife *noun* a thick sharp knife used for boning meat

booze *noun* alcoholic drink (*informal*)

boozy *adjective* containing alcohol or flavoured with alcohol

borage *noun* a European flowering plant with leaves that are used as a herb (NOTE: Its botanical name is *Borago officinalis*.)

borborygmus *noun* a rumbling noise in the abdomen, caused by gas in the intestine

Bord Bia *noun* the Irish Food Board, providing a link between food manufacturers and their existing and potential customers

boric acid *noun* a chemical once used as a preservative, no longer thought to be safe

borlotti bean *noun* a speckled, pinkish-brown bean related to the kidney bean and haricot bean, used in Mediterranean and East African cooking

boron *noun* a chemical element that is essential as a trace element for healthy plant growth (NOTE: The chemical symbol is **B**.)

borosilicate glass *noun* a heatproof and shockproof type of glass used for cooking utensils, marketed under the tradename Pyrex

borscht *noun* Russian soup, made with beetroot, other vegetables and small pieces of meat or sausage, eaten either cold or hot, with sour cream

bottle *noun* a narrow-necked container for liquids, made of glass or plastic ■ *verb* **1.** to put drink into bottles **2.** to preserve food by heating it inside a glass jar with a suction cap

bottle feeding *noun* the act of giving a baby milk from a bottle, as opposed to breast feeding. Compare **breast feeding**

bottler's sugar *noun* sugar that is subject to higher microbiological controls than other types of sugar so that it does not spoiled bottled goods

bottling *noun* a way of preserving food by sealing it in sterile glass bottles

botulinum *noun* a bacterium that causes botulism when it is present in food

botulinum cook *noun* the process of heating food until all the botulism spores are destroyed

botulism *noun* a type of food poisoning caused by badly canned or preserved food

bouillabaisse *noun* French fish soup, flavoured with olive oil and saffron

bouillie *noun* a type of pastry cream made from sugar, flour, eggs and milk heated gently

bouillon *noun* a clear liquid that is traditionally made by boiling meat, bones and vegetables together. It is sometimes served as a soup, but usually used as a stock for soups and stews.

bouillon cube *noun* same as **stock cube**

bouquet garni *noun* a bundle of herbs used for flavouring soups and stews, usually consisting of thyme, parsley and bay leaves

bovine *adjective* relating or belonging to the genus of ruminant animals that includes cattle, oxen, and buffalo

bovine somatotropin *noun* a growth hormone of cattle, formerly added to feed to improve milk production but banned in the EU since 2000. Abbreviation **BST**

bovine spongiform encephalopathy *noun* full form of **BSE**

bowel cancer *noun* cancer of the intestine, causing the formation of polyps on the intestinal wall

box scheme *noun* a regular arrangement in which a consumer pays to receive boxes of organic vegetables of a standard value, containing whichever vegetables are available and in season

BPC *abbreviation* British Potato Council

bradypepsia *noun* the fact of having a slow-working digestive system

bradyphagy *noun* extreme slowness when eating

bradyuria *noun* slowness while urinating

brain *noun* the part of the central nervous system situated inside the skull

braise *verb* to cook meat or vegetables in a covered pot with very little liquid

braising steak *noun* good-quality beef suitable for braising

bramble *noun* a wild blackberry

bran *noun* the outside covering of the wheat seed, removed when making white flour, but an important source of roughage and some vitamin B

branched-chain *adjective* used for describing a molecular structure that has side chains or branches attached to specific atoms of the original chain

branched-chain amino acid *noun* an amino acid that is an essential part of muscle protein, often used in bodybuilding supplements. Abbreviation **BCAA**

brand *noun* a well-known make of product, recognisable by its name or by its design

branded *adjective* displaying a brand name

branding griddle *noun* a cast-iron plate with raised parallel ribs, used for giving brown lines on grilled steaks or fish

brand name *noun* the name of a particular make of product

brandy *noun* an alcoholic spirit that is distilled from the fermented juice of grapes or other fruit. ◊ **cognac**, **Armagnac**

brassica *noun* any plant of the family that includes cabbage, kale, broccoli, cauliflower and mustard

brat pan *noun* a cooking pan for stewing, braising, poaching, etc., which can be tilted to drain off liquid

brawn *noun* chopped meat from the head of an animal, mixed with jelly to form a loaf

brazil nut *noun* a hard nut with a rough crescent-shaped shell from a tropical tree

BRC *abbreviation* British Retail Consortium

BRC Global Standard – Food *noun* a technical standard for companies supplying retailer-branded food products

bread *noun* food made from flour, water, a little fat or oil and usually a raising agent such as yeast or soda, then cooked in an oven

breadcrumbs *plural noun* dried bread, crushed into powder, used for covering fish or meat before frying

breaded *adjective* covered with breadcrumbs before cooking

bread flour *noun* flour used for making bread, made from hard wheat that generally contains a high proportion of protein that aids rising

bread knife *noun* **1.** a large knife with a serrated edge like a saw, used for cutting slices of bread from a loaf **2.** a small knife put on the bread plate, used for spreading butter on pieces of bread and cutting them

bread sauce *noun* sauce made from white breadcrumbs, butter and milk, flavoured with onion, served hot as an accompaniment to roast chicken or turkey

breadspread *noun* butter, margarine or low-fat spread

bread stick *noun* a long thin cylindrical biscuit, eaten as an appetiser

breakfast cereal *noun* a breakfast food made from cereal grains, principally, maize, rice, wheat or oats, especially one that is commercially processed by precooking, pressing, drying and coating, generally eaten with milk

bream *noun* **1.** a deep-bodied seawater fish with a silver underside, of the genera *Pagellus* and *Spondyliosoma*, found in the North East atlantic. Also called **red bream 2.** a similar yellowish freshwater fish of the carp family, *Abramis brama*

breast *noun* meat from the chest part of a bird or animal

breast cancer *noun* a malignant tumour in a breast

breast feeding *noun* the practice of feeding a baby from the mother's breasts, as opposed to from a bottle. Compare **bottle feeding**

breast milk *noun* the milk produced in the breasts of a woman who has recently had a baby

breatharianism *noun* a belief that intake of food and water is not necessary and that all the necessary nutrients can be obtained from sunlight

breathe *verb* (*of wine*) to rest in an open bottle, carafe or decanter before being served, believed by some to improve the flavour and bouquet

breed *noun* a group of animals of a particular species that have been developed by people over a period of time so that they have desirable characteristics ■ *verb* to reproduce, or cause animals or plants to reproduce

brettanomyces *noun* yeast that can produce unpleasant flavours in wine

brevibacterium *noun* a halophilic bacterium that grows on the outside of cheese when smeared with brine, causing the characteristic 'smelly feet' odour

brew *verb* **1.** to prepare tea or coffee for drinking by infusing it to develop its flavour, or to infuse in order to develop flavour **2.** to make beer or similar alcoholic drinks by a process of steeping, boiling, and fermenting grain with hops, sugar, and other ingredients

brewer's yeast *noun* the yeast that is used in brewing beer, also used as a dietary source of vitamins, especially vitamin B

brigade *noun* a team of people working in a restaurant, generally divided into the kitchen brigade and the restaurant brigade

brill *noun* an edible flatfish that is closely related to the turbot, native to Europe (NOTE: Its scientific name is *Scophthalmus rhombus.*)

brilliant acid green BS *noun* a food colouring used in sweets, toiletries and perfumes

brilliant black PN *noun* ♦ E151

brilliant blue FCF *noun* ♦ E133

brine *noun* salt water used for preserving meat, fish and vegetables

brining *noun* the process of soaking vegetables in brine before pickling to remove water

brioche *noun* a sweet French bread roll made from a dough enriched with eggs and butter

brisket *noun* beef from the breast of an animal

British Association for Nutritional Therapy *noun* a not-for-profit organisation that provides lists of accredited nutrition practitioners. Abbreviation **BANT**

British Cheese Board *noun* a membership organisation representing cheese manufacturers in the UK. Abbreviation **BCB**

British Egg Information Service *noun* a body that provides nutritional information and recipes for eggs, and also industry statistics. Abbreviation **BEIS**

British Food Journal *noun* a scientific publication reporting research affecting the British food production industries. Abbreviation **BFJ**

British Hospitality Association *noun* an association representing the British hotel, restaurant and catering industry. Abbreviation **BHA**

British Journal of Nutrition *noun* a scientific publication reporting research affecting the British nutrition industry

British Liver Trust *noun* a charitable research body

British Meat Education Service *noun* an industrial sponsor of food-related education in Britain. Abbreviation **BMES**

British Meat Nutrition Education Service *noun* a body working for the British meat industry to provide public guidance on having a healthy diet. Abbreviation **BMNES**

British Nutrition Foundation *noun* an organisation that works in partnership with scientific institutions, the government and the food industry to disseminate nutritional information. Abbreviation **BNF**

British Potato Council *noun* a non-departmental government body which works to promote British potatoes. Abbreviation **BPC**

British Poultry Council *noun* a membership-based trade association representing British poultry farmers and processors. Abbreviation **BPC**

British Retail Consortium *noun* a trade association representing the whole range of retailers. Abbreviation **BRC**

British Soft Drinks Association *noun* a body representing the interests of UK soft drink manufacturers. Abbreviation **BSDA**

brittle bone disease *noun* same as **osteoporosis**

Brix scale *noun* a hydrometer scale used for measuring the sugar content of a solution at a particular temperature

broach *noun* a spit for roasting meat over a fire

broad bean *noun* a large flat green seed cooked and eaten as a vegetable

broccoli *noun* a vegetable that has a cluster of tight green, purple or white flower buds on the end of a broad stalk

brochette *noun* a small skewer on which chunks of food, especially meat or fish, are grilled and roasted

broil *verb* to grill meat

broiler *noun* a chicken that is young and tender and may be cooked by grilling

bromatology *noun* the science of food and nutrition

bromatotoxin *noun* a toxin created by bacteria fermenting in food

bromatotoxism *noun* food poisoning caused by a bromatotoxin

bromelain *noun* an enzyme extracted from pineapples, used in alternative medicine to help the digestion of proteins, reduce blood clotting, counter inflammation, and boost immunity

bromine *noun* a pungent substance used to fumigate grain, which can build up to toxic levels in the human body

bromopnea *noun* same as **halitosis**

broth *noun* a light soup

brown *adjective* **1.** with a colour like earth or wood **2.** unprocessed

brown adipose tissue *noun* fat stored in the body that is metabolically active and burned if needed. Compare **white adipose tissue**

brown braising *noun* the practice of sealing meat in oil by browning it on all sides prior to braising on a bed of chopped root vegetables

brown bread *noun* bread made from brown flour

brown fat *noun* same as **brown adipose tissue**

brown FK *noun* ♦ E154

brown flour *noun* wheat flour containing between 80% and 90% of the dehusked grain and all of the wheat germ. Also called **wheatmeal flour**

brown HT *noun* ♦ E133

brownie *noun* a small chocolate cake

browning reaction *noun* a chemical reaction in food that causes it to turn brown. ◊ **Maillard reaction**

brown rice *noun* rice that still has its outer covering

brown roux *noun* a roux consisting of four parts of fat with five parts of soft plain flour cooked until the flour is light brown in colour, used for thickening soups

brown stock *noun* stock made with bones and vegetables that have been browned in the oven

brown sugar *noun* an unrefined or partly refined sugar in the form of large brown crystals. ◊ **demerara sugar**

brucellosis *noun* a disease that can be caught from cattle or goats or from drinking infected milk, spread by a species of the bacterium *Brucella*

bruise *verb* to crush food slightly to extract juice from it or bring out its flavour

brunch *noun* a meal that is a combination of breakfast and lunch, served at some point between mid morning and early afternoon

bruschetta *noun* Italian bread toasted and drizzled with olive oil, usually served with added garlic and chopped tomatoes

brush *verb* to coat foods before, during or after cooking with a substance such as milk, fat, oil or beaten egg using a small brush

Brussels sprout *noun* a small round green edible shoot from a type of cabbage

BS 5750 *noun* the British Standard of excellence in quality management

BSDA *abbreviation* British Soft Drinks Association

BSE *noun* a disease that affects the nervous system of cattle, believed to be caused by a transmissible protein particle and related to Creutzfeldt-Jakob disease in humans. Full form **bovine spongiform encephalopathy**

BST *abbreviation* bovine somatotropin

buckwheat *noun* a grain crop that is ground into flour, used for making pancakes and, in Japan, noodles

buffalo mozzarella *noun* a fresh mozzarella cheese made from a combination of water buffalo milk and cow's milk

buffalo wings *plural noun* fried chicken wings, usually served in barbecue sauce

buffer *noun* 1. a substance that keeps a constant balance between acid and alkali 2. a solution in which the pH is not changed by adding acid or alkali ■ *verb* to prevent a solution from becoming acid

buffet *noun* a meal in which the food is laid out in dishes on a table and each person helps himself or herself

bulgur, bulgur wheat *noun* wheat that has been parboiled, dried and cracked into small pieces, a common ingredient in southwestern Asian and vegetarian cooking

bulimia, bulimia nervosa *noun* a psychological condition in which a person overeats uncontrollably and follows this with behaviour designed to prevent weight gain, e.g. vomiting, use of laxatives or excessive exercise

bulk-forming laxative *noun* a laxative substance such as bran that works by swelling and moistening the contents of the bowel

bulking agent *noun* an additive that causes a substance to stick together as a mass

bulk sweetener *noun* a sweetening agent used in the food manufacturing industry

bun tray *noun* an oven baking tray with small reservoirs for making individual buns

burdock *noun* a detoxifying supplement

burger *noun* a round, flat cake of minced beef, grilled or fried and usually served in a toasted bread roll. Also called **beefburger, hamburger**

burn *verb* to cook something too much, so that it becomes brown or black ■ *noun* an injury to skin and tissue caused by light, heat, radiation, electricity or chemicals

burning foot syndrome *noun* neuralgic pain in the feet caused by severe deficiency of protein and B vitamins

burning mouth syndrome, burning tongue syndrome *noun* a burning pain in the mouth, lips and tongue, thought to be caused by nutritional deficiencies. Abbreviation **BMS**

burp *noun* a noise made through the mouth when air is suddenly forced up through the oesophagus from the stomach ■ *verb* **1.** to make a noise through the mouth when air is suddenly forced up through the oesophagus from the stomach **2.** to remove the excess oxygen in modified atmosphere packaging

burrito *noun* in Mexican cooking, a flour tortilla with a filling of meat, beans or cheese

butcher *noun* someone whose job is preparing and selling uncooked meat ■ *verb* to slaughter and prepare the meat of an animal for food

butcher's knife *noun* a specialist chef's knife suitable for cutting large pieces of meat

butchery *noun* the work of using knives or other tools to remove meat from an animal's carcass

butter *noun* solid yellow fat made from cream

butter-basted poultry *noun* ready-basted poultry in which the injected basting mixture contains butterfat

butter bean *noun* a large flat cream-coloured bean, dried before cooking

butter cream *noun* a cake filling or coating made by whisking butter with an equal part of icing sugar or caster sugar (NOTE: It can be made less rich by replacing some of the butter with milk or coffee.)

butterfat *noun* the natural fats found in dairy products

butterfly *verb* to split a piece of food such as meat or fish along its length, separating it into halves that remain joined

butterfly chop *noun* a thick chop cut through until almost separated, opened out and flattened to look like a pair of butterfly wings prior to cooking

butterfly cut *noun* a preparation technique in which a piece of meat, fish or seafood is cut through until almost separated then flattened out to look like a butterfly

butter knife *noun* a small knife with a broad blunt blade, used for spreading butter

buttermilk *noun* thin milk left after butter has been churned

butternut squash *noun* a beige-coloured squash that is shaped like a club and has firm yellow-orange flesh

button mushroom *noun* a small white mushroom with a round cap

butylated hydroxyanisole *noun* an antioxidant and preservative in food, currently undergoing research to determine its carcinogenic properties. Abbreviation **BHA**

butylated hydroxytoluene *noun* a common additive used in processed foods containing fat to prevent the fat from oxidising. Abbreviation **BHT**

butyrate *noun* a salt or ester of butyric acid

butyric acid *noun* a fatty acid found in milk

buy one get one free *noun* a special offer in which two items may be purchased for the price of one. Abbreviation **BOGOF**

BV *abbreviation* biological value

B vitamin *noun* a water-soluble vitamin belonging to a group that is essential to the working of some enzymes (NOTE: The B vitamins are B1 thiamine, B2 riboflavin, B6 pyridoxine, B12 cobalamin, B5 pantothenic acid, folic acid and biotin.)

by-catch *noun* fish or sea mammals caught during fishing but not required and thrown back dead into the sea

by-product *noun* something additional produced during a process, often something useful or commercially valuable

C

cabbage *noun* a green leafy vegetable with a round heart or head

cachexia *noun* severe wasting caused by serious illness

cacogastric *adjective* having poor digestion

cacogeusia *noun* an unpleasant taste in the mouth

cadmium *noun* a toxic compound which may contaminate soil and which leads to severe poisoning and organ failure

caecum *noun* a wide part of the intestine that leads to the colon

caesar salad *noun* a salad made with lettuce, croutons, Parmesan cheese and anchovies, with an egg-based dressing

caesium *noun* a highly-reactive element which can enter the food chain through radiation disasters such as Chernobyl, rendering the food unsafe for consumption

cafeteria *noun* a self-service restaurant, especially used by the staff in an office building or factory

cafeteria service *noun* a way of serving food in which the customer takes a tray and helps himself or herself to hot or cold food from a buffet and pays for it at a till on leaving the buffet

cafetiere *noun* a coffee pot in which you push down a filter once the coffee has brewed

caffeine *noun* a stimulant found in coffee, tea and cola nuts

Cajun *adjective* cooked in a style that was developed by the French Canadians who settled during the 18th century in Southern USA and is based on rice, okra and crayfish

cake *noun* a sweet food made from flour, sugar, eggs, milk and other ingredients, baked in an oven ■ *verb* to form into a solid mass

cake stand *noun* **1.** a round rotating platform on which a cake is placed for decoration **2.** a round platform on a pedestal for displaying a cake

cake tin *noun* a tin for baking or keeping cakes in

cal *abbreviation* calorie

calabrese *noun* a variety of broccoli with a large central head

calamari *plural noun* squid served as food, especially in Mediterranean cookery

calcinosis *noun* deposits of calcium in body tissues

calciol *noun* naturally occurring vitamin D

calcium *noun* a metallic chemical element that is a major component of bones and teeth and is essential for various bodily processes, e.g. as blood clotting (NOTE: The chemical symbol is **Ca**.)

calcium acetate *noun* ♦ E263

calcium alginate *noun* ♦ E404

calcium benzoate *noun* ♦ E213

calcium-binding protein *noun* a protein which is activated by calcium ions and interacts with other proteins controlling neuronal function

calcium bisulphite *noun* a chemical preservative used diluted with water

calcium carbonate *noun* a white insoluble solid formed from animal organisms that is naturally abundant and is found in chalk, limestone and marble, used in the production of antacids and toothpaste

calcium chloride *noun* ♦ E509

calcium citrate *noun* ♦ E333

calcium disodium EDTA *noun* ♦ E385

calcium formate *noun* ♦ E238

calcium gluconate *noun* ♦ E578

calcium hydrogen malate *noun* ♦ E352

calcium hydrogen orthophosphate *noun* a food additive used as an acidity regulator

calcium hydrogen sulphite *noun* ♦ E227

calcium hydroxide *noun* a white alkaline powder used in acid soil treatment and in glass manufacture. Also called **slaked lime**

calcium lactate *noun* ♦ E327

calcium L-ascorbate *noun* ♦ E302

calcium magnesium carbonate *noun* a stone sometimes sold ground as a calcium supplement

calcium malate *noun* ♦ E352

calcium oxide *noun* a chemical used in many industrial processes and also spread on soil to reduce acidity. Also called **quicklime**

calcium polyphosphate *noun* ♦ E544

calcium salt *noun* a crystalline compound formed from the neutralisation of an acid solution containing calcium

calcium silicate *noun* ♦ E552

calcium sorbate *noun* ♦ E203

calcium stearoyl-2-lactylate *noun* ♦ E482

calcium sulphate *noun* ♦ E516

calcium sulphite *noun* ♦ E226

calcium tetrahydrogen diorthophosphate *noun* a type of calcium phosphate

calculus *noun* a hard stone formed in the kidneys, gallbladder or ureters

calf *noun* a young cow or bull of a domestic breed of cattle. ◊ **veal** (NOTE: The plural is **calves**.)

calmodulin *noun* a calcium-binding protein found in the cells of most living organisms that controls many enzyme processes

calorie *noun* a unit of measurement of energy in food. Abbreviation **cal**

calorie-controlled *adjective* used for describing a diet that is low in calories for the purposes of losing weight

calorie-dense *adjective* used for describing food and drink that is high in calories with comparatively few essential nutrients

Calorie Restriction for Longevity *noun* a dietary plan that is rich in nutrients but low in calories, on the premise that this can extend a person's life expectancy. Abbreviation **CRL**

calorific *adjective* used for describing food and drink that contains many calories and is therefore likely to be fattening

calorific value *noun* the number of calories that a particular amount of a food or drink contains

Cambridge diet *noun* a dietary plan that is very low in calories while providing enough of each nutrient to prevent tissue damage

camomile tea *noun* a tea made from camomile flowers, used as an antioxidant, anti-inflammatory and mild sedative

cAMP *noun* a derivative of adenosine triphosphate that plays an important role in glycogenolysis and lipolysis. Full form **cyclic adenosine monophosphate**

campylobacter *noun* a bacterium that is a common cause of food poisoning in humans

campylobacter enteritis *noun* an intestinal infection by the organism *Campylobacter jejuni*, usually acquired from contaminated water, milk or poultry

can *noun* a metal container for food or drink ■ *verb* to preserve food or drink by sealing it in special metal containers

canapé *noun* a small piece of bread or savoury biscuit with a topping, served as a snack, especially with drinks

cancer *noun* a malignant growth or tumour that develops in tissue and destroys it, can spread by metastasis to other parts of the body and cannot be controlled by the body itself

cancer cell *noun* a mutated cell in the body that quickly multiplies, forming a tumour that may spread into surrounding tissue

can defect *noun* a fault in a can such as a split seam that may lead to contamination of the contents

candied *adjective* cooked in sugar until crystallised as a method of preservation

candied fruit *noun* decorative pieces of fruit covered with crystalline sugar, achieved by soaking them in a heavy sugar syrup until all the water is replaced with the syrup, then drying them. Also called **crystallised fruit**, **preserved fruit**

candling *noun* a checking process in which eggs are passed over a source of light that detects blood spots in the egg or cracks in the shell

candy *noun* **1.** a sweet food, made with sugar **2.** a piece of this food

cane sugar *noun* sucrose obtained from sugar cane or sugar beet

cannellini bean *noun* a large variety of haricot bean that is widely used in Italy (NOTE: Its botanical name is *Phaseolus vulgaris*.)

cannelloni *noun* a type of wide tube-shaped pasta, stuffed with a meat, cheese or spinach filling

canner's sugar *noun* sugar that is subject to higher microbiological controls than other types of sugar so that it does not spoiled canned food

cannery *noun* a factory where food is packaged into tins

canning *noun* a way of preserving food by sealing it in sterile metal containers

can opener *noun* a tool for opening cans. Also called **tin opener**

cantaloupe *noun* a small round melon with a ridged scaly rind and aromatic orange flesh (NOTE: The plant's botanical name is *Cucumis melo cantalupensis.*)

canthaxanthin *noun* a reddish pigment in water insects that colours the yolks of duck eggs

CAP *abbreviation* Common Agricultural Policy

caper *noun* the flowerbud of a Mediterranean bush, pickled and used in sauces or as a garnish for fish and meat

capillary *noun* an extremely narrow thin-walled blood vessel that connects small arteries (**arterioles**) with small veins (**venules**) to form a network throughout the body

capon *noun* an edible cockerel that grows and increases in weight more rapidly than other birds because it has been castrated

cappuccino *noun* frothy Italian coffee, with whipped milk and a sprinkling of powdered chocolate

capric acid *noun* a type of fatty acid

caproic acid *noun* a type of fatty acid

caprylic acid *noun* a type of fatty acid

capsaicin *noun* the primary and hottest type of capsaicinoid

capsaicinoid *noun* a chemical compound that produces a burning sensation, responsible for the heat in chilli peppers

capsanthin *noun* a peppery flavouring and pink food colouring obtained from paprika. Also called **capsorubin**

capsicum *noun* strictly, any of various pod-like vegetables but, commonly, a red, yellow or green pepper

carafe *noun* a narrow-necked glass jar used for serving wine or water

caramel *noun* **1.** a sweet made with sugar and butter **2.** burnt sugar

caramelise *verb* **1.** to heat sugar until it becomes brown **2.** to cook food such as onions slowly until they become brown

caraway *noun* a plant with seeds that are used as a flavouring in bread and cakes

caraway seed *noun* a spice that is the dried seed of the caraway plant

carb *noun* a carbohydrate, or a high-carbohydrate food (*informal*)

carb blocker *noun* a sports supplement that helps weight loss by blocking the breakdown of carbohydrates

carbohydrase *noun* an enzyme that aids the breakdown of a carbohydrate

carbohydrate *noun* an organic compound derived from sugar, the main ingredient of many types of food

carbohydrate loading *noun* a controversial practice of first starving the body of carbohydrates, then following a high-carbohydrate diet just before an athletic event in an attempt to increase performance

carbon *noun* one of the common non-metallic elements, an essential component of living matter and organic chemical compounds (NOTE: The chemical symbol is **C**.)

carbonade *noun* a stew made with beef and onions cooked in beer

carbon adsorption *noun* the process of removing impurities from water using finely powdered carbon

carbonated *adjective* used for describing a liquid that has had carbon dioxide put into it to make it fizzy

carbon black *noun* a fine carbon powder derived from petroleum or natural gas and used as a pigment and in making rubber

carbon dioxide *noun* a colourless gas produced when carbon is burnt with oxygen (NOTE: Its chemical symbol is CO_2.)

carborundum stone *noun* a hard stone used for sharpening knives, made from finely powdered silicon carbide fused together (NOTE: It is often shaped like a steel and is used in the same way, but it causes more wear than a conventional steel.)

carboxyglutamate *noun* a derivative of glutamate

carboxypeptidase *noun* a protein-digesting enzyme secreted from the pancreas

carcass *noun* the dead body of an animal, especially one slaughtered and prepared for use as meat

carcinogen *noun* a substance that causes cancer

carcinogenic *adjective* causing cancer

cardamom *noun* the aromatic pods and seeds of a tropical plant, used whole or crushed as a spice or flavouring

cardiac *adjective* of the heart, or relating to the heart

cardiac sphincter *noun* same as **lower oesophageal sphincter**

cardiomyopathy *noun* a disorder of the heart muscle

cardioprotective *adjective* used for describing food that is healthy for the heart

cardiospasm *noun* same as **achalasia**

cardiovascular *adjective* relating to the heart and the blood circulation system

cardiovascular disease *noun* reduced function of the heart and arteries caused by excessive intake of saturated fats. Abbreviation **CVD**

caries *noun* dental decay

cariogenic *adjective* used for describing a substance that causes caries

carminative *noun* a drug that relieves excess wind in the digestive tract

carmoisine *noun* ♦ E122

carnauba wax *noun* wax obtained from the young leaves of a Brazilian palm tree, used as a glazing agent. Also called **E903**

carnitine *noun* a derivative of lysine

carnivore *noun* an animal that eats meat. ◊ **herbivore, omnivore**

carnivorous *adjective* **1.** used for describing animals that eat meat **2.** used for describing plants that trap and digest insects

carnosine *noun* a sports supplement

carob *noun* an edible powder with a taste similar to that of chocolate, made from the seeds and pods of an evergreen tree

Caroline Walker Trust *noun* an organisation offering nutrition education for vulnerable groups, e.g. children and elderly people. Abbreviation **CWT**

carotene *noun* an orange or red pigment in carrots, egg yolk and some oils, converted by the liver into vitamin A

carotenoid *noun* an orange or red plant pigment belonging to a group that includes carotenes

carp *noun* a large fish with a single fin on its back, found worldwide in lakes and slow-moving rivers and widely bred for food (NOTE: Its scientific name is *Cyprinus carpio*.)

carpaccio *noun* a dish of raw beef sliced thinly, moistened with olive oil and lemon juice and seasoned

carrageenan *noun* a complex carbohydrate obtained from edible red seaweeds, especially the seaweed Irish moss, used in the commercial preparation of food and drink

carrot *noun* a bright orange root vegetable eaten boiled, steamed or braised, and also shredded cold for use in salads

carte du jour *noun* 'menu of the day', a list of special dishes prepared for the day and not listed in the printed menu

cartilage *noun* the tough elastic tissue that is found in the nose, throat, and ear and in other parts of the body

cartouche *noun* a round or oval piece of paper that is placed on top of food while it is being cooked in liquid, to keep the solid ingredients submerged

carve *verb* to cut up meat and poultry

carvery *noun* a restaurant or section of a restaurant where roast or baked joints of meat or poultry are sliced to order and served

carving fork *noun* a large fork used for holding meat still when carving

carving knife *noun* a large sharp knife used for carving

CAS *abbreviation* controlled atmosphere storage

casease *noun* a bacterial enzyme that aids the breakdown of casein

case-control study *noun* an epidemiological research method in which people who have developed a disease such as cancer are studied alongside people who have not, and the differences and possible causes analysed

casein *noun* a protein found in milk

casein mark *noun* a mark on the rind of a cheese that gives the date and place of manufacture and any quality designations

caseose *noun* a chemical produced in the digestion of cheese

CASH *abbreviation* Consensus Action on Salt and Health

cash crop *noun* a crop which is grown to be sold for money, rather than to provide food for the farmer

cashew *noun* a kidney-shaped nut that is edible when roasted

casing *noun* the tube that encloses the meat mixture of a sausage or similar product, nowadays often plastic but traditionally a part of an animal's alimentary canal from the gullet to the rectum

cassava *noun* a large thick-skinned tuber that is poisonous when raw and untreated but like the potato when boiled, used as a vegetable in many tropical countries, and as a source of tapioca. Also called **manioc**

casserole *noun* **1.** an ovenproof covered dish **2.** food cooked in a covered dish in the oven ■ *verb* to cook something in a casserole

cassoulet *noun* a French stew of haricot beans cooked in a casserole with meat

caster sugar *noun* finely ground white sugar, often used in baking

castor oil *noun* an oil derived from the seeds of the castor oil plant, used as a common purgative (NOTE: The plant's botanical name is *Ricinus communis*.)

catabolism *noun* the part of metabolism that releases energy from food

catalase *noun* an enzyme that splits hydrogen peroxide

catalyse *verb* to act as a catalyst in helping to make a chemical process take place

catalyst *noun* a substance that produces or helps a chemical reaction without itself changing

catecholamine *noun* a compound belonging to a class that act as neurotransmitters or hormones

caterer *noun* a person or company supplying food and drink, especially for parties or similar events

catering *noun* the business of supplying food and drink for parties or similar events

catering urn *noun* a large container for holding or boiling water

cater to *verb* to provide and serve prepared food for a group of people as part of an event, e.g. a private party or a business

catfish *noun* a scaleless, usually freshwater fish with long whiskers around its mouth

cathepsin *noun* an enzyme that hydrolyses proteins

cauldron *noun* a large deep pan for cooking

cauliflower *noun* a cabbage-like vegetable with an edible large white flower head

caustic soda *noun* a compound of sodium and water used to make soap and to clear blocked drains. Also called **sodium hydroxide**

caviar *noun* **1.** the salted roe of a large fish, particularly the sturgeon, eaten as a delicacy **2.** any prepared fish roe in which the eggs are separated so as to resemble sturgeon caviar, e.g. lumpfish roe

cavity *noun* a hole or space inside the body

cayenne pepper *noun* a very hot-tasting red spice made from the seeds and pods of the chilli, different from chilli powder in that the latter often also contains oregano and garlic

CCP *abbreviation* critical control point

CDC *abbreviation* Center for Disease Control and Prevention

CDP *abbreviation* chef de partie

CDRC *abbreviation* Coeliac Disease Resource Centre

celeriac *noun* a vegetable with a thick root tasting like celery, often eaten grated as a salad or used to make a purée

celery *noun* a white- or green-stemmed plant eaten cooked as a vegetable or, more frequently, raw in salads

celery seeds *plural noun* the small brown seeds of a wild celery plant native to southern Europe, used as a flavouring in pickles, tomato ketchup and tomato juice (NOTE: The plant's botanical name is *Apium graveolens*.)

cell *noun* a tiny unit of matter which is the base of all plant and animal tissue

cell division *noun* the way in which a cell reproduces itself

cell membrane *noun* a membrane enclosing the cytoplasm of a cell

cellulase *noun* an enzyme that converts cellulose into sugars

cellulite *noun* fatty deposits beneath the skin that give a lumpy or grainy appearance to the skin surface, especially on the thighs or buttocks

cellulose *noun* a carbohydrate that makes up a large percentage of plant matter

cell wall *noun* the outermost layer of a cell in plants and some fungi, algae and bacteria, providing the cell with protection and support

Celsius scale *noun* a scale of temperature where the freezing point of water is 0° and the boiling point is 100°. ◊ **Fahrenheit scale**

Center for Disease Control and Prevention *noun* part of the US Department of Health and Human Services, which conducts research into public health threats. Abbreviation **CDC**

Center for Food Safety and Applied Nutrition *noun* a centre forming part of the US Food and Drug Administration, with responsibility for the safety of foods, cosmetics and medicines. Abbreviation **CFSAN**

centigrade *noun* ♦ **Celsius scale**

centilitre *noun* a unit of measure equal to 10 millilitres or one hundredth of a litre. Abbreviation **cl**

centralised service *noun* a way of serving food in which trays or plates of food are completely prepared and laid out in the main kitchen and dispatched from there

central obesity *noun* the condition of being 'apple-shaped', with subcutaneous fat being deposited mainly around the abdomen

centrifugation *noun* the separation of the components of a liquid in a centrifuge. Also called **centrifuging**

centrifuge *noun* a device that separates the components of a liquid by spinning it rapidly ■ *verb* to separate liquids by using centrifugal force

cep *noun* an edible woodland mushroom with a shiny brown cap and a creamy-coloured underside

cephalopod *noun* any of a class of marine invertebrate animals with a well-developed head and tentacles, e.g. an octopus, squid or cuttlefish

cereal *noun* a grain crop, e.g. wheat, barley or maize

cereal product *noun* any foodstuff made from cereals, e.g. flour, rice and couscous

cerelose *noun* a commercial preparation of glucose

ceviche *noun* a South American dish of raw fish or shrimp marinated in lemon or lime juice and served as a type of salad with chopped onions and tomatoes

CFA *abbreviation* Chilled Food Association

CFSAN *abbreviation* Center for Food Safety and Applied Nutrition

chafing dish *noun* a dish that keeps food hot at the table

chafing lamp *noun* a small alcohol-burning lamp lit under a chafing dish. Also called **flambé lamp**

chalasia *noun* relaxation of the lower oesophageal sphincter causing gastric reflux

chambré *adjective* served at room temperature

champ *noun* an Irish dish of mashed potatoes with milk and spring onions, eaten with melted butter

champignon *noun* a mushroom, especially one cultivated for eating

change of life *noun* same as **menopause**

Chantilly *noun* sweetened whipped cream that is often flavoured with vanilla

chapati *noun* a piece of flat unleavened Indian bread made from cereal flour and water

charbroil *verb* same as **chargrill**

charcuterie *noun* cold cooked, cured, or processed meat and meat products

chargrill *verb* to grill food over charcoal on a barbecue, or to roast it in a ridged pan that makes it look as if it has been barbecued

charlotte *noun* a dessert made with fruit or cream in a thin biscuit or pastry case

Chateaubriand *noun* a thick beefsteak cut from the widest middle part of the fillet

CHD *abbreviation* coronary heart disease

cheddar *noun* a hard pale yellow or orange-red cheese with a flavour that ranges from mild to very strong, depending on its maturity

cheddaring *noun* the process of allowing the curds to settle and become dense and rubbery in cheese-making

cheese *noun* a solid food made from cow's milk curds, also made from goat's milk and more rarely from ewe's milk or buffalo milk

cheese analogue *noun* a cheese substitute made from other proteins

cheeseboard *noun* **1.** a flat piece of wood on which cheese is served **2.** a selection of cheeses served on a cheeseboard

cheesecake *noun* a dessert consisting of a layer of sweetened soft cheese mixed with cream and eggs on a biscuit or pastry base

cheese cutter *noun* a board to which a piece of wire is attached for cutting cheese

cheese grater *noun* ♦ **grater**

cheese knife *noun* a knife with two points at the end of the blade, used for cutting and serving cheese

cheesemaking *noun* the process of making cheese from milk using rennet and a starter culture

chef *noun* **1.** someone who prepares food in a restaurant **2.** a name given to various special-ised waiters

chef de cuisine *noun* same as **chef**

chef de partie *noun* the chef in charge of a particular section of a kitchen. Abbreviation **CDP**

chef de rang *noun* same as **station waiter**

chef d'étage *noun* same as **floor attendant**

chef entremétier *noun* same as **vegetable chef**

chef garde-manger *noun* same as **larder chef**

chef pâtissier *noun* same as **pastry chef**

chef poissonnier *noun* same as **fish chef**

chef potager *noun* same as **soup chef**

chef restaurateur *noun* the chef in charge of the à la carte menu

chef rôtisseur *noun* same as **roast chef**

chef saucier *noun* same as **sauce chef**

chef's hat *noun* a tall white hat traditionally worn by the main chef in a kitchen. Also called **toque**

chef's salad *noun* a tossed green salad with added tomatoes, sliced hard-boiled eggs and thin strips of meat and cheese

chef's special *noun* a special dish listed separately on a menu, sometimes a dish that the chef is famous for

chef tournant *noun* a chef who is available to work in any of the sections of a kitchen, helping out when other chefs are ill or on holiday

chef traiteur *noun* the chef in charge of outside functions that are prepared in the kitchen but served in a different venue

cheilosis *noun* cracking at the corners of the mouth caused by vitamin B2 deficiency

chelated mineral *noun* an essential mineral that has been treated to make it more absorbable by the body when used as a dietary supplement

chemical hazard *noun* a health risk posed by chemical traces in foods, e.g. pesticide residues

chemical ice *noun* ice containing preservatives

Chemical Score *noun* a measure of protein quality, expressed as its limiting amino acid content as compared to egg protein

chemical treatment *noun* the treatment of food with synthetic substances such as preservatives

chemzyme *noun* a substance that acts like an enzyme to increase the effectiveness of a drug

cherry *noun* a small summer fruit, usually dark red, but also light red or almost white, growing on a long stalk

cherry tomato *noun* a variety of very small tomato

chervil *noun* a herb of the parsley variety used for flavouring mild foods

chestnut *noun* a bright reddish-brown nut of various trees of the beech family

chestnut purée *noun* a purée made of cooked sweet chestnuts, usually with added sugar and vanilla

chest sweetbread *noun* the thymus gland of an animal, used as food

chewing and spitting *noun* an eating disorder in which the person will chew food and spit it out without swallowing to avoid taking in the calories

chicken *noun* a common farm bird that is eaten as food and produces the eggs that are most commonly used in cooking

chicken Kiev *noun* a boned piece of chicken, filled with garlic and butter, covered in breadcrumbs and deep-fried

chicken nugget *noun* a small piece of food consisting of chopped and shaped chicken coated with breadcrumbs, baked or fried

chickpea *noun* a pale yellow seed about the size of a large pea, cooked as a vegetable

chicory *noun* a vegetable with a conical white head of crisp leaves, eaten raw as a salad or cooked and served with a sauce. ◊ **endive**

chiffon *adjective* used for describing food with a light fluffy texture, usually created by adding whipped egg whites or gelatin

chiffonade *noun* vegetables that have been shredded or finely chopped, often used as a garnish for other foods

child poverty *noun* a lack of resources to provide children in a family or larger community with basic necessities such as clean food and water, leading to increased health risks

chill *verb* to cool food or drink in a refrigerator, or to be left to cool there

chilled *adjective* used for describing food or drinks made colder using ice or a refrigerator

chilled food *noun* cooked food kept at a temperature between 0°C and 5°C and reheated prior to serving

Chilled Food Association *noun* an organisation that monitors hygiene standards in chilled food preparation. Abbreviation **CFA**

chilled storage *noun* a place where food can be stored at low temperatures

chiller *noun* a machine for chilling food. ◊ **blast chiller**

chilli *noun* a very hot-tasting pod with seeds in it, available fresh as green or red chillies, dried or preserved in cans or bottles. Also called **chilli pepper** (NOTE: The US spelling is **chili**.)

chilli con carne *noun* a Mexican dish of beans, minced beef and chilli sauce

chilling *noun* the process of cooling something

chilli powder *noun* a spice consisting of dried ground chillies, often made milder by the addition of ground sweet red peppers, oregano and garlic

chilli sauce *noun* a tomato sauce flavoured with chilli

chillproofing *noun* the addition of tannins or enzymes to beer so that it does not become cloudy when chilled

chill storage *noun* a method of preserving foods by storing it at temperatures between – 1°C and +4°C

chime beading *noun* same as **beading**

chine *noun* the spinal column in an animal carcass, or a cut of meat containing this ■ *verb* to remove the spinal column from an animal carcass during the butchering process

chine bone *noun* a joint of meat consisting of the backbone of an animal with some of the surrounding muscle, usually stewed or braised

Chinese ginseng *noun* same as **jiaogulan**

Chinese gooseberry *noun* same as **kiwi fruit**

Chinese Restaurant Syndrome *noun* a collection of symptoms suffered by people consuming too much monosodium glutamate, an ingredient commonly used in Chinese food

chinoise, chinois *noun* a conical metal strainer with one handle, made either of perforated metal or fine wire mesh

chip *noun* **1.** a small stick-shaped piece of potato, fried in oil or fat **2.** a crisp **3.** a small piece of something

chip basket *noun* a wire basket used for holding food such as chips when frying in deep fat. Also called **frying basket**

chipolata *noun* a small thin sausage, usually made of finely ground pork

chitin *noun* a tough waterproof substance that forms part of the outer skeleton of insects and the cell walls of fungi

chitosan *noun* a substance derived from the chitin of crab, lobster, and other crustaceans, used as dietary supplement

chitterlings *plural noun* the small intestines of pigs, used for food

chive *noun* an onion-like with thin leaves that are used as a garnish or in soups and salads

chloride *noun* a salt of hydrochloric acid

chlorination *noun* sterilisation that involves the use of chlorine

chlorine *noun* a powerful greenish gas, used for sterilising water

chlorine dioxide *noun* ♦ **E926**

chlorophyll *noun* a green pigment in plants and some algae

chlorpropamide *noun* an insulin-boosting drug used for treating diabetes

chocamine *noun* an anorectic supplement

chocolate *noun* **1.** a popular sweet food made from the cocoa bean **2.** a small sweet made from chocolate

choke *noun* the central inedible part of a globe artichoke ■ *verb* to stop breathing properly because something such as a piece of food is blocking the throat

cholecalciferol *noun* a form of vitamin D found naturally in fish-liver oils and egg yolks

cholecystectomy *noun* the surgical removal of the gallbladder

cholecystitis *noun* inflammation of the gallbladder and abdominal walls

cholecystoduodenostomy *noun* a surgical operation to join the gallbladder to the duodenum to allow bile to pass into the intestine when the main bile duct is blocked

cholecystokinin *noun* a hormone released by cells at the top of the small intestine, responsible for stimulating the gallbladder, making it contract and release bile

choledocholithiasis *noun* a condition in which a gallstone has passed into the bile duct

cholelithiasis *noun* a medical condition caused by stones in the gallbladder

cholera *noun* a serious bacterial disease spread through food or water that has been infected by *Vibrio cholerae*

cholestasis *noun* failure of bile to reach the stomach, owing to an obstruction

cholesterol *noun* a fatty substance found in fats and oils, also produced by the liver and forming an essential part of all cells

choline *noun* a compound involved in fat metabolism and the precursor for acetylcholine

cholinesterase *noun* an enzyme which breaks down a choline ester

chop *noun* a cut of meat, usually pork or lamb, that contains a rib. Also called **rib** ■ *verb* to cut something roughly into small pieces with a knife or other sharp tool

chopping block *noun* a heavy block of wood, sometimes mounted on legs, for chopping food on

chopping board *noun* a piece of thick wood, used in a kitchen to cut up food on. Also called **cutting board**

chopsticks *noun* a pair of long thin sticks used in Southeast Asia to eat food or to stir food when cooking

chorizo *noun* a very spicy Spanish or Mexican pork sausage

choux pastry *noun* a soft glossy egg-rich pastry that puffs up into a hollow case when baked

chowder *noun* any thick fish soup

chromium deficiency *noun* a rare condition resulting in poor metabolisation of sugar

chromium picolinate *noun* a sports supplement that maintains insulin sensitivity

chronic *adjective* **1.** used for describing a disease or condition that lasts for a long time. Compare **acute 2.** used for describing severe pain

chronic cholecystitis *noun* long-term inflammation of the gallbladder and abdominal walls

chronic disease *noun* a long-term, manageable health condition such as diabetes or asthma

chronic toxicity *noun* high exposure to harmful levels of a toxic substance over a period of time

chrysin *noun* an oestrogen inhibitor

chump *noun* a thick end of a piece of meat, particularly of a leg of lamb or mutton

churn *verb* to stir or beat milk or cream vigorously to make butter

chutney *noun* a sweet and spicy relish made from fruit, spices, sugar and vinegar

chyle *noun* a fluid in the lymph vessels in the intestine, containing fat

chylomicron *noun* a particle of chyle present in the blood

chyme *noun* a thick fluid containing partially digested food and gastric secretions that is passed from the stomach to the small intestine

chymification *noun* the conversion of food to chyme by enzymic action

chymopapain *noun* an enzyme found in papayas that helps digest proteins, used as a meat tenderiser

chymorrhoea *noun* the flow of chyme from the stomach to the duodenum

chymosin *noun* an enzyme in the stomachs of calves that clots milk

chymotrypsin *noun* a protein-digesting enzyme produced by the pancreas

chymotrypsinogen *noun* the inactive form of chymotrypsin that is converted into chymotrypsin by the enzyme trypsin

CIAA *abbreviation* Confédération des Industries Agro-Alimentaires

ciabatta *noun* a flat white Italian bread made with olive oil

cibarious *adjective* edible (*technical*)

cibophobia *noun* a fear or dislike of food

cider *noun* an alcoholic drink made from apple juice

cider vinegar *noun* a light vinegar made from apple juice

cilantro *noun* **1.** same as **coriander 2.** a herb from Costa Rica, Dominica and Mexico with a similar flavour to coriander, very common in Trinidad (NOTE: Its botanical name is *Eryngium foetidum.*)

cinnamon *noun* a spice made from the bark of a tropical tree

circulation *noun* the flow of blood around the body

cirrhosis *noun* a chronic progressive disease of the liver in which healthy cells are replaced by scar tissue, typically caused by alcohol abuse, poor diet or chronic infection

cis isomer *noun* an isomer in which the atom groups are on the same side of the central bond

cissa *noun* same as **allotriophagy**

citric acid *noun* an acid found in citrus fruit such as oranges, lemons and grapefruit

citric acid cycle *noun* same as **Krebs cycle**

citronella *noun* a tropical grass that has bluish-green lemon-scented leaves and contains oil, native to Asia

citrullinaemia *noun* a genetic illness that affects the conversion of protein to urea

citrus fruit *noun* the edible fruits of evergreen citrus trees, of which the most important are oranges, lemons, grapefruit and limes (NOTE: Citrus fruit have thick skins, are very acidic and are an important source of Vitamin C.)

CJD *abbreviation* Creutzfeldt-Jakob disease

CLA *abbreviation* conjugated linoleic acid

clam *noun* any of various invertebrate animals with a shell in two parts and a muscular foot used for burrowing into sand, some of which are edible

clarification *noun* the process of removing suspended particles from a liquid

clarified butter *noun* pure butter fat that contains no other solids, liquid or foam and is transparent when molten

clarify *verb* to make a liquid clear and pure, usually by filtering it

clarifying agent *noun* a substance that removes impurities in liquids (NOTE: Egg white is the most common clarifying agent used in food preparation.)

cleaning and separation *noun* the process of removing any foreign bodies, e.g. earth and stones, from harvested crops

clean-label *adjective* used for describing packaged or processed foods that deliberately do not contain any undesirable additives, allergenic agents or other ingredients that might put consumers off

clean meats *plural noun* meats that are acceptable to eat according to religious dietary laws

cleaver *noun* a heavy knife with a broad blade, used by butchers

clementine *noun* an orange-coloured citrus fruit that is a cross between a tangerine and a Seville orange

climacteric *adjective* continuing to ripen after harvesting

climate change *noun* a long-term alteration in global weather patterns, occurring naturally, as in a glacial or post-glacial period, or as a result of atmospheric pollution (NOTE: Sometimes climate change is used interchangeably with 'global warming', but scientists tend to use the term in the wider sense to include natural changes in the climate.)

cling film *noun* a clear plastic film that sticks to itself and to other surfaces, used for wrapping food

clinical nutrition *noun* the use of nutrition as a means of treating illnesses

clinical trial *noun* a trial carried out in a medical laboratory on a person or on tissue from a person

clonorchiasis *noun* a severe infection of the biliary tract caused by a fluke found in raw fish

Clostridium botulinum *noun* the bacterium that causes botulism

Clostridium perfringens *noun* a food-poisoning bacterium found in cooked and reheated meats and meat products

clot *verb* to change from a liquid to a semi-solid state, or to cause a liquid to do this ■ *noun* a soft mass of coagulated blood in a vein or an artery

clotted cream *noun* thick solid cream made from milk that has been heated to boiling point, produced especially in the south-west of England

cloves *plural noun* the dried unopened flower buds of an evergreen tree, *Eugenia caryophyllus*, used whole or ground in desserts and savoury dishes for their strong, sweet, aromatic smell and flavour

club sandwich *noun* a sandwich made of three slices of bread with fillings between them. Also called **doubledecker**

club soda *noun* same as **soda water**

coacervation *noun* the building up of amylopectin in bread, causing it to become stale

coagulase *noun* an enzyme that makes blood plasma clot

coagulate *verb* **1.** to change from liquid to semi-solid, or cause a liquid to do this. ◊ **clot 2.** to group together as a mass, as egg white does when heated

coagulation *noun* the action of clotting

coat *verb* to cover food with a layer of other food

coating batter *noun* a viscous mixture of flour, water or milk, sometimes with egg, cream or sugar added, used for coating food before frying, deep-frying or baking

coating consistency *noun* the body and viscosity of a liquid such that when it coats a solid it will not drain off (NOTE: It is tested by inverting a spoonful of the mixture. If the body and viscosity are correct, the mixture should not leave the spoon.)

cobalt *noun* an element which is found in vitamin B12 and which is also used in some methods of food sterilisation

cobbler *noun* a baked fruit dessert with a soft thick crust

cocarcinagen *noun* a substance that is not carcinogenic but enhances the effect of a carcinogen

coccidiosis *noun* a parasitic disease of livestock and poultry that affects their intestines

cochineal *noun* a red colouring matter obtained from the dried body of the female concilla insect of Mexico, Central America and the West Indies

Cockayne syndrome *noun* a genetic disease that inhibits growth

cockle *noun* a small edible shellfish with a double shell

cocktail *noun* **1.** a mixture of alcoholic drinks, containing at least one spirit, usually served before a meal **2.** a mixture of food

cocktail shaker *noun* a metal container into which you put the various ingredients of a cocktail and shake them vigorously to mix them

cocktail stick *noun* a short thin sharp stick stuck into foods such as small sausages to make them easier to serve

cocoa *noun* **1.** a powder made from chocolate beans **2.** a drink made from this powder

cocoa bean *noun* the bean-shaped seed of the cacao tree, used for making cocoa powder and chocolate

cocoa butter *noun* a thick oily solid obtained from cocoa beans, used in making chocolate, cosmetics and suntan oils

cocoa cake *noun* a chocolate-flavoured cake made using cocoa powder

cocoa mass, cocoa liquor *noun* a paste produced by grinding roasted cocoa beans, used for making chocolate or separated into cocoa powder and cocoa butter

cocoa powder *noun* cocoa beans ground to a fine powder, used as a flavouring and to make drinks (NOTE: The beans are defatted, treated with an alkali and dried.)

coconut *noun* a large nut from a tropical palm tree containing a white edible pulp

coconut milk *noun* **1.** a cloudy whitish liquid inside a coconut **2.** a white creamy liquid made from coconut pulp, used in Malaysian and Thai cooking

cocotte *noun* a heat-proof dish in which food can be cooked and served in small portions

cod *noun* a large white sea fish (NOTE: Its scientific name is *Gadus morhua*.)

coddle *verb* to heat food in water that is just below boiling point

code marking *noun* embossed figures on a can end showing the use-by date or similar information

code of practice *noun* a set of rules according to which people in a particular profession are expected to behave

Codex Alimentarius, Codex *noun* a collection of standards and codes of practice relating to all aspects of food production, documented by the FAO and WHO

Codex Alimentarius Committee *noun* the subsidiary body of the FAO and WHO responsible for creating the Codex Alimentarius

cod liver oil *noun* a fish oil that is rich in calories and vitamins A and D

coeliac *adjective* relating to the abdomen

coeliac disease *noun* an allergic disease, mainly affecting children, in which the lining of the intestine is sensitive to gluten, preventing the small intestine from digesting fat. Also called **gluten-induced enteropathy**

Coeliac Disease Resource Centre *noun* a password-only site for healthcare professionals involved with the treatment of coeliac disease. Abbreviation **CDRC**

Coeliac UK *noun* a charitable research body

coenzyme *noun* a non-protein compound that combines with the protein part of an enzyme to make it active

coenzyme A *noun* a complex compound that acts with specific enzymes in energy-producing biochemical reactions. Abbreviation **CoA**

cofactor *noun* a substance that acts with and is essential to the activity of an enzyme, e.g. a coenzyme or metal ion

coffee *noun* **1.** the crushed beans of the plant *Coffea*, used for making a hot drink **2.** a drink made from ground coffee beans or powder, mixed with hot water

coffee beans *plural noun* the small fruits of the plant *Coffea*, dried and roasted to make coffee

coffee grinder *noun* a machine for grinding coffee beans into powder for making coffee

Coffee Science Information Centre *noun* a service that presents research on coffee and the effects of caffeine on the human body. Abbreviation **CoSIC**

cognac *noun* brandy made in western France

cohort study *noun* a study of people over an extended period of time

cola *noun* **1.** a tree from West Africa, the West Indies and South America with a nut-like fruit that contains caffeine, chewed or used for making cola drinks **2.** a fizzy sweet drink containing an extract of the cola nut or a similar flavouring

colander *noun* a bowl-shaped dish with holes in it, used for draining food cooked in water and washing vegetables or fruit

cold holding *noun* same as **chilling**

cold pack *noun* the packing and sterilisation of uncooked food in jars or tins

cold-pressed *adjective* used for describing olive oil that has been extracted from olives without the use of heat

cold room *noun* a room where stores of food are kept cool, so as to prevent the food from going bad. Also called **cold store**

cold shortening *noun* the process by which carcass meat becomes tough if it is chilled too rapidly after slaughter, especially in the case of beef, lamb and mutton

cold-smoke *verb* to lightly smoke food at a temperature not greater than 33°C so as not to cook the flesh, used mainly for salmon, kippers, gammon and some sausages

cold storage *noun* the keeping of food in a cold place to prevent it from going bad

cold store *noun* same as **cold room**

cold-water fish *noun* fish such as trout and salmon that thrive in cold water conditions, usually containing a high proportion of fish oils in their flesh

colectomy *noun* surgical removal of the colon or part of the colon

coleslaw *noun* a salad of shredded white cabbage mixed with mayonnaise, often also containing carrot and onion

coley *noun* a type of sea fish similar to cod

colforsin *noun* a vasodilatory sports supplement

colic *noun* **1.** pain in any part of the intestinal tract. Also called **enteralgia**, **tormina 2.** stomach pains in babies, causing crying and irritability

coliform bacteria *plural noun* aerobic bacteria formed in faeces, some types of which are toxic

colistin *noun* an antibiotic that is effective against a wide range of organisms and is used for treating gastrointestinal infections

colitis *noun* inflammation of the colon, characterised by lower-bowel spasms and upper abdominal cramps

collar *noun* a cut of meat, especially bacon, taken from an animal's neck ■ *verb* to pickle meat by soaking it in salt or brine with seasonings and flavouring ingredients, then rolling, boiling and pressing it

collar bacon *noun* the top front section of a side of bacon cut into bacon joints or sliced into rather rectangular-shaped rashers

colloid *noun* a mixture in which very fine particles of a gas, liquid or solid are dispersed in another substance, as milk solids are in milk and oil droplets are in mayonnaise

colloidal system *noun* a dispersion of particles in another medium, which can be solid, liquid or gas

colon *noun* the main part of the large intestine, running from the caecum at the end of the small intestine to the rectum

colonic *adjective* relating to the colon

colonic inertia *noun* a total loss of muscle function in the bowel, causing chronic constipation requiring medical treatment

colonic irrigation *noun* the washing out of the contents of the large intestine using a tube inserted in the anus

colonorrhoea *noun* diarrhoea caused by a disease affecting the colon

colonoscope *noun* a surgical instrument for examining the interior of the colon

colonoscopy *noun* an examination of the inside of the colon, using a colonoscope passed through the rectum (NOTE: The plural is **colonoscopies**.)

colorectal *adjective* relating to both the colon and rectum

colorectal cancer *noun* ♦ **bowel cancer**

colostomy *noun* a surgical operation to make an opening between the colon and the abdominal wall to allow faeces to be passed out without going through the rectum (NOTE: The plural is **colostomies**.)

colostrum *noun* a yellowish fluid that is rich in antibodies and minerals produced by a mother's breasts after giving birth and prior to the production of true milk

colouring *noun* a substance that colours a processed food

colporrhoea *noun* a discharge of mucus from the colon

COMA *abbreviation* Committee on Medical Aspects of Food and Nutrition

combination *noun* the act of bringing two or more substances together

combination menu *noun* a menu in which popular items are repeated each day and others changed on a regular or irregular basis

combination oven *noun* a standard fan-assisted electric oven combined with a microwave energy source to give very fast cooking together with the surface browning and hardening of a conventional oven

combine *verb* to mix ingredients together

comfrey *noun* a medicinal herb of the genus *Boraginaceae* that is also used in salads and for composting

commercial sterility *noun* a level of sterility in packaged foods where they are not completely sterile but where they do not contain microorganisms that could cause health problems

commis chef *noun* an assistant chef to a chef de partie

commis de salle *noun* an assistant to a chef de rang, helping him or her to organise a restaurant

commis saucier *noun* an assistant to the chef saucier, helping him or her prepare sauces

commis waiter *noun* an assistant to a station waiter

Committee on Medical Aspects of Food and Nutrition *noun* the former name for the Scientific Advisory Committee on Nutrition. Abbreviation **COMA**

commodity *noun* a substance sold in very large quantities, e.g. raw materials or foodstuffs such as corn, rice, butter

Common Agricultural Policy *noun* a set of regulations and mechanisms agreed between members of the European Union to control the supply, marketing and pricing of farm produce. Abbreviation **CAP**

community dietitian *noun* same as **public health nutritionist**

community medicine *noun* the study of medical practice which examines groups of people and the health of the community, including housing, pollution and other environmental factors

comparative product sampling *noun* food tasting that compares a product against other available products

complementary action of proteins *noun* the act of eating different types of protein in the same meal so as to raise their biological value, by supplementing each others' limiting amino acid levels

complete protein *noun* a protein that contains all of the essential amino acids

complex carbohydrate *noun* any carbohydrate with large molecules containing many linked sugar units, broken down more slowly by the body

composition *noun* the make-up or structure of something

compote *noun* fruit cooked in sugar or syrup, served as a hot or cold dessert

compound *noun* a chemical substance made up of two or more components ■ *adjective* made up of two or more components ■ *verb* to make something by combining parts

compulsive overeating *noun* a condition in which a person routinely consumes too much food as a result of emotional disturbance

concarnivorous *adjective* only eating food that contains meat

concentrate *verb* to remove water from a liquid or substance so that it becomes thicker and has a stronger flavour ■ *noun* a food substance or liquid that has been concentrated to make it thicker or stronger in flavour

concentrated milk *noun* milk that has been condensed and evaporated

conch *verb* to mechanically treat chocolate with heavy rollers to make it smooth

condensation *noun* **1.** the action of making vapour into liquid **2.** the water that forms when warm damp air meets a cold surface such as a wall or window

condense *verb* to make something, especially a food, denser by removing water

condensed milk *noun* milk that is thickened by evaporating most of the water content and then sweetened

condiment *noun* a seasoning used for giving taste to food and put directly onto food at the table by the eater, e.g. salt, pepper or mustard. Compare **cruet**

condiment set *noun* a decorative carrier holding two or more small pots or bottles for condiments such as salt and pepper or oil and vinegar

condition *verb* to improve the quality of meat, cheese or alcoholic drink by ageing it at a controlled temperature (NOTE: With meat this process occurs naturally after slaughter.)

conditioning *noun* the process of making meat more tender by keeping it for some time at a low temperature. ◊ **air-conditioning**

conduction *noun* the process of passing heat, sound or nervous impulses from one part of the body to another

cone *noun* same as **cornet**

confectioners' sugar *noun* same as **icing sugar**

confectionery *noun* **1.** a shop selling sweets and chocolates **2.** sweets and chocolates

Confédération des Industries Agro-Alimentaires *noun* same as **Confederation of the Food and Drink Industries of the EU**

Confederation of the Food and Drink Industries of the EU *noun* a professional body that represents the interests of food and drink industries both within the EU and at an international level

confit *noun* meat such as goose, duck or pork that has been cooked and preserved in its own fat

congeal *verb* to become thick and solid, or cause a liquid to thicken and solidify

congener *noun* a flavour substance in alcoholic spirits

congenital *adjective* existing at or before birth

congenital anomaly *noun* a medical condition arising during development of the fetus and present at birth

conjugated *adjective* containing at least two double or triple chemical bonds alternating with single bonds

conjugated linoleic acid *noun* a form of linoleic acid that is reputed to reduce lipid levels in the blood, leading to weight loss. Abbreviation **CLA**

connective tissue *noun* tissue that forms the main part of bones and cartilage, ligaments and tendons, in which a large proportion of fibrous material surrounds the tissue cells

connoisseur *noun* someone with a lot of knowledge of good foods and wines and an ability to tell good from bad or ordinary

Consensus Action on Salt and Health *noun* a body that lobbies for the reduction of salt levels in processed foods. Abbreviation **CASH**

conserve *verb* **1.** to keep and not waste something **2.** to look after and keep something in the same state ■ *noun* a food consisting of fruit in a thick sugar syrup, like jam but less firmly set and usually containing larger pieces of fruit

consistency *noun* the degree of thickness or smoothness of a mixture

consommé *noun* a clear soup made from meat, poultry, fish or vegetables

constipation *noun* difficulty in passing faeces

consultant dietitian *noun* same as **freelance dietitian**

consultation *noun* a meeting between a doctor and a patient, in which the doctor may examine the patient, discuss his or her condition and prescribe treatment

consume *verb* to eat a food or drink a drink

consumer *noun* a person or company that buys and uses goods and services

consumer testing *noun* sensory analysis of a food product by a panel of untrained consumers, giving 'gut reactions'

consumption *noun* **1.** the act of consuming something **2.** the quantity something consumed

contaminant *noun* a substance that contaminates

Contaminants in Food (England) Regulations 3062/2004 *noun* an EU statute that makes provision for the setting of maximum levels for contaminants in foods

contamination *noun* **1.** the act of making something impure by touching it or by adding something to it **2.** a state of impurity caused by the presence of substances that are harmful to living organisms

continuous grill *noun* a grill, used e.g. in burger bars, in which food is loaded on a conveyor and cooks on both sides as it travels to the unloading position

controlled atmosphere storage *noun* the storage of fresh fruits and vegetables in an airtight room, which slows their ripening by reducing the amount of available oxygen. Abbreviation **CAS**

controlled gas storage *noun* the storing of meat, fruit and vegetables in a carbon-dioxide-rich controlled environment

controlled temperature storage *noun* the storage of food at temperatures between $-1°C$ and $+4°C$

control point *noun* in food production, a point in the process at which control should be exercised to keep food safety and quality at optimum levels. Abbreviation **CP**

convection *noun* the process by which hot air rises and cool air descends

convection oven *noun* an oven with a fan that circulates heat throughout the oven, so that food on all levels cooks uniformly. Also called **forced convection oven**

convenience food *noun* food that is prepared and cooked before it is sold, so that it needs only heating to be made ready to eat

convenience store *noun* a small shop selling food and household goods that is open until late at night or even 24 hours a day

conventional farming *noun* farming that does not use specific organic practices

conveying *noun* the transporting of food substances using a moving belt or bed of air

cook *noun* someone whose job is to prepare food in a restaurant ■ *verb* to heat food in order to prepare it for eating

cook-and-hold oven *noun* an oven that cooks food and then keeps it warm for a long period by reducing the temperature and often adjusting the humidity, often used in carveries

cook-chill *noun* a method of processing food by bulk cooking it, then chilling it for the purposes of packaging and storage, to be later reheated by the consumer

cooked-chilled *adjective* referring to food that is cooked, packaged and refrigerated, and then reheated before serving

cooker *noun* a device for cooking food, which runs on gas, electricity, charcoal, etc. Also called **stove**

cook-freeze *noun* a method of processing food by cooking it in bulk, then freezing it for the purposes of packaging and storage, to be later reheated by the consumer

cooking apple *noun* a sour apple used for cooking. Also called **baking apple**

cooking chocolate *noun* unsweetened chocolate available in block form or as chips (NOTE: Not to be confused with the cheap, brown chocolate-flavoured substance often sold under this name.)

cooking fat *noun* a hard, tasteless, normally white unsalted fat made by hydrogenating vegetable or fish oils

cook out *verb* to completely cook a food, e.g. a sauce, so that no suggestion of the uncooked ingredients remains

cook's knife *noun* an all-purpose kitchen knife

cookware *noun* utensils used in cooking, e.g. pots, pans, and dishes

cool *verb* to reduce the temperature of food by any of a variety of means, e.g. by placing it in a refrigerator, plunging it in cold water or standing its container in cold water

cooler *noun* a device or machine that cools

copper *noun* a metallic trace element (NOTE: The chemical symbol is **Cu**.)

copper gluconate *noun* a metabolisable form of copper used as a supplement to treat deficiency

copra *noun* the dried pulp of a coconut, from which oil is extracted by pressing

coprolith *noun* a mass of hard matter in the intestine or rectum, caused by severe constipation

CoQ10 *noun* a protein compound that is required for the proper functioning of enzymes in the body, speeding up energy release

coq au vin *noun* a dish of chicken cooked in red wine with other ingredients

coral *noun* the unfertilised eggs of a lobster or crab that turn pinkish-orange when cooked

cordial *noun* a fruit drink, especially one that is sold in concentrated form and diluted with water

cordon bleu *adjective* **1.** done or working to a very high standard **2.** used for describing a way of preparing meat, especially veal, by rolling a thin slice around cheese and ham and then coating in breadcrumbs

core *noun* the central part of a fruit such as an apple or pear ■ *verb* to remove the core from something such as an apple or pear

Core *noun* the working name of the Digestive Disorders Foundation, a charitable research body

corepressor *noun* a metabolite that combines with and activates a genetic repressor apoprotein, inhibiting protein synthesis

coriander *noun* an aromatic plant whose seeds, green leaves and roots are used in cookery (NOTE: The US term is **cilantro**.)

Cori cycle *noun* the way in which excess lactic acid produced by muscles is converted back to glucose so that it can be reused for energy production

corked *adjective* **1.** with a cork in it **2.** used for describing wine that has an unpleasant sour taste because of a dirty or faulty cork

corkscrew *noun* a device for taking corks out of bottles

cork taint *noun* the taste of vinegar, must or mould in wine caused by a dirty or faulty cork

corn *noun* same as **maize**

corn cob *noun* a woody stem of maize, to which the seeds are attached

corned beef *noun* beef that has been salted and usually canned

corner gammon *noun* a triangular cut of gammon

cornet *noun* a large cone-shaped wafer in which ice cream is served so that it can be eaten as a snack. Also called **cone**

corn-fed *adjective* fed or fattened on cereal grains

cornflakes *plural noun* a breakfast cereal made of flat crisp pieces of corn, eaten with milk and sugar

cornflour *noun* a very smooth type of flour made from maize, used in cooking to make sauces thicker

cornichon *noun* same as **gherkin**

Cornish pasty *noun* a pie of meat and potatoes wrapped in pastry, a common food in pubs

cornmeal *noun* white or yellow dried maize kernels ground to varying degrees of fineness

corn oil *noun* an edible oil made from corn

corn on the cob *noun* a piece of maize, with seeds on it, served hot, with butter and salt

corn syrup *noun* a sweet liquid made from corn

coronary arteries *plural noun* two arteries which supply blood to the heart muscles

coronary heart disease *noun* any disease affecting the coronary arteries, which can lead to strain on the heart or a heart attack. Abbreviation **CHD**

coronary thrombosis *noun* same as **atherosclerosis**

corporate social responsibility *noun* the extent to which an organisation behaves in a socially, environmentally and financially responsible way. Abbreviation **CSR**

corrosion *noun* a process in which the surface of a material, generally a metal, is changed by the action of moisture, air or a chemical

cortex *noun* the outer layer of an organ

corticosteroid *noun* **1.** any steroid hormone produced by the cortex of the adrenal glands **2.** a drug that reduces inflammation, used in treating asthma, gastrointestinal disease and in adrenocortical insufficiency

cos *noun* a type of lettuce with long stiff dark green leaves. Also called **romaine**

CoSIC *abbreviation* Coffee Science Information Centre

cottage cheese *noun* mild white cheese formed into soft grains, made from skimmed milk and therefore having a very low fat content

cottage pie *noun* a dish of minced beef with a layer of mashed potatoes on top. Compare **shepherd's pie**

coulis *noun* a thin purée of fruit or vegetables used as a garnish

counter guard *noun* a transparent glass or plastic shield that protects unwrapped food on display from the coughs, sneezes and other contaminants emitted by customers. Also called **sneeze guard**

counter service *noun* a method of service in which customers sit at a counter from behind which food is served and sometimes cooked

courgette *noun* the fruit of the marrow at a very immature stage in its development, cut when green or yellow in colour and between 10 and 20 cm long

course *noun* **1.** one part of a meal. ◊ **main course 2.** a series of lessons

court bouillon *noun* a liquid used for poaching fish, made with water flavoured with vegetables, herbs and wine or vinegar

couscous *noun* **1.** very small grains of wheat cooked by steaming **2.** a North African dish of meat and vegetables stewed in a spicy sauce, served with steamed couscous

cover *noun* a place for a customer at a restaurant table, with the cutlery and glasses already set out

cover charge *noun* an extra charge for service in a restaurant, added to the cost of food or drinks

cow beef *noun* beef from dairy cows no longer needed for milk production

cow's milk *noun* milk from dairy cows

CP *abbreviation* control point

crab *noun* **1.** an edible ten-footed crustacean with large pincers **2.** same as **crabmeat**

crabmeat *noun* the flesh of a crab used as food

crab stick *noun* a stick-shaped piece of processed fish that has been flavoured and coloured to resemble crabmeat

cracked wheat *noun* coarsely crushed grains of wheat served hot as a breakfast cereal, served as an accompaniment to other dishes or sprinkled on rolls or bread prior to baking. Also called **kibbled wheat**

cracker *noun* a dry unsweetened biscuit

crackling *noun* the crisp skin of a roast joint of pork, bacon or ham, served as an accompaniment to the roast

craft bread *noun* bread baked using traditional bakery methods, rather than on an industrial production line

cramp *noun* a painful involuntary spasm in the muscles, in which the muscle may stay contracted for some time

cranberry *noun* a wild red berry, used for making a sharp sweet sauce and juiced for use as a drink

cranberry sauce *noun* a sharp sweet red sauce, eaten with meat, in particular turkey

crash diet *noun* a dietary plan that drastically reduces calorie intake for a short period, leading to rapid but unsustainable weight loss

craving *noun* a strong desire for a particular food or drink

crayfish *noun* a kind of freshwater crustacean like a small lobster (NOTE: The plural form is **crayfish**. The US English spelling is **crawfish**.)

cream *noun* the rich fat part of milk ■ *verb* to mix ingredients together until they form a smooth mixture

cream cheese *noun* a soft smooth cheese that can be spread easily

cream cracker *noun* a crisp savoury biscuit usually eaten with cheese

creamed potatoes *plural noun* same as **mashed potatoes**

creamer *noun* **1.** a dry white powder used as a substitute for cream or milk in coffee and tea, made from glucose and vegetable fats **2.** a device that separates cream from milk

creamery *noun* a factory where butter and other products are made from milk

creaming *noun* the tendency of fat globules to rise to the top of a solution such as milk

creaming method of making cakes *noun* a method of making cakes that gives a soft, light, fluffy texture by vigorously beating together fat and sugar to incorporate air, incorporating well-beaten eggs slowly with continuous beating (NOTE: The trapped air expands with steam during the baking and setting process.)

cream of tartar *noun* potassium tartrate or potassium bitartrate when used as a raising agent in cooking

cream of tartare *noun* potassium hydrogen tartrate, used as a stabilising and raising agent

creamy *adjective* **1.** with a texture, colour, taste or consistency like that of cream **2.** containing a large amount of cream

creatine *noun* a compound of nitrogen found in the muscles, produced by protein metabolism and excreted as creatinine

creatine kinase *noun* an enzyme that breaks down phosphocreatine into creatine and phosphoric acid, releasing energy

crème à l'anglaise, crème anglaise *noun* a type of custard made with milk, cream, eggs, sugar and cornflour

crème brûlée *noun* a dessert of egg custard with a topping of caramelised sugar

crème fraîche *noun* thick slightly sour cream used in cooking and as an accompaniment to desserts

crème pâtissière, crème pâtisserie *noun* a custard-like filling for cakes and tarts, made from egg yolks, caster sugar, milk and butter

crepe *noun* ♦ pancake

crêpe suzette *noun* a pancake prepared with orange sauce and flambéed with an orange-flavoured liqueur or brandy

cress *noun* a plant whose seedlings are used for salads, especially together with seedlings of mustard. ◊ **mustard and cress, watercress**

cretinism *noun* impairment of mental faculties caused by long-term iodine deficiency, which affects the production of thyroid hormones causing hypothyroidism

Creutzfeldt-Jakob disease *noun* a disease of the nervous system caused by a slow-acting prion that eventually affects the brain, thought to be linked to BSE in cows. Abbreviation **CJD**

crimp *verb* to fold or press the ends or edges of something, e.g. pastry, together

crisp *adjective* used for describing food that is hard, is able to be broken into pieces and makes a noise when you bite it ■ *noun* a thin slice of potato, fried till crisp and eaten cold as a snack

crispy bacon *noun* thin slices of bacon, fried or grilled until they are hard and crisp

crista *noun* a ridge, e.g. the border of a bone

critical control point *noun* in food production, a point in the process at which control is essential to prevent a health risk or to reduce it to acceptable levels. Abbreviation **CCP**

critical moisture content *noun* the percentage of water in a food item or substance at which it becomes unsuitable for sale or use

CRL *abbreviation* Calorie Restriction for Longevity

crockery *noun* plates, cups, saucers, and other household items made of china or earthenware

Crohn's disease *noun* an inflammatory disease of the bowel that inhibits the absorption of nutrients

croissant *noun* a crescent-shaped sweetish pastry often served as a breakfast food

crop *noun* 1. a plant grown for food 2. a yield of produce from plants 3. the bag-shaped part of a bird's throat where food is stored before digestion ▪ *verb* to produce fruit

crop residue *noun* minute traces of pesticide or fertiliser on crops that may find their way into the food chain

croquette *noun* a small ball or cake of mashed potato, minced meat, vegetables or fish, covered with breadcrumbs and fried

cross-contamination *noun* contamination from one type of food to another and back again

crouton *noun* a small piece of fried or toasted bread, served with soup or as part of a salad

crown roast *noun* a dish of lamb, formed of two pieces of best end of neck, tied together to form a shape like a crown

cruciferous *adjective* used for describing vegetables of the cabbage family, e.g. cabbage, kale and broccoli

crudités *plural noun* small pieces of raw vegetables, e.g. carrots and cucumber, eaten as an appetiser or snack, often with a dip

cruet *noun* a set of containers for salt, pepper and other condiments, put on the table or kept on a special stand. Compare **condiment**

crumble *noun* a dessert made of fruit covered with a cake mixture of flour, fat and sugar

crumpet *noun* a flat bun with small holes in its surface that is made from a batter risen with yeast and is eaten toasted with butter

crunchy *adjective* used for describing food that makes a noise when you eat it

crush *noun* a drink containing the juice from crushed fruit

crush, tear, curl *noun* ♦ CTC machine

crust *noun* 1. the hard outer part of a loaf of bread, of a roll or of a slice of bread 2. the pastry top of a pie

crustacean *noun* any animal with a hard shell, usually living in the sea, e.g. a lobster, crab or shrimp

cryogenic freezing *noun* the process of freezing something to very low temperatures

cryptosporidiosis *noun* a common disease with symptoms of diarrhoea, caused by microorganisms in drinking water

cryptosporidium *noun* a water-borne protozoan parasite that contaminates drinking water supplies, causing intestinal infections in human beings and domestic animals

cryptoxanthin *noun* ♦ E161(c)

crystalline *adjective* formed of crystals

crystallisation *noun* the formation of crystals

crystallise *verb* 1. to form crystals 2. to coat or impregnate something with crystals, especially sugar crystals

crystallised fruit *noun* same as **candied fruit**

crystallised ginger *noun* ginger that has been preserved by soaking in a strong sugar solution

CSR *abbreviation* corporate social responsibility

c-store *abbreviation* convenience store

CTC machine *noun* a machine with rotating rollers used for preparing tea leaves. Full form **crush, tear, curl**

cube sugar *noun* white or brown crystals of sugar compressed into small cubes. Also called **sugar lump**, **loaf sugar**

cucumber *noun* a long cylindrical green vegetable used in salads or, when small, for pickling

Cucurbitaceae *plural noun* the botanical name of family of vine plants with fruits that include cucumbers, melons, marrows, courgettes and pumpkins

cuisine *noun* a style of cooking

culinary *adjective* relating to cooking

culture *noun* the traditional customs and way of life of a people or group ■ *verb* to grow microorganisms or tissues in a culture medium

culture medium *noun* a nutrient substance in which scientists grow microorganisms, fungi, cells or tissue in a laboratory

cumin *noun* the seeds of a plant of the carrot family used as a spice

cup *noun* a unit of measurement used in US recipes, equal to around 240 ml

curative *adjective* able to cure medical conditions

curcumin *noun* a natural yellow food colouring obtained from turmeric

curd *noun* the solid substance formed when milk coagulates, used for making cheese. Compare **whey**

curd cheese *noun* same as **cottage cheese**

curdle *verb* to make food, especially milk products, go sour

curds *plural noun* same as **curd**

cure *verb* **1.** to preserve fish or meat by salting or smoking it **2.** to make someone healthy ■ *noun* a particular way of making someone well or of stopping an illness

curing salts *plural noun* nitrates used for curing meat

currant *noun* a small dried black grape. ◊ **blackcurrant**, **redcurrant**

curry *noun* **1.** a dish containing meat, fish or vegetables in a highly spiced sauce **2.** a mixture of spices used to prepare curry. It may be a sauce, paste, powder or other form.

curry powder *noun* a mixture of finely ground spices, usually turmeric, cumin, coriander, chilli and ginger, used for making curry

cushion *noun* a cut of beef from near the udder

custard *noun* a sweet yellow sauce made with milk, cornflour and vanilla

cut *noun* a place where the skin has been penetrated by a sharp instrument ■ *verb* **1.** to remove pieces from something, or divide it into pieces, with a knife **2.** to damage the skin with something sharp

cut and fold *verb* to mix dry ingredients into a batter or foamed mixture by sprinkling them on and slowly turning over the mixture with a metal spoon, spatula or knife

cut fruit *noun* fruit that has been peeled or chopped and is subject to browning

cut in *verb* to mix fat into other ingredients by cutting it with a knife

cutlet *noun* a flat cake of minced meat or fish, covered with breadcrumbs and fried

cutlet bat *noun* a heavy kitchen tool with a flat face and a handle used for flattening a piece of meat or fish to allow it to cook faster. ◊ **bat out**

cutlet frill *noun* a small piece of frilled white paper shaped like a chef's hat, used for covering the end of the bare, scraped rib bone on a cutlet or roast joint after it has been cooked. Also called **frill**, **paper frill**

cutter *noun* a pig prepared for both the fresh meat and the processing markets

cutting board *noun* same as **chopping board**

CVD *abbreviation* cardiovascular disease

CWT *abbreviation* Caroline Walker Trust

cyanide *noun* a poison which kills very rapidly when drunk or inhaled

cyanocobalamin *noun* same as **vitamin B12**

cyanogenic glycoside *noun* a phytotoxin found in vegetables including cassava and sorghum

cyclamate *noun* a sweetening substance used instead of sugar, believed to be carcinogenic and banned in the USA, UK and elsewhere as a food additive

cyclamic acid *noun* a synthetic crystalline acid used as a food additive

cyclic adenosine monophosphate *noun* full form of **cAMP**

cyclopeptide *noun* a type of polypeptide that has antibiotic and antifungal properties

cyclospora *noun* a parasitic microbe that affects soft fruit and salad vegetables, causing infection in humans

cyclosporiasis *noun* gastrointestinal infection with cyclospora microbes, causing pain, diarrhoea and fatigue

cystathioninuria *noun* a genetic disease that makes the body unable to convert methionine to cysteine, and may cause mental disorders

cysteine *noun* a sulphur-containing amino acid that is converted to cystine during metabolism

cysteine hydrochloride *noun* ♦ E920

cystic duct *noun* a duct which takes bile from the gallbladder to the common bile duct

cysticercosis *noun* infestation by tapeworms at the larval stage

cystic fibrosis *noun* a genetic disease that thickens bodily mucus and impairs digestion

cystine *noun* an amino acid

cystinuria *noun* a genetic disease involving high levels of cysteine in the urine, causing kidney stones

cytochrome *noun* an iron-containing protein, several types of which are crucial to cell respiration

cytoplasm *noun* a substance inside the cell membrane that surrounds the nucleus of a cell

cytoplasmic streaming *noun* the movement of cytoplasm within living cells resulting in the transport of nutrients and enzymes

D

DADS *abbreviation* diallyl disulfide

daily value *noun* the American equivalent of recommended daily intake

dairy *noun* a room or building where butter and cheese are made ■ *adjective* **1.** relating to or containing milk or milk products **2.** relating to those foods, including milk products, eggs, fish and vegetables, that Jewish dietary law allows on occasions when milk is consumed

dairy drink *noun* a drink made from dairy products such as soya milk or lactose-free milk

dairy product *noun* a food prepared from milk, e.g. butter, cream, cheese or yoghurt

damiana *noun* a herbal supplement from Mexico used as a treatment for depression and erectile dysfunction

dandelion leaf tea *noun* an infusion of dandelion leaves used as a diuretic

danger zone *noun* the range of temperatures most suitable for bacterial growth, 7°C to 60°C or 45°F to 140°F, within which food should not be stored for any length of time

dariole *noun* a small pastry with custard cooked in a dariole mould

dariole mould *noun* a small cup-shaped mould in which individual portions of a dish can be cooked and then served

dark, firm, dry *noun* ♦ DFD meat

dark adaptation *noun* a test for how long it takes the eye to adjust to the dark, a measure of vitamin A deficiency

dark chocolate *noun* chocolate that has no added milk and is darker and less sweet than milk chocolate

dark meat *noun* meat from the legs and thighs of poultry, darker colour than the meat of the breast

date *noun* the small sweet brown fruit of the date palm, a staple food of many people in the Middle East

date mark *noun* a date stamped on a packaged food item indicating either the use-by date, best-before date, best-before-end date or display-until date

date marking, date tagging *noun* the practice of printing the best-before and use-by dates of a food product, a required element in food labelling in the UK

daube *noun* in French cookery, a dish of braised meat or vegetables, especially a traditional French dish of beef braised in wine

dauphinois *adjective* used, in French cuisine, for describing potatoes that are thinly sliced and baked in milk or cream, sometimes with garlic or cheese

deactivate *verb* to turn off a system or a piece of equipment, stopping it from being ready to operate

dealcoholise *verb* to remove some or all of the alcohol from a drink

deaminase *noun* an enzyme that breaks down amino compounds such as amino acids

debone *verb* to take the bones out of meat or fish

decaf *noun* a decaffeinated drink, especially coffee (*informal*)

decaffeinated *adjective* from which the caffeine has been removed

decant *verb* **1.** to pour wine from a bottle into another container, so as to remove the sediment, worth doing only with wine that is several years old **2.** to put a food such as jam or pickle from large jars into small serving dishes for each table

decay *noun* **1.** the process by which tissues become rotten, caused by the action of microorganisms and oxygen **2.** damage caused to tissue or a tooth by the action of microorganisms, especially bacteria ■ *verb* to rot

decentralised service *noun* a method of serving food, used e.g. in hospitals, in which food is prepared in bulk and sent to serving points where it is placed onto dishes or trays for onward dispatch

decilitre *noun* a unit of measure equal to 100 millilitres or one tenth of a litre. Abbreviation **dl**

decimal reduction time *noun* ♦ **D value**

decoction *noun* **1.** the extraction of an essence or active ingredient from a substance by boiling **2.** a concentrated substance that results from decoction

decolourisation *noun* a method of filtering sugars and syrups by passing carbon through them to remove impurities

decompose *verb* to break down organic matter from a complex to a simpler form, mainly through the action of fungi and bacteria, or to be broken down in this way

decorate *verb* to put coloured icing on a cake

deep-fat fryer *noun* same as **deep fryer**

deep-freeze *noun* a powerful refrigerator for freezing food and keeping it frozen ■ *verb* to freeze food and keep it frozen

deep-fried *adjective* cooked in deep oil or fat

deep-fry *verb* to cook food in a deep pan of boiling oil or fat

deep fryer *noun* an electrical appliance for deep-frying food. Also called **deep-fat fryer**

deer *noun* any of various ruminant animals the males of which have distinctive antlers (NOTE: The meat of deer is venison.)

defat *verb* to remove the fat or fats from something

defecate *verb* **1.** to expel faeces from the bowel through the rectum **2.** to remove impurities from a solution, especially a solution that contains sugar

defect eliminator *noun* a device on a food production line that automatically scans for product defects

deficiency *noun* a lack of something necessary, especially a nutrient

deficiency disease *noun* a disease caused by lack of an essential element in the diet such as vitamins or essential amino and fatty acids

deficient *adjective* not meeting the required standard

Defra *abbreviation* Department of the Environment, Food and Rural Affairs

defreeze *verb* to thaw frozen food

defrost *verb* **1.** to remove ice that has formed inside a refrigerator or freezer **2.** to thaw frozen food

deglaze *verb* to dissolve fragments remaining in a frying or roasting pan by heating them and adding a liquid in order to make a sauce

deglutition *noun* the physical action or process of swallowing

dégorger *verb* to salt and drain a vegetable such as aubergine to remove bitter juices

degrease *verb* to remove fat from the surface of a liquid, either by skimming, decanting or soaking it into paper

dehumidify *verb* to remove water vapour from air, either by passing the air over a chemical that absorbs water or over a cold surface that condenses it

dehusk *verb* to remove the husks from fruits, nuts, or grains

dehydrate *verb* **1.** to remove water from something in order to preserve it **2.** to lose water

dehydrated milk *noun* milk that has been dried and reduced to a powder. Also called **dried milk**

dehydration *noun* **1.** the removal of water from something in order to preserve it **2.** a dangerous lack of water in the body resulting from inadequate intake of fluids or excessive loss through sweating, vomiting or diarrhoea

dehydrator *noun* an electrical appliance for drying food, consisting of a stack of interlocking trays through which heated air is circulated

dehydrocanning *noun* the process of removing half the water content from food before canning

dehydrofreezing *noun* the process of removing half the water content from food before freezing

deionised water *noun* purified water that has been through a process that removes mineral salts. Also called **demineralised water**

Delaney Amendment *noun* a US law forbidding the use of carcinogenic additives in food

Delhi belly *noun* diarrhoea that affects people travelling in foreign countries, caused by consuming unwashed fruit or drinking water that has not been boiled (*informal*)

deli *noun* same as **delicatessen**

delicatessen *noun* a shop selling cold meats and imported or specialised food products, and usually also sandwiches and snacks

deli counter *noun* a counter in a supermarket or food shop that sells delicatessen products

delta-tocopherol *noun* ♦ **E309**

demerara sugar *noun* light brown sugar with coarse crystals, originally from Demerara in Guyana but now produced widely from raw cane sugar (NOTE: It is used for coffee and various desserts and is less moist than muscovado.)

demersal *adjective* used for describing fish that live on or near the seabed. Compare **pelagic**

demi chef *noun* a chef who specialises in a particular type of cooking as part of a kitchen's staff

demi chef de rang *noun* the deputy to a chef de rang

demineralised water *noun* same as **deionised water**

demographic *adjective* relating to the details of a population

demographics *plural noun* the details of the population of a country, in particular its size, density, distribution, and the birth, death and marriage rates, all of which affect marketing

denaturation *noun* a loss of biological function in a protein after treatment with heat, acid or alkali

denature *verb* **1.** to add a poisonous substance to alcohol to make it unsuitable for humans to drink **2.** to change the natural structure of a protein or nucleic acid by high temperature, chemicals or extremes of pH **3.** to convert a protein into an amino acid

denatured alcohol *noun* ethyl alcohol with an additive, usually methyl alcohol, that makes it unfit for people to drink

density *noun* mass or weight per unit of volume (NOTE: Water has a density of 1 kg per litre, saturated brine about 1.22 kg per litre and vegetable oil about 0.8 kg per litre.)

dental caries, dental decay *noun* the rotting of a tooth

dental erosion *noun* the loss of tooth enamel after attack by acids, sometimes caused by repeated vomiting related to an eating disorder

dental plaque *noun* a hard smooth bacterial deposit on teeth, the probable cause of caries

deoxyribonucleic acid *noun* full form of **DNA**

deoxyribose *noun* a simple sugar with five carbon atoms per molecule that is a structural component of DNA

Department for Education and Skills *noun* a UK government department responsible for education at all levels and ages, and training people for work. Abbreviation **DfES**

Department of Health *noun* a UK government department in charge of health services. Abbreviation **DH**

Department of the Environment, Food and Rural Affairs *noun* a UK government department responsible for farming, the environment, animal welfare and rural development in England and Wales. Abbreviation **Defra**

Department of Trade and Industry *noun* a UK government department that deals with areas such as commerce, international trade and the stock exchange. Abbreviation **DTI**

depectinisation *noun* the process of removing the cloudiness from fruit juice using enzymes

dependence *noun* the fact that a person is addicted to a substance

derivative *noun* a substance that is derived from another substance

dermatitis herpetiformis *noun* an itchy skin condition associated with coeliac disease, which responds to the withdrawal of gluten from the diet. Abbreviation **DH**

desalination *noun* the removal of salt from a substance such as sea water or soil

descale *verb* **1.** to remove the lime scale that has accumulated in a household appliance such as a kettle **2.** same as **scale**

descriptive analysis *noun* technical sensory analysis of a food product by a panel of trained testers

descriptor *noun* a standard term used in sensory analysis of foods to describe what it reminds the tester of

desiccate *verb* **1.** to preserve food by removing moisture from it **2.** to dry out

desiccated coconut *noun* the white flesh of a coconut that has been dried

designer egg *noun* an egg with increased levels of vitamins and minerals, created by adding particular compounds to the chicken's feed

desmutagen *noun* a compound that makes a mutagen less effective

dessert *noun* a sweet dish eaten at the end of a meal

dessert fork *noun* a small, three-pronged fork used for eating solid desserts such as cheesecake

dessertspoon *noun* a spoon for eating desserts, smaller than a soup spoon but larger than a teaspoon

deterioration *noun* the fact of becoming worse

detox *noun* same as **detoxification**

detoxication *noun* the process in which toxic compounds in the body are metabolised into ones that can be excreted

detoxification *noun* **1.** the process of removing a toxic substance from something or counteracting its toxic effects **2.** the process of subjecting yourself to withdrawal from a toxic or addictive substance such as alcohol or drugs

devein *verb* to remove the dark thready gut from the back of the tail meat of a prawn

devil *verb* to cook or prepare a food with spicy seasonings

devil's claw *noun* a plant of the sesame family with tuberous roots used for stimulating digestion (NOTE: Its botanical name is *Harpagophytum procumbens*.)

dextran *noun* a branched polysaccharide produced by the action of bacteria on sucrose, used as a blood plasma substitute and a food additive

dextrin *noun* a product that is an intermediate in the formation of maltose, used in syrups and beers

dextrinisation *noun* ♦ **Maillard reaction**

dextrose *noun* same as **glucose**

DFD meat *noun* meat with a high pH due to lack of glycogen. Full form **dark, firm, dry**

DfES *abbreviation* Department for Education and Skills

D-glucono-1,5-lactone *noun* a substance that is hydrolysed to produce gluconic acid

DH *abbreviation* **1.** dermatitis herpetiformis **2.** Department of Health

DHA *noun* a polyunsaturated essential fatty acid found in cold-water fish that has been linked to the reduction of cardiovascular disease and other health benefits. Full form **docosahaexanoic acid**

dhal *noun* **1.** a term used in South Asian cooking for dehusked and split pigeon peas, lentils or similar small pulses (NOTE: From the Hindi word meaning 'to split'.) **2.** a South Asian dish of cooked dehusked split pulses with aromatic flavourings, onions and other vegetables

dhool *noun* tea leaves in their fresh state, before being dried for use

di- *prefix* containing two atoms, radicals or groups

diabetes *noun* any of a group of diseases in which the body cannot control sugar absorption because the pancreas does not secrete enough insulin. ◊ **Type I diabetes, Type II diabetes**

diabetes mellitus *noun* the most common form of diabetes. ◊ **Type I diabetes, Type II diabetes**

Diabetes UK *noun* a registered charity that funds research and raises awareness of diabetes

diabetic food *noun* food with low carbohydrate and sugar levels suitable for diabetics

diacetyl *noun* a substance produced in wine by lactic acid bacteria, which can make it unpleasantly sweet and buttery-tasting

diacetyl tartaric acid *noun* a substance that is combined with monoglyceride to create an acid-resistant emulsifying ester

diallyl disulfide *noun* a compound found chiefly in plants of the allium family such as garlic. Abbreviation **DADS**

dialyse *verb* to treat someone using a kidney machine

dialysis *noun* a procedure in which a membrane is used as a filter to separate soluble waste substances from the blood

diarrhoea *noun* a condition in which someone frequently passes liquid faeces

diarrhoeal disease *noun* any disease caused by bacteria, viruses or parasites that has diarrhoea as the main symptom

diastolic blood pressure *noun* the pressure of blood in a person's artery when the heart contracts, shown written over the systolic blood pressure reading. Compare **systolic blood pressure**

dicalcium citrate *noun* ♦ **E330**

dicalcium diphosphate *noun* ♦ **E540**

dice *verb* to cut food into small cubes

dicer *noun* a kitchen implement used for cutting vegetables into small cubes

diet *noun* **1.** the amount and type of food eaten **2.** the act of eating only particular types of food, in order to become thinner, to cure an illness or to improve a condition ■ *verb* to reduce the quantity of food you eat, or to change the type of food you eat, in order to become thinner or healthier ■ *adjective* used for describing a food or drink that is intended for people trying to lose weight, usually because it is low in calories or fat, or contains a sugar substitute

dietary *adjective* relating to food eaten

dietary cholesterol *noun* inessential cholesterol which is not synthesized by the liver, but passes into the bloodstream from the diet

dietary fat *noun* fat from food, which is an essential nutrient and also transports other nutrients such as fat-soluble vitamins

dietary fibre *noun* food materials that cannot by hydrolysed by digestive enzymes and are therefore important for digestive health, found in fruit and grains. Also called **roughage**, **non-dietary polysaccharides**

dietary guidelines *plural noun* public advice on healthy eating

dietary intake *noun* the amount of a nutrient that a person receives through their diet

dietary laws *plural noun* the rules governing which items of food members of a particular religion are permitted to eat

dietary recall survey *noun* a description of everything that a person has eaten over a specific period, given by the person themselves, for the purposes of evaluating their diet

dietary reference value *noun* the amount of a particular nutrient that is recommended per person per day by official bodies

dietary supplement *noun* ♦ **supplement**

dietary survey *noun* a consumer profile charting diet against such factors as age, gender and income

diet drink *noun* a drink that is low in calories or is a reduced-calorie version of a popular drink

dieter *noun* someone who is on a diet, especially a weight-loss diet

dietetic *adjective* referring to diets

dietetic assistant *noun* an employee in a clinical setting who assists a Registered Nutritionist

dietetic food *noun* any food designed for people with specific nutritional requirements

dietetics *noun* the study of food and its nutritional value

diethylpropion *noun* an anorectic drug used for treating obesity

dietician *noun* another spelling of **dietitian**

diet-induced thermogenesis *noun* an increase in heat production in the body after eating. Abbreviation **DIT**

dietitian *noun* someone who specialises in the study of diet, especially someone in a hospital who supervises diets as part of the medical treatment of patients. ◊ **nutritionist**

diet sheet *noun* a printed sheet of dietary advice distributed by healthcare professionals

digest *verb* to break down food in the stomach and intestine and convert it into elements that can be absorbed by the body

digestibility *noun* the percentage of a food that is digested and absorbed

digestible *adjective* possible to digest

digestif *noun* an alcoholic drink taken after a meal to help the digestion, e.g. brandy or a liqueur

digestion *noun* the act of breaking down food in the stomach and intestine and converting it into elements that can be absorbed by the body

digestive *adjective* helping you to digest something

Digestive Disorders Foundation *noun* ♦ **Core**

digestive enzyme *noun* an enzyme in the digestive system which aids the biochemical breakdown of food in the body

digestive juices *plural noun* bile, saliva, intestinal juice and gastric juice

digestive system *noun* the set of organs that comprises the stomach, liver and pancreas, responsible for the digestion of food. Also called **alimentary system**

diglyceride *noun* an ester of fatty acids with glycerol

Dijon mustard *noun* a pale, smooth French mustard that is the most common mustard used in cooking, made with brown mustard seed, salt, spices, water and white wine

dill *noun* a herb of the parsley family used as flavouring or a garnish

diluent *noun* a substance used for diluting a liquid, e.g. water

dilute *verb* to make something thinner or weaker by adding water or another liquid, or to become thinner or weaker in this way

dimethylpolysiloxane *noun* ♦ **E900**

dim sum *noun* a light meal or appetiser of small dishes of southern Chinese style

dioxin *noun* an extremely poisonous gas that is a by-product of various industrial processes

dip *noun* a creamy mixture into which vegetables or pieces of bread can be dipped

dipeptidase *noun* an enzyme that breaks down dipeptides in the final stage of protein digestion

dipeptide *noun* a compound composed of two amino acids

diphenyl *noun* a white crystalline substance used as a fungicide. Also called **biphenyl, phenylbenzene**. ◊ **E230**

dipotassium hydrogen orthophosphate *noun* a chemical used for purifying water for human consumption

dipper *noun* a cup or ladle for dipping into liquid

dipsesis *noun* an unusually great thirst, or a craving for unusual drinks

dipsetic *adjective* provoking thirst

-dipsia *suffix* relating to the sense of thirst

dipsogen *noun* something that provokes thirst

dipsomania *noun* a craving for alcohol

disaccharide *noun* a sugar consisting of two linked monosaccharide units

disaccharide intolerance *noun* an inability to digest lactose, maltose or sucrose, which then ferment in the gut causing diarrhoea

disc mill *noun* a grinder with two rotating circular plates

discolour *verb* to change the colour of something

discrimination test *noun* a product test designed to show how one product differs from another

disease of civilisation *noun* any condition caused by the poor diet and low exercise rate associated with developed countries, e.g. diabetes, heart disease and hypertension

dish *noun* 1. a large plate for serving food 2. a part of a meal, or a plate of prepared food

disinfect *verb* to make the surface of something or somewhere free from microorganisms

disinfectant *noun* a substance designed to kill germs

disjoint *verb* to cut meat, game or poultry into pieces by severing the joints between bones

disodium citrate *noun* ♦ E331

disodium dihydrogen diphosphate *noun* ♦ E450(i)

disodium guanylate *noun* ♦ E627

disodium hydrogen orthophosphate *noun* a chemical used for purifying water for human consumption

disodium inosinate *noun* a food additive used as a flavour enhancer, often in conjunction with monosodium glutamate

disodium tartrate *noun* an additive used as a binding agent and emulsifier

dispensable amino acids *plural noun* same as **non-essential amino acids**

display-until date *noun* a date mark used on packaged food for stock control purposes and not an indication of shelf life. ◊ **best-before date, use-by date**

dissolve *verb* to absorb or disperse something in liquid

distension *noun* a condition in which something is swollen

distil *verb* to make strong alcohol by heating wine or other alcoholic liquid and condensing it

distillation *noun* the act of distilling water or alcohol

distillery *noun* a factory for distilling alcohol (NOTE: The plural form is **distilleries**.)

distribution channel *noun* 1. the route by which a product reaches a customer after it leaves the producer or supplier 2. an area where controlled amounts of feed are made available to livestock

DIT *abbreviation* diet-induced thermogenesis

diuresis *noun* an increase in the production of urine

diuretic *noun* a substance that increases the production of urine ■ *adjective* causing increased production of urine

diverticulitis, diverticulosis *noun* inflammation of protrusions called **diverticula** in the lining of the large intestine, causing severe abdominal pain, often with fever and constipation

DNA *noun* a chemical substance that is contained in the cells of all living things and carries their genetic information. Full form **deoxyribonucleic acid**

dock *verb* to make holes in rolled-out pastry to allow any air bubbles in the pastry to collapse and thus prevent irregularities when it is baked (NOTE: The holes are made either with a fork, a hand roller with many short spines or an industrial-scale machine.)

dockage *noun* waste material that is removed from grain as it is being processed before milling

docosahexanoic acid *noun* full form of **DHA**

dodecyl gallate *noun* ♦ E312

dog fish *noun* same as **huss**

doily *noun* a decorative lacy mat that is put on plates under cakes or party food to display the food attractively

dolomite *noun* same as **calcium magnesium carbonate**

doner kebab *noun* a Turkish meat dish consisting of slices of spit-roasted meat served with pitta bread and salad, usually as a takeaway

dose-related response *noun* a human response to a stimulant that varies according to the amount it is exposed to

dot *verb* to put small pieces of butter over the surface of food to be grilled

double *noun* a double measure of alcoholic spirits

double-acting baking powder *noun* a chemical raising agent that releases carbon dioxide firstly on being moistened and secondly on being heated. Compare **single-acting baking powder**

double-blind testing *noun* a form of blind testing in which the researchers are not aware which subjects are receiving the supplement and which are receiving a placebo until the results have been collected and analysed. Compare **single-blind testing**

double boiler *noun* a cooking utensil made up of two saucepans, one of which fits on top of the other, the lower pan containing hot water and the top pan containing the food to be cooked. Also called **double saucepan**

double cream *noun* thick cream with a high fat content

doubledecker *noun* same as **club sandwich**

double grid *noun* a wire-mesh frame with a handle in which food can be placed for barbecuing to allow it to be turned over easily and without damage

double loin *noun* a cut of meat incorporating the loin chops from both sides of the animal

double saucepan *noun* same as **double boiler**

dough *noun* an uncooked mixture of water and flour for making bread or pizza

dough hook *noun* a hook-shaped heavy metal arm used in mixing machines for mixing and kneading bread doughs

dough knife *noun* a kitchen utensil used for cutting and scraping dough when baking

doughnut *noun* a small round or ring-shaped cake cooked by frying in oil

Dover sole *noun* a seawater flatfish found in northwest Europe and the Mediterranean, highly prized for its lean white flesh. Also called **sole** (NOTE: Two species exist, *Solea solea* and *Solea vulgaris*, both having a mud-coloured upper surface and a whitish underside.)

drain *verb* to empty or dry something by allowing the water to flow out of or off it, or become empty or dry in this way

dram *noun* a small amount of an alcoholic drink, particularly whisky or brandy

draw *verb* to remove the innards from a carcass before cooking it

drawn butter *noun* melted butter that has had the solids removed, served as a sauce, sometimes with herbs and seasoning

dredge *verb* to sprinkle or cover food with a coating of icing sugar, flour or sugar

dredger *noun* a container with small holes in the top used for sprinkling icing sugar, flour or sugar onto food

dress *verb* to prepare something such as a chicken for cooking

dressed crab, dressed lobster *noun* cooked crab or lobster with the legs removed and the flesh broken up and put back into the shell

dressing *noun* a sauce for salad

dressing out *noun* the process of butchering a carcass into edible meat cuts

dressing percentage *noun* the proportion of a live animal's weight that translates into edible meat cuts, after blood drainage, removal of hide, feet and other inedible parts, usually between 50% and 60%

dried fruit *noun* fruit that has been dehydrated to preserve it for later use

dried milk *noun* same as **dehydrated milk**

dried vine fruit *plural noun* dried fruits that come from grapes, e.g. raisins, sultanas and currants

drinkable *adjective* able to be drunk, or pleasant to drink

drinkableness *noun* the extent to which a liquid is safe to drink or of a good enough quality to drink

Drinkaware Trust *noun* a charitable organisation campaigning for education about alcohol consumption limits

drinking chocolate *noun* sweet chocolate powder, used for making a hot drink

drinking water *noun* water that is safe to drink, as opposed to water for washing

dripping *noun* the fat that melts off meat when it is being cooked and hardens when cold, used for frying, basting and making pastry

dropping consistency *noun* the consistency of a cake or pudding mixture such that a spoonful of the mixture held upside down should drop off the spoon in more than 1 and fewer than 5 seconds

drown *verb* to put far too much liquid onto food

drug-nutrient interaction *noun* the effect of a medication on the proper function, absorption or use of a nutrient

drupe *noun* a fruit with a single seed and a fleshy body, e.g. a peach, plum or olive

dry *adjective* **1.** used for describing wine that is not sweet **2.** used for describing a place in which the drinking of alcohol is forbidden ■ *verb* to remove water from something

dry-blanche-dry process *noun* a way of preserving fruit

dry brining *noun* the practice of covering vegetables in salt before pickling to remove water

dry-cure *verb* to preserve fish or meat in salt crystals as opposed to brine

dry fry *verb* to fry food using no oil in a non-stick silicone pan

dry goods *plural noun* any dry foods that can be stored for long periods without deterioration

drying *noun* a method of preserving food by removing moisture, either by leaving it in the sun, as for dried fruit, or by passing it through an industrial process

dry-roast *verb* to roast food, e.g. spices, coffee beans or nuts, with no oil or fat at all

dry-salt *verb* to use salt to dry and preserve food

DTI *abbreviation* Department of Trade and Industry

Dublin Bay prawn *noun* a large prawn, often served as scampi

duchesse potatoes *plural noun* creamed potatoes with beaten egg added, piped into small mounds and baked in an oven

duck *noun* **1.** any of various species of common water bird **2.** the meat of this bird used as food

due diligence *noun* a requirement of the food safety legislation that food producers must take all reasonable care that the food they produce is safe, and is produced and packed in a way that prevents contamination

dumpling *noun* a small ball of paste, often with a filling, that is boiled or steamed

dunst *noun* fine semolina flour

duodenum *noun* the first part of the small intestine, going from the stomach to the jejunum

durability date *noun* ♦ best-before date, use-by date

duration-related response *noun* a human response to a stimulant that varies according to the time spent exposed to it

durum wheat *noun* a hard type of wheat grown in southern Europe and used for making pasta

dust *verb* to sprinkle a powdery substance over something, e.g. sugar over a cake

duxelles *noun* a paste made from mushrooms sautéed with shallots and herbs in butter and used with stuffings, sauces and soups, or as a garnish

D value *noun* a number that shows how long and at what temperature food should be heated to reduce the number of micro-organisms by 90%

dye *noun* a substance used for changing the colour of something

dysentery *noun* an infection and inflammation of the colon causing bleeding and diarrhoea

dysgeusia *noun* impairment of the sense of taste

dyslipidaemia *noun* an imbalance of lipids

dysmesesis *noun* difficulty in chewing food

dysorexia *noun* any eating disorder

dysoxia *noun* a condition in which bodily tissues cannot make use of available oxygen in the bloodstream

dyspepsia *noun* pain or discomfort in the stomach when eating

dyspeptic *adjective* relating to dyspepsia

dysphagia *noun* difficulty with swallowing

dystrophy *noun* the wasting of an organ, muscle or tissue due to lack of nutrients in that part of the body

dysuria *noun* pain while urinating

dysvitaminosis *noun* a disease caused by either a deficiency or excess of a particular vitamin

E

E100 *noun* same as **curcumin**

E101 *noun* riboflavin and riboflavin-5'phosphate, used as a food colouring. Also called **vitamin B2**

E102 *noun* same as **tartrazine**

E104 *noun* quinoline yellow, a synthetic food colouring

E110 *noun* sunset yellow FCF or orange yellow s, synthetic food colourings used in biscuits

E120 *noun* cochineal, the red food colouring extracted from an insect. Same as **cochineal**

E122 *noun* carmoisine or azorubine, synthetic red food colourings

E123 *noun* amaranth, a synthetic red food colouring banned in the USA, used in alcoholic drinks

E124 *noun* ponceau 4R, a synthetic red food colouring used in dessert mixes

E127 *noun* erythrosine BS, a synthetic red food colouring used in glacé cherries

E128 *noun* red 2G, a synthetic dye used for colouring sausages

E131 *noun* patent blue V, a synthetic food colouring

E132 *noun* indigo carmine or indigotine, a synthetic blue food colouring

E133 *noun* brilliant blue FCF, a synthetic food dye used in conjunction with yellows to colour tinned vegetables

E140 *noun* same as **chlorophyll**

E141 *noun* copper complexes of chlorophyll used as food colourings

E142 *noun* green S, acid brilliant green BS and lissamine green, synthetic green food colourings

E150 *noun* same as **caramel**

E151 *noun* black PN or brilliant black PN, synthetic black food colourings

E153 *noun* carbon black or vegetable carbon, used as a food colouring, e.g. in liquorice

E154 *noun* brown FK, a synthetic food dye used on kippers

E155 *noun* brown HT, a synthetic food dye used in chocolate cake

E160(a) *noun* any of various carotenes, orange food colourings obtained from plants

E160(b) *noun* annatto, bixin and norbixin, golden yellow food colourings used in crisps, obtained from the seeds of achiote

E160(c) *noun* capsanthin or capsorubin, pink peppery-flavoured food colouring obtained from paprika

E160(d) *noun* lycopene, a natural red food colour, one of the carotenoids extracted from ripe fruit especially tomatoes

E160(e) *noun* beta-apo-8'-carotenal, an orange carotene compound extracted from fruit and vegetables

E160(f) *noun* the ethyl ester of E160(e), an orange food colouring

E161(a) *noun* flavoxanthin, a natural carotenoid yellow food colouring

E161(b) *noun* lutein, a natural carotenoid yellow or red food colouring extracted from flower petals. Also called **xanthophyll**

E161(c) *noun* cryptoxanthin, a natural yellow carotenoid food colouring extracted from the petals and berries of the Physalis

E161(d) *noun* rubixanthin, a natural carotenoid yellow food colouring extracted from rose hips

E161(e) *noun* violaxanthin, a natural carotenoid yellowish brown food colouring

E161(f) *noun* rhodoxanthin, a natural carotenoid violet food colouring

E161(g) *noun* canthaxanthin, a natural orange food colouring extracted from shellfish, used in fish food to give colour to farmed salmon

E162 *noun* beetroot red or betanin, a red food colouring extracted from beetroot, used for ice cream and liquorice

E163 *noun* any of various anthocyanins, red, violet or blue vegetable food colourings extracted from grape skins, used in yoghurt

E170 *noun* calcium carbonate used as an acidity regulator, firming agent, release agent and diluent

E171 *noun* titanium dioxide, an inert white pigment used in sweets

E172 *noun* iron oxide and hydroxides, natural red, brown, yellow and black food colourings and pigments

E173 *noun* aluminium, a silvery metal sometimes used in very thin layers as a food decoration

E174 *noun* silver, sometimes used in very thin layers as a food decoration

E175 *noun* gold, sometimes used in very thin layers in the decoration of cakes

E180 *noun* pigment rubine or lithol rubine BK, synthetic red colours used for colouring the rind of hard cheeses

E200 *noun* sorbic acid, used as a preservative in baked and fruit products, soft drinks and processed cheese slices

E201 *noun* sodium sorbate, the sodium salt of sorbic acid used as a preservative in frozen pizzas and flour confectionery

E202 *noun* potassium sorbate, the potassium salt of sorbic acid, used as a preservative in frozen pizzas and flour confectionery

E203 *noun* calcium sorbate, the calcium salt of sorbic acid, used as a preservative in frozen pizzas and flour confectionery

E210 *noun* benzoic acid, a naturally occurring organic acid also made synthetically, used as a preservative in beer, jam, salad cream, soft drinks, fruit products and marinated fish

E211 *noun* sodium benzoate, the sodium salt of benzoic acid, used in the same way as E210

E212 *noun* potassium benzoate, the potassium salt of benzoic acid, used in the same way as E210

E213 *noun* calcium benzoate, the calcium salt of benzoic acid, used in the same way as E210

E214 *noun* ethyl 4-hydroxybenzoate, a synthetic derivative of benzoic acid used as a food preservative

E215 *noun* sodium ethyl 4-hydroxybenzoate, the sodium salt of E214, used in the same way as E210

E216 *noun* propyl 4-hydroxybenzoate, a synthetic derivative of benzoic acid, used in the same way as E210

E217 *noun* sodium propyl 4-hydroxybenzoate, the sodium salt of E216, used in the same way as E210

E218 *noun* methyl 4-hydroxybenzoate, a synthetic derivative of benzoic acid, used in the same way as E210

E219 *noun* sodium methyl 4-hydroxybenzoate, the sodium salt of E218, used in the same way as E210

E220 *noun* sulphur dioxide, a pungent and irritating gas that is one of the most common food preservatives, used in dried fruit, dehydrated vegetables, fruit products, juices and syrups, sausages, cider, beer and wine, to prevent the browning of peeled potatoes and to condition biscuit doughs

E221 *noun* sodium sulphite, a compound formed from caustic soda and sulphur dioxide, used in the same way as E220

E222 *noun* sodium hydrogen sulphite, a similar food preservative to E221 but with a higher proportion of sulphur dioxide

E223 *noun* sodium metabisulphite, a compound that contains twice as much sulphur dioxide as E221

E224 *noun* potassium metabisulphite, a similar compound to E223

E226 *noun* calcium sulphite, a food preservative similar to E221

E227 *noun* calcium hydrogen sulphite, a food preservative similar to E222

E228 *noun* potassium bisulphite, a food preservative used in wines

E230 *noun* diphenyl, a fungicide that is often used on the wrappings of oranges and bananas or in their packing cases. Also called **biphenyl, phenyl benzene**

E231 *noun* 2-hydroxy diphenol, a synthetic compound used in the same way as E230. Also called **orthophenyl phenol**

E232 *noun* sodium diphenyl-2-yl oxide, a synthetic compound used in the same way as E230. Also called **sodium orthophenylphenate**

E233 *noun* 2–(thiazol-4-yl) benzimidazole, a synthetic compound used in the same way as E230. Also called **thiabendazole**

E234 *noun* nisin, a food preservative used in cheese and clotted cream (NOTE: It is licensed for use in the UK but not generally in the EU.)

E236 *noun* formic acid, a natural chemical found in some fruit but made synthetically for use as a flavour enhancer

E237 *noun* sodium formate, the sodium salt of formic acid, used as a flavour enhancer

E238 *noun* calcium formate, the calcium salt of formic acid, used as a flavour enhancer

E239 *noun* hexamine, a synthetic chemical used as a preservative in preserved fish and Provolone cheese

E249 *noun* potassium nitrite, the potassium salt of nitrous acid, used for maintaining the pink colour of cured meats and in some cheeses

E250 *noun* sodium nitrite, the sodium salt of nitrous acid, used for maintaining the pink colour of cured meat by reacting with the haemoglobin in it

E251 *noun* sodium nitrate, the sodium salt of nitric acid, used for curing and preserving meat

E252 *noun* potassium nitrate, the potassium salt of nitric acid, used for curing and preserving meat. Also called **saltpetre**

E260 *noun* acetic acid, the acid component of vinegar, used as an acidity regulator, as a flavouring and to prevent mould growth

E261 *noun* potassium acetate, the potassium salt of acetic acid, used as a preservative and firming agent

E262 *noun* sodium acetate used in the same way as potassium acetate, E261 (NOTE: It is licensed for use in the UK but not generally in the EU.)

E263 *noun* calcium acetate, the calcium salt of acetic acid, used as a firming agent and as a calcium source in quick-setting jelly mixes

E270 *noun* lactic acid, a substance produced by the anaerobic metabolism of some microorganisms and animal muscle, widely used as an acidifying agent, flavouring and as a protection against mould growth, e.g. in salad dressings and soft margarine

E280 *noun* proprionic acid, a simple fatty acid that occurs naturally in dairy products but is also synthesised for use as a flour improver and preservative

E281 *noun* sodium proprionate, the sodium salt of proprionic acid, used as a flour improver and preservative

E282 *noun* calcium proprionate, the calcium salt of proprionic acid, used as a flour improver and preservative

E283 *noun* potassium proprionate, the potassium salt of proprionic acid, used as a flour improver and preservative

E290 *noun* carbon dioxide, the gas that makes yeasted goods rise, also used as a propellant, in sealed packs where oxygen must be excluded, and in fizzy drinks

E296 *noun* malic acid, an acid found in fruit and also produced synthetically, used as a flavouring in soft drinks, biscuits, dessert mixes and pie fillings

E297 *noun* fumaric acid, used in the same way as E296

E300 *noun* L-ascorbic acid, used for preventing oxidation and browning in food, and as a flour improver. Also called **vitamin C**

E301 *noun* sodium L-ascorbate, the sodium salt of ascorbic acid, used in the same way as E300

E302 *noun* calcium L-ascorbate, the calcium salt of L-ascorbic acid, used in the same way as E300

E304 *noun* 6-o-palmitoyl L-ascorbic acid, an oil soluble ester of ascorbic acid, used in the same way as E300, especially in Scotch eggs

E306 *noun* any extract of a natural substance that is rich in tocopherols, e.g. vitamin E, used as a vitamin additive in foods and as an antioxidant in vegetable oils

E307 *noun* synthetic alpha-tocopherol, used as an antioxidant in cereal-based baby foods

E308 *noun* synthetic gamma-tocopherol, used in the same way as E306

E309 *noun* synthetic delta-tocopherol, used in the same way as E306

E310 *noun* propyl gallate, the propyl ester of gallic acid, used as an antioxidant in oils, fats and essential oils

E311 *noun* octyl gallate, the octyl ester of gallic acid, used as an antioxidant in oils, fats and essential oils

E312 *noun* dodecyl gallate, the dodecyl ester of gallic acid, used as an antioxidant in oils, fats and essential oils

E320 *noun* BHA, butylated hydroxyanisole, a controversial antioxidant, allowed for used in fats, oils and essential oils only

E321 *noun* BHT, butylated hydroxytoluene, a controversial antioxidant, allowed for use in fats, oil, essential oils and chewing gum

E322 *noun* same as **lecithin**

E325 *noun* sodium lactate, the sodium salt of lactic acid, used as a buffer in foods and as a humectant in jams, preserves and flour confectionery

E326 *noun* potassium lactate, the potassium salt of lactic acid, used as a buffer in jams, preserves and jellies

E327 *noun* calcium lactate, the calcium salt of lactic acid, used as a buffer and as a firming agent in tinned fruits and pie fillings

E330 *noun* citric acid, the acid present in citrus and other fruit and in animals, used as an acidifying agent, as an emulsifier, as a flavour enhancer, and to protect foods from reaction with metals in, e.g., soft drinks, biscuit fillings and processed cheeses

E331 *noun* any of various sodium salts of citric acid used in the same way as E330

E332 *noun* either of two potassium salts of citric acid used in the same way as E330

E333 *noun* any of various calcium salts of citric acid used in the same way as E330 and also as a firming agent

E334 *noun* tartaric acid, an acid naturally present in many fruits, used in the same way as E330

E335 *noun* either of two sodium salts of tartaric acid, used in the same way as E334

E336 *noun* either of two potassium salts of tartaric acid used in the same way as E334, one of which, potassium hydrogen tartrate, is the cream of tartar used as a constituent of baking powder

E337 *noun* potassium sodium tartrate, a mixed salt of tartaric acid, used in the same way as E334

E338 *noun* orthophosphoric acid, an inorganic acid used as an acidity regulator in soft drinks and cocoa

E339(a) *noun* sodium dihydrogen orthophosphate, a sodium salt of orthophosphoric acid, used as a buffer, sequestrant and emulsifying agent

E339(b) *noun* disodium hydrogen orthophosphate, used in the same way as E339(a)

E339(c) *noun* trisodium orthophosphate, used in a similar way to as E339(a) but not as a buffer

E340(a) *noun* potassium dihydrogen orthophosphate, a potassium salt of orthophosphoric acid used in the same way as E339(a)

E340(b) *noun* dipotassium hydrogen orthophosphate, used in the same way as E339(a)

E340(c) *noun* tripotassium orthophosphate, used in a similar way to as E339(a) but not as a buffer

E341(a) *noun* calcium tetrahydrogen diorthophosphate, a calcium salt of orthophosphoric acid used as a firming agent, anticaking agent and raising agent

E341(b) *noun* calcium hydrogen orthophosphate, used in the same way as E341(a)

E341(c) *noun* tricalcium orthophosphate, used in the same way as E341(a)

E350 *noun* either of two sodium salts of malic acid used as buffers and humectants in sweets, cakes and biscuits

E351 *noun* potassium malate, used in the same way as E350

E352 *noun* either of two calcium salts of malic acid E296, used as firming agents in processed fruit and vegetables

E353 *noun* metatartaric acid, a sequestering agent used in wine

E355 *noun* adipic acid, an organic acid used as a buffer and flavouring in sweets and synthetic cream desserts

E363 *noun* succinic acid, an organic acid used as a buffer and flavouring in dry foods and beverage mixes

E370 *noun* 1,4-heptanolactone, used as an acid and sequestering agent in dried soups and instant desserts

E375 *noun* nicotinic acid used as a colour stabiliser in bread, flour and breakfast cereals. Also called **vitamin B3**

E380 *noun* triammonium citrate, an ammonium salt of citric acid used as a buffer and emulsifier in processed cheese

E381 *noun* ammonium ferric citrate, used as an iron supplement in bread

E385 *noun* calcium disodium EDTA, used as a sequestering agent in tinned shellfish

E400 *noun* alginic acid, a water-loving carbohydrate acid extracted from seaweeds in the form of mixed sodium, potassium and magnesium salts, used for its thickening and gelling properties, e.g. in ice cream and soft cheeses

E401 *noun* sodium alginate, the sodium salt of alginic acid used as an emulsifier and stabiliser in cake mixes and in ice cream to provide a creamy texture and to prevent the formation of ice crystals

E402 *noun* potassium alginate, the potassium salt of alginic acid used as a thickener and stabiliser

E403 *noun* ammonium alginate, the ammonium salt of alginic acid used as a more soluble thickener and stabiliser

E404 *noun* calcium alginate, the calcium salt of alginic acid, which gives a much more solid gel than the other alginates

E405 *noun* propane-1, 2-diol alginate, an ester of alginic acid that mixes more freely with fats and oils than simple salts do, used in salad dressings and cottage cheese

E406 *noun* same as **agar-agar**

E407 *noun* carrageenan, a polysaccharide used as an emulsifier in oil and water mixtures and for gelling and thickening, extracted from some types of seaweed

E410 *noun* locust bean gum, a plant gum used as a thickener or gelling agent, e.g. in salad cream

E412 *noun* same as **guar gum**

E413 *noun* gum tragacanth, a vegetable gum obtained from an Asian shrub, used for thickening creams and jellies, to prevent the crystallisation of sugars in jam and ice creams

E414 *noun* same as **gum arabic**

E415 *noun* same as **xanthan gum**

E416 *noun* karaya gum, used as an emulsifier and stabiliser, e.g. in soft cheeses and brown condiment sauce

E420(i) *noun* same as **sorbitol**

E420(ii) *noun* sorbitol syrup, a water solution of sorbitol

E421 *noun* mannitol, found in many plants and plant exudates, now synthesised from sucrose, used as a humectant and in sugar-free confectionery

E422 *noun* glycerol, a naturally occurring alcohol used as a humectant in cake icing and confectionery

E432 *noun* polyoxyethylene sorbitan monolaurate, a synthetic emulsifier used in icecream

E433 *noun* polyoxyethylene sorbitan monooleate, a synthetic emulsifier used in bakery products

E434 *noun* polyoxyethylene sorbitan monopalmitate, an antifoaming agent

E435 *noun* polyoxyethylene sorbitan monostearate, an emulsifier and thickener used in dairy products and soups

E436 *noun* polyoxyethylene sorbitan tristearate, a close relative of E435 and used in the same way

E440(i) *noun* same as **pectin**

E450(i) *noun* any of various salts of phosphoric acid used for flavouring, as stabilisers, buffers, sequestrants, emulsifiers, texturisers and raising agents in fish and meat products, whipping cream, bread, tinned vegetables and processed cheese

E450(ii) *noun* pentasodium triphosphate and pentapotassium triphosphate, used in the same way as E450(a)

E450(iii) *noun* either of two mixtures of phosphoric acid salts, used in the same way as E450(a) and to stabilise added water in poultry, ham, bacon and other similar meat products where it appears as a white exudate on cooking

E452 *noun* any of various polyphosphates, used as a stabiliser and emulsifier

E460(i) *noun* microcrystalline cellulose, used for adding bulk to and for stabilising slimming foods, convenience foods and desserts and also in grated cheese

E460(ii) *noun* powdered cellulose, used in the same way as E460(i)

E461 *noun* methyl cellulose, a methyl derivative of cellulose used as a thickener, e.g. in low-fat spreads

E463 *noun* hydroxypropyl cellulose, a derivative of cellulose, used in the same way as E461

E464 *noun* hydroxypropylmethyl cellulose, a mixed derivative of cellulose, used as a thickener in ice cream

E465 *noun* ethylmethyl cellulose, a mixed derivative of cellulose, used as a thickener in gateaux

E466 *noun* sodium carboxymethyl cellulose, the sodium salt of a derivative of cellulose, used as a thickener and bulking agent in jellies and gateaux

E470 *noun* any of various salts of fatty acids used as emulsifiers in cake mixes

E471 *noun* any of various manufactured synthetic fats widely used in place of fats and oils in baked goods and desserts to improve keeping qualities and to soften and stabilise them

E472(i) *noun* any of various manufactured synthetic fats and oils used in the same way as E471

E472(ii) *noun* any of various lactic acid esters used in the same way as E471 and in convenience toppings

E472(iii) *noun* any of various citric acid esters used in the same way as E471 and in continental sausages

E472(iv) *noun* any of various tartaric acid esters used in the same way as E471

E472(v) *noun* any of various diacetyl tartaric acid esters used in the same way as E471, especially in bread and frozen pizzas

E472(vi) *noun* any of various mixed acetic and tartaric esters used in the same way as E471

E473 *noun* any of various sucrose esters of fatty acids used in the same way as E471

E474 *noun* any of various sucroglycerides, used in the same way as E471, especially in ice cream

E475 *noun* any of various polyglycerol esters of fatty acids, used in the same way as E471, especially in cakes and gateaux

E476 *noun* any of various polyglycerol esters of castor oil, used in chocolate-flavoured coatings for cakes

E477 *noun* propane-1, 2-diol esters of fatty acids, used in the same way as E471, especially in instant desserts

E481 *noun* sodium stearoyl-2-lactylate, the sodium salt of a derivative of lactic and stearic acids, used for stabilising doughs, emulsions and whipped products

E482 *noun* calcium stearoyl-2-lactylate, the calcium salt that corresponds to E481, used in gravy granules

E483 *noun* stearyl tartrate, a derivative of stearic and tartaric acids, used in cake mixes

E491 *noun* sorbitan monostearate, a fatty aid ester used as an emulsifier in bakery products and cosmetics

E492 *noun* sorbitan tristearate, a fatty acid ester used as an emulsifier for water/oil emulsions

E493 *noun* sorbitan monolaurate, a fatty acid used as an emulsifier and stabiliser

E494 *noun* sorbitan mono-oleate, used as an emulsifier, stabiliser and thickener

E495 *noun* sorbitan monopalmitate, a fatty acid used as an emulsifier and stabiliser

E500 *noun* any of various compounds of sodium used as bases, aerating agents and diluents in jams, jellies, self-raising flour, wine and cocoa

E501 *noun* potassium carbonate or potassium hydrogen carbonate, used in the same way as E500

E503 *noun* ammonium carbonate or ammonium hydrogen carbonate, used as a buffers and aerating agents in cocoa and biscuits

E504 *noun* magnesium carbonate, used as a base and anticaking agent in wafer biscuits and icing sugar

E507 *noun* same as **hydrochloric acid**

E508 *noun* potassium chloride, used as a gelling agent and as a substitute for salt (**sodium chloride**)

E509 *noun* calcium chloride, used as a firming agent in tinned fruit and vegetables

E510 *noun* ammonium chloride, used as a yeast nutrient in bread making

E513 *noun* same as **sulphuric acid**

E514 *noun* sodium sulphate, used as a diluent for food colours

E515 *noun* potassium sulphate, used as a fertiliser

E516 *noun* calcium sulphate, used as a firming agent and as a yeast food in bread making

E518 *noun* magnesium sulphate, used as a firming agent. Also called **Epsom salts**

E524 *noun* sodium hydroxide, a very strong base used for adjusting acidity in cocoa, jams and sweets

E525 *noun* potassium hydroxide, a very strong base used for adjusting acidity in sweets

E526 *noun* calcium hydroxide, a weak base used as a firming agent in sweets

E527 *noun* ammonium hydroxide, a weak base used as a diluent and solvent for food colours and as an acidity regulator for cocoa

E528 *noun* magnesium hydroxide, a weak base used for regulating acidity in sweets

E529 *noun* calcium oxide, a weak base used for regulating acidity in sweets

E530 *noun* magnesium oxide, a fine white powder used as an anticaking agent in cocoa products

E535 *noun* sodium ferrocyanide, used as an anticaking agent in salt and used in winemaking

E536 *noun* potassium ferrocyanide, used as an anticaking agent in salt and used in winemaking

E540 *noun* dicalcium diphosphate, a calcium salt of phosphoric acid, used as a buffer and neutralising agent in cheese

E541 *noun* sodium aluminium phosphate, used as an acid and raising agent in cake mixes, self-raising flour and biscuits

E542 *noun* edible bone phosphate, a fine powder made from boiled dried and ground bones, used as an anticaking agent

E544 *noun* calcium polyphosphate, used as an emulsifier in processed cheese

E545 *noun* ammonium polyphosphate, used as an emulsifier, a texturiser and to help retain water in frozen chickens

E551 *noun* silicon dioxide, very finely powdered purified sand, used as an anticaking agent in skimmed milk powder and sweeteners

E552 *noun* calcium silicate, used as an anticaking agent in icing sugar and as a release agent in sweets

E553(a) *noun* magnesium silicate and magnesium trisilicate, used as anticaking agents and in sugar confectionery

E554 *noun* aluminium sodium silicate, used as an anticaking agent

E556 *noun* aluminium calcium silicate, used as an anticaking agent

E558 *noun* bentonite, a very fine white clay-like mineral used as an anticaking agent

E559 *noun* same as **kaolin**

E572 *noun* magnesium stearate, a type of soap used as an emulsifier and release agent

E575 *noun* d-glucono-1,5-lactone, an acid and sequestering agent used in cake mixes and continental-style sausages. Also called **glucono delta-lactone**

E576 *noun* sodium gluconate, used as a sequestering agent

E577 *noun* potassium gluconate, used as a sequestering agent

E578 *noun* calcium gluconate, used as a buffer, firming agent and sequestering agent in jams and dessert mixes

E620 *noun* glutamic acid, an amino acid used as a flavour enhancer

E621 *noun* same as **monosodium glutamate**

E622 *noun* same as **monopotassium glutamate**

E627 *noun* guanosine 5'-disodium phosphate, used as a flavour enhancer in savoury foods, snacks, soups, sauces and meat products. Also called **sodium guanylate** (NOTE: It is produced when the genetic material of cells breaks down.)

E631 *noun* inosine 5'-disodium phosphate, a flavour enhancer similar to E627. Also called **sodium inosinate**

E635 *noun* sodium 5'-ribonucleotide, a flavour enhancer similar to E627

E900 *noun* dimethylpolysiloxane, used as an anti-foaming agent in liquid foodstuffs and ingredients

E901 *noun* same as **beeswax**

E903 *noun* same as **carnauba wax**

E904 *noun* same as **shellac**

E905 *noun* any of various mineral hydrocarbons used for preventing dried vine fruits from sticking together and as a glazing and release agent

E907 *noun* a refined microcrystalline wax derived from crude oil, used as a release agent and in chewing gum

E920 *noun* cysteine hydrochloride, the acid salt of the amino acid cysteine used as a flour improver. Also called **L-cysteine hydrochloride**

E925 *noun* same as **chlorine**

E926 *noun* chlorine dioxide, used as a flour improver

E927 *noun* azodicarbonamide, used as a flour improver

EA *abbreviation* Environment Agency

EAR *abbreviation* estimated average requirements

earthy *adjective* relating to or consisting of soil

easy open lightweight end *noun* used for describing a can with a ring-pull opening. Abbreviation **EOLE**

eating apple *noun* a sweet apple that may be eaten raw

eating disorder *noun* an illness that causes the usual pattern of eating to be disturbed, e.g. anorexia or bulimia

Eating Disorder Not Otherwise Specified *noun* an eating disorder that meets most but not all of the diagnostic criteria for anorexia, bulimia or binge eating disorder, e.g. where the person displays some anorexic behaviour but is still a healthy weight or has regular periods. Abbreviation **EDNOS**

Eating Disorders Association *noun* an organisation that provides support and information for people suffering from eating disorders and their families. Abbreviation **EDA**

eating pattern *noun* the times of day at which a person eats and the amount that they eat at each sitting

ECA stack *noun* a thermogenic sports supplement containing ephedrine, caffeine and aspirin

echinacea *noun* a herbal remedy prepared from the pulverised leaves and stems of purple coneflowers, thought to bolster the immune system

éclair *noun* a long thin cylinder of choux pastry filled with whipped cream and topped with chocolate or coffee icing

E coli *abbreviation* Esherichia coli

E coli 0157 *noun* a form of E coli found in the digestive tracts of cattle, which causes haemorrhagic colitis and can be fatal to children and the elderly

ecological *adjective* relating to the environment and the ways in which plants, animals and people exist together

ectomorph *noun* a body type that is tall, thin and possibly underweight. Compare **endomorph**

ecuelle *noun* a deep dish used for serving vegetables

ED *abbreviation* electrodialysis

EDA *abbreviation* Eating Disorders Association

Edam *noun* a mild Dutch cheese with a slightly rubbery texture, typically formed into balls covered with red wax

edible *adjective* used for describing something that can be safely eaten

edible bone phosphate *noun* ♦ **E542**

EDNOS *abbreviation* Eating Disorder Not Otherwise Specified

EDTA *noun* a chemical compound used as a preservative and stabiliser. Full form **ethylene diamine tetra-acetate**

eel *noun* a fish with a long thin body resembling that of a snake, smooth skin without scales, and very small fins (NOTE: Eels belong to the order *Anguilliformes*.)

EFA *abbreviation* essential fatty acid

EFLA *abbreviation* European Food Law Association

EFSA *abbreviation* European Food Safety Authority

EFSIS *noun* a technical standard for companies supplying retailer-branded food products. Full form **European Food Safety Inspection Scheme**

egg *noun* **1.** an oval object with a hard shell, produced by a female bird and from which a baby bird comes **2.** an egg produced by a domestic hen, the type of egg most commonly used as food for humans

egg foam *noun* egg white that has been whipped until it is foamy and stiff, used as a basis for soufflés

egg noodles *plural noun* noodles made with flour, water and egg

eggplant *noun* same as **aubergine**

eggs Benedict *noun* a dish consisting of ham and a poached egg in hollandaise sauce on a slice of toast or a split toasted muffin

egg separator *noun* a kitchen tool shaped like a large spoon or small ladle with a slot or holes to allow the white of an egg to pass through, leaving the yolk in the spoon

egg slicer *noun* a small kitchen tool for slicing a hard-boiled egg, with a hollow base and multiple wires on a hinged frame

egg-wash *verb* to brush beaten egg over a food to be baked, to glaze it and give it a brown colour

egg white *noun* the part of an egg that is not yellow. Also called **white**

egg yolk *noun* the central part of an egg, usually light yellow or orange, semi-liquid and held separate from the white in a fragile membrane (NOTE: It contains about 16% protein, mainly lecithin, 33% fat including cholesterol, plus vitamins, trace elements and water. It represents about 30% of the total weight of a hen's egg.)

EHEC *abbreviation* enterohaemorrhagic E coli

EHEDG *abbreviation* European Hygienic Engineering and Design Group

eicosanoid *noun* a compound of long-chain fatty acids

eicosapentaenoic acid *noun* full form of **EPA**

eiswein *noun* very sweet German wine made from frozen grapes

elastic *adjective* able to stretch and contract

elastin *noun* a protein that occurs in elastic fibres

electric mixer *noun* a handheld kitchen tool with rotating whisks or blades for processing food

electric whisk *noun* a handheld kitchen tool with two rotating whisks for beating liquids

electrodialysis *noun* a method of purifying liquids using a filtering membrane with an electrical charge. Abbreviation **ED**

electrolyte *noun* a substance in cells, blood or other organic material that helps to control fluid levels in the body and maintain normal pH levels

electrolyte balance *noun* the levels of electrolytes in the blood, which should be neither too high, to avoid overloading the kidneys, nor too low, to avoid weakness and malnutrition

electrolytic tinplate *noun* a corrosion-resistent metal used for making tins. Abbreviation **ETP**

electropure process *noun* a method of sterilising milk using electrical current

eleuthero *noun* a stimulant sports supplement that may increase metabolism

elimination *noun* the methodical process of removing an item or items from a list of possibilities, as a way of narrowing down a search

elimination diet *noun* a structured diet where different foods are eliminated one at a time in order to see the effect on symptoms, used in conditions such as allergies and attention deficit hyperactivity disorder

ELISA *abbreviation* enzyme-linked immunosorbent assay

elixir *noun* an alcoholic extract of a naturally occurring substance

ellagic acid *noun* a yellow crystalline compound used for reducing bleeding

emaciation *noun* bodily wasting caused by malnutrition

e mark *noun* a mark like a small 'e' before the weight of a food product on its label, indicating that it conforms to European standards of minimum weight

embolism *noun* a condition in which an artery is blocked by a blood clot, interrupting normal blood circulation

embryo *noun* **1.** an unborn baby during the first eight weeks after conception (NOTE: After eight weeks, the unborn baby is called a **foetus**.) **2.** a plant in its earliest stages of development

emetatrophia *noun* bodily wasting caused by an inability to keep food down

emetic *noun* a substance that causes vomiting ■ *adjective* causing vomiting

emetocathartic *adjective* used for describing a medicine that purges the stomach and intestines by provoking vomiting and diarrhoea

Emmental *noun* a type of hard cheese from Switzerland with large holes and a mild nutty flavour

emollient laxative *noun* a substance that softens the contents of the bowel by mixing fatty deposits evenly, promoting its free passage

empty calorie *noun* food that contains energy, but no nutrients

emulsification *noun* the process of converting two or more liquids into an emulsion, or becoming an emulsion

emulsifier, emulsifying agent *noun* a substance added to mixtures of food such as water and oil to hold them together. ◊ **stabiliser** (NOTE: Emulsifiers are used in sauces and added to meat to increase the water content so that the meat is heavier. In the European Union, emulsifiers and stabilisers have E numbers E322 to E495.)

emulsify *verb* to convert two or more liquids into an emulsion, or to become an emulsion

emulsion *noun* a combination of liquids such as oil and water that do not usually mix

enamel *noun* a glass-like covering for steel, sometimes used for trays, saucepans, casseroles and other kitchen utensils

encapsulate *verb* to enclose a nutrient, enzyme or other desirable substance within a vehicle such as a lipid, so that it is most efficiently delivered to its source

encapsulation efficiency *noun* the percentage of ingested nutrients that are encapsulated and delivered

encapsulation technology *noun* methods of enriching foods by encapsulating extra nutrients inside vehicles such as lipids

endive *noun* **1.** a green salad plant similar to a lettuce, with curly bitter-tasting leaves **2.** a vegetable with a conical head of white crisp leaves packed firmly together, eaten raw in salads or cooked with a sauce. ◊ **chicory**

endocrine gland *noun* a gland such as the pituitary gland that produces hormones introduced directly into the bloodstream

endomorph *noun* a body type that is short, stocky and easily puts on weight. Compare **ectomorph**

endoscope *noun* an instrument used for examining the inside of the body, made of a thin tube containing a fibreoptic light, passed into the body down a passage

endoscopy *noun* an examination of the inside of the body using an endoscope

endosperm *noun* a storage tissue in plant seeds that provides nourishment for the developing embryo

energy balance *noun* a series of measurements showing the movement of energy between organisms and their environment (NOTE: In farming a common use of the energy balance is to assess the ratio between the amount of energy used to grow a crop and the amount of energy that crop produces.)

energy bar *noun* a bar-shaped snack made of ingredients intended to boost physical energy

energy expenditure *noun* the amount of energy used during a particular activity such as running or walking

energy requirements *plural noun* the number of calories that are needed to sustain a person leading a particular lifestyle

energy value *noun* the amount of energy produced by a given amount of a particular food

English mustard *noun* a mixture of dehusked and ground brown and white mustard seeds mixed with wheat flour and turmeric, sold dry or mixed with water and preservatives, used for flavouring or as a condiment

English service *noun* a way of serving food in which the host apportions food onto plates that are then distributed by a waiter

Englyst method *noun* a method of determining the amount of fibre of a food by measuring its polysaccharide content

enhancer *noun* an artificial substance that increases the flavour of food, or even the flavour of artificial flavouring that has been added to food

enolase *noun* an enzyme involved in the metabolism of carbohydrates

enrich *verb* **1.** to improve the nutritional quality of food **2.** to improve the living conditions of farm animals, e.g. by providing them with larger living areas

enriched *adjective* of food, having had vitamins and minerals added to make it more nutritious

enrobe *verb* to coat food with something such as chocolate or sauce

Ensure *noun* a nutritionally-complete milkshake supplement used as a therapeutic food

enteralgia *noun* same as **colic**

enteral nutrition *noun* tube feeding directly into the intestine through the abdominal wall

enterectomy *noun* total or partial surgical removal of the intestine

enteric *adjective* relating to the intestine

enteritis *noun* an inflammation of the mucous membrane of the intestine

enterobiasis *noun* a common children's disease, caused by threadworms in the large intestine that cause itching round the anus. Also called **oxyuriasis**

enterocolitis *noun* inflammation of the small and large intestine

enterodynia *noun* pain in the intestine

enterohaemorrhagic E coli *noun* a type of toxic bacteria that causes gastrointestinal infection with blood in the bowel movements, found in the gut of cattle. Abbreviation **EHEC**

enterokinase *noun* an enzyme in the upper small intestine that converts trypsinogen to trypsin

enteropathy *noun* any disorder of the intestine

enterorrhoea *noun* excessive secretion of mucus in the intestine

enterostomy *noun* a surgical operation to make an opening between the small intestine and the abdominal wall

enterotomy *noun* a surgical incision in the intestine

enterotoxin *noun* a substance that is toxic to intestinal mucosa

enterotropic *adjective* related to or affecting the intestinal tract

enterovirus *noun* a virus that prefers to live in the intestine

entoleter *noun* a machine that removes insects and eggs from grain

entrecote *noun* a steak cut from the middle part of a sirloin of beef

E number *noun* a classification number given to a food additive by the European Union

Environment Agency *noun* in England and Wales, the government agency responsible for protection of the environment, including flood and sea defences. Abbreviation **EA**

environmental allergen *noun* an airborne allergen such as dust, insect spores or pet hair

environmental inequality *noun* the situation in which some societies consume more natural resources and emit more pollutants than others

enzymatic browning *noun* the browning of fruit and vegetables that occurs when cut surfaces are exposed to air, which can be inhibited by acids, e.g. lemon juice or vinegar

enzyme *noun* a protein substance produced by living cells that aids a biochemical reaction in the body

enzyme activation assay *noun* a test of enzyme activity in red blood cells that reveals vitamin deficiencies

enzyme defect *noun* a metabolic disorder caused by a deficiency of a particular enzyme

enzyme-linked immunosorbent assay *noun* full form of **ELISA**

enzyme precursor *noun* same as **proenzyme**

enzymic browning *noun* same as **enzymatic browning**

enzymology *noun* the study of enzymes

enzymolysis *noun* the breakdown of a substance into smaller particles, caused by an enzyme

enzymopathy *noun* a disruption in enzyme function

EOLE *abbreviation* easy open lightweight end

eosinophil *noun* white blood cells produced in response to bodily infections

eosinophilia *noun* an elevated level of eosinophils in the blood, symptomatic of parasite infection

eosinophilia-myalgia syndrome *noun* a neurological condition linked to tryptophan supplements that led to them being withdrawn from sale

EPA *noun* a polyunsaturated essential fatty acid found in cold-water fish that has been linked to the reduction of cardiovascular disease and other health benefits. Full form **eicosapentaenoic acid**

ephedra *noun* a plant used as a stimulant and slimming aid, containing ephedrine

ephedrine *noun* a drug that relieves asthma and blocked noses by causing the air passages to widen

epidemic *adjective* spreading quickly through a large part of the population ■ *noun* an outbreak of an infectious disease that spreads very quickly and affects a large number of people

epidemiology *noun* the study of diseases in the community, in particular how they spread and how they can be controlled

epiglottis *noun* a flap of cartilage at the root of the tongue that moves to block the windpipe when food is swallowed, so that the food does not go down the trachea

epinephrine *noun* same as **adrenaline**

epizootics *noun* the study of disease epidemics in animals that may spread to humans

Epsom salts *noun* same as **magnesium sulphate**

erepsin *noun* the mixture of enzymes in the intestines

ergocalciferol *noun* ♦ **vitamin D2**

ergogenic *adjective* used for describing a stimulant that gives greater energy or improved mental capacity

ergosterol *noun* a substance found in yeast and moulds that forms vitamin D_2 when exposed to ultraviolet light

ergot *noun* a fungus that grows on cereals, especially rye, producing a mycotoxin that causes hallucinations and sometimes death if eaten

ergotism *noun* poisoning by eating cereals or bread contaminated by ergot

erythropoiesis *noun* the formation of red blood cells in bone marrow

erythrosine BS *noun* ♦ **E127**

escalope *noun* a thin slice of meat, especially veal, pork, chicken or turkey. ◊ **Wiener schnitzel**

esculent *adjective* edible (*technical*)

Esherichia coli *noun* a bacterium found in the colon of human beings and animals that becomes a serious contaminant when found in the food or water supply. Abbreviation **E coli**

esophago-gastro-duodenoscopy *noun* a diagnostic medical procedure in which an endoscope is passed through the alimentary canal to the stomach and into the small intestine

espresso *noun* **1.** a type of strong Italian coffee, made in a machine in which steam or boiling water is forced through ground coffee under pressure **2.** a cup of this coffee

essence *noun* a concentrated plant extract containing its unique flavour and fragrance

essential amino acid index *noun* a measure of protein quality, expressed as its total amino acid content as compared to egg protein

essential amino acids *plural noun* the eight amino acids that are essential for growth but cannot be synthesised and so must be obtained from food or medicinal substances

essential fatty acid *noun* an unsaturated fatty acid that is essential for growth but cannot be synthesised and so must be obtained from food or medicinal substances

essential oil *noun* a volatile oil with the characteristic odour of the plant from which it is distilled

ester *noun* an organic compound formed during the reaction between an acid and an alcohol with loss of water, often having a fragrant smell

esterase *noun* an enzyme that breaks down esters into their component acids and alcohols, thus destroying or modifying the flavour or aroma of food

esterify *verb* to change or make a substance change into an ester

estimated average requirements *plural noun* the amount of a particular nutrient that is estimated to be consumed per person per day by official bodies. Abbreviation **EAR**

ethane *noun* a highly flammable gas that is colourless and odourless used as a fuel and in refrigeration

ethanol *noun* a colourless liquid, present in alcoholic drinks such as whisky, gin and vodka, and also used in medicines and as a disinfectant. Also called **ethyl alcohol**

ethanolamine *noun* a base used as a softening and peeling agent

ethical *adjective* **1.** concerning ethics, or reasonable or acceptable from a moral point of view **2.** used for describing a drug that available on prescription only

ethical sourcing *noun* ♦ **fair trade**

ethical trading *noun* business practices that are socially responsible and protect the environment and the rights of workers

ethnic food *noun* from a Western perspective, food from a country that is not European or North American, e.g. Chinese or Indian food

ethoxyquin *noun* a chemical used for preventing discoloration on apples and pears

ethyl *adjective* relating to the group of atoms derived from ethane after the loss of a hydrogen atom

ethyl 4-hydroxybenzoate *noun* ♦ **E214**

ethyl acetate *noun* a volatile colourless liquid with a pleasant fruity smell, used as a solvent

ethyl alcohol *noun* same as **ethanol**

ethylene *noun* a gas given off by ripening fruit that is also used for accelerating ripening (NOTE: An overripe banana is often used in an enclosed space to provide this gas for artificial ripening.)

ethylene bromide *noun* a fumigant gas

ethylene diamine tetra-acetate *noun* full form of **EDTA**

ethylene oxide *noun* a fumigant gas

ethyl formate *noun* a flavouring constituent also used for fumigation against insects

ethylmethyl cellulose *noun* ♦ **E465**

ETP *abbreviation* electrolytic tinplate

EU *abbreviation* European Union

EUFIC *abbreviation* European Food Information Council

eupepsia *noun* having a healthy or normal digestive system

eupeptic *adjective* relating to or producing good digestion

euphagia *noun* a normal eating style and pattern

European Food Information Council *noun* a not-for-profit organisation that provides information on healthy eating, nutrition and fitness. Abbreviation **EUFIC**

European Food Law Association *noun* an organisation situated in Belgium whose role is to advise the European Commission on issues relating to food safety laws. Abbreviation **EFLA**

European Food Safety Authority *noun* a consultative body, funded by the European Community, that advises policymakers on health and food safety issues. Abbreviation **EFSA**

European Food Safety Inspection Scheme *noun* full form of **EFSIS**

European Hygienic Engineering and Design Group *noun* a consortium of engineers and food manufacturers working towards improved hygiene in food engineering. Abbreviation **EHEDG**

European Journal of Clinical Nutrition *noun* a scientific publication reporting research affecting the European clinical nutrition industries. Abbreviation **EJCN**

European Nutrigenomics Organisation *noun* an international community of nutrigenomic scientists. Abbreviation **NuGO**

European Society for Clinical Nutrition and Metabolism *noun* an organisation that promotes the diffusion of knowledge in the fields of clinical nutrition and metabolic processes (NOTE: Note that it still uses the acronym ESPEN although the company name has changed.)

European Union *noun* a group of European countries linked together by the Treaty of Rome, basing their cooperation on the four fundamental freedoms of movement: of goods, capital, people and services. Abbreviation **EU**

euryphagy *noun* the practice of eating a wide variety of foods

eusitia *noun* the state of having a normal appetite

eutectic ice *noun* ice made from salted water, which does not melt readily, used as a refrigerant

eutrophia *noun* a normal state of nutrition

evaluation *noun* the act of examining and calculating the quantity or level of something

evaporate *verb* to change from being a liquid to being a vapour, or to change a liquid into a vapour. Compare **condense**

evaporated milk *noun* milk that has been thickened by removing some of the water by evaporation

evening primrose oil *noun* a supplement that is rich is gamma linolenic acid, taken to relieve menstrual symptoms

event catering *noun* catering provided for large events such as weddings and conferences

eviscerate *verb* to remove the internal organs from a carcass

evodiamine *noun* a thermogenic stimulant used by athletes

ewe *noun* an adult female sheep

exchange list *noun* a table showing foods that are equivalent to each other in calorie or fat content or nutritional value, used by dieters

exclusion diet *noun* a diet that eliminates foods suspected of causing of food allergies or intolerance

excrete *verb* to pass waste matter out of the body, especially to discharge faeces

excretion *noun* the act of passing waste matter, e.g. faeces, urine or sweat, out of the body.

executive chef *noun* the main chef in charge of a large restaurant, with many other chefs reporting to him or her

exocrine gland *noun* a gland that discharges its secretion through a duct into a body cavity or to the exterior, e.g. the sweat glands and salivary glands

exogenous nitrogen *noun* nitrogen in the body that comes from dietary sources, as opposed to metabolic nitrogen

expansion rings *plural noun* rings stamped onto the end of a can that expand slightly during heat processing, stopping the can from bursting or deforming

expiry date *noun* the last date on which something can be used. ◊ **best-before date, display-until date, use-by date**

export *noun* **1.** a product made in one country and sold to another. Compare **import 2.** the business of selling goods to other countries ■ *verb* to send goods to buyers in other countries. Compare **import**

exsanguination *noun* the process of draining the blood from a slaughtered animal

extended shelf-life technology *noun* methods such as pasteurisation or the use of active packaging that extend the shelf life of a product

extender *noun* a food additive that makes the food bigger or heavier without adding to its nutritional value

extract *verb* to take something out ■ *noun* a concentrated product obtained by first dissolving a substance and then evaporating the liquid in which it is dissolved

extraction *noun* the removal of the useful part from the whole, as with juice from fruit

extraction rate *noun* the percentage of flour produced as a result of milling grain

extractive *noun* the flavouring components in meat and browned vegetables that dissolve in the cooking liquor to give it flavour

extra virgin olive oil *noun* olive oil produced from the first pressing, which has a low acidity and is regarded as being of the best quality

extrinsic sugars *plural noun* sugars that are added to a foodstuff to enhance the flavour

extrude *verb* to make something by forcing a semisoft substance such as sausage meat through a specially shaped mould or nozzle

extrusion *noun* the process of forcing food through a mould or membrane to process it

exudate *noun* fluid that is released from food when it is cooked

F

F-100 *noun* an enriched milk product that is highly nutritious, distributed by humanitarian agencies during times of famine

FAB *abbreviation* Flour Advisory Bureau

factory *noun* a building or complex of buildings where goods are manufactured on a large scale using machinery or automation

factory hygiene *noun* industrial practices needed in order to maintain total hygiene in a food processing plant

fact sheet *noun* a printed sheet or booklet giving information about something, especially a subject covered in a broadcast programme

FAD *abbreviation* flavin adenine dinucleotide

faddy *adjective* tending to have strongly held likes and dislikes about food

faeces *plural noun* solid waste matter passed from the bowels through the anus

FAGEP *abbreviation* Flour and Grain Education Program

Fahrenheit scale *noun* a scale of temperature in which the freezing point of water is 32° and the boiling point 212°. ◊ **Celsius scale**

failure to thrive *noun* same as **marasmus**

fair trade *noun* an international system in which food companies agree to pay producers in developing countries a fair price for their products

Fairtrade Foundation *noun* a registered charity organisation that promotes fair trade and licenses the Fairtrade mark for use on food packaging

fajitas *plural noun* a Mexican dish consisting of beef or other meat, especially chicken, that has been marinated, grilled, cut into strips and served in a soft tortilla

falafel *noun* a deep-fried ball of ground chickpeas seasoned with onions and spices, originating in Southwest Asia

famine *noun* a period of severe shortage of food

famine response *noun* same as **ketosis**

FAO *abbreviation* Food and Agriculture Organisation of the United Nations

FareShare *noun* an organisation that redistributes waste food from suppliers to people in need

farina *noun* **1.** flour or meal made from wheat, nuts or vegetables **2.** starch, especially that made from potatoes

farinaceous *adjective* used for describing flour that contains starch

farinaceous food *noun* a food such as bread that is made of flour and has a high starch content

farinose *adjective* consisting of or producing food starch

farm assurance *noun* a scheme whereby specific criteria are applied in order to guarantee quality control for farm produce

farmed fish *noun* fish that have been bred or reared in special pools for sale as food

farmed salmon *noun* a salmon grown in cages in sea lochs or inlets, mainly in Scotland and Norway, distinguishable from wild salmon by its pinker flesh and perfect tail fins

farmers' market *noun* a market, usually held outdoors, where farmers sell fresh produce direct to the public

farm shop *noun* a shop that sell foodstuffs directly from the producers, without using distributors or other third parties

farm to fork *noun* the chain of food supply, from the farm where it is produced to the consumer

Fasciola gigantica *noun* a liver fluke that affects cattle and can be transmitted to humans

Fasciola hepatica *noun* a liver fluke that affects sheep and can be transmitted to humans

fascioliasis *noun* a disease caused by an infestation of parasitic liver flukes

fast *noun* a period of going without food, undergone in order to lose weight or for religious reasons ■ *verb* to go without food

fast food *noun* cooked food that can be prepared, bought and eaten quickly

fast-freeze *verb* to freeze food very rapidly, which prevents the formation of large ice crystals that would destroy the structure of the food on thawing

fasting *noun* the practice of going without food

fat *noun* **1.** a white oily substance in the body that stores energy and protects the body against cold **2.** a solid or liquid substance that is derived from animals or plants and is used as a cooking medium or ingredient, e.g. butter or sunflower oil ■ *adjective* **1.** having a body weight greater than is considered desirable or advisable **2.** containing a lot of fat **3.** thick

fat content *noun* the amount of fat in a foodstuff, usually measured in grams

fat extender *noun* any food additive that allows the fat content of food to be reduced without affecting the texture

fat-free *adjective* used for describing foods that contain no animal or vegetable fat

fat free mass *noun* all body tissues not containing fat, including bone, muscle, organs, hair, blood and retained water

fatigue *noun* very great tiredness ■ *verb* to tire someone out

fat replacer *noun* an ingredient used in food processing to give fat-reduced foods a better flavour or texture

fat separator *noun* a kitchen utensil used for draining away fat which has risen to the top of sauces

fat-soluble vitamins *plural noun* vitamins A, D, E and K, which are not soluble in water

fatty acid *noun* any of a group of acids that are important substances in the body, e.g. stearic acid. ◊ **essential fatty acid**

fatty acid oxidation *noun* a chemical process in which a fatty acid reacts with oxygen, losing some electrons to release energy

fatty acid salts *plural noun* ♦ **E470**

fava bean *noun* same as **broad bean**

favism *noun* a type of inherited anaemia caused by an allergy to beans

FCP *abbreviation* Free-Choice Profiling

FDA *abbreviation* Food and Drug Administration

FDF *abbreviation* Food and Drink Federation

feathered game *noun* birds that are hunted for sport and food, e.g. grouse, pheasant and partridge

Federation of Bakers *noun* an association representing the interests of industrial producers of bread and bread products. Abbreviation **FOB**

feed *noun* 1. a meal given to babies 2. food given to animals and birds ■ *verb* to give food to a person or an animal

feed-food chain *noun* the relationship between the substances that are fed to animals before they are slaughtered for food and the substances that might be passed to humans in this way

feeding tube *noun* a plastic tube used for administering enteral nutrition

feedstock *noun* a raw material used in the industrial manufacture of a product

fennel *noun* a herb with seeds and feathery leaves that have a light aniseed flavour

fennel seed *noun* a herb used as a supplement to ease bloating and gas production

fenugreek *noun* a plant of the eastern Mediterranean and Asia with leaves that are used as a herb and seeds that are crushed for use as a spice

ferment *verb* to change something into alcohol by the effect of yeast on sugar

fermentation *noun* a chemical change brought about in liquids, usually leading to the production of alcohol

ferric ammonium citrate *noun* iron in food additive form (red or green flakes)

fertiliser *noun* a chemical or natural substance spread and mixed with soil to stimulate plant growth

ferulic acid *noun* a type of phenol found in citrus fruits that may help reduce heart disease

feta *noun* a firm crumbly salty cheese made from sheep's or goat's milk and preserved in brine, originally from Greece

fettuccine *noun* pasta made in narrow flat strips, slightly narrower and thicker than tagliatelle

FFA *abbreviation* free fatty acids

FFB *abbreviation* Food From Britain

fibre *noun* 1. a structure in the body shaped like a thread 2. same as **dietary fibre**

field mushroom *noun* a common edible mushroom

fig *noun* the juicy sweet fruit of a semi-tropical tree grown mainly in Mediterranean countries and eaten either fresh or dried

filé powder *noun* a spice and thickening agent used in Creole cuisine

fill *verb* to put a filling inside food

fillet *noun* 1. a piece of good-quality meat, with no bones 2. a piece of fish from which the bones have been removed ■ *verb* to take the bones out of a fish

filleting knife *noun* a thin sharp knife used for removing the bones and innards from fish

filling *noun* food used to put inside some other food, e.g. in a sandwich, pie or cake

filo pastry *noun* thin translucent pastry that is usually sold ready prepared in sheets, used for many Mediterranean and Middle Eastern specialities

filter *noun* **1.** a piece of cloth, plastic or paper or a mass of crystals through which water or air passes and which holds back solid particles such as dirt **2.** a piece of paper through which coffee passes in a coffee machine and which separates off the coffee grounds ■ *verb* to pass liquid through a paper or cloth filter, or through crystals, to remove impurities

filth test *noun* a test of the hygienic handling of food by measuring its contamination with substances such as droppings, hairs and insect parts

filtrate *noun* any liquid that is passed through a filter

filtration *noun* the action of passing a liquid through a filter

finger *noun* a small portion of food about as long and thick as an adult human finger

fireless cooker *noun* an insulated container in which hot, partially-cooked food is placed to continue cooking in its own heat

fire point *noun* the temperature at which a cooking oil will ignite and sustain a flame

firming agent *noun* a chemical compound used for maintaining crispness in tinned and bottled vegetables

fish *noun* a cold-blooded animal with fins and scales that lives in water ■ *verb* to try to catch fish

fishcake *noun* a round cake of fish and potato mixed together and fried

fish chef *noun* the chef in charge of preparing fish dishes. Also called **chef poissonnier**

fisherman's pie *noun* same as **fish pie**

fish farm *noun* a place where fish are raised in large numbers in special tanks

fish finger *noun* a rectangular stick of filleted or minced fish covered in breadcrumbs or batter, usually bought frozen in packs

fish fork *noun* a fork with flat prongs used with a fish knife for eating fish

fish kettle *noun* a long metal container for cooking a whole fish

fish knife *noun* a special wide knife with a blunt blade, used for eating fish

fishmonger *noun* **1.** someone whose job is to sell fish to people for food **2.** a shop where fish is sold

fish oil *noun* oil obtained from fish, considered beneficial to health because it contains essential fatty acids and vitamins A and D

fish pie *noun* a dish of various types of fish, cooked in a white sauce with a topping of potatoes. Also called **fisherman's pie**

fish sauce *noun* a salty fishy-tasting liquid that drains off fermented and salted fish, widely used as a flavouring in Southeast Asia

fish slice *noun* a wide flat utensil used for turning fish and removing it from a frying pan

fish stick *noun* same as **fish finger**

fish stocks *plural noun* the population of fish in a particular area of ocean, which may suffer from overfishing

FISS *abbreviation* Food Industry Sustainability Strategy

five-a-day *noun* the government-recommended guideline of eating at least 5 portions of fruit and vegetables a day for health

five freedoms *plural noun* ♦ **Freedom Food**

five-spice powder *noun* a spice that is a mixture of cinnamon, black pepper, cloves, fennel seed and star anise

fizz *noun* champagne (*informal*)

fizzy drink *noun* a drink that has had carbon dioxide put in it so that it is full of small bubbles

flageolet bean *noun* a light green oval bean from semi-mature French bean pods, picked after the pod has become stringy but before it dries off and eaten fresh or dried

flake *noun* **1.** a thin piece of tissue **2.** an apparatus for drying fish ■ *verb* to break something such as fish into flakes

flakiness *noun* the quality of breaking into thin pieces of tissue easily

flaky pastry *noun* a type of soft pastry that breaks into flakes easily when cooked

flambé *adjective* used for describing food that has had brandy or other alcohol poured over it and and has been set alight ■ *verb* to pour brandy or other alcohol over food and set it alight

flambé lamp *noun* same as **chafing lamp**

flameless ration heater *noun* a self-contained device for heating food without a flame, used for army rations. Abbreviation **FRH**

flan *noun* **1.** an open tart **2.** a French word for a custard tart

flank *noun* a cut of meat, especially beef, from an animal's side that is typically tough and requires slow cooking in liquid

flash *verb* to brown the surface of a cooked dish very quickly under a very hot grill or in a very hot oven

FlashBake *noun* a device that can cook food in minutes using infrared radiation

flash evaporation *noun* the rapid evaporation of volatile components from a substance, e.g. fruit juice, that are added back after concentration

flash-freeze *verb* to freeze produce very rapidly, just after it has been picked or caught

flash-fry *verb* to cook food quickly over a very high heat

flash point *noun* the temperature at which a cooking oil will ignite, although not sustain a flame

flat *noun* any flat dish with low straight sides

flatfish *noun* a type of fish with a flattish back that lives on the bed of the sea or of a lake and has both eyes on the top of its body, e.g. a plaice

flat leaf parsley *noun* a variety of parsley with flat leaves (NOTE: Its botanical name is *Petroselinum crispum Neapolitanum.*)

flat mushroom *noun* a fully mature mushroom in which the cap is fully open so that all the gills are exposed on one side

flatogen *noun* a substance that increases gas production in the intestine

flat sour *noun* a bacterium that spoils food without producing gas, with the result that the packaging is not deformed

flatulence *noun* gas or air that collects in the stomach or intestines causing discomfort

flatulent *adjective* having flatulence, or caused by flatulence

flatus *noun* gas produced in the intestine

flatware *noun* flat pieces of crockery, e.g. plates

flatworm *noun* any of several types of parasitic worm with a flat body, e.g. a tapeworm. Compare **roundworm**

flavan-3-ol *noun* an active polyphenol found in red wine and ripened fruit and vegetables

flavanone *noun* a substance derived from flavone

flavido *noun* same as **zest**

flavin adenine dinucleotide *noun* a coenzyme that is required for oxidation and reduction reactions in the body. Abbreviation **FAD**

flavone *noun* a crystalline compound from which yellow pigments are derived

flavonoid *noun* a natural compound derived from phenol, belonging to a group that includes many plant pigments

flavonol *noun* a type of flavonoid found in cocoa

flavour *noun* the property of a substance that stimulates the sense of taste. ◊ **odour** (NOTE: The main flavour qualities are salt, sweet, sour and bitter.) ■ *verb* to add spices and seasoning in cooking to add a flavour to something

flavour enhancer *noun* a substance that has little or no flavour itself but intensifies other flavours with which it is combined, commonly used in processed and convenience foods (NOTE: Monosodium glutamate is the most common and is used to enhance the flavour of vegetables and meat, especially in Chinese cooking.)

flavouring *noun* a substance added to food to give a particular taste

flavour modifier *noun* same as **flavour enhancer**

flavour profile *noun* a breakdown of the character notes of a flavour

flavour profile testing *noun* a method of sensory testing in which the testers choose from a single lexicon of flavour descriptors for all competing products, making the similarities and differences clear

flavour scalping *noun* the absorption of strong flavours from food by its packaging

flavoxanthin *noun* ♦ **E161(a)**

flaxseed *noun* seed from the flax plant, crushed to produce linseed oil

flaxseed oil *noun* oil obtained from the seeds of the flax plant, especially as used in products to promote human and animal health

fleishig *adjective* under Jewish dietary laws, relating to, containing, or used only for meat or meat products. Compare **milchig, pareve**

flesh *noun* **1.** the soft part of the body covering the bones **2.** the soft part of a fruit

fleshy fruit *noun* a fruit that has a mass of soft flesh, e.g. a peach, cherry or grape

flipper *noun* a swell can with one bulging end that can be forced back into place causing the other end to spring out

floor attendant *noun* a waiter responsible for room service in a series of hotel rooms on the same floor. Also called **chef d'étage**

floridean starch *noun* a polysaccharide resembling glycogen

flounder *noun* **1.** an edible flatfish that has a greyish-brown mottled skin with orange spots and prickly scales, native to Europe (NOTE: Its scientific name is *Platichthys flesus*) **2.** the general term for any flatfish **3.** a small coastal flatfish that is excellent for eating but rather small (NOTE: Its scientific name is *Pseudorhombus arsius.*)

flour *noun* a grain crushed to powder, used for making bread, cakes and similar products

Flour Advisory Bureau *noun* an organisation that promotes bread and flour-based products as part of a healthy diet. Abbreviation **FAB**

Flour and Grain Education Program *noun* an information service provided by the Flour Advisory Bureau and the Home-Grown Cereals Authority. Abbreviation **FAGEP**

flour confectionery *noun* food which contains flour and which is sold ready to eat either immediately or after reheating

flour enrichment *noun* the addition of vitamins and minerals such as niacin to flour

flour improver *noun* an additive agent, often a form of vitamin C, that makes dough more elastic and manageable

flour strength *noun* the ability of the proteins in flour to retain gas, making the bread more textured and substantial

floury *adjective* like flour

fluid *noun* 1. a liquid 2. any gas, liquid or powder that flows

fluid bed dryer *noun* an apparatus for drying and gently mixing solid particles using a cushion of hot air

fluid milk *noun* milk that has not been dried or processed into cheese

fluid ounce *noun* a unit of liquid measurement in the imperial system that is equal to one twentieth of a pint or 28.41 ml

fluke *noun* a parasitic flatworm that settles inside the liver, in the bloodstream and in other parts of the body

fluoridation *noun* the addition of sodium fluoride to drinking water to help prevent tooth decay

fluoride *noun* a chemical compound of fluorine and sodium, potassium or tin

fluorosis *noun* a condition caused by excessive fluoride in drinking water

flush *noun* a red colour in the skin ■ *verb* 1. to wash a wound with liquid 2. to turn red ■ *adjective* level or in line with something

flute *noun* an indentation pressed into the edge of pie or pasty for decoration or to help seal two edges of pastry together

FNIC *abbreviation* Food and Nutrition Information Center

foam *noun* 1. a mass of bubbles of air or gas in a liquid film 2. a light, porous, semi-rigid or spongy material used for thermal insulation or shock absorption

foam-mat drying *noun* a way of drying liquid foods by adding a foaming agent and drying the foam on a mat

FOB *abbreviation* Federation of Bakers

focaccia *noun* a flat Italian bread, often sprinkled with a topping before baking, and served hot or cold

foetal alcohol syndrome *noun* damage caused to the foetus by alcohol in the blood of the mother, which affects the growth of the embryo, including its facial and brain development. Abbreviation **FAS**

foie gras *noun* goose liver that is swollen because the bird has been forced to eat large amounts of maize

folate *noun* 1. same as **folic acid** 2. a salt or ester of folic acid

fold in *verb* to add a food ingredient to a mixture carefully and lightly

folding in *noun* a way of combining flour with a soft mixture that cannot be treated roughly because it will lose air, e.g. in the making of a soufflé

folic acid *noun* a vitamin in the vitamin B complex found in milk, liver, yeast and green vegetables such as spinach, essential for creating new blood cells

follow-on milk *noun* an enriched milk drink given to babies during the dietary transition from milk to solid food

fondant *noun* a smooth paste made from boiled sugar syrup, often coloured or flavoured, used as a filling for chocolates or a coating for cakes, nuts, or fruit

fondue *noun* a dish eaten by dipping small pieces of food into a pot that contains a sauce, often cheese sauce, or hot oil

food additive *noun* same as **additive**

food aid *noun* food that is provided by aid agencies during times of war or famine

Food Alert *noun* information issued by the Food Standards Agency to local authorities and consumers when there is a health issue associated with a food product

food allergen *noun* a substance in food that produces an allergy

food allergy *noun* a reaction caused by sensitivity to particular foods, some of the commonest being nuts, strawberries, chocolate, milk, eggs and oranges

Food and Agriculture Organisation of the United Nations *noun* an international organisation that is an agency of the United Nations, established with the purpose of improving standards of nutrition and eradicating malnutrition and hunger. Abbreviation **FAO**

Food and Drink Federation *noun* a body that represents the food and drink manufacturing industry in the UK. Abbreviation **FDF**

Food and Drug Administration *noun* a US government department that protects the public against unsafe foods, drugs and cosmetics. Abbreviation **FDA**

Food and Nutrition Information Center *noun* an online resource provided by the library of the US Department of Agriculture, providing nutritional information and guidance. Abbreviation **FNIC**

food aversion *noun* a dislike for a particular type of food

food bank *noun* a place where food is collected before being distributed to people in need

food-borne disease *noun* a disease caused by microorganisms in ingested food

food choice *noun* the type of foods that a person chooses to eat, based on factors such as level of hunger, appearance of food and packaging, advertising, nutritional education and personal health choices

food chopper *noun* a food processor in which the bowl revolves in the opposite direction to the rotating cutting blades, used for high volume work in commercial kitchens

food combining *noun* the practice of eating different types of food at different times in the belief that this aids digestion and weight loss

Food Commission *noun* an organisation campaigning for safety and sustainability in food production practices

food composition *noun* the percentages of each nutrient present in a particular foodstuff

food court *noun* the part of a shopping centre where snacks and light meals can be bought from a number of different outlets, often with a communal eating area

food diary *noun* a note of all food eaten by a person over a particular period, used by a dietetic professional to assess their diet

food drop *noun* packages of food dropped by aid agencies into areas known to have a food crisis

food energy *noun* the amount of digestible energy provided by food

Food Ethics Council *noun* an independent research and campaign group that examines the ethics of food production processes

food finishing *noun* the action of making a preprepared food product ready to be served, e.g. by browning the surface, arranging it attractively and decorating or garnishing

FoodFitness *noun* an initiative by the Food and Drink Federation to educate the public about healthy eating

Food for Assets *noun* a project run by the World Food Programme, in which underprivileged communities are given food in exchange for work done to create sustainable resources

food formulation *noun* the scientific creation of a food product

food frequency questionnaire *noun* a survey designed to find out how often a person eats particular types of foods

Food From Britain *noun* a trade organisation that promotes British food and drink products. Abbreviation **FFB**

FoodFuture *noun* an initiative by the Food and Drink Federation to provide the public with information about GM foods

food group *noun* a general category under which foods are grouped, e.g. fats, proteins, dairy, fruits, vegetables and grains

food hall *noun* the part of a department store where food is sold

food handler *noun* someone who touches food as part of his or her job

food handling *noun* the act of touching food as part of your job

food hygiene *noun* healthy conditions for handling, storing and serving food

foodie *noun* someone with a lively interest in cooking and eating good food (*informal*)

food industry *noun* businesses at all stages of the food production chain, including farmers, food processing factories, packagers, distributors, retailers and caterers

Food Industry Sustainability Strategy *noun* a policy developed by Defra that covers the secondary and tertiary food industries. Abbreviation **FISS**

Food in Schools *noun* a programme run jointly by DfES and DoH to improve the quality of school meals

food intolerance *noun* a sensitivity to, or an inability to digest, a particular food, ingredient or substance, which means that it should be excluded from the diet

food labelling *noun* the practice, required under EU rules, of labelling packaged food with information such as a list of ingredients in descending order of weight, the net quantity, a best-before or best-before-end date, special conditions of storage or use, the name and address of the packager or seller, and often its place of origin

Food Labelling Regulations 1996 *noun* a UK statute that sets out labelling requirements on food packaging, including mandatory information and the accuracy of descriptions and health claims

food law *noun* any national law that restricts how food can be prepared, packaged, labelled or sold

food line *noun* ♦ feeding tube

Food Manufacture *noun* a journal on the subject

food mile *noun* a measure of the distance travelled by foodstuffs from producer to consumer, long distances being regarded as detrimental to quality, wasteful of energy, and prejudicial to local producers

food mixer *noun* an electrical kitchen appliance used for beating eggs or cream or for mixing together the ingredients for cakes and batters, typically with two detachable beaters that are rotated electrically at varying speeds

food parcel *noun* a small package of essential, highly nutritious food items distributed by the government or aid agencies to vulnerable people at times of war or famine

food poisoning *noun* an illness caused by eating food that is contaminated with bacteria

food preparation *noun* the act of making food ready to eat, by handling, processing and cooking it

food preservation *noun* methods of preventing food from spoiling, using natural and chemical agents and specially-designed packaging and storage methods

food preservation science *noun* the science that deals with methods of destroying or inhibiting the growth of harmful microorganisms in food

food processing *noun* the actions of chopping, cutting, slicing and mixing food, either by hand or automatically

food processor *noun* a kitchen appliance in which food can be cut, sliced, shredded, grated, blended, beaten or liquidised automatically by a variety of removable revolving blades

food product *noun* a retail product that is edible

food pyramid *noun* a chart of a food chain showing the number of organisms at each level

food safety *noun* the issues surrounding the production, handling, storage and cooking of food that determine whether or not it is safe to eat

Food Safety Act 1994 (Amendment) Regulations 2990/2004 (2990) *noun* a statutory amendment that brought the UK Food Safety Act into line with EC food safety regulation 178/2002

food science *noun* the chemical reactions that take place during food creation and processing

foodservice *noun* food served outside the home, e.g. in restaurants and cafés

food slicer *noun* same as **slicing machine**

food spoilage *noun* deterioration in the quality of food, making it unpleasant or unsafe to eat, happening naturally over time or caused by bacterial contamination or poor storage

food stacking *noun* the idea of eating nutrients in a particular order to allow them to be digested in the most efficient manner

food stamp *noun* a coupon issued by the US federal government to poor people so that they can buy food at a discounted price

Food Standards Agency *noun* a British government agency set up in 2000 to offer advice on food safety and make sure that food sold is safe to eat. Abbreviation **FSA**

foodstuff *noun* something that can be used as food

food surveillance *noun* the act of monitoring food at all stages of the supply chain to check for the risk of contamination

food technologist *noun* a person who works in a food technology industry

food technology *noun* the practical application of food science to the process of creating and preparing food

forced convection oven *noun* same as **convection oven**

force-feed *verb* to make someone swallow food against their will, e.g. by using a tube to put it directly down their throat

forcemeat *noun* a mixture of breadcrumbs, onions and flavouring used for stuffing meat and poultry

forcing bag *noun* a soft bag of fabric or plastic, to which various nozzles can be attached, used for squeezing out a soft substance such as icing or puréed potato in a decorative way

foreign contamination *noun* contamination of a can with grease, oil, glue or dirt from the production line

forerib *noun* a cut of beef from the back of the animal

forged knife *noun* the best-quality kitchen knife, made of a single piece of steel that forms the blade and centre of the handle

fork *noun* a piece of cutlery, with a handle at one end and sharp points at the other, used for picking food up

formic acid *noun* a colourless corrosive liquid with an unpleasant smell that is naturally present in ants and in some plants. Also called **methanoic acid** (NOTE: It is used in tanning, electroplating, paper, textiles, insecticides and refrigerants.)

forming machine *noun* a piece of food processing equipment that forms soft foods into shapes such as nuggets

formula *noun* **1.** a way of indicating the composition of a chemical compound using letters and numbers, e.g. H_2SO_4 (NOTE: The plural is **formulas** or **formulae**.) **2.** powdered milk for babies

formula diet *noun* a diet of simple substances that do not need digesting

formula milk *noun* a preparation used as an alternative to human breast milk and intended to provide all the nutrients an infant requires

fortified wine *noun* wine that has an alcoholic spirit added to it, e.g. port or sherry

fortify *verb* to add further ingredients to food or drink in order to improve its flavour or add nutrients

FOS *abbreviation* fructo-oligosaccharide

fowl *noun* a bird kept for its meat and eggs, especially a chicken

FPEO *abbreviation* full-panel easy open

fractional test meal *noun* a way of measuring stomach activity by examining the stomach contents via a tube at intervals after a meal

fragrant *adjective* with a sweet smell

frangipane *noun* an almond-flavoured cream or paste used in pastries, cakes and other sweet foods

Frankenstein food *noun* food or a food product produced using genetic engineering (*informal*)

Free-Choice Profiling *noun* a method of sensory testing in which the testers choose from a different list of descriptors for each product. Abbreviation **FCP**

Freedom Food *noun* an RSPCA scheme that sets out guidelines for the welfare of livestock and labels food that comes from participating suppliers

free fatty acids *plural noun* fatty acids in the blood that are unattached to any other molecule, an important source of fuel. Abbreviation **FFA**

freelance dietitian *noun* a dietitian who is not affiliated full-time to a particular organisation but takes on short-term contract work for different companies and individuals

free radical *noun* an atom or group of atoms that is highly reactive owing to the presence of an unpaired electron (NOTE: Because of the effect they have on cells in the body, free radicals are thought to be a contributory cause of medical conditions such as cancer, atherosclerosis and Alzheimer's.)

free-range *adjective* **1.** used for describing a hen or other farm animal that is free to move about and feed at will, not confined in a battery or pen **2.** produced by free-range poultry or livestock

freeze *verb* **1.** to change the state of something from liquid to solid because of the cold **2.** to become very cold **3.** to store food at below freezing point. ◊ **flash-freeze**

freeze-concentrate *verb* to concentrate fruit juice or another water-based liquid by freezing out part of the water as crystals and removing them

freeze concentration *noun* a method of removing water from fruit juice, by chilling it until the water forms ice crystals which can be removed

freeze-dry *verb* to preserve food by freezing it and then reducing the air pressure around it, which reduces its water content greatly and thereby inhibits the action of microorganisms and enzymes that would otherwise degrade it

freezer *noun* an appliance or room in which food is kept at very low temperatures

freezer burn *noun* the pale dry spots that form when moisture evaporates from frozen food that is not properly wrapped

freezer tunnel *noun* part of a factory production line that flash-freezes food as it passes along a conveyor belt

freezing *noun* a way of preserving food by lowering its temperature to halt microbiological activity

french *verb* to cut meat across the fibres

French beans *plural noun* same as **green beans**

French dressing *noun* same as **vinaigrette**

French fries *plural noun* thin stick-shaped pieces of potato, fried in deep oil or fat

French mustard *noun* a mild-tasting mustard made with wine or unripe grape juice

French paradox *noun* the observation that people in southern France suffer a lower incidence of heart disease, despite eating larger amounts of saturated fat, possibly due to their increased consumption of red wine

French service *noun* **1.** a style of laying the table with a plate, cutlery, glasses and a napkin on the plate **2.** a way of serving food in which guests help themselves from food offered on a dish or flat from the left by a waiter

French trim *noun* a method of preparing a rack of meat by removing the skin and membranes to leave the bones exposed, for presentation purposes

fresh *adjective, adverb* used for describing food that has been made recently, has been recently picked, killed or caught, or is not frozen or tinned

fresh-chilled *adjective* used for describing meat that is chilled when fresh, rather than being frozen or hung

fresh fruit *noun* fruit that has not been processed or preserved after harvesting

fresh water fish *noun* fish such as trout, bass and carp that live in rivers and lakes rather than in the sea

FRH *abbreviation* flameless ration heater

fricassee *noun* a dish of pieces of meat cooked in a rich white sauce ■ *verb* to stew meat, usually chicken, with vegetables in a little water that is then used to make a rich white sauce

fried *adjective* cooked in oil or fat. ◊ **fry**

fried egg *noun* an egg that has been shallow-fried, with the white, on the top, cooked either by basting with hot fat or by turning the egg over when almost finished

friendly bacteria *plural noun* ♦ **probiotic** (*informal*)

frigi-canning *noun* the process of sealing heat-treated food aseptically in a tin and then storing in a chilled place

frill *noun* same as **cutlet frill**

frittata *noun* a firm thick Italian omelette that may contain any of a variety of chopped ingredients, including meat or vegetables

fritter *noun* a piece of fruit, meat or vegetable dipped in a mixture of flour, egg and milk and fried

fromage frais *noun* a fresh cheese with a light creamy taste and a texture like thick cream or yoghurt

front-of-pack information *noun* basic nutritional information presented on the front of packaged food for easy reference

frost *verb* to give an item, especially a soft fruit or the rim of a glass or coupe, a frosty appearance by dipping it in lightly whipped egg white then in caster sugar and leaving it to dry

froth *verb* to dredge meat with flour before basting and roasting

frozen *adjective* 1. very cold 2. at a temperature below freezing point

frozen food *noun* foods, typically processed or made-up dishes, that have been frozen to −20°C and can be stored for six weeks or more

frozen yoghurt *noun* a dessert similar to ice cream made from a mixture of yoghurt, sugar and flavourings

fructo-oligosaccharide *noun* a type of prebiotic. Abbreviation **FOS**

fructosan *noun* a polysaccharide of fructose that is not digestible

fructose *noun* the sugar found in honey and fruits such as figs

fruit *noun* the part of a plant that contains the seeds and is often eaten raw ■ *verb* to produce fruit

fruitarian *noun* someone who eats only fruit

fruit juice *noun* juice from fruit, often served as an appetiser or starter

fruit salad *noun* a mixture of pieces of fresh or tinned fruit, usually in fruit juice or syrup, served as a dessert

fry *verb* to cook in oil or fat in a shallow pan. ◊ **deep-fry**

fryer *noun* a large device for frying quantities of food at the same time

frying basket *noun* same as **chip basket**

frying pan *noun* a shallow, open pan used for frying

FSA *abbreviation* Food Standards Agency

fuel *noun* a substance that can be burnt to provide heat or power, e.g. wood, coal, gas or oil ■ *verb* to use a fuel to power something

fugu *noun* a Japanese fish that is considered a delicacy and must be prepared by a licensed chef as it contains a paralysing, potentially lethal toxin

full-cream *adjective* used for describing milk that has had none of the cream or fat removed, or for describing products made with this kind of milk

fuller's earth *noun* an absorbent clay used for treating cloth and filtering liquids

full-panel easy open *noun* used for describing a can that opens using a key. Abbreviation **FPEO**

fumaric acid *noun* ♦ **E297**

fumigant *noun* a chemical compound that becomes a gas or smoke when heated and is used to kill insects

fumous *adjective* tending to produce gas in the digestive system

functional food *noun* food, often containing additives, that is said to be beneficial to health and able to prevent or reduce diseases such as tooth decay and cancer

fungicide *noun* a substance used for killing fungi

fungus *noun* an organism such as yeast or mould, some of which cause disease (NOTE: The plural is **fungi**.)

furan *noun* a ring compound produced during Maillard browning that supplies a caramel flavour

furcellaran *noun* a polysaccharide used as a gelling agent

furred game *noun* animals that have fur and are hunted for sport and food, e.g. deer and rabbit

fusel oil *noun* a solution of congeners in alcohol that gives flavour to spirits and also causes hangovers

fusilli *plural noun* pasta in the form of short spiral shapes

fusion cuisine *noun* the addition of a product from a different country to a particular type of cooking, or the mixing of dishes from different countries in the same menu

G

g *abbreviation* gram

GABA *abbreviation* gamma-aminobutryic acid

galactans *plural noun* galactose derivatives found in carrageenan

galactosaemia *noun* an inability to digest galactose

galactose *noun* a sugar that forms part of milk and is converted into glucose by the liver

galactosidase *noun* an enzyme that breaks down lactose

galangal *noun* the pungent underground stem of a ginger plant, sold fresh or dried and ground

galantine *noun* a dish of boned and cooked white meat, poultry or fish, usually stuffed, moulded into shape and served cold in its own jelly

galenicals *plural noun* tinctures and other preparations made from medicinal plants

gallbladder *noun* a small muscular sac on the right underside of the liver, in which bile secreted by the liver is stored and concentrated until needed for the digestive process

gallbladder sludge *noun* a thick substance that is not broken down by bile and can build up in the gallbladder, causing pain

gallic acid *noun* a colourless crystalline solid

gallon *noun* a unit of liquid volume in the Imperial System, approximately equal to 4.5 litres

gallstone *noun* a hard stone in the gallbladder formed of bile components

game *noun* **1.** animals that are hunted and killed for sport and food **2.** food from animals such as deer or pheasants that have been hunted and killed

game farming *noun* the breeding and care of furred or feathered game for use in sport shooting

gamey *adjective* used for describing the desired smell and flavour of game that has been hung for the correct time and is sufficiently tenderised

gamma-aminobutryic acid *noun* a stimulant and secretagogue used by athletes. Abbreviation **GABA**

gamma linolenic acid *noun* full form of **GLA**

gamma rays *plural noun* electromagnetic rays that are shorter than X-rays, given off by radioactive substances and used in food irradiation

gamma-tocopherol *noun* ♦ **E308**

gammon *noun* smoked or cured ham, either whole or cut into slices

gammon steak *noun* a thick slice of gammon

GAP *abbreviation* Good Agricultural Practices

garam masala *noun* a mixture of spices used in South Asian cooking to give a hot pungent flavour to a dish

garlic *noun* a plant whose bulb has a strong smell and taste, used as a flavouring

garlic press *noun* a small kitchen tool, usually made of metal or plastic, that minces a clove of garlic by squeezing it through small holes

garlic salt *noun* a preparation of salt and powdered garlic used as a food seasoning

garnish *noun* a small piece of food used as a decoration ■ *verb* to add things to decorate food

gasified *adjective* same as **carbonated**

gasket compound *noun* same as **sealing compound**

gas mark *noun* a mark on the temperature regulator of the oven of a gas cooker, indicating a gradation of heat. Also called **regulo**

gastral *noun* same as **gastric**

gastralgia *noun* pain in the stomach

gastric *adjective* relating to the stomach

gastric band *noun* a band fitted around the stomach to reduce its capacity in gastric bypass surgery

gastric bypass *noun* surgery to reduce the capacity of the stomach, used for treating morbid obesity

gastric feeding tube *noun* a plastic tube used for administering long-term enteral nutrition, which enters the stomach via an opening in the abdomen created by a gastrostomy procedure

gastric inhibitory peptide *noun* a hormone that stimulates insulin production, secreted by the duodenum. Abbreviation **GIP**

gastric juice *noun* the mixture of hydrochloric acid, pepsin, intrinsic factor and mucus secreted by the cells of the lining membrane of the stomach to help the digestion of food (NOTE: Often used in the plural.)

gastric lavage *noun* the action of washing out the stomach contents, e.g. to remove an ingested toxin

gastric ulcer *noun* an ulcer in the stomach. Abbreviation **GU**

gastrin *noun* a hormone that stimulates the gastric glands to release hydrochloric acid

gastritis *noun* inflammation of the stomach lining

gastroadenitis *noun* inflammation of the glands of the stomach

gastroblennorrhoea *noun* excessive production of mucus by the stomach

gastrodynia *noun* same as **gastralgia**

gastroenteritis *noun* inflammation of the membrane lining the intestines and the stomach, caused by a viral infection and resulting in diarrhoea and vomiting

gastroenterology *noun* the study of diseases of the stomach and intestines

gastroesthesia *noun* having a sensitive stomach

gastrogenic *adjective* caused by or relating to the stomach

gastrointestinal *adjective* relating to the stomach and intestine

gastrointestinal tract *noun* the digestive tract, comprising the stomach and intestines

gastrokinesograph *noun* a medical device that measures movements of the stomach

gastromalacia *noun* a softening of the walls of the stomach

gastronome *noun* an expert on food and drink

gastro-oesophageal reflux disease *noun* a tendency towards acid reflux causing long-term oesophageal damage. Abbreviation **GORD**

gastropathy *noun* a disease of the stomach

gastroplasty *noun* surgery carried out to change, usually reduce, the capacity of the stomach

gastrostomy *noun* a surgical operation to create an opening into the stomach from the wall of the abdomen, so that food can be introduced without passing through the mouth and throat

gastrostomy feeding *noun* tube feeding directly into the stomach through the abdominal wall

gateau *noun* **1.** a rich cake, usually consisting of several layers held together with a cream filling **2.** savoury food baked and served in a form resembling a cake

Gaucher disease *noun* a genetic metabolic disorder in which a fatty substance accumulates in the body, especially the spleen, liver, lungs and bone marrow, characterised by bruising, fatigue, anaemia, low blood platelets and enlargement of the liver and spleen

gauntlet *noun* an industrial oven glove covering the arm to the elbow

gavage *noun* same as **gastrostomy feeding**

gazpacho *noun* a Spanish-style soup consisting of tomatoes, onions, cucumber, garlic, oil and vinegar, served cold

GDA *abbreviation* guideline daily amount

gel *noun* a suspension that sets into a jelly-like solid

gelatiera *noun* an ice-cream maker

gelatin, gelatine *noun* a protein that is soluble in water, made from collagen

gelatinisation *noun* the addition of gelatin or a similar substance to a food to turn it into a gel

gelatinise *verb* to make something gelatinous, or to become gelatinous

gelatinous *adjective* used for describing something with a texture like jelly

gelato *noun* an Italian ice cream made from milk, gelatin, sugar, and fruit ■ *adjective* iced, frozen or chilled

gelling agent *noun* any substance that is dissolved in a liquid to cause it to set into a gel

GEMS/Food *noun* an official body that collates data on trends in food contamination. Full form **Global Environment Monitoring System – Food Contamination Monitoring and Assessment Programme**

gene *noun* a unit of DNA on a chromosome that governs the synthesis of a protein sequence and determines a particular characteristic

General Food Law Regulations 3279/2004 *noun* a set of EU regulations that confers on health authorities the right to enforce EU food laws, and sets out the offences and punishments for contravening these

generic descriptor *noun* the name for a vitamin that covers several different chemical forms with the same function

genetic *adjective* relating to or contained in genes

genetically modified *adjective* used for describing a plant that has received genetic material from a totally different organism, or for describing products made from such plants. Abbreviation **GM**

genetically modified organism *noun* a plant or animal produced by the technique of genetic modification. Abbreviation **GMO**

genetic disease *noun* a disease caused by a genetic variation, e.g. an intolerance to, or an inability to metabolise, some substance

genetic modification, genetic engineering *noun* the alteration of the genetic material of a plant or animal under laboratory conditions, resulting in a plant or animal with new characteristics. Abbreviation **GM**

genetic pollution *noun* unintended effects caused by genetically modified organisms breeding with related or even unrelated species

genistein *noun* an isoflavonoid in soya beans found to have phyto-oestrogenic properties, linked to reduced fertility in men

genotoxicity *noun* the toxic effect of a substance on genetic cellular structure, leading to the risk of physical or developmental disorders

geosmin *noun* a compound that can produce unpleasant flavours in wine

geranium taint *noun* a defect of wine in which it has a geranium aroma, caused by lactic acid bacteria

germ *noun* **1.** a microorganism that causes a disease, e.g. a virus or bacterium **2.** a part of an organism capable of developing into a new organism

gerontology *noun* the study of the process of ageing and the diseases of old people

gestational diabetes *noun* diabetes which develops during pregnancy in previously-unaffected wmen, thought to be caused by hormone levels affecting the production of insulin

geumaphobia *noun* a fear of unfamiliar flavours or textures in food

ghee *noun* clarified butter, especially as used in South Asian cooking

gherkin *noun* a small vegetable of the cucumber family used for pickling

ghrelin *noun* a hormone that controls the production of growth hormone

GI *abbreviation* glycaemic index

giardiasis *noun* a disorder of the intestine caused by a parasite, usually with no symptoms but in heavy infections the absorption of fat may be affected, causing diarrhoea

giberellin *noun* a plant growth stimulator derived from fungus

giblets *plural noun* the liver, heart and other internal organs of poultry, removed before the bird is cooked

GI diet *noun* a dietary plan based on choosing foods according to their glycaemic index rating, with foods with a low rating giving a slow, steady release of energy, reducing blood sugar peaks and troughs that cause food cravings and weight gain

gild *verb* **1.** to glaze food with beaten egg before baking, to give a rich golden colour **2.** to coat the surface of a hard food with gold leaf, for decoration and historically for parading the wealth of the person serving it

Gillette method *noun* same as **high-performance liquid chromatography**

gills *plural noun* **1.** the breathing apparatus of fish and other animals living in water, consisting of a series of layers of tissue that extract oxygen from water as it passes over them **2.** a series of thin structures on the underside of the cap of a fungus, carrying the spores

gin *noun* a strong colourless alcohol distilled from grain and flavoured with juniper

ginger *noun* **1.** a plant with a hot-tasting root used in cooking and medicine **2.** a spice made from the powdered root of this plant

gingerbread *noun* a cake made with treacle and flavoured with ginger

gingivitis *noun* swelling and bleeding of the gums, sometimes caused by poor nutrition

ginkgo *noun* a Chinese tree with leaves that are used in herbal remedies and seeds that are used in Southeast Asian cooking for their health benefits

ginkgo biloba *noun* a herbal preparation made from the pulverised leaves of the ginkgo tree

gin-nan *noun* food poisoning caused by eating raw (toxic) ginkgo seeds

ginseng *noun* the fleshy root of an Asian plant, believed to have various health benefits, or a herbal preparation made from the root

GIP *abbreviation* gastric inhibitory peptide

GLA *noun* a fatty acid obtained from the seeds of the evening primrose, used as a medicine. Full form **gamma linolenic acid**

glacé *adjective* **1.** coated with a sugar solution that results in a glazed finish **2.** made by mixing icing sugar and a liquid, usually water

glacé cherry *noun* a candied cherry given a glossy appearance by dipping it in sugar solution, used for decorating cakes and desserts and sometimes in cake mixtures

glacé icing *noun* a simple mixture of sugar and water or strained fruit juice of coating consistency that gives a glossy appearance when spread on cakes and biscuits. Also called **water icing**

glasshouse *noun* a large structure made of glass inside which plants are grown, especially commercially or for scientific purposes

glassine *noun* a transparent paper treated with a glaze to make it greaseproof and resistant to the passage of air, used in food packaging

glaze *noun* a shiny surface on food ■ *verb* to cover food with a shiny coating

gliadin *noun* a simple cereal protein

Global Environment Monitoring System – Food Contamination Monitoring and Assessment Programme *noun* full form of **GEMS/Food**

globalisation *noun* the development of a similar culture and economy across the whole world as a result of technological advances in communications

globe artichoke *noun* ♦ **artichoke**

glossitis *noun* inflammation of the tongue

glucagon *noun* a hormone secreted by the islets of Langerhans in the pancreas, which increases the level of blood sugar by stimulating the breakdown of glycogen

glucaric acid *noun* dicarboxylic acid derived from glucose

gluco- *prefix* glucose

glucocorticoid *noun* a natural steroid hormone that regulates carbohydrate digestion

glucokinase *noun* an enzyme in the liver that plays a key role in carbohydrate metabolism

gluconeogenesis *noun* the production of glucose in the liver from protein or fat reserves

gluconic acid *noun* an acid formed by the oxidation of glucose

glucono delta-lactone *noun* ♦ **E575**

glucos *noun* same as **glucosinolate**

glucosamine *noun* a glucose derivative found in supportive tissues and plant cell walls

glucosamine sulphate *noun* a supplement used by athletes that is thought to help rebuild damaged cartilage

glucose *noun* a simple sugar found in some fruit, but also broken down from white sugar or carbohydrate and absorbed into the body or secreted by the kidneys

glucose oxydase *noun* the enzyme that oxidises glucose

glucose syrup *noun* a syrup containing dextrose, maltose, dextrin and water that is obtained from starch and is used in food manufacture

glucose tolerance *noun* the ability to metabolise a high dose of glucose, which is a test for diabetes

glucosidase *noun* an enzyme that splits glucose off glucosides

glucosinolate *noun* a compound left in rape meal after the oil has been extracted. Also called **glucos**

glucosuria *noun* the presence of glucose in the urine, an indicator of diabetes

glutamate *noun* a salt or ester of glutamic acid, especially its sodium salt (**monosodium glutamate**)

glutamic acid *noun* an amino acid

glutamine *noun* an amino acid

glutathione *noun* a peptide consisting of glutamic acid, cysteine and glycine that is an important antioxidant

glutathione reductase *noun* an enzyme in red blood cells

gluten *noun* a protein found in some cereals that makes the grains form a sticky paste when water is added

gluten-free *adjective* used for describing foods that do not contain gluten

glutenin *noun* a protein that is present in gluten, responsible for the elasticity of dough

gluten-induced enteropathy *noun* same as **coeliac disease**

glutton *noun* someone who habitually eats or drinks too much

gluttonous *adjective* greedy, especially for food and drink

gluttony *noun* the behaviour of someone who eats and drinks too much

glycaemic effect *noun* the extent to which a food containing carbohydrate can raise blood sugar levels

glycaemic index *noun* a points rating for different types of food, based on their glycaemic effect. Abbreviation **GI**

glycaemic load *noun* a rating for different types of food based on the amount of carbohydrate that they contain, as well as the extent to which this raises blood sugar levels

glyceraldehyde *noun* an intermediate in carbohydrate metabolism

glycerine, glycerol *noun* a sweetish colourless oily liquid used as a humectant to prevent foods from drying out, used especially royal icing. Also called **glycerol**

glyceryl lactostearate *noun* ♦ E472(ii)

glycine *noun* an amino acid

glyco- *prefix* sugar, or glycogen

glycoalkaloid *noun* a toxin produced in potatoes on exposure to sunlight

glycogen *noun* a type of starch, converted from glucose by the action of insulin, and stored in the liver as a source of energy

glycogenesis *noun* the synthesis of glycogen from glucose by insulin

glycogenolysis *noun* the breakdown of glycogen into glucose

glycogen storage disease *noun* a condition in which the liver and muscles accumulate excess amounts of glycogen

glycolysis *noun* the metabolic breakdown of glucose to release energy

glycoprotein *noun* a protein that is linked to a carbohydrate

glycorrhoea *noun* the expulsion of unusually large quantities of sugar from the body

glycosuria *noun* same as **glucosuria**

glysocholic acid *noun* an acid present in bile

GM *abbreviation* genetically modified

GMO *abbreviation* genetically modified organism

GMP *abbreviation* Good Manufacturing Practices

gnocchi *plural noun* in Italian cookery, dumplings made of potato, semolina or flour, usually boiled and served with soup or a sauce

goat's milk *noun* milk from a goat, used for drinking and for making cheese

goitre *noun* enlargement of the thyroid gland caused by iodine deficiency

goitrogen *noun* a substance that interferes with the thyroid gland's uptake of iodine

golden rice *noun* rice fortified with beta-carotene, developed as a humanitarian food to combat vitamin A deficiency

golden syrup *noun* thick golden juice from sugar, used for making dishes such as treacle tart

Gomez classification *noun* categories of malnutrition in children, based on the ratio of actual weight to expected or average weight

Good Agricultural Practices *plural noun* a set of codes which provide practical guidance for farmers on the proper maintenance of soil, water and air. Abbreviation **GAP**

good cholesterol *noun* cholesterol that is transported away from cells and tissue by high density lipoprotein (*informal*)

Good Manufacturing Practices *plural noun* a set of standards used by the FDA to assess processes in food manufacturing. Abbreviation **GMP**

goodness *noun* the nutritional value of food

goods *plural noun* things that are produced for sale

goose *noun* **1.** a web-footed water bird, larger than a duck (NOTE: The plural form is **geese**.) **2.** meat from this bird

gooseberry *noun* a small soft fruit from a small prickly bush, green or red in colour and usually cooked or preserved

GORD *abbreviation* gastro-oesophageal reflux disease

Gorgonzola *noun* a moist Italian blue cheese with a strong flavour

gosling *noun* a young goose

Gouda *noun* a mild Dutch cheese, typically sold in a thick round shape covered in yellow wax

goujon *noun* a long strip of fish or chicken coated in egg and breadcrumbs and deep-fried

goulash *noun* a Hungarian dish of meat and vegetables, flavoured with paprika

gourmet *noun* someone who knows a lot about and appreciates food and wine

gout *noun* pain caused by crystallisation of uric acid in the joints

Graham diet *noun* a dietary plan that is wholly vegetarian and allows fats only in small quantities

grain *noun* **1.** a measure of weight equal to 0.0648 grams. Abbreviation **gr 2.** a small hard seed

Grain Information Service *noun* an organisation that provides information on wheat intolerance and associated diseases

graining *noun* the crystallisation of sugar that takes place when it is boiled and cooled

gram *noun* a metric measure of weight equal to one thousandth of a kilogram. Abbreviation **g**

gram flour *noun* a gluten-free flour, used in South Asian cookery, that is usually made from ground chickpeas and is pale yellow in colour

Gram's stain *noun* a way of identifying bacteria by whether their cell walls are stained by a particular dye or not

granary bread *noun* bread made from granary flour

granary flour a trade name for a brown flour with malted wheat grains added to give a nutty flavour

granulate *verb* to form into small particles or granules by crystallisation or agglomeration

granulated sugar *noun* refined sugar in small white crystals. Also called **white sugar**

grape *noun* any of numerous species of small fruit of vine plants of the *Vitis* genus, grown for eating and widely used for making wine and related drinks

grapefruit *noun* a citrus fruit similar to and about twice as large as an orange, but not as sweet, that is lemon-yellow when ripe and very juicy, and has flesh that is usually pale greenish-yellow, but can also be pink (NOTE: The plural form is **grapefruit**.)

grape skin *noun* a good source of resveratrol, an antioxidant agent

grate *verb* to shred a firm textured food such as a carrot, a piece of cheese or a nutmeg using either a handheld tool or a food processor

grater *noun* a tool with a rough metal surface, or with rough holes, used for grating food such as cheese

gratin *noun* **1.** food that has been topped with breadcrumbs, cream sauce or cheese, and browned under a grill or in an oven **2.** a low flat dish in which food can be browned under a grill

gratinate *verb* to cause a crust to form on the surface of baked food, usually by sprinkling the surface with grated cheese or breadcrumbs and browning it under the grill or in the oven

gravadlax *noun* a Scandinavian dish consisting of thin slices of dried salmon marinated in sugar, salt, pepper, and herbs, especially dill, and usually served as an appetiser. Also called **gravlax**

gravity feed slicer *noun* a type of slicer for cooked meat such as ham, where the meat is placed on a sloping tray and slides further down after each slice is cut

gravlax *noun* same as **gravadlax**

gravy *noun* the juices that come from meat during cooking, or a brown sauce made using these that is served with meat

gravy browning *noun* a solution of dark caramel with salt, used for colouring gravy and sauces

grease *noun* thick soft animal fat, e.g. from cooked meat ■ *verb* to put a coating of fat or oil on the surface of a container, e.g. a baking tin, to prevent food sticking to it

greaseproof paper *noun* paper that does not allow oil or grease to soak into it or pass through it, used in cooking, preparing, and wrapping food. Also called **waxed paper**

Greek salad *noun* a salad of tomatoes, lettuce, cucumber, olives, oregano and feta cheese

Greek yoghurt *noun* a thick sour yoghurt made from sheep's milk

green *adjective* showing concern about or sensitivity towards environmental issues

green beans *plural noun* beans grown on low bushes and eaten when green in their pods. Also called **French beans**, **string beans**

greengage *noun* a bitter green plum, used for cooking, making pies, jam, etc.

green goose *noun* a young goose up to three months old that has been fed on pasture, less fatty than a Christmas goose and traditionally eaten at Michaelmas, September 29th

greenhouse *noun* a structure made of glass inside which plants are grown

green maté *noun* a South American tea that contains high levels of caffeine

green pepper *noun* an unripe sweet pepper with a green skin, eaten raw or cooked

greens *plural noun* plants with green leaves that are eaten as vegetables, e.g. cabbage and kale

green S *noun* ♦ E142

green salad *noun* a salad made of lettuce or other green leaves, sometimes including other raw green vegetables such as cucumber or green pepper

green tea *noun* any type of tea in which the leaves are heated to prevent fermentation

griddle *noun* a flat metal sheet or pan on which food is cooked over a flame

griddle scraper *noun* a spatula-like utensil used for scraping burned food deposits from a griddle surface

grill *noun* **1.** an open metal surface with heat above or below, used for cooking food **2.** a dish of food cooked on a grill **3.** a restaurant, or part of a restaurant, that specialises in grilled food ■ *verb* to cook food on or under a grill

griller *noun* a kitchen device with an open metal rack with heat beneath, used for cooking food

grill pan *noun* a metal tray used for putting food on while cooking it under a grill

grind *verb* to pass food through a machine that reduces it to powder or pulp

grinder *noun* **1.** a machine for grinding food such as coffee or spices **2.** same as **mincer**

gripe *noun* same as **colic**

gripe water *noun* a solution of sodium barcarbonate used for relieving colic in infants

gristle *noun* tough cartilage, especially in meat prepared for eating

grocer *noun* an owner or manager of a shop selling food and other household goods

Grocer, The *noun* the leading business magazine for the UK food and drink industry

groceries *plural noun* goods, especially food, sold in a grocer's shop

grocery *noun* **1.** a shop that sells food and other household goods **2.** the trade or profession of a grocer

ground almonds *plural noun* dried sweet almonds dehusked and ground

groundnut *noun* same as **peanut**

ground rice *noun* rice flour or meal used for milk puddings, as a thickener and to give a crisp texture to biscuits, shortbread and batters

grouse *noun* a small black game bird, found in the UK, especially in the north of England and in Scotland (NOTE: The plural is **grouse**.)

growth *noun* the process of increasing in size

growth hormone *noun* same as **somatotrophin**

gruel *noun* a thin porridge made by boiling meal, especially oatmeal, in water

guacamole *noun* mashed or puréed avocado with chillies, used as a dip or as a filling for tacos

guanosine 5'-disodium phosphate *noun* ♦ E627

guanosine monophosphate, guanylic acid *noun* a constituent of the nucleic acids DNA and RNA that plays a part in various metabolic reactions and is composed of guanosine linked to a phosphate group. Abbreviation **GMP**

guarana *noun* a herbal supplement that contains caffeine

guar gum *noun* gum extracted from the seeds of a plant that is widely grown in South Asia, used for thickening and stabilising processed foods

guava *noun* an orange-coloured tropical fruit with pink flesh

guideline daily amount *noun* ♦ **dietary reference value**

guinea fowl *noun* a small black bird with white spots, bred for its meat that has a delicate flavour similar to that of game birds

gum *noun* the soft tissue covering the part of the jaw that surrounds the teeth

gum arabic, gum acacia *noun* a sticky substance taken from some acacia trees, used in confectionery and medicines. Also called **acacia gum**

gumbo *noun* **1.** same as **okra 2.** a type of thick soup or stew, made with meat or fish and okra, from the southern USA

gum tragacanth *noun* ♦ E413

gustation *noun* in sensory analysis, the sense of taste

gut *noun* the tubular organ for the digestion and absorption of food. Also called **digestive tract**, **alimentary canal**, **intestine**

Guthrie test *noun* a test for genetic diseases performed on infants, which measures amino acid levels in the blood. Also called **heel-prick test**

gut sweetbread *noun* the pancreas of an animal, used as food

gutting *noun* the action of removing the innards of an animal while butchering it

gutting knife *noun* ♦ **filleting knife**

gut wall *noun* the inner surface of the intestine, through which nutrients are absorbed

H

HACCP *abbreviation* Hazard Analysis and Critical Control Point

hachoir *noun* a chopping tool consisting of a curved blade with a vertical handle at each end, used with a rocking motion. Also called **mezzaluna**

haddock *noun* a white sea fish found in North Atlantic waters (NOTE: The plural form is **haddock**.)

haem *noun* a substance that carries oxygen in blood and bone marrow

haematemesis *noun* bleeding in the upper gastrointestinal tract causing vomiting of blood

haematin *noun* a iron-rich compound produced when blood is oxidised

haematinic *adjective* promoting the healthy growth of blood cells in bone marrow

haemato- *prefix* blood

haem iron *noun* dietary iron found in meat and seafood. Compare **non-haem iron**

haemo- *prefix* blood

haemochromatosis *noun* an excess of iron in the body, which can cause tissue damage and discoloration of the skin

haemoglobin *noun* a red pigment in red blood cells that gives blood its red colour and carries oxygen to the tissues. Abbreviation **Hb**

haemolytic anaemia *noun* anaemia caused by the destruction of red blood cells

haemolytic uraemic syndrome *noun* a serious kidney disease caused by infection of the intestine with EHEC, most commonly found in young children. Abbreviation **HUS**

haemorrhoids *plural noun* swollen veins around the anus. Also called **piles**

haemosiderin *noun* an insoluble protein that contains iron, produced by the action of phagocytes on haematin

haggis *noun* a Scottish dish consisting of a mixture of sheep's heart, liver and other organs and oatmeal, traditionally in a sheep's stomach but now often in a synthetic bag, boiled in water (NOTE: In Scotland, haggis is served on special occasions, especially on Burns' Night.)

hair tube *noun* a piping-bag nozzle with multiple small openings that makes a hair- or grass-like icing decoration

hake *noun* a large white sea fish with flesh similar to that of cod but with a slightly coarser texture (NOTE: The plural form is **hake**.)

halal *adjective* prepared according to Islamic law. Compare **haram**

half-fat *adjective* containing half the amount of fat of a comparable product

half-fat milk *noun* milk from which some of the fat has been removed

half-life *noun* the time taken for half the cells in a tissue sample to die and be replaced

halibut *noun* a type of flat white sea fish, the largest of all flatfish (NOTE: The plural form is **halibut**.)

haliphagy *noun* the consumption of an excessive amount of salt

halitosis *noun* a condition in which a person has breath that smells unpleasant

halophilic *adjective* used for describing bacteria that are able to grow in a salty environment

halva *noun* a sweet food made from crushed sesame seeds or almonds combined with boiled sugar syrup, sold sliced from a block

ham *noun* meat from this part of the pig, usually cured in brine and sometimes dried in smoke

hamburger *noun* a small flat cake of minced beef that is grilled or fried. Also called **beefburger**

hamburger roll *noun* a soft round bread roll suitable for serving a hamburger in

ham slice *noun* a thin slice of ham for use in sandwiches

hand sanitiser *noun* an antimicrobial liquid that can be used to disinfect the hands without rinsing

hand whisk *noun* ♦ **whisk**

hang *verb* to suspend meat or a recently killed game animal until the flesh begins to decompose slightly and becomes more tender and highly flavoured

hanging *noun* the process of draining the blood from a slaughtered animal by hanging it by the hocks

hangover *noun* a condition occurring after a person has drunk too much alcohol, with dehydration causing symptoms including headache, nausea and trembling of the hands

haram *adjective* used for describing foods forbidden by Islam. Compare **halal**

hard *adjective* used for describing wheat that is hard to the bite

hard-boiled *adjective* used for describing an egg that has been cooked in boiling water until the white and yolk are set

hard cheese *noun* cheese that has been pressed and so has a firm texture

hard swell *noun* a can swell that is hard and cannot be forced back into shape by hand. ◊ **swell**

hard water *noun* tap water that contains a high percentage of calcium and magnesium (NOTE: Hard water makes it difficult for soap to lather and also causes deposits in pipes, boilers and kettles.)

hard wheat *noun* a wheat with hard kernels and a high gluten content, used for making flour for bread

hare *noun* a common field mammal of the genus *Lepus* that resembles a large, long-eared rabbit

haricot bean *noun* a white bean of the type used for making baked beans

harissa *noun* a spicy oily paste made from chilli and tomatoes, used as an ingredient in North African cooking

harvesting *noun* the practice of cutting marketing investment on a particular product prior to withdrawing it from the market

hash *noun* a dish prepared from chopped meat and vegetables

hash browns *plural noun* boiled potatoes, diced or mashed and fried till crisp and brown

haunch *noun* one of the back legs of a four-legged animal, either when it is alive, or as a cut of meat

haute cuisine *noun* high-class French cooking

haybox cooker *noun* ♦ **fireless cooker**

Hay diet *noun* a dietary plan that classifies foods as acidic, alkaline or neutral and advises appropriate combinations

Hazard Analysis and Critical Control Point *noun* a formal food safety methodology in which critical control points are identified and adhered to. Abbreviation **HACCP**

haze *noun* cloudiness in beer

hazelnut *noun* a small round nut with a smooth shiny shell

HDL *abbreviation* high-density lipoprotein

HDR *abbreviation* Humanitarian Daily Ration

head chef *noun* the main chef in a restaurant

head waiter *noun* same as **maître d'hôtel**

health *noun* the fact of being well or being free from any illness

health-conscious *adjective* used for describing someone who is keen to eat healthy and nutritious foods and to look after his or her health in other ways, e.g. by exercising

health counsellor *noun* a general adviser on matters of health, fitness and nutrition in an institution such as a school

Health Education Board for Scotland *noun* a government agency in Scotland responsible for health advice, education and promotion. Abbreviation **HEBS**

Health Education Trust *noun* a charitable research body. Abbreviation **HET**

health food *noun* food with no additives or natural foods, which are good for your health

Health Food Manufacturers' Association *noun* a society representing specialist health food producers. Abbreviation **HFMA**

Health Professions Council *noun* a regulatory body in the UK that sets standards for training in the health industries and qualifies people to practice under particular job titles. Abbreviation **HPC**

health risk *noun* a situation in which there is a risk to health caused by something such as not following safety procedures

health trainer *noun* a person who acts as a link between health professionals and the community, giving personal advice and support to people looking to improve their health

healthy *adjective* **1.** in good physical condition **2.** helping to maintain or bring about good health

healthy eating *noun* the practice of eating food that is rich in essential nutrients and within recommended dietary guidelines

Healthy Living Scotland *noun* a government information service promoting fitness and a healthy diet, available online

heaped *adjective* used for describing an amount large enough to rise up in a small heap

heart *noun* the compact central part of a vegetable such as lettuce, cabbage or celery, where the leaves or stalks curl in tightly

heartburn *noun* indigestion that causes a burning feeling in the stomach and oesophagus and a flow of acid saliva into the mouth

heart disease *noun* a general term for any disease of the heart

heart-smart *adjective* used for describing food that is low in fat and cholesterol and therefore reduces the risk of heart disease

hearty *adjective* **1.** showing physical health, strength, and vigour **2.** used for describing food that is substantial and gives considerable satisfaction and nourishment

heat *noun* the spiciness of food

heat labile *noun* same as **thermolabile**

heat lamp *noun* a source of infra-red radiation usually suspended above a food-serving or food-holding area to keep the food warm

heat-sealing *noun* a method of closing plastic food containers in which air is removed from a plastic bag with the food inside and the bag is then pressed by a hot plate that melts the plastic and seals the contents in the vacuum

heat transfer *noun* the process of passing heat from one medium or substance to another

heat treated *adjective* heated in order to reduce bacterial action to acceptable levels

HEBS *abbreviation* Health Education Board for Scotland

heel-prick test *noun* same as **Guthrie test**

height *noun* how tall someone or something is

height-for-weight *noun* an index of a child's height against the average height for a child of that weight, showing whether they are being adequately nourished for growth

helminth *noun* a parasitic worm

helping *noun* a portion of food served to one person

hemiageusia *noun* a loss of taste from one side of the tongue only

hemicellulose *noun* a polysaccharide carbohydrate found in fruit and vegetables, of which pectin is a form

hen *noun* **1.** a female of the common domestic fowl **2.** any female bird, e.g. a hen pheasant

hepatic duct *noun* a duct which links the liver to the bile duct leading to the duodenum

hepatic portal vein *noun* a vein that drains blood from the digestive system and carries it to the liver

hepatitis *noun* inflammation of the liver through disease or drugs

hepatolithiasis *noun* the presence of calculi in the liver

hepatomegaly *noun* enlargement of the liver caused by congestion or inflammation

hepatorrhoea *noun* an excessive flow of bile from the liver

herb *noun* a plant that can be used to give a particular taste to food or to give a particular scent

herbal extract *noun* the active ingredients of a herb preserved in a water, alcohol or oil solution

herbicide *noun* a chemical that kills plants, especially used for controlling weeds

herbivore *noun* an animal that feeds only on plants. ◊ **carnivore, omnivore**

hermetic *adjective* airtight

herring *noun* a small oily sea fish found in the temperate, shallow waters of the North Atlantic and the Baltic Sea (NOTE: The plural form is **herring**.)

herringworm *noun* a marine roundworm that can infect humans if it is ingested in raw fish, causing severe abdominal pain

herringworm disease *noun* infestation of the abdominal wall with herringworm larvae

hesperidin *noun* a white or colourless crystalline glycoside found in citrus fruits

Hess test *noun* a test for scurvy in which the skin is pressed to see if broken capilliaries appear

HET *abbreviation* Health Education Trust

heterolysis *noun* the breaking of a chemical bond in a compound, producing particles or ions of opposite charge, e.g. the formation of sodium and chloride ions in a salt solution

hexamine *noun* ♦ E239

HFCS *abbreviation* high fructose corn syrup

HFMA *abbreviation* Health Food Manufacturers' Association

HFSS *adjective* used for describing calorie-dense snack foods. Full form **high in fat, salt or sugar**

HGCA *abbreviation* Home-Grown Cereals Authority

HGH *abbreviation* human growth hormone

HGH booster *noun* same as **secretagogue**

hide *noun* the skin of an animal, important commercially both in its raw state and as leather

high *adjective* used for describing meat, especially game, that has been kept until it is beginning to rot and has a strong flavour

high biological value *noun* the fact of containing large amounts of bioavailable proteins

high blood pressure *noun* same as **hypertension**

high-density lipoprotein *noun* an aggregate of fat and protein that transports cholesterol away from the arteries, high levels of which are associated with a decreased risk of heart disease. Abbreviation **HDL**. ◊ **low-density lipoprotein**

high electric field pulses *plural noun* a method of enhancing the antibacterial action of preservatives by passing an electrical charge through the preserved food

high-energy *adjective* used in marketing to describe foods such as glucose drinks or high-sugar items such as honey that can be broken down easily by the body to provide a rapid supply of energy

high-energy food *noun* food containing a large number of calories that give a lot of energy when they are broken down by the digestive system

high-fibre *adjective* used for describing foods that are rich in dietary fibre and therefore help to maintain a healthy colon

high fructose corn syrup *noun* a sweetener used in the soft drinks industry, extracted from maize. Abbreviation **HFCS**

high in fat, salt or sugar full form of **HFSS**

high-performance liquid chromatography *noun* a way of measuring the hotness of a spice or chilli pepper, using a scientific analysis of the proportions of heat-producing chemicals. Abbreviation **HPLC**

high pressure treatment *noun* a method of sterilising food without affecting its natural textures or nutritional value by subjecting it to intense pressure, which deactivates most bacteria

high-protein diet *noun* a dietary plan that is high in protein, used for building muscle mass especially while training

high quality protein *noun* protein that is bioavailable and contains high levels of all essential amino acids

high-ratio shortening *noun* fat with a higher-than-usual proportion of monoglycerides and diglycerides, able to absorb a lot of sugar

high temperature short time method *noun* the usual method of pasteurising milk, where the milk is heated to 72°C for 15 seconds and then rapidly cooled. Abbreviation **HTST method**

high-temperature short-time treatment *noun* a sterilisation technique that destroys bacteria rapidly without causing damage to food texture. Abbreviation **HTST**

histamine *noun* a substance released in response to allergens, causing blood vessels to dilate and leading to an increase in acid secretions in the stomach

histidinaemia *noun* a genetic disease causing histidine intolerance

histidine *noun* an amino acid from which histamine is derived

histotrophic *adjective* causing the growth or nourishment of tissue

hives *noun* an allergic reaction in which raised red welts are produced on the skin

HMB *abbreviation* beta-hydroxy beta-methylbutyrate

hob *noun* the flat top on a cooker

hock *noun* the lower part of a leg of a pig, used for food

hoisin sauce *noun* a thick dark sweet and spicy sauce made from fermented soya beans and used for flavouring Chinese dishes

holistic *adjective* used for describing a medical treatment that takes account of someone's mental and personal circumstances, in addition to their physical symptoms

hollandaise sauce *noun* a sauce for meat, fish or vegetables, made of egg yolks, butter, lemon juice and sometimes vinegar

hollowware *noun* metal or china dishes from which food is served

holozoic *adjective* used for describing organisms such as animals that feed on other organisms or organic matter

holy basil *noun* a variety of basil with a dark leaf and a sharp, slightly aniseed flavour, native to Southeast Asia

home-baked *adjective* baked by hand, individually or as part of a small batch, as opposed to factory-produced

home-cooked meal *noun* a meal cooked on the premises or presented as having been cooked on the premises

home economics *noun* the study of cookery as taught in schools, often also including the study of other aspects of running a home

home economist *noun* a person who teaches or specialises in home economics

Home-Grown Cereals Authority *noun* an organisation that promotes and funds research into the UK arable industry. Abbreviation **HGCA**

homeopath *noun* a practitioner of homeopathy

homeopathic *adjective* relating to homeopathy or prepared using the principles of homeopathy

homeopathy *noun* a type of medical treatment that involves using natural substances that produce a very mild form of the condition that the patient already has

homeostasis *noun* the process by which the functions and chemistry of a cell or internal organ are kept stable, even when external conditions vary greatly

homocysteine *noun* an amino acid produced in the body during the metabolism of methionine

homocystinuria *noun* a genetic disease that makes the body unable to convert methionine to cysteine and may cause mental problems

homogenisation *noun* the treatment of milk so that the cream does not separate

homogenise *verb* to mix various parts until they become a single whole, especially to treat milk so that the cream does not separate

honey *noun* a sweet runny sticky substance produced by bees

honeycomb *noun* a structure made up of waxy hexagonal cells containing honey that is extracted from a bees' hive or nest and can be eaten

honey dipper *noun* a wooden utensil with a rounded, grooved end designed for dipping into honey

hookworm *noun* a parasitic worm that lives in the small intestine

hop *noun* a climbing plant that has long thin groups of green flowers which are used dried in brewing to add flavour to beer (NOTE: The plant's botanical name is *Humulus lupulus*.)

hormonal *adjective* relating to hormones

hormone *noun* a substance that is produced by one part of the body, especially the endocrine glands and is carried to another part of the body by the bloodstream where it has particular effects or functions

hormone-sensitive lipase *noun* a lipase that is controlled by insulin and adrenaline

hors d'oeuvre *noun* a small portion of food served cold or hot before a meal to stimulate the appetite

horse mackerel *noun* a name given to various large long-bodied fish of the mackerel family, found in tropical and subtropical seas

horseradish *noun* a plant with a large root that is grated to make a sharp sauce

hospitalise *verb* to send someone to hospital

hotdog *noun* a long sausage usually served hot on a bread roll with toppings such as fried onions, mustard or ketchup

hot holding *noun* the process of maintaining a foodstuff at a constant high temperature to prevent bacteria from multiplying

hotplate *noun* a piece of metal heated usually by electricity, used for cooking food or keeping it hot

hotpot *noun* a meat stew with sliced potatoes on top, cooked in the oven

hot-smoke *verb* to smoke food at a temperature between 40°C and 105°C, thus cooking it at the same time (NOTE: Food to be hot-smoked is usually cold-smoked first, and fish is not heated above 80°C.)

hot water pastry *noun* a strong dense pastry used for hand-raised meat pies, made from flour, fat and water or milk boiled together (NOTE: The mixture is moulded while warm.)

Howard mould count *noun* a test for mould contamination of food

HPC *abbreviation* Health Professions Council

HPLC *abbreviation* high-performance liquid chromatography

HTST *abbreviation* high-temperature short-time treatment

HTST method *abbreviation* high temperature short time method

hull *noun* 1. the outer covering of a cereal seed 2. the pod of a pea or bean

human growth hormone *noun* same as **somatotrophin**

Humanitarian Daily Ration *noun* a food package dropped by aid agencies into famine areas. Abbreviation **HDR**

humectant *adjective* able to absorb or retain moisture ■ *noun* a substance that can absorb or retain moisture, used as a food additive

hummus *noun* a thick paste made by combining mashed chickpeas, oil, lemon juice and garlic

hundredweight *noun* a unit of mass in the British imperial system equal to 112 lb or 50.80 kg. Abbreviation **cwt**

hungover *adjective* feeling ill as a result of having drunk too much alcohol earlier

hurdle *noun* something such as an unfavourable pH level or a modified environment that acts as an obstacle to the growth of microorganisms in food

hurdle effect *noun* the combination of more than one hurdle, having a stronger effect than either one in isolation

HUS *abbreviation* haemolytic uraemic syndrome

husk *noun* the dry outer covering of a cereal grain, removed during threshing ■ *verb* to remove the husk from seeds

huss *noun* a name given to various large sea fish. Also called **dogfish**

hyaluronic acid *noun* a substance which binds connective tissue

hyaluronidase *noun* an enzyme that destroys hyaluronic acid

hybrid *noun* an organism that is a result of a cross between individuals that are not genetically the same as each other ■ *adjective* used for describing a plant or animal that is the result of a cross between organisms that have different genotypes

Hybu Cig Cymru *noun* the red meat promotion board for Wales. Abbreviation **HCC**

hydragogue *noun* a substance that produces watery faeces

hydrase *noun* an enzyme that catalyses the addition or removal of water

hydrochloric acid *noun* an acid found in the gastric juices that helps to break apart the food

hydrocolloid *noun* a substance that forms a gel when mixed with water

hydrocooling *noun* the process of chilling food, especially fruit and vegetables, by putting them in chilled water, which stops the process of ripening

hydrodyne process *noun* a way of tenderising meat using shock waves to break the fibres

hydrogen *noun* a chemical element that combines with oxygen to form water, and with other elements to form acids, and is present in all animal tissue (NOTE: The chemical symbol is **H**.)

hydrogenate *verb* to add hydrogen to a compound in a chemical reaction

hydrogenated fat *noun* a liquid oil that has been converted to a hard fat by hydrogenation

hydrogenated glucose syrup *noun* a modified glucose syrup used in sugar-free confectionery

hydrogenation *noun* the process of chemically combining hydrogen with unsaturated oils and soft fats to make them more saturated and harder, used for making margarine and lard substitutes from oils

hydrogen sulphide *noun* a foul-smelling gas responsible for the smell of rotten eggs, produced by anaerobic bacterial action

hydrogen sulphites *plural noun* salts that are similar to sulphites but contain a higher proportion of sulphur dioxide, used as preservatives in the food industry. ◊ **E227**

hydrogen swell *noun* a can swell caused by a reaction of acid fruits such as pineapple with the can, producing harmless hydrogen. ◊ **swell**

hydrolase *noun* an enzyme that controls hydrolysis, e.g. an esterase

hydrolyse *verb* to undergo hydrolysis, or make a substance undergo hydrolysis

hydrolysed protein *noun* a protein that has been broken down into smaller peptides, usually by treatment with water at high temperature, to produce highly flavoured compounds, as in yeast and meat extracts (NOTE: The process also occurs when proteins are fermented, as in soy sauce, and to a limited extent when proteins are cooked.)

hydrolysis *noun* a chemical reaction in which a compound reacts with water, causing decomposition and the production of two or more other compounds, e.g. in the conversion of starch to glucose

hydrometer *noun* a device, usually a sealed graduated tube containing a weighted bulb, used to determine the specific gravity or density of a liquid

hydrophilic *adjective* used for describing molecules that are soluble in water

hydrophobia *noun* fear of drinking water

hydrostatic sterilisation *noun* ♦ **high pressure treatment**

hydroxyapatite *noun* a hydrated calcium phosphate mineral

hydroxyproline *noun* an amino acid present in some proteins, especially in collagen

hydroxyproline index *noun* a test of malnutrition in children that measures the excretion of hydroxyproline

hydroxypropyl cellulose *noun* ♦ **E463**

hyfoma *noun* the hygienic manufacture of food

hygiene *noun* **1.** methods and practices that keep people and places clean and healthy **2.** the science of health

hygienic *adjective* **1.** clean and safe because all germs have been destroyed **2.** producing or fostering healthy conditions

hygroscopic *adjective* easily absorbing water

hyoscyamine *noun* an anti-cramping agent found in lettuce

hyper- *prefix* higher or too much

hyperactivity *noun* a condition in which someone is unusually active, restless and lacking the ability to concentrate for any length of time, especially as a result of attention deficit disorder

hyperalimentation *noun* the deliberate feeding of larger-than-average amounts of food to somebody

hyperammonaemia *noun* high levels of ammonia in the blood, caused by inadequate metabolisation of proteins

hyperchlorhydria *noun* a larger-than-average secretion of gastric juices causing high levels of hydrochloric acid in the stomach

hypercholesterolaemia *noun* a higher-than-average presence of cholesterol in the blood

hypergeusia *noun* a heightened sense of taste

hyperglycaemia *noun* an excess of glucose in the blood

hyperglycaemic *adjective* having hyperglycaemia

hyperinsulinaemia *noun* an unusually high level of insulin in the blood, causing hypoglycaemia

hyperinsulinism *noun* the reaction of a diabetic to an excessive dose of insulin or to hypoglycaemia

hyperkalaemia *noun* a higher-than-average presence of potassium in the blood

hyperlipidaemia *noun* large concentrations of lipids in blood plasma

hypermarket *noun* a very large supermarket, usually on the outskirts of a large town

hyperoxaluria *noun* a genetic disease in which too much oxalic acid is produced, leading to kidney stone formation

hyperoxemia *noun* a condition in which there is an unusually high concentration of oxygen in the blood and bodily tissues

hyperpepsinia *noun* the presence of excess pepsin in gastric juices

hyperphagia *noun* overeating (*technical*)

hyperphosphataemia *noun* a higher-than-average presence of phosphate in the blood

hyperpiesia *noun* same as **hypertension**

hypersensitivity *noun* same as **allergy**

hypertension *noun* arterial blood pressure that is higher than the usual range for gender and age. Also called **high blood pressure**, **hyperpiesia**. Compare **hypotension**

hyperthyroidism *noun* a condition in which the thyroid gland is too active and releases unusual amounts of thyroid hormones into the blood, giving rise to a rapid heartbeat, sweating and trembling. Also called **thyrotoxicosis**

hypertonic *noun* a liquid supplement that has more concentrated nutrients than are normally found in the body

hypervitaminosis *noun* excessively high intakes of vitamins, which can be toxic in large doses

hypo- *prefix* less, too little or beneath

hypoallergenic *adjective* not likely to cause an allergic reaction

hypocalcaemia *noun* a lower-than-average level of calcium in the blood

hypochlorhydria *noun* a lower-than-average secretion of hydrochloric acid in the stomach

hypogeusia *noun* an impaired sense of taste

hypoglycaemia *noun* a low concentration of glucose in the blood

hypoglycaemic *adjective* having hypoglycaemia

hypokalaemia *noun* a lower-than-average presence of potassium in the blood

hypopepsinia *noun* the condition of having too little pepsin in gastric juices

hypophosphataemia *noun* a lower-than-average presence of phosphate in the blood

hypoproteinaemia *noun* a low concentration of protein in blood plasma

hypotension *noun* a condition in which the pressure of the blood is unusually low

hypothalamus *noun* the part of the brain that controls the production of hormones by the pituitary gland and regulates important bodily functions such as hunger, thirst and sleep

hypothyroidism *noun* underactivity of the thyroid gland, causing a decrease in the metabolic rate and corresponding sluggishness and weight gain

hypotonic *noun* a liquid supplement that has more dilute nutrients than are normally found in the body

hypovitaminosis *noun* an unhealthily low intake of vitamins

hypoxia *noun* a condition in which there is an unusually low concentration of oxygen in the blood and bodily tissues

I

IAFP *abbreviation* International Association for Food Protection

IASO *abbreviation* International Association for the Study of Obesity

iatrogenic *adjective* caused by medical interference or drug use

IBD *abbreviation* inflammatory bowel disease

IBS *abbreviation* irritable bowel syndrome

ice *noun* **1.** water that is frozen and has become solid **2.** ice cream ■ *verb* **1.** to add ice to something, e.g. a drink **2.** to put icing on a cake

iceberg lettuce *noun* a large round lettuce with a tight head of pale crisp juicy leaves

ice cream *noun* a mixture of cream, eggs, sugar and flavouring or of milk, sugar, water and flavouring, frozen until quite hard

ice crystals *plural noun* large clumps of ice that can form in frozen foods, affecting the texture

ice-glaze *verb* to add a thin layer of ice to frozen food by spraying it with or dipping it in water (NOTE: The process is widely used with frozen prawns.)

ice-structuring protein *noun* a protein found in deep-water fish that restructures ice crystals, with the potential for use in frozen food products

ichthysarcotoxins *plural noun* toxins found in fish

icing *noun* a covering of sugar and flavouring, spread over a cake or biscuits

icing bag *noun* a cloth bag with a nozzle used for piping soft foods

icing sugar *noun* a fine powdered white sugar, mixed with water or egg white and flavouring, used for covering cakes or biscuits

ICO *abbreviation* International Coffee Organisation

ideal body weight *noun* a healthy weight for a person based on a formula such as body mass index

ideopathic hypercalcaemia *noun* high levels of calcium in the blood plasma, potentially fatal in infants

IDF *abbreviation* International Dairy Federation

IDFA *abbreviation* Infant and Dietetic Foods Association

idiosyncrasy *noun* an individual reaction to food

IFIC *abbreviation* International Food Information Council

IFR *abbreviation* Institute of Food Research

IFS *abbreviation* International Food Standard

IFST *abbreviation* Institute of Food Science and Technology

IGD *abbreviation* Institute of Grocery Distribution

IgE *abbreviation* immunoglobulin E

IgE-mediated *adjective* used for describing an allergic condition or reaction caused by immunoglobulin E

ileitis *noun* inflammation of the ileum

ileostomy *noun* a surgical operation that creates an opening to the ileum through the abdominal wall

ileum *noun* the lower part of the small intestine, between the jejunum and the caecum (NOTE: The plural is **ilea**.)

ileus *noun* an intestinal obstruction

ILSI *abbreviation* International Life Sciences Institute

immature *adjective* not old enough to have acquired the maximum flavour

immune system *noun* a complex network of cells and cell products that protects the body from disease, including the thymus, spleen, lymph nodes, white blood cells and antibodies

immunocompromised *adjective* with a lowered immune system

immunodeficiency *noun* a lack of immunity to a disease

immunoglobulin E *noun* a type of antibody that causes strong allergic reactions. Abbreviation **IgE**

immunomagnetic separation *noun* a way of separating pathogens from food using magnetism

impairment *noun* a condition in which a sense or function is harmed so that it does not work properly

import *noun* an article or type of goods brought into a country from abroad ■ *verb* to bring goods from abroad into a country for sale ► compare (all senses) **export**

improver *noun* an additive that improves the performance of foodstuffs when mixed with others

impulse food *noun* ↓ **convenience food**

impurity *noun* a substance that is not pure or clean

inactivate *verb* to make bacteria unable to multiply

inanition *noun* a state of exhaustion caused by starvation

incise *verb* to cut deep slits in raw food, e.g. to allow a marinade to penetrate or to allow garlic, herbs or spices to be inserted

incisor *noun* a flat sharp-edged tooth in the front of the mouth for cutting and tearing food

inconcocted *adjective* not properly digested

incorporate *verb* to combine something with something else, e.g. when adding liquid ingredients to dry ingredients when making a cake

incubation period *noun* the period between the time someone is infected with a disease and the appearance of its first symptoms

independent retailer *noun* a shop or outlet that is not part of a larger chain

index of nutritional quality *noun* a way of describing the nutrient content of a particular food. Abbreviation **INQ**

indigestible *adjective* used for describing food that cannot be digested, e.g. roughage

indigestion *noun* a disturbance of the normal process of digestion that causes the person to experience pain or discomfort in the stomach. ◊ **dyspepsia**

indigestive *adjective* experiencing or resulting from indigestion

indigo carmine *noun* a blue dye that is injected into a person to test how well their kidneys are working

indigotine *noun* ◆ **indigo carmine**

indispensable amino acids *plural noun* same as **essential amino acids**

induction period *noun* the time during which a food remains protected by an additive before it begins to deteriorate

industrial catering *noun* commercial catering on a large scale

industry nutritionist *noun* a professional who works with the food manufacture industry providing nutritional information when developing new products

inedia *noun* the theory that a person can live without food or water, as in breatharian beliefs

inedible *adjective* not fit to be eaten

inert *adjective* not active or not producing a chemical reaction

Infant and Dietetic Foods Association *noun* a society representing specialist dietetic food producers, especially those formulated for infants. Abbreviation **IDFA**

infant formula *noun* powdered milk for babies

infantile paralysis *noun* same as **poliomyelitis**

infant nutrition *noun* the provision of a healthy and nutritionally complete diet for small babies

infection *noun* a state in which microorganisms enter into the body and multiply, usually causing unpleasant symptoms

infestation *noun* the state of having large numbers of parasites or vermin

inflammatory bowel disease *noun* a set of disorders in which the bowel is sore and inflamed, including ulcerative colitis and Crohn's Disease. Abbreviation **IBD**

INFOODS *abbreviation* International Network of Food Data Systems

informed choice *noun* the ability of a consumer to choose which foods to eat because they have access to information about their nutritional content

infra-red radiation *noun* heat, the radiation that is transferred from a hot surface to food

infuse *verb* to soak tea or herbs in liquid to extract the flavour or other qualities from them

infuser *noun* a small perforated closed container that allows boiling water to come into contact with a substance such as tea, herbs or spices, extracting flavour from it

infusion *noun* a drink made by pouring boiling water on a dry substance such as a herbal tea or a powdered drug

ingest *verb* to take in or absorb food

ingesta *plural noun* food or liquid that enters the body via the mouth (*technical*)

ingredient *noun* an item used in making a dish of food

ingredients *noun* a list of all ingredients in a food product, listed in decreasing order of proportional size, a required element in food labelling in the UK

ingredient technology *noun* ◆ **food technology**

inhibited starch *noun* same as **modified starch**

inhibitor *noun* a molecule that attaches to an enzyme and make it less active, widely used in drugs

innards *plural noun* the internal organs of the body, especially the intestines

inorganic *adjective* used for describing a substance that is not made from animal or vegetable sources

inosine *noun* an organic compound nucleoside involved in the formation of purines and energy metabolism, used in sports supplements

inosine 5'-disodium phosphate *noun* ♦ E631

inositol *noun* a carbohydrate found in fruits and cereals (NOTE: It has a role in fat metabolism and in the transmission of nerve impulses.)

INQ *abbreviation* index of nutritional quality

insalivate *verb* to mix food with saliva in the process of chewing

insalivation *noun* the act of mixing saliva with food while chewing

insecticide *noun* a liquid or powder that kills insects

insolation *noun* a method of drying food by exposing it to the sun, used for meat, fish and fruit

insoluble *adjective* not able to be dissolved in liquid

insoluble fibre *noun* the fibre in bread and cereals that is not digested but swells inside the intestine

instant *adjective* used for describing food that is quickly and easily prepared, and is usually sold in a premixed, precooked or powdered form

instant food *noun* food that has been dehydrated and reconstitutes quickly with water

Institute for Optimum Nutrition *noun* an independent educational body that specialises in clinical and therapeutic nutrition. Abbreviation **ION**

Institute of Food Research *noun* a registered charity that undertakes research on food safety, diet and health issues. Abbreviation **IFR**

Institute of Food Science and Technology *noun* a professional body for the food science industry that also runs courses and accredits courses run elsewhere. Abbreviation **IFST**

Institute of Grocery Distribution *noun* an organisation that brings together companies in the food and grocery industries and shares resources

instructions for use *plural noun* a suggested way to prepare a food product for eating, often seen in food labelling in the UK

insulin *noun* a hormone produced in the pancreas that regulates the body's metabolism of carbohydrates and has widespread effects on the body

insulin-dependent diabetes *noun* same as **diabetes mellitus**

insulin resistance *noun* a medical condition in which bodily or injected insulin has a reduced effect in metabolising glucose, a possible cause of metabolic syndrome

insulism *noun* same as **hyperinsulinism**

intake *noun* **1.** the amount of a substance taken in by the body **2.** the process of taking a substance into the body

integrated pest management *noun* a holistic system of controlling pests, intended to minimise the build-up of pesticides on foodstuffs. Abbreviation **IPM**

integument *noun* an outer protective layer or part of an animal or plant, e.g. a shell, rind, husk or skin

intellectual property *noun* ideas, designs, and inventions, including copyrights, patents and trademarks, that were created by and legally belong to an individual or an organisation

intense sweetener *noun* same as **low-calorie sweetener**

intensive farming *noun* the farming of small areas of expensive land, using machines and fertilisers to obtain high crops

intercellular air space *noun* part of the cellular structure of a fruit of vegetable, which affects its texture and may change on cooking or ripening

intermediate *noun* a chemical compound that is formed during a chemical reaction and is used in another reaction to obtain another compound

International Association for Food Protection *noun* a food safety organisation. Abbreviation **IAFP**

International Association for the Study of Obesity *noun* an umbrella organisation representing national obesity associations. Abbreviation **IASO**

International Coffee Organisation *noun* an association representing the interests of coffee importers and exporters, based in London. Abbreviation **ICO**

International Dairy Federation *noun* an international forum for national dairy associations. Abbreviation **IDF**

International Food Information Council *noun* an information resource for nutritionists and related professions that publishes a monthly newsletter. Abbreviation **IFIC**

International Food Standard *noun* a set of quality control standards applied to food manufacturers and retailers across Europe. Abbreviation **IFS**

International Journal of Food Sciences and Nutrition *noun* an industry journal that seeks to integrate the two fields of nutrition and food science

International Life Sciences Institute *noun* a not-for-profit organisation that promotes the advance of science in the fields of nutrition, food safety and the environment. Abbreviation **ILSI**

International Network of Food Data Systems *noun* an organisation that promotes the integration of, and free access to, food analysis data systems. Abbreviation **INFOODS**

International Obesity Taskforce *noun* a group established to combat worldwide obesity. Abbreviation **IOTF**

International Society of Organic Agriculture Research *noun* an association which promotes the advancement of research into organic methods and practices. Abbreviation **ISOFAR**

International Union of Food Science and Technology *noun* an international association aiming to foster international cooperation and sharing of data between food scientists worldwide. Abbreviation **IUFoST**

international unit *noun* a standard amount of a biologically-active substance, such as a vitamin, which produces a particular response. Abbreviation **IU**

intervention study *noun* a comparison study between two groups of people on different dietary regimes

intestinal defences *plural noun* immune responses and friendly bacteria in the gut

intestinal flora *plural noun* microorganisms found in the gastrointestinal tract

intestinal juice *noun* an alkaline liquid secreted by the small intestine that helps to digest food

intestinal lavage *noun* the process of washing out the small intestine to remove toxins in the blood surrounding it

intestinal pseudoobstruction *noun* a decreased ability of the intestinal muscles to push food along, causing dilation of the colon

intestine *noun* the part of the digestive system between the stomach and the anus that digests and absorbs food. ◊ **large intestine, small intestine** (NOTE: For other terms referring to the intestines, see words beginning with **entero-**.)

intolerance *noun* ♦ **food intolerance**

intolerant *adjective* unable to eat or drink a particular food, ingredient or substance, or to take a particular drug without having an allergic reaction or becoming ill

intoxicant *noun* a substance that induces a state of intoxication or poisoning, e.g. an alcoholic drink

intravenous nutrition *noun* same as **parenteral nutrition**

intrinsic factor *noun* a protein produced in the gastric glands that reacts with vitamin B12, controls the absorption of extrinsic factor, and, if lacking, causes pernicious anaemia

intrinsic sugars *plural noun* sugars that are naturally found in a foodstuff

inulase *noun* an enzyme that brings about the breakdown of inulin

inulin *noun* a fructose polysaccharide that is a food reserve found in the roots and tubers of various plants

invertase *noun* an enzyme in the intestine that splits sucrose

invert sugar *noun* hydrolysed sucrose, a mixture of glucose and fructose

iodine *noun* a chemical element that is essential to the body, especially to the functioning of the thyroid gland (NOTE: Lack of iodine in the diet can cause goitre. The chemical symbol is I.)

iodised salt *noun* salt to which potassium iodide or iodate is added in order to overcome any deficiencies of iodine in the diet

ION *abbreviation* Institute for Optimum Nutrition

ionisation *noun* a process in which an atom or molecule loses or gains electrons, acquiring an electric charge or changing an existing charge

ionising radiation *noun* electromagnetic radiation that kills living organisms, used in the sterilisation of food in hermetically sealed packs, for reducing spoilage in perishable foods, for eliminating pathogens in foods, for controlling infestation in stored cereals, for preventing the sprouting of root vegetables in storage, and for slowing the development of picked mushrooms (NOTE: There is no current legislation requiring the labelling of foods treated in this way.)

IOTF *abbreviation* International Obesity Taskforce

IPM *abbreviation* integrated pest management

Irish coffee *noun* hot coffee, served in a glass, with Irish whiskey added to it and whipped cream poured on top

Irish cream *noun* cream flavoured with Irish whiskey and sweeteners, used as a drink or in coffee

Irish Food Board *noun* ♦ **Bord Bia**

iron *noun* a chemical element essential to the body, present in foods such as liver and eggs

iron ammonium citrate *noun* same as **ferric ammonium citrate**

iron-deficiency anaemia *noun* anaemia caused by a lack of iron in red blood cells

iron hydroxide *noun* ♦ **E172**

iron rations *plural noun* food designed to be used in an emergency, especially by military personnel

irradiate *verb* to treat food with electromagnetic radiation in order to kill germs and slow down the process of ripening and decay

irradiated milk *noun* milk that has been treated with UV light to promote the development of vitamin D

irradiation *noun* the use of electromagnetic radiation to kill bacteria in food

irritable bowel syndrome *noun* a condition of the bowel in which there is recurrent pain with constipation or diarrhoea or alternating attacks of these. Abbreviation **IBS**

irritant *noun* a substance that can cause an irritation

ischaemia *noun* insufficient blood supply to an organ

ischaemic heart disease *noun* a disease of the heart caused by a failure in the blood supply, as in coronary thrombosis. Abbreviation **IHD**

isoenzyme *noun* a form of an enzyme that is chemically different to other forms but functions in the same way

ISOFAR *abbreviation* International Society of Organic Agriculture Research

isoflavone *noun* an organic compound belonging to a group that occurs in legumes, especially soya beans, that may have positive effects against cancer and heart disease. Also called **phytoestrogen**

isoflavonoid *noun* an organic compound belonging to a group that occurs in legumes, especially soya beans, and is converted by bacteria in the intestines into substances that act rather like oestrogen

isolate *verb* **1.** to keep one person apart from others because he or she has a dangerous infectious disease **2.** to identify a single virus, bacterium or other pathogen among many ■ *noun* a pure culture of a microorganism

isoleucine *noun* an essential amino acid

isomalt *noun* a commercial sweetener that does not promote tooth decay

isomer *noun* each of two or more molecules that have the same number of atoms but have different chemical structures and therefore different properties

isomerase *noun* an enzyme that converts one isomer into another

isomerise *verb* to convert one isomer into another

isopropyl alcohol *noun* a colourless flammable alcohol used as a rubbing alcohol and a solvent

isopropyl citrate *noun* an ester used for preventing oils from becoming rancid

isotonic drink *noun* a liquid supplement that has nutrients in the same proportions in which they are normally found in the body

isozyme *noun* a form of an enzyme that is chemically different from other forms but functions in the same way

ispaghula *noun* a polysaccharide gum used as a thickening agent and laxative

Italian dressing *noun* a salad dressing typically made with oil and vinegar, garlic and oregano

-ite *suffix* salt or ester of an acid with a name ending in *-ous*

IU *abbreviation* international unit

IUFoST *abbreviation* International Union of Food Science and Technology

J

J *abbreviation* joule

jacket potato *noun* same as **baked potato**

jalapeño *noun* a small hot pepper that is picked when green and is used extensively in Mexican cooking

jam *noun* a sweet food made with fruit and sugar

Jamaica pepper *noun* same as **allspice**

jambalaya *noun* a Creole dish of rice with a mixture of fish and meat such as shrimps, chicken, ham and spicy sausage

Japanese puffer fish *noun* same as **fugu**

jaundice *noun* a condition in which there is an excess of bile pigment in the blood, and in which the pigment is deposited in the skin and the whites of the eyes, which have a yellow colour

JECFA *abbreviation* Joint Expert Committee on Food Additives

jejunal *adjective* relating to the jejunum

jejuno-ileostomy *noun* a surgical operation to remove part of the ileum or jejunum

jejunostomy *noun* a surgical operation to make an artificial passage to the jejunum through the wall of the abdomen (NOTE: The plural is **jejunostomies**.)

jejunum *noun* the part of the small intestine between the duodenum and the ileum, about two metres long

jellied *adjective* cooked or preserved in a jelly

jelly *noun* **1.** a semi-solid substance, especially a type of sweet food made of gelatin, water and fruit flavouring, etc. (NOTE: The plural form is **jellies**.) **2.** a type of preserve made of fruit juice boiled with sugar **3.** same as **jam**

jelly bag *noun* a bag used for straining the juice when making jelly or jam

jellying *noun* a way of preserving food by cooking it in a substance such as aspic that forms a gel when cooled

jelly mould *noun* a shape for making jelly

JEMRA *noun* a scientific committee that reports on risk assessment methods related to food safety. Full form **Joint FAO/WHO Expert Meetings on Microbiological Risk Assessment**

jerk seasoning *noun* a spice mixture used for coating meat prior to frying or grilling, consisting of some or all of ground cayenne and black pepper, allspice, cinnamon, oregano, bay leaf, nutmeg, onion and garlic, available as a paste or powder

Jerusalem artichoke *noun* ↓ **artichoke**

JHCI *abbreviation* Joint Health Claims Initiative

jiaogulan *noun* a herbal supplement used in Chinese medicine, closely related to ginseng

JMPR *abbreviation* Joint Meeting on Pesticide Residues

John Dory *noun* a deep-sea fish with a large flat olive-yellow body, long dorsal spines and large jaws, native to the eastern Atlantic and the Mediterranean (NOTE: Its scientific name is *Zeus faber.*)

joint *noun* a piece of meat, especially one suitable for roasting ■ *verb* to cut a carcass into pieces of meat for cooking

Joint Expert Committee on Food Additives *noun* an association of scientists who provide WHO and the FAO with information on food additives, contaminants and toxicants. Abbreviation **JECFA**

Joint FAO/WHO Expert Meetings on Microbiological Risk Assessment *noun* full form of **JEMRA**

Joint Health Claims Initiative *noun* a joint venture between manufacturers of food products, trade associations and regulatory authorities to ensure that health claims are scientifically true when applied to food, legally acceptable under the current UK food law, and meaningful and not confusing to consumers. Abbreviation **JHCI**

Joint Meeting on Pesticide Residues *noun* a committee of the FAO that produces reports on the long-term toxicological effects of pesticide use. Abbreviation **JMPR**

joule *noun* the SI unit of measurement of work or energy. Abbreviation **J** (NOTE: 4.184 joules equals one calorie.)

Journal of Food Protection *noun* a scientific journal produced by the International Association for Food Protection

Journal of Human Nutrition and Dietetics *noun* a journal of peer-reviewed research papers published on behalf of the British Dietetic Association

jugged hare *noun* hare cooked slowly in a covered dish

juice *noun* the liquid inside a fruit or vegetable, or inside meat or poultry ■ *verb* to extract the juice from a fruit or vegetable

juice drink *noun* a flavoured drink containing between 6% and 30% fruit juice, water, sugar and flavourings

juice extractor *noun* a device for extracting juice from a fruit or vegetable

juice press *noun* ↓ **press**

julienne *adjective* used for describing food such as vegetables which have been cut into long thin strips ■ *verb* to cut vegetables into long thin strips

juniper berries *plural noun* the dried berries of a shrub of the cypress family, used for flavouring gin and as a pickling spice, its piney flavour also making it a pleasant accompaniment to game and pork (NOTE: The plant's botanical name is *Juniperus communis.*)

junk food *noun* food of little nutritional value, e.g. high-fat processed snacks, eaten between or instead of meals

jus *noun* traditional gravy, the reduced juice from cooked meat, served as an accompaniment to meat

K

kale *noun* a plant of the cabbage family with large curly dark-green leaves, used as a green vegetable and also grown as animal forage

kallikrein *noun* an enzyme present in blood, urine, and body tissue that, when activated, dilates blood vessels

kaolin *noun* a fine soft clay used in the making of medical preparations, especially for the treatment of diarrhoea

karaya gum *noun* ♦ E416

Kashin-Beck disease *noun* selenium deficiency that causes damage to the cartilage in joints

kashruth, kashrut *noun* the set of Jewish laws that relate to the preparation and fitness of foods and to items such as textiles and ritual scrolls to be used by Jewish people

kava *noun* **1.** a herbal medicine made from the dried roots and rhizome of a bush of the pepper family, used for relieving anxiety and improving sleep **2.** a narcotic drink made from the roots of a bush of the pepper family

kcal *abbreviation* kilocalorie

kebab *noun* a dish of pieces of meat, fish or vegetables stuck on a skewer and cooked over a charcoal grill

kedgeree *noun* a spicy mixture of rice, fish, curry and eggs, traditionally eaten at breakfast

kelp *noun* a brown seaweed with large leathery fronds that is a source of iodine and potash

keratomalacia *noun* damage to the cornea caused by vitamin A deficiency

kernel *noun* the softer edible part inside a nut

Keshan disease *noun* selenium deficiency that causes damage to the heart

ketchup *noun* thick savoury tomato sauce, eaten especially with fried food

ketoacidosis *noun* an accumulation of ketone bodies in tissue in diabetes, causing acidosis

ketogenic diet *noun* a diet which causes the body to go into ketosis, typically one which is very low in carbohydrates

ketoglutaric acid *noun* a compound that combines with ammonia to form glutaric acid

ketone *noun* an organic compound containing a carbon atom connected to an oxygen atom by a double bond and to two carbon atoms

ketone bodies *plural noun* ketone compounds formed from fatty acids

ketonuria *noun* the excretion of ketone bodies in urine

ketosis *noun* the metabolisation of ketone bodies to provide the brain with energy when sufficient glucose is not available through the diet

key lime pie *noun* a pie made from thickened sweetened condensed milk flavoured with juice from limes, traditionally a small variety called the key lime

kg *abbreviation* kilogram

kibble *verb* to grind something such as grain into small pieces

kibbled *adjective* coarsely ground

kibbled wheat *noun* same as **cracked wheat**

kidney *noun* **1.** one of a pair of organs in animals that extract impurities from the blood **2.** this organ used as food

kidney bean *noun* a type of bean with reddish seeds, shaped like kidneys, used e.g. in chilli con carne

kidney failure *noun* a situation in which the kidneys do not function properly

kidney stone *noun* a hard stone in the kidneys formed of calcium, uric acid or cysteine

kilocalorie *noun* a unit of measurement of heat equal to 1000 calories. Abbreviation **kcal** (NOTE: In scientific use, the SI unit **joule** is now more usual. 1 calorie equals 4.186 joules.)

kilogram *noun* an SI unit of measurement of weight equal to 1000 grams. Abbreviation **kg**

kilojoule *noun* an SI unit of measurement of energy or heat equal to 1000 joules. Abbreviation **kJ**

kinase *noun* an enzyme belonging to a large family of related substances that bind to the energy-providing molecule ATP and regulate functions such as cell division and signalling between cells

king prawn *noun* a type of very large prawn, the type that is served as scampi

kipper *noun* a smoked herring that has been opened up and is flat

kitchen clerk *noun* the person in the kitchen who shouts the order from the waiter to the chefs, and pins the waiter's written order on a hook relating to a particular table. Also called **aboyeur**

kitchen foil *noun* same as **aluminium foil**

kitchen scales *noun* a machine for weighing, used in the kitchen to weigh ingredients

kitchenware *noun* frying pans, saucepans and other cooking or preparing containers, used in a kitchen

kiwi fruit *noun* a brownish oval fruit with green juicy flesh, the fruit of a subtropical climbing plant. Also called **Chinese gooseberry**

kJ *abbreviation* kilojoule

Kjeldahl determination *noun* a way of measuring the amount of nitrogen in a substance by converting it to measurable ammonia

knead *verb* to press and fold dough before it is cooked to make bread

knife *noun* an implement with a sharp blade, used for cutting and spreading

knife block *noun* a heavy block with slots in which sharp knives are stored safely

knife sharpener *noun* a device for grinding the edges of kitchen knives to make them sharp

knock back, knock down *verb* to lightly knead risen dough a second time in order to eliminate gas bubbles and help further develop the gluten

knuckle *noun* a joint on the leg of an animal

kohlrabi *noun* a variety of cabbage with a swollen stem and green or purple leaves, used as a fodder crop, and also sometimes eaten as a vegetable

koilonychia *noun* brittleness and warping of the fingernails caused by iron deficiency

Konzo *noun* a debilitating illness caused by eating untreated cassava root that contains cyanide

Korsakoff's psychosis *noun* a loss of long-term memory and embroidering of short-term memory, caused by a deficiency of vitamin B1

kosher *adjective* prepared according to Jewish law

Krebs cycle *noun* an important series of reactions in which the intermediate products of fats, carbohydrates and amino acid metabolism are converted to carbon dioxide and water in the mitochondria. Also called **citric acid cycle**

krill *noun* a tiny ocean crustacean resembling a shrimp that is the primary food of baleen whales and other animals that filter their food from seawater

krill oil *noun* oil from krill that is rich in omega 3 essential fatty acids, taken as a food supplement

kumquat *noun* a small oval orange fruit, related to citrus fruits, with sweet skin and tart flesh, eaten whole or preserved

kuru *noun* a degenerative neurone disease believed to be caused by prions ingested from human tissue

kwashiorkor *noun* malnutrition of small children, mostly in tropical countries, causing anaemia, wasting of the body and swollen liver

L

L. *abbreviation* Lactobacillus

labelling *noun* the work of putting labels on products, especially food products, to show what the products contain or how or where they are made

labile *adjective* unstable under certain conditions

laccase *noun* an enzyme containing copper, found in plants

lace *verb* to add a small amount of alcohol or a drug to a drink or to food

L. acidophilus *noun* a lactic acid bacteria and probiotic

lacquer *noun* a protective layer of hard gum that stops the food inside a tin from corroding it

lactalbumin *noun* a milk protein that contains all the essential amino acids

lactase *noun* an enzyme, secreted in the small intestine, that converts milk sugar into glucose and galactose

lactate *noun* any of various salts of lactic acid used as buffers and firming agents

lactation *noun* **1.** the production of milk in the body **2.** the period during which a mother is breastfeeding a baby

lacteal *noun* a lymphatic vessel in the small intestine that absorbs fats

lactic acid *noun* a sugar that forms in cells and tissue, and also in sour milk, cheese and yoghurt

lactitol *noun* a modified lactose used in sugar-free confectionery

Lactobacillus *noun* a type of probiotic found in dairy products. Abbreviation **L.**

Lactococcus *noun* a bacterium that turns milk sour

lactogen *noun* a substance that promotes the production of milk

lactoglobulin *noun* any of a group of globular proteins that occur in milk

lacto-ovo-vegetarian *noun* a person who does not eat animal flesh, poultry or fish but does eat eggs and milk products. ◊ **vegetarian, vegan**

lactose *noun* a type of sugar found in milk

lactose intolerance *noun* a condition in which a person cannot digest lactose because lactase is absent in the intestine or because of an allergy to milk, causing diarrhoea

lactovegetarian *noun* a person who eats vegetables, grains, fruit, nuts and milk products but not meat or eggs. ◊ **vegetarian, vegan**

lactucarium *noun* a mild sedative agent found in lettuce

lactulose *noun* an artificially produced sugar used as a laxative

ladies' fingers *noun* same as **okra**

ladle *noun* a spoon with a large bowl, used for serving soup

lager *noun* **1.** a pale type of beer that is highly carbonated and typically slightly sweeter than bitter beer **2.** a glass of this beer

lamb *noun* meat from a sheep, especially from a young sheep

langoustine *noun* a very large prawn

laparoenterostomy *noun* a surgical operation that creates an opening in the abdominal wall into the intestine

laparogastroscomy *noun* the creation of a permanent opening in the abdominal wall for tube feeding

laparogastroscopy *noun* the insertion of an endoscope into an incision in the abdominal wall in order to medically examine the stomach

lard *noun* pig fat used in cooking ■ *verb* to cover meat with bacon, lard or other fat before cooking it in the oven

larder *noun* a cool room or cupboard for storing food

larder chef *noun* the chef in charge of cold dishes, salads and salad sauces, sandwiches, and who cuts meat and fish ready for cooking in the kitchen. Also called **chef garde-manger**

larder fridge *noun* a fridge for keeping food in until needed

larding *noun* the action of threading strips of fat into the surface of meat to prevent it drying out during cooking

lardon *noun* a strip of fat or fatty bacon threaded through lean meat to prevent it drying out and to add flavour during cooking

lardoon *noun* a narrow strip of bacon fat used in larding

large bowel *noun* ♦ **large intestine**

large intestine *noun* the section of the digestive system from the caecum to the rectum

lasagne *noun* a type of flat pasta, served cooked with meat or vegetable sauce in layers

L-ascorbic acid *noun* ♦ **vitamin C**

lassi *noun* a South Asian drink consisting of flavoured yoghurt or buttermilk diluted with water

lateral abuse *noun* denting of a food tin caused by rough handling

lathyrism *noun* nerve damage caused by a high intake of native pulses in Asia and northern Africa

latte *noun* **1.** a type of Italian coffee consisting of an espresso with steamed milk added, topped with froth, and often served in a tall cup or glass **2.** a cup of this coffee

laurel *noun* same as **bay**

lavage *noun* the process of washing out a hollow organ such as the stomach

laver bread *noun* a Welsh dish made from boiled seaweed mixed with oatmeal, formed into cakes, and fried, traditionally in bacon fat

laxative *adjective* causing a bowel movement ■ *noun* a medicine that causes a bowel movement ▶ also called (all senses) **purgative**

lax bowel *noun* same as **diarrhoea**

layer *noun* **1.** a flat mass of food under or over another mass **2.** a bird that is laying eggs

lazy bowel *noun* same as **atonic non-functioning colon**

lazy Susan *noun* a revolving tray, placed in the centre of a dining table to hold condiments, extra dishes, hors d'oeuvres and other foods

lb *abbreviation* pound

L-cysteine hydrochloride *noun* ♦ **E920**

LDL *abbreviation* low-density lipoprotein

lead *noun* a very heavy soft metallic element that is poisonous in compounds (NOTE: The chemical symbol is **Pb**.)

lead poisoning *noun* poisoning caused by taking in lead salts

leaf gelatin *noun* purified gelatin in the form of sheets that look rather like stiff cellophane, softened in water for five minutes prior to using

leafy *adjective* used for describing a vegetable with large leaves, especially when the leaves are the edible part

lean *adjective* used for describing meat with little fat ■ *noun* lean meat

lean body mass *noun* ♦ **fat free mass**

Leatherhead Food International *noun* a research and advisory service for the UK food industry. Abbreviation **LFI**

leavening agent *noun* same as **raising agent**

lecithin *noun* a chemical that is a constituent of all animal and plant cells and is involved in the transport and absorption of fats

lecithinase *noun* same as **phospholipase**

lectin *noun* a protein found widely in nature, especially in seeds, that belongs to a group that bind to specific carbohydrates and cause clumping of blood cells (NOTE: Lectins might sometimes trigger immune reactions and dietary intolerance. They are used in testing for blood type.)

leek *noun* a vegetable with a white stem and long green leaves, related to the onion

leftovers *plural noun* food that has not been eaten

legume *noun* a seed, pod or other part of a plant such as a pea or bean, used as food

lemon *noun* the yellow edible fruit of an evergreen citrus tree, with sour-tasting flesh and juice

lemonade *noun* **1.** a drink made from fresh lemon juice, sugar and water **2.** a commercially produced fizzy drink with the flavour of lemons

lemon balm *noun* a widely cultivated plant of the mint family that has lemon-scented leaves. Also called **melissa**

lemon grass *noun* a green lemon-flavoured herb, used especially in Thai cooking

lemon juice *noun* the juice of lemons, used for flavouring, for preventing cut fruit and vegetables from browning, and for whitening fish and fish bones for stock

lemon sole *noun* a small flatfish with delicate flesh

lemon squeezer *noun* a device for removing the juice from a lemon

lemon thyme *noun* a variety of thyme that smells of lemon

lemon verbena *noun* a widely cultivated bush with leaves that produce a fragrance resembling lemons when crushed

lentil *noun* the small round dried yellow or green seed of a plant of the pea family, used as food, especially in soups and stews

leptin *noun* a hormone produced by fat cells that signals the body's level of hunger to the hypothalamus of the brain

let down *verb* to dilute a substance

lettuce *noun* any of several varieties of plant with large leaves used in salads

leucine *noun* an essential amino acid

leucocyte *noun* a white blood cell

leucocytosis *noun* an increase in the numbers of leucocytes in the blood above the usual upper limit, which occurs when the body needs to fight an infection

leucopenia *noun* a reduction in the number of leucocytes in the blood, usually as the result of a disease

leucovorin *noun* a synthetic form of folic acid

lexicon *noun* a finite list of descriptors used in sensory evaluation of a foodstuff

LFI *abbreviation* Leatherhead Food International

liaise *verb* to thicken a substance

liaison *noun* a thickening agent used in soups and sauces, e.g. egg yolks or flour

licensed *adjective* given official permission to produce or sell something

licorice *noun* another spelling of **liquorice**

lientery *noun* incompletely digested intestinal contents expelled in faeces, indicative of a digestive disorder

life expectancy *noun* the number of years a person of a particular age is likely to live

lift *noun* the rising of a cooked mixture, especially the rising of puff pastry

light *adjective* with a pleasant open texture that does not give a feeling of heaviness in the stomach when eaten

lignan *noun* a phenolic compound of a group found mainly in plants that are believed to protect human beings from tumours and viruses

lignin *noun* the material in plant cell walls that makes plants woody and gives them rigidity and strength

lime *noun* a green citrus fruit similar to, but smaller than, a lemon

limiting amino acid *noun* the amino acid that is present in the smallest amount in a particular foodstuff, limiting the amount of protein that can be absorbed

limonene *noun* an antioxidant found in lemons

limosis *noun* a strong, abnormal desire for food

line *verb* to cover the inside of a cake tin, pudding bowl or other container with something edible, e.g. bacon, or something non-edible, e.g. greaseproof paper, usually to prevent the enclosed food from sticking to the container

liner *noun* a dish on which another dish is placed containing food ready for serving

linguine *plural noun* pasta made in long narrow flat strips

linoleic acid *noun* an omega-6 fatty acid, found in grains

linolenic acid *noun* an omega-3 fatty acid, found in oils and seeds

linseed oil *noun* oil from the seeds of the flax plant, rich in omega 3 essential fatty acids and taken as a food supplement

Lion Quality *noun* the symbol used on eggs in the UK to show that they come from a supplier approved by the British Egg Industry Council

lipaciduria *noun* the excretion of fatty acids in the urine

lipaemia *noun* an increase of lipids in the blood

liparia *noun* same as **obesity**

lipase *noun* an enzyme that breaks down fats in the intestine. Also called **lipolytic enzyme**

LIPGENE *noun* a research consortium based at the University of Dublin, looking into the relationship between obesity and genetics

lipid *noun* any organic compound that is insoluble in water, e.g. fat, oil or wax

lipidema *plural noun* subcutaneous fat deposits that form in the lower extremities of the body

lipo- *prefix* fat, fatty tissue

lipodology *noun* the study of fat and its effects on the body

lipodystrophy *noun* any condition in which fat is ineffectively metabolised

lipoic acid *noun* a sulphur-containing fatty acid that plays a role in carbohydrate metabolism

lipolysis *noun* the breakdown of fatty acids in the body

lipolytic enzyme *noun* same as **lipase**

lipolytic rancidity *noun* food spoilage caused by the hydrolysation of fats by lipase

lipophilic *adjective* used for describing molecules that are soluble in fats

lipoprotein *noun* a protein that combines with lipids and carries them in the bloodstream and lymph system (NOTE: Lipoproteins are classified according to the percentage of protein they carry.)

lipoprotein lipase *noun* an enzyme found in the lining of blood vessels which hydrolyses blood lipids (NOTE: Lipoproteins are classified according to the percentage of protein they carry.)

liposoluble *adjective* soluble in fat

liposome *noun* a microscopic spherical sac bounded by a double layer of lipids, sometimes used to carry a drug to targeted body tissues

liquefy *verb* to make a gas into liquid, or to become liquid

liqueur *noun* any strong sweet alcohol made from fruit or herbs

liquid *noun* a substance that flows easily like water and is neither a gas nor a solid ■ *adjective* flowing easily and neither gas nor solid

liquidise *verb* to reduce fruit or vegetables to liquid

liquidiser *noun* a machine that liquidises fruit or vegetables

liquid paraffin *noun* a lubricating mineral oil used as a mild laxative

liquor *noun* **1.** alcohol **2.** a liquid produced in cooking

liquorice *noun* the root of a perennial plant native to southern Europe and Asia, with a slightly aniseed flavour that makes it useful in sweets and soft drinks (NOTE: The plant's botanical name is *Glycyrrhiza glabra*.)

lissamine green *noun* ♦ E142

listeria *noun* a bacterium found in human and animal faeces, one species of which can cause meningitis if ingested in contaminated food

listeriosis *noun* an infectious disease transmitted from animals to humans by the listeria bacterium

lithium *noun* a soft silver-white metallic element that forms compounds, used as a medical treatment for bipolar disorder

live bacteria *plural noun* probiotic bacteria in a food or food supplement

liver *noun* **1.** an organ in the body that helps the digestion by producing bile **2.** an animal's liver used as food

liver failure *noun* a medical condition in which the liver stops working efficiently, resulting in jaundice, weak blood vessels and failing general health

liver salts *plural noun* a solution of mineral salts used for relieving indigestion

Livestock and Meat Commission for Northern Ireland *noun* a marketing and advisory service promoting the meat industry in Northern Ireland. Abbreviation **LMC**

living food diet *noun* same as **raw food diet**

living salad *noun* salad vegetables sold still growing in a small pot, to be harvested when needed

LMC *abbreviation* Livestock and Meat Commission for Northern Ireland

loaf *noun* a large single piece of bread, cut into slices before being eaten

loaf tin *noun* a rectangular tin for baking bread and other foods in loaf form, with slightly outward sloping sides that allow for easy removal of the food

loaf tray *noun* a rectangular baking tray with deep sides for baking loaves of bread

lobster *noun* a shellfish with a long body, two large claws, and eight legs, used as food

local food *noun* the principle of buying food from local suppliers, to reduce the environmental impact of long-distance transport and also sustain the local economy

loganberry *noun* a soft red fruit, a cross between a blackberry and a raspberry

loin *noun* a cut of meat taken between the neck and the leg

lollo rosso *noun* a type of lettuce with curly red-tipped leaves

long chain fatty acids *noun* fatty acids with more than 6 carbon bonds

long-grain rice *noun* rice with long grains used in savoury dishes

long-life *adjective* specially treated to last for a long time. Also called **ultra high temperature**, **ultra heat treated**

loonzein *noun* rice grains with the husk removed

loose seam *noun* an improperly soldered seam on a tin that makes it vulnerable to contamination

loperamide *noun* an opiate drug that slows down the movements of the intestines, used in the treatment of acute and chronic diarrhoea

LOS *abbreviation* lower oesophageal sphincter

lot code, lot mark *noun* same as **batch code**

lot marking *noun* the marking of food packaging with a batch code, required by law in the UK

lot number *noun* ♦ **batch code**

lovage *noun* a herb used as a vegetable and for making herbal teas

low biological value *noun* the fact of containing a relatively low amount of bioavailable proteins

low-calorie, low-cal *adjective* with a low energy value, in the EU generally less than 40 kcal per 100g of food

low-calorie sweetener *noun* any sweet substance that is not made from sugar and contains fewer calories, e.g. aspartame

low-density lipoprotein *noun* the lipoprotein that carries cholesterol to cells and tissue. Abbreviation **LDL**

lower oesophageal sphincter *noun* a ring of muscle at the lower end of the oesophagus that prevents stomach contents from refluxing. Abbreviation **LOS**

lower-reference nutrient intake *noun* an amount of a nutrient that is sufficient for people with low nutrition requirements, but not for the majority of people. Abbreviation **LRNI**

low-fat *adjective* containing very little fat

low-sugar *adjective* containing very little sugar

L. plantarum *noun* a protective intestinal probiotic. Full form **Lactobillus plantarum**

L. rhamnosus *noun* a protective intestinal probiotic. Full form **Lactobillus rhamnosus**

LRNI *abbreviation* lower-reference nutrient intake

lubricant laxative *noun* a substance such as liquid paraffin that lubricates the walls of the colon and prevents water reabsorption

lumpy *adjective* used for describing semiliquid foods such as sauces and soups that lack the normal appetising smoothness of texture

luncheon meat *noun* a tinned meat loaf containing mostly minced pork

lupeose *noun* same as **stachyose**

lute *verb* **1.** to seal the gap between the lid and body of a cooking dish with a flour and water paste that bakes hard in the oven **2.** to place a strip of pastry around the rim of a pie dish to seal the pastry cover

lutein *noun* a yellow pigment in the corpus luteum

luting *noun* strips of pastry used for sealing down the lid of an oven container for slow-cook dishes

lychee *noun* the fruit of a tropical tree native to Southeast Asia, with sweet translucent white flesh that is rich in vitamin C

lycopene *noun* a powerful antioxidant of the carotenoid group, found in tomatoes and used in many antioxidant dietary supplements. ◊ **E160(d)**

lye-peeling *noun* the process of removing the skin from fruit and vegetables using a chemical solution of lye

lymph, lymph fluid *noun* a colourless liquid containing white blood cells that circulates in the lymph system from all body tissues, carrying waste matter away from tissues to the veins

lyonnaise *adjective* used for describing potatoes that are cooked with onions

lyophilisation *noun* the process of freeze-drying food

lyophilise *verb* to freeze-dry food

lysin *noun* **1.** a protein in the blood that destroys the cell against which it is directed **2.** a toxin that causes the lysis of cells

lysine *noun* an essential amino acid

lysozyme *noun* an enzyme found in the whites of eggs that destroys specific bacteria

M

macadamia *noun* same as **macadamia nut**

macadamia nut *noun* a nut rather like a large hazelnut, from an evergreen tree originally grown in Australia, developed in Hawaii and now grown worldwide (NOTE: There are two species of tree, *Macadamia ternifolia*, with hard-shelled nuts, and *Macadamia integrifolia*, with softer-shelled nuts.)

macaroni *noun* short thick tubes of pasta, often served with a cheese sauce

macaroon *noun* a small sweet almond biscuit

mace *noun* a spice made from the covering of the nutmeg seed, used in the form of dried pieces or as a yellow-orange powder

macerase *noun* an enzyme used for breaking down the pectin in fruit

macerate *verb* to make something soft by letting it lie in a liquid for a time

mackerel *noun* a sea fish with dark flesh, eaten grilled or smoked and also used for canning

macro- *prefix* large, inclusive or long

macrobiotic *adjective* relating to macrobiotics

macrobiotics *noun* a dietary system based on vegetarian foods without artificial additives or preservatives, especially organically grown whole grains, fruit and vegetables

macronutrient *noun* a substance that an organism needs in large amounts for normal growth and development, e.g. nitrogen, carbon or potassium. Compare **micronutrient**

mad cow disease *noun* same as **BSE**

Madeira *noun* a fortified wine from Madeira, used for flavouring foods, especially sauces

Madeira cake *noun* a rich yellow sponge cake flavoured with lemon juice and zest and decorated with candied citron peel

madeleine mould *noun* a hinged scallop-shaped mould that completely encloses the cake baked in it

magma *noun* a syrup of sugar containing crystals, produced during sugar refinement

magnesium *noun* a chemical element found in green vegetables, essential for the correct functioning of muscles (NOTE: The chemical symbol is **Mg**.)

magnesium carbonate *noun* a crystalline white salt used in glass making and in indigestion remedies

magnesium deficiency *noun* a condition that can cause heart arrhythmia and electrolyte disturbances

magnesium hydroxide *noun* a white powder used as an indigestion remedy and laxative. Also called **milk of magnesia**

magnesium oxide *noun* a white powder used in indigestion remedies and laxatives

magnesium salt *noun* a crystalline compound formed from the neutralisation of an acid solution containing magnesium

magnesium silicate *noun* ◆ E553(a)

magnesium stearate *noun* ◆ E572

magnesium sulphate *noun* a magnesium salt used as a laxative when diluted with water

magnesium trisilicate *noun* a magnesium compound used for treating peptic ulcers

Maillard reaction, Maillard browning *noun* a reaction between a sugar and an amino acid, responsible for the browning of meat, bread, chocolate, coffee and other roasted food

main course *noun* the central and most substantial dish of a meal, usually containing a fair amount of meat, fish or pulse protein

maître d'hôtel, maître d' *noun* the person in charge of a restaurant, who is responsible for all the service and takes orders himself from customers. Also called **head waiter**

maître d'hôtel de carré *noun* a chief waiter who is in charge of a station, and takes the orders from customers. Also called **station head waiter**

maize *noun* a widely grown cereal crop. Also called **corn**

maize protein *noun* the protein found in corn

malabsorption *noun* a situation in which the intestines are unable to absorb the fluids and nutrients in food properly

malabsorption syndrome *noun* a set of symptoms caused by not taking in enough of a particular nutrient

malassimilation *noun* the poor or inadequate incorporation of food constituents such as proteins and minerals into bones, muscles and other body structures

maldigestion *noun* poor digestion and absorption of a nutrient

malic acid *noun* a colourless crystalline solid found in fruits, particularly apples

malnourished *adjective* not having enough to eat or having only poor-quality food, and therefore ill

malnutrition *noun* **1.** a lack of food or of good-quality food, leading to ill-health **2.** the state of not having enough to eat

malo-lactic fermentation *noun* the conversion of malic acid into lactic acid over time in wines, making them less acidic

mal rosso *noun* same as **pellagra**

malt *noun* a grain that has been prepared for making beer or whisky by being allowed to sprout and then dried ■ *verb* to treat grain such as barley by allowing it to sprout and then drying it

maltase *noun* an enzyme in the small intestine that converts maltose into glucose

malt bread *noun* a soft moist loaf enriched with malt extract, black treacle and dried vine fruits

malted *adjective* tasting of malt

malted wheatgrain *noun* same as **granary flour**

malt extract a sweet sticky substance produced from malt, used as an additive in cooking or brewing

maltitol *noun* a low-calorie bulk sweetener

maltose *noun* a sugar formed by digesting starch or glycogen

maltose intolerance *noun* same as **disaccharide intolerance**

malt vinegar *noun* brown vinegar made by partially oxidising ale, containing about 5% acetic acid

mandarin *noun* any of a group of orange citrus fruits that are small, sweet and have very easily separable thin skins and segments (NOTE: They are the satsuma or unshui mandarin, *Citrus unshui*, the Mediterranean mandarin, *Citrus deliciosa*, king mandarin, *Citrus nobilis*, and common mandarin, *Citrus reticulata*.)

mandatory fortification *noun* the enrichment of food products that is required by government policy, e.g. the enrichment of bread with folic acid

mandatory labelling *noun* ♦ **food labelling**

mandolin, mandoline *noun* a kitchen tool for slicing vegetables, consisting of adjustable blades in a frame

manganese *noun* a metallic trace element (NOTE: The chemical symbol is **Mn**.)

mangetout *noun* a variety of pea in which the whole pod is eaten

mango *noun* a large, yellow or yellowish-green tropical fruit with a soft orange pulp surrounding a very large flat seed

mangosteen *noun* a fruit that has a dark shiny rind and a soft sweet white flesh

mannitol *noun* a diuretic drug used in the treatment of oedema of the brain

mannotetrose *noun* same as **stachyose**

manufacturing *noun* the production of machine-made products for sale

MAO inhibitor *abbreviation* monoamine oxidase inhibitor

MAP *abbreviation* modified atmosphere packaging

maple syrup *noun* a sweet syrup made from the sap of the sugar maple tree

maraschino *noun* a colourless liqueur flavoured with maraschino cherries and their crushed kernels, used for flavouring

maraschino cherry *noun* a cherry preserved in a red-coloured sugar syrup flavoured with almond oil, or in maraschino liqueur

marasmic kwashiorkor *noun* the most severe form of kwashiorkor, with weight under 60% of the expected figure

marasmus *noun* a wasting disease that affects small children who have difficulty in absorbing nutrients or who are malnourished. Also called **failure to thrive**

marbled *adjective* **1.** used for describing lean meat that contains streaks of fat **2.** in pastry or cake-making, made from two contrasting coloured pastes mixed together to resemble marble when cooked

margarine *noun* a mixture of animal or vegetable fat used instead of butter

marinade *noun* a mixture of wine and herbs in which meat or fish is soaked before cooking ■ *verb* same as **marinate**

marinate *verb* to soak meat, fish or vegetables in a mixture that adds flavour

Marine Conservation Society *noun* a UK charity that campaigns for responsible and sustainable fishing practices. Abbreviation **MCS**

marinière *adjective* cooked with a little wine, herbs and chopped onion or shallot in a closed pan, so that the main ingredient, usually mussels, is partly poached and partly steamed

marjoram *noun* a herb related to oregano, used in Mediterranean cooking for its delicate citrus and pine flavours

market basket *noun* the theoretical food requirements for a family

market garden *noun* a place for the commercial cultivation of plants, usually vegetables, soft fruit, salad crops and flowers, found near a large urban centre that provides a steady outlet for the sale of its produce

marketing *noun* the techniques used in selling a product, e.g. packaging and advertising

marketing campaign *noun* a series of co-ordinated activities intended to advertise and promote a product

market measure *noun* the pre-metric system of volume measures used for large quantities of goods

market research *noun* the work of examining the possible sales of a product before it is put on the market

marmalade *noun* jam made of oranges, or other citrus fruit such as lemon or grapefruit

marquise *noun* a cold French dessert consisting of whipped cream folded into fruit-flavoured ice

marrons glacés *plural noun* shelled chestnuts boiled in sugar syrup and drained for use as a dessert, as a decoration, or, when puréed and sieved, as a flavouring and bulking agent for meringue and whipped cream

marrow *noun* a large green cylindrical vegetable with spongy white flesh from a plant of the melon family

marrow bone *noun* any large hollow bone that contains bone marrow, soft spongy tissue in which new blood cells are produced

marsala *noun* a sweet Italian wine

marshmallow *noun* a soft spongy sweet made from sugar syrup, egg whites and flavouring

marzipan *noun* a paste made from ground almonds, sugar and egg, used for covering a fruit cake before icing or to make individual little sweets

masala *noun* a mixture of spices ground into a paste, used for flavouring South Asian dishes, or a dish flavoured with this kind of a paste

mascarpone *noun* a rich fatty unsalted Italian cream cheese with a spreadable texture

mash *noun* mashed potatoes ■ *verb* to crush food to a soft paste

mashed potatoes *plural noun* potatoes that have been peeled, boiled and then crushed with butter and milk until they form a soft cream. Also called **creamed potatoes**

mask *verb* to coat the inside of a mould with savoury jelly

maslin pan *noun* a heavy-duty metal pan for making jam

mass production *noun* the process of manufacturing large quantities of identical products

mast cell *noun* a large cell in connective tissue that carries histamine and reacts to allergens

mastic *noun* a tree resin used in Turkish delight

masticate *verb* to chew food

mastication *noun* the act of chewing food

maturation *noun* the process of becoming mature or fully developed

mature *adjective* old enough to have acquired the maximum flavour

matzo *noun* a large thin piece of very dry unleavened Jewish bread eaten during Passover

matzo meal *noun* finely powdered matzos often used as a flour substitute in Jewish cooking and as the equivalent of dried breadcrumbs

maximum residue level *noun* the maximum amount of a pesticide that can remain in crops or foodstuffs under European Union regulations. Abbreviation **MRL**

mayo *noun* mayonnaise (*informal*)

mayonnaise *noun* a sauce for cold dishes, made of oil, eggs and lemon juice or vinegar

MCS *abbreviation* Marine Conservation Society

ME *abbreviation* myalgic encephalopathy

meal *noun* **1.** an amount of food eaten at a particular time of day **2.** roughly ground flour

Meal Ready-to-Eat *noun* a self-contained packaged meal used in army rations. Abbreviation **MRE**

meal replacement *noun* a convenience food product or a slimming or bodybuilding supplement that takes the place of a whole meal

meal replacement product *noun* a bodybuilding supplement containing concentrated proteins, vitamins and minerals, usually powdered and taken mixed with water or milk. Abbreviation **MRP**

mealy *adjective* **1.** powdery or granular, like meal or grain **2.** containing, made of, or covered with meal

mealy endosperm *noun* an endosperm with an open structure

measure *noun* **1.** a way of calculating size or quantity **2.** a serving of alcohol or wine ■ *verb* to find out the size or quantity of something

measuring cup *noun* the standard volume measure used in North America and Australasia, equal to 236 ml

measuring jug *noun* a jug with a scale of volume measures inscribed on the side

measuring spoon *noun* a hemispherical spoon, often one of a set, used for measuring small quantities of liquid or powder

meat *noun* food from an animal's body

meat alternative *noun* a vegetarian food product that provides protein and takes the place of meat. Also called **meat replacement**

meat analogue *noun* a vegetarian food product that tries to simulate the flavour and texture of meat, made from vegetable proteins

Meat and Livestock Commission *noun* an organisation that provides services to livestock breeders, including the evaluation of breeding stock potential and carcass grading and classification. Abbreviation **MLC**

meatball *noun* a small ball of minced meat with flavourings

meat bar *noun* a compressed bar of cooked meat and fat, eaten for energy

meat cleaver *noun* a heavy chopping implement that can cut through bone

meat conditioning *noun* the practice of allowing the glycogen in the muscles of a slaughtered animal to convert to lactic acid, which improves its texture

meat extender *noun* any edible material or mixture added to meat preparations to increase their bulk

meat extract *noun* a thick dark syrupy paste consisting of the soluble components of meat, used for spreading, making drinks and as a flavouring

meat glaze *noun* white or brown beef stock, reduced by boiling until sticky, used as a base for sauces or to improve their flavour

meat hammer *noun* a heavy hammer with a textured or spiked head, used for tenderising meat

meat loaf *noun* a solid block of minced meat, vegetables and flavourings cooked and usually served hot

meat pie *noun* a pie filled with precooked meat, gravy, flavouring and seasoning prior to baking

meat-processing plant *noun* a factory in which raw and cooked meats are processed and packaged

meat products *plural noun* foods made from meat, e.g. pies, sausages and pâtés

meat replacement *noun* same as **meat alternative**

meat safe *noun* a cupboard for storing meat, well ventilated and in a cool place, used in the time before refrigerators were in common use

meat tenderiser *noun* a form of proteinase in a water solution, used for tenderising meat by breaking down the muscle fibres

meat thermometer *noun* a metal thermometer with the measuring element in a sharp point and a circular indicating dial, placed with its point in the thick part of a joint so as to indicate its internal temperature (NOTE: The required temperature for beef and lamb is 51°C, 60°C and 70°C for rare, medium and well done respectively. For pork and veal it is 75°C. For chicken, duck and turkey it is 80°, and for goose 85°C.)

mechanical ileus *noun* an ileus caused by a physical obstruction in the bowel

mechanically-recovered meat *noun* the scraps of meat that remain on an animal's carcass after the prime cuts have been removed, which are removed using machinery, ground and used as cheap filler for foods such as burgers, pies and sausages. Abbreviation **MRM**

medallion, médaillon *noun* a small round piece of tender meat, especially beef or veal, easily cooked by frying or grilling

mediate *verb* to act as a medium that transfers something from one place to another in the body

medical food *noun* food specially processed or formulated to be given, under medical supervision, to patients who require a special diet

Mediterranean diet *noun* a diet high in fibre and monounsaturated fat from fish, vegetables, grains and olive oil

medium *adjective* used for describing steak that is cooked so that it is brown on the outside but slightly pink and moist inside

medium-fat *adjective* containing between 10% and 20% butterfat

medium oily *adjective* used for describing fish flesh that contains between 2% and 6% fat or oil

medium rare *adjective* used for describing steak that is cooked so that the centre of the meat is just pink but set

medulla *noun* the soft inner part of an organ, as opposed to the outer cortex

megadose *noun* a large dose of something such as a vitamin

megajoule *noun* a unit of measurement of energy equal to one million joules. Abbreviation **MJ**

megaloblastic anaemia *noun* anaemia caused by the immaturity of red blood cells

megavitamin *noun* a dose of a vitamin or vitamins that is much higher than the usual dose

Melba sauce *noun* raspberry sauce

melba toast *noun* toast made by grilling a slice of bread once, then slicing it in half and grilling it again quickly, so as to produce a sort of cracker

melena *noun* black faeces containing blood, an indication of bleeding in the gastrointestinal tract

melon *noun* a large sweet round or cylindrical fruit with flesh varying from green to orange or white

melon baller *noun* a cutter used for making melon balls

melt *verb* to heat a solid so that it becomes liquid ■ *noun* an open toasted sandwich, often with cheese melted on top

melting point *noun* the temperature at which a solid turns to liquid

membrane *noun* a thin layer of tissue that lines or covers an organ

menadione *noun* a yellow crystalline solid used as a fungicide and a vitamin K supplement in medicines and animal feedstuffs

ménage *noun* the cleaning and preparing of a restaurant for guests

menaquinone *noun* a form of vitamin K produced by bacteria in the large intestine

Menkes' syndrome *noun* severe copper deficiency, causing a change in hair texture as well as fragile connective tissue

menopause *noun* a period, usually between 45 and 55 years of age, when a woman stops menstruating and can no longer bear children. Also called **change of life**

menstruation *noun* bleeding from the uterus that occurs in a woman each month when the lining of the uterus is shed because no fertilised egg is present

menu *noun* a printed list of food available in a restaurant

menu pricing *noun* the work of giving prices to dishes on the menu so as to produce a profit, but not so high as to deter customers

mercury *noun* a poisonous liquid metal, used in thermometers (NOTE: The chemical symbol is **Hg**.)

meringue *noun* a mixture of whipped egg white and caster sugar baked slowly until crisp

meromyosin *noun* either of two protein subunits of myosin produced through digestion by trypsin

mesomorph *noun* a body type that is muscular and powerful

mesophile *noun* a microorganism that grows at temperatures between 25°C and 40°C

mesophilic *adjective* used for describing microorganisms that prefer medium temperatures

metabisulphites *plural noun* ♦ **E223**

metabolic imbalance teratogen *noun* a nutritional imbalance that may cause defects in a developing baby

metabolic nitrogen *noun* nitrogen in the body that comes from internal sources and not the diet, e.g. from intestinal bacteria

metabolic pathway *noun* a series of chemical reactions in the body, controlled by enzymes

metabolic rate *noun* a measure of how fast the chemical reactions in living cells happen

metabolic syndrome *noun* a medical condition characterised by symptoms such as obesity, diabetes, hypertension and high cholesterol

metabolisation *noun* the act of metabolising food

metabolise *verb* when the body metabolises food, it converts food into new or repaired cell material and tissues and energy after it has been broken down in the gut and transported in the blood to the cells of the body

metabolism *noun* the chemical processes that are continually taking place in the human body and are essential to life, especially the processes that convert food into energy

metabolite *noun* a substance produced by metabolism, or a substance taken into the body in food and then metabolised

metatartaric acid *noun* ♦ E353

meteorism *noun* same as **tympanites**

methane *noun* a colourless flammable gas with no smell

methanoic acid *noun* same as **formic acid**

methionine *noun* an essential amino acid

methyl 4-hydroxybenzoate *noun* ♦ E218

methyl cellulose *noun* ♦ E461

meunière *adjective* used for describing a fish dish in which the fish is dredged in flour, fried in butter, and sprinkled with lemon juice and chopped parsley

meze *noun* an assortment of snacks, typically stuffed vine leaves, small pastries, or grilled sausages, served with drinks as an appetiser or a light meal in Greece and Southwest Asia

mezzaluna *noun* same as **hachoir**

mg *abbreviation* milligram

micelle *noun* a molecular grouping of nutrients in milk

Michelin star *noun* an award made to the very best restaurants, graded from one to three stars

micro- *prefix* small or minute, or using a microscope or requiring magnification

micro-aerophiles *plural noun* microorganisms that do not need much oxygen to grow and can spoil even sealed food

microbe *noun* a microorganism that may cause disease and can only be seen with a microscope, e.g. a bacterium

microbial *adjective* relating to microbes

Microbiological Risk Assessment *noun* a formal set of guidelines for assessing the risk of contamination in a food preparation facility. Abbreviation **MRA**

microbiological swabbing *noun* a test for contamination in a food preparation facility in which a sample of food is taken and scientifically analysed

microbiology *noun* the scientific study of microorganisms

microbrewery *noun* a small, usually independently owned brewery that produces limited quantities of often specialised beers, often selling them on the premises

microbrewing *noun* the practice of brewing a limited quantity of beer on a small premises, often specialised beer

microcapsule *noun* a tiny capsule used to release a drug, flavour or chemical

microcrystalline cellulose *noun* ♦ E460(i)

microcrystalline wax *noun* ♦ E907

microencapsulate *verb* to enclose a substance in microcapsules

microflora *noun* same as **intestinal flora**

microgram *noun* a unit of measurement of weight equal to one millionth of a gram

micronisation *noun* the process of rapidly heating food using infra-red radiation

micronutrient *noun* a substance that an organism needs for normal growth and development, but only in very small quantities, e.g. a vitamin or mineral. Compare **macronutrient**

microorganism *noun* a microscopic form of life, e.g. a bacterium, virus or yeast

microwave *noun* an oven that heats food by means of very-high-frequency electromagnetic radiation ■ *verb* to heat a dish in a microwave

microwaveable, microwavable *adjective* able to be cooked in a microwave

microwave cooking *noun* cooking, usually reheating precooked convenience food, using a microwave oven

microwaves *plural noun* very-high-frequency electromagnetic radiation used for heating up and cooking food (NOTE: Microwaves transfer their energy to food by causing certain types of molecules to vibrate at their frequency.)

microwave thermometer *noun* a thermometer with no metal parts, used inside a microwave oven

MID *abbreviation* minimum infective dose

middle bacon *noun* bacon from the centre of the pig, combining streaky and back bacon

middle gammon *noun* a lean cut of bacon from between the corner gammon and the hock

middle loin *noun* meat from the middle section of the loin

mid-upper-arm-circumference *noun* a quick way of diagnosing potential malnutrition in children. Abbreviation **MUAC**

milchig *adjective* under Jewish dietary laws, relating to, containing, or derived from dairy products and so not to be used with meat products. Compare **fleishig, pareve**

mild-cure *adjective* cured using a solution of salt, saltpetre, flavourings and sometimes polyphosphates, which is either injected into the food or in which the food is immersed

mildew *noun* a fungus that grows on food exposed to a warm humid atmosphere, usually in the form of green furry blotches

milk *noun* a white liquid produced by female mammals for feeding their young, especially the milk produced by cows ■ *verb* to take the milk from an animal

milk alternative *noun* a product such as soya milk, substituted for cow's milk to avoid the allergies and lactose intolerance the latter may trigger

milk chocolate *noun* a sweet pale brown chocolate made with milk

milk fat content *noun* the proportion of fat in cow's milk

milk foam *noun* milk that has been whipped until it is stiff, containing lots of small air bubbles

milk of magnesia *noun* magnesium hydroxide used as a laxative

milk pan *noun* a small, usually non-stick pan for warming milk

milk products *plural noun* milk and other foodstuffs produced from it, e.g. liquid milk, butter, cheese, cream, ice cream, condensed milk and milk powder

milkshake *noun* a drink made from milk mixed with flavouring and sometimes ice cream

milk solids *noun* the portion of milk that is not water, made of fat, protein and minerals

milkstone *noun* the residue of calcium and protein left by milk when it is heated and evaporated

milk substitute *noun* same as **creamer**

milk thistle *noun* a herb that is reputed to cleanse the liver, taken in supplement form

mill *noun* **1.** a factory where a substance is crushed to make a powder, especially one for making flour from the dried grains of cereals **2.** a small device for grinding something such as coffee, pepper, or salt into granules ■ *verb* to grind cereal grains in a mill to make flour

millefeuille *noun* a dessert or pastry consisting of several layers of puff pastry with a filling of cream and jam, topped with icing sugar or icing

millerator *noun* a machine that cleans wheat and sorts it by particle size

millet *noun* a common cereal crop grown in many of the hot, dry regions of Africa and Asia, where it is a staple food

milligram¹ *noun* a unit of measurement of weight equal to one thousandth of a gram. Abbreviation **mg**

milligram² *noun* a unit of measurement of weight equal to one thousandth of a gram. Abbreviation **mg**

Minamata disease *noun* a form of mercury poisoning from eating polluted fish, first identified in Japan

mince *noun* meat, usually beef, that has been shredded into very small pieces ■ *verb* to shred meat into very small pieces

minced meat *noun* meat that has been shredded by being passed through a mincer, used for burgers, pies and meat sauces

mincemeat *noun* a mixture of dried fruit, suet, nuts and spices, used for making pies at Christmas time

mince pie *noun* a small round pastry tart with a pastry top, filled with mincemeat, baked and sprinkled with icing sugar

mincer, mincing machine *noun* a machine for shredding meat into very small pieces

mineral *noun* an inorganic substance with a characteristic chemical composition that occurs naturally and is an essential part of the human diet

mineral hydrocarbon *noun* any highly purified oil with a high boiling point, usually colourless and transparent, used as a release agent to prevent dried vine fruits from sticking together. ◊ **E905**

mineralisation *noun* ♦ bone mineralisation

mineral salt *noun* a crystalline compound formed from the neutralisation of an acid solution containing a mineral

mineral water *noun* water that comes naturally from the ground and is sold in bottles

miner's cramp *noun* a cramping of the muscles due to salt loss through excess sweating

minestrone *noun* a soup of Italian origin made of vegetables, beans, pasta and herbs and served with grated parmesan cheese

minimum infective dose *noun* the number of bacteria that need to be present in a foodstuff in order for it to be unsafe for consumption. Abbreviation **MID**

mint *noun* any of various varieties of common herb used in cooking as a flavouring, and to flavour commercially made sweets (NOTE: The varieties belong to the genus *Mentha*.)

minute steak *noun* a very lean piece of beef that has been passed through spiked rollers to break down its fibres and make for fast grilling or frying

miscible *adjective* able to be completely mixed together (NOTE: This term is usually applied to liquids.)

mise en place *noun* **1.** the act of setting out chairs, tables and linen in a restaurant, ready for customers (NOTE: From the French phrase meaning 'putting in place'.) **2.** the act of preparing ovens, pans and other utensils in a kitchen, ready to start cooking for the day **3.** the act of preparing the basic ingredients, ready for cooking

miso *noun* Japanese fermented soya bean paste used mainly in vegetarian cooking

misuse *noun* of an addictive substance

mitochondrion *noun* a tiny rod-shaped part of a cell's cytoplasm responsible for cell respiration (NOTE: The plural is **mitochondria**.)

mix *noun* any commercially produced mixture of dry ingredients to which water, milk, eggs or a combination of these is added to produce a food ■ *verb* to combine two or more ingredients so that they become mingled and cannot be separated

mixed grill *noun* a mixture of small portions of various grilled meats, often served with grilled mushrooms and tomatoes, as a main meal or breakfast dish

mixed herbs *plural noun* a mixture of dried herbs used for flavouring, often prepared for a particular type of dish

mixer *noun* **1.** a non-alcoholic drink, e.g. tonic water or ginger ale, used in a cocktail along with alcohol **2.** ◆ **electric mixer**

mixing *noun* the act of thoroughly combining two or more ingredients

mixing bowl *noun* a large bowl, usually made of glass, for mixing ingredients

mixiria *noun* a way of preserving meat by roasting it and sealing it in a jar with a layer of fat

MJ *abbreviation* megajoule

MLC *abbreviation* Meat and Livestock Commission

mmol *abbreviation* millimole

mobile shop *noun* a van fitted out like a small shop that travels round selling meat, fish, groceries or vegetables

modern biotechnology *noun* the genetic modification of living organisms

modern food materials *plural noun* food substances created by genetic modification or other recent scientific advances, e.g. probiotic-enriched foods

modified atmosphere packaging *noun* packaging inside which there is a mixture of gases that prevents the perishable contents from decaying. Abbreviation **MAP**

modified enzyme *noun* the chemical treatment of an enzyme to change its function or level of activity

modified starch *noun* potato or wheat starch that has had chemicals added to alter its function for increased efficiency

moist *adjective* slightly wet or damp

moisten *verb* to add a little liquid to a dry mixture of foods so as to soften or flavour it

moisture *noun* water or other liquid

molar *adjective* **1.** used for describing the large back teeth **2.** relating to the mole, the SI unit of amount of a substance ■ *noun* one of the large back teeth, used for grinding food

molasses *noun* a thick dark-brown syrup produced when sugar is refined (NOTE: The British English is **treacle**.)

mole *noun* a unit of measurement of molecular weight, meaning a quantity of particles numbering 6.02×10 to the power of 23

molecular structure *noun* the way in which a molecule is composed of two or more atoms joined by shared electrons

molecule *noun* the smallest particle into which a substance can be divided without changing its chemical and physical properties

Moller-Barlow disease *noun* same as **Barlow's disease**

mollusc *noun* an animal with a shell, e.g. an oyster or a snail

molybdenum *noun* a metallic trace element (NOTE: The chemical symbol is **Mo**.)

monkfish *noun* **1.** a large wide-bodied fish with a very wide mouth, found in the Atlantic waters of Europe, Africa and North America (NOTE: Its scientific name is *Lophius piscatorius*.) **2.** a name sometimes given to the angel fish, a type of shark

mono- *prefix* containing a single atom, radical or group

monoamine oxidase *noun* an enzyme that breaks down the catecholamines to their inactive forms. Abbreviation **MAO**

monoamine oxidase inhibitor *noun* any of various drugs that inhibit monoamine oxidase and are used for treating depression, e.g. phenelzine. Abbreviation **MAOI**. Also called **MAO inhibitor**

monoglyceride *noun* a compound derived from glycerol in which one hydroxyl group has been esterified

monophagia *noun* the desire to eat only one type of food

monopotassium glutamate *noun* a food additive used as flavour enhancer. Abbreviation **MPG**. Also called **E622**

monosaccharide *noun* a simple sugar of the type that includes glucose, fructose and galactose

monosodium glutamate *noun* a substance added to processed food to enhance the flavour, but causing a reaction in hypersensitive people. Abbreviation **MSG**. Also called **E621**

monosodium tartrate *noun* same as **E334**

monoterpene *noun* a class of hydrocarbon components that are a constituent of essential oils

monounsaturated fat *noun* a fat or oil containing a single double bond in the chain of carbon atoms that make up the fatty acid part (NOTE: Olive oil is the commonest example.)

monté *adjective* used for describing a sauce to which butter has been added before serving to enrich, thicken and gloss it

Montevideo *noun* a strain of salmonella

Montezuma's revenge *noun* diarrhoea associated with travel in Mexico or eating Mexican food (*informal*)

Montignac diet *noun* a dietary plan that advises that carbohydrates and proteins or fats should not be eaten at the same time

mood swing *noun* a sudden and extreme change in someone's mood, possibly as a result of their diet

moral *adjective* good or right, when judged by the standards of the average person or society at large

moratorium *noun* a period when everyone agrees to stop a specific activity

morbidity *noun* the condition of being diseased or sick

morbid obesity *noun* severe obesity, as much as twice the ideal body weight of a person

morel *noun* an edible mushroom with a brown pitted spongy cap

morello cherry *noun* the best cooking variety of cherry, almost black in colour and slightly tart when ripe

Mornay *adjective* used for describing a dish of food cooked with a white sauce containing cheese

mother *noun* the name often given to a undefined mass of microorganisms, e.g. yeast or bacteria, used for starting the process of fermentation

mould *noun* **1.** a fungus, especially one that produces a fine powdery layer on the surface of an organism **2.** a container that is used to give a shape to a liquid substance poured into it to set or harden ■ *verb* to shape something, often using a mould

mould bran *noun* an amylase from mould grown on wheat bran

mould-ripened *adjective* used for describing cheese that is allowed to mature with blue or white mould that develops its flavour and texture

moule *noun* same as **mussel**

moussaka *noun* a Greek dish made of aubergines and minced meat in layers

mousse *noun* a light food made of whipped egg whites and cream with a gelatine base, flavoured with fruit, vegetables, fish or shellfish and served as a cold dessert or as a starter

mousseline *noun* a type of light hollandaise sauce made with whipped cream and egg whites

mouth *noun* an opening at the head of the alimentary canal, through which food and drink are taken in, and through which a person speaks and can breathe

mouth-feel *noun* the texture of a foodstuff in the mouth

mozzarella *noun* a rubbery white unsalted Italian cheese used in salads, cooking, and especially on pizza

MRA *abbreviation* Microbiological Risk Assessment

MRE *abbreviation* Meal Ready-to-Eat

MRL *abbreviation* maximum residue level

MRM *abbreviation* mechanically-recovered meat

MRP *abbreviation* meal replacement product

MSA *abbreviation* Margarine and Spreads Association

MSG *abbreviation* monosodium glutamate

MUAC *abbreviation* mid-upper-arm-circumference

mucin *noun* a glycoprotein that is a constituent of mucus

mucosa *noun* same as **mucous membrane**

mucosal ulceration *noun* lesions on the mucus membrane of the gastrointestinal tract, causing pain and bleeding present in blood and stools

mucous colitis *noun* same as **irritable bowel syndrome**

mucous membrane *noun* a wet membrane that lines internal passages in the body, e.g. the nose, mouth, stomach and throat, and secretes mucus. Also called **mucosa**

mucus *noun* a slippery liquid secreted by mucous membranes inside the body in order to protect them

muesli *noun* a breakfast food of grains and dried fruit, eaten with milk

muffin *noun* **1.** a small round flat bun eaten warm with butter **2.** a small sweet cake that often contains fruit

mulled wine *noun* sweetened red wine served warm, traditionally flavoured with cinnamon, dried ginger, cloves and orange zest

mulligatawny *noun* a spicy soup made with curry

multigrain *adjective* used for describing bread that is made from several different types of grain

multinational *noun* a company that has branches or subsidiary companies in several countries

multivitamin *noun* a preparation containing several vitamins and sometimes minerals, used as a dietary supplement ■ *adjective* used for describing a preparation containing several vitamins, and sometimes minerals

mung bean *noun* a small green or yellow bean that is dried and sometimes split, also germinated to produce bean sprouts

muscarine *noun* a poison found in fungi

muscle fibre *noun* a component fibre of muscles (NOTE: There are two types of fibre, one forming striated muscles and one forming smooth muscles.)

muscle function *noun* the smooth expansion or contraction of muscles in the body to create movement

muscle tissue *noun* the specialised type of tissue which forms the muscles and which can contract and expand

muscovado sugar *noun* a soft and sticky partially refined cane sugar with fine crystals, available in both light and dark varieties

mushroom *noun* a small white fungus that grows wild in fields but is usually grown commercially in mushroom farms

muslin *noun* woven cotton with an open texture, used for straining liquids or for wrapping dried foods from which the flavour is to be extracted in a simmering liquid

mussel *noun* a small shellfish with a blue shell

mustard *noun* a very spicy yellow condiment, eaten with meat

mustard and cress *noun* seedlings of the mustard and cress plants sold for cutting to use as a garnish

mustard seeds *plural noun* small seeds used extensively in Indian cooking, usually fried to bring out their pungent flavour

mutagen *noun* an agent that makes DNA more liable to abnormal mutation

mutate *verb* to undergo a genetic change

mutton *noun* meat from a fully-grown sheep (NOTE: The word is not much used, as most meat from sheep is called **lamb** even when it comes from an older animal.)

myalgic encephalopathy *noun* a complex disorder with symptoms of profound fatigue, claimed to be alleviated by some food supplements. Abbreviation **ME**

mycoprotein *noun* a food, especially a meat substitute, made by fermenting a fungus and heating, draining and texturing the resultant product

mycotoxin *noun* a toxic substance produced by a fungus growing on crops in the field or in storage

myenteric plexus *noun* the bundles of nerves and neuron cells that detect food in the digestive tract and instruct the intestinal muscles to pass it along

myiasis *noun* an infestation by the larvae of flies

myoglobulin *noun* a set of proteins found in muscle tissue

myosin *noun* a protein in muscles that helps them contract

mystery shopper *noun* a person employed by a market-research company to visit shops anonymously to test the quality of service

myxoedema *noun* a slowing of the metabolic rate caused by iodine deficiency

N

naan *noun* a type of flat bread made with wheat flour, served with South Asian food

NAASO *abbreviation* North American Association for the Study of Obesity

NACC *abbreviation* National Association for Colitis and Crohns Disease

nacho *noun* a tortilla chip, usually eaten covered with melted cheese, salsa, or sliced pickled jalapeño peppers

NACNE *abbreviation* National Advisory Committee on Nutrition Education

NAD *noun* a substance in cells that helps glycolysis. Full form **nicotinamide adenine dinucleotide**

NADP *noun* a substance in cells that helps anabolic reactions. Full form **nicotinamide adenine dinucleotide phosphate**

nam pla *noun* a thin sauce of fermented fish with has a strong flavour and smell and a salty taste, widely used in Southeast Asian cookery

nap *verb* to cover a food item, usually a piece of meat or fish on a plate or dish, with sauce

naprapathy *noun* a system of therapy that combines diet with manipulation of joints, ligaments, and muscles to assist the body's natural regenerative ability

narcotic *noun* a pain-relieving drug that makes someone sleep or become unconscious ■ *adjective* causing sleep or unconsciousness

nasogastric tube *noun* a plastic feeding that passes through the nose to the stomach

nasolabial seborrhoea *noun* redness and cracking of the skin in the nasolabial cavity, caused by a vitamin B deficiency

nasturtium *noun* any of various annual and perennial flowering plants with red, orange or yellow flowers that are sometimes used in salads

National Advisory Committee on Nutrition Education *noun* an advisory group, set up in the early 1980s, that published nutritional guidelines advising a cut in saturated fat and sugar in processed foods. Abbreviation **NACNE**

National Association for Colitis and Crohns Disease *noun* an information and support service for sufferers of inflammatory bowel disease. Abbreviation **NACC**

National Diet and Nutrition Survey *noun* a nationwide survey carried out by the Food Standards Agency into the eating habits of British people. Abbreviation **NDNS**

National Institute for Health and Clinical Excellence *noun* a special health authority under the NHS that offers clinical guidance and recommendations for health services across the UK. Abbreviation **NICE**

natural additive *noun* a food additive that is a natural extract of a raw material, rather than a synthesized chemical

natural foods diet *noun* same as **raw food diet**

natural toxin *noun* a toxic substance produced naturally by a plant or animal

natural yoghurt *noun* yoghurt which contains no additives such as sugar or fruit

nature identical additive *noun* a synthesised additive that is chemically identical to one naturally occurring in food

naturopath *noun* a person who practices naturopathy

naturopathy *noun* a method of treatment of diseases and disorders that does not use medical or surgical means but natural forces such as light, heat, massage, eating natural foods and using herbal remedies

nausea *noun* a feeling that you want to vomit

nauseant *noun* a substance that induces vomiting

nauseate *verb* to have the unsettling feeling in the stomach that accompanies the urge to vomit, or to make someone have this feeling

nausifugic *noun* used for describing medicine that relieves nausea

navarin *noun* a lamb or mutton stew with onions and potatoes

navel orange *noun* a sweet seedless orange with a small bump at the top enclosing a smaller secondary fruit

N balance *abbreviation* nitrogen balance

NCHS standards *noun* tables of height and weight by age used for assessing the physical development of children, created by the National Center for Health Statistics

NDNS *abbreviation* National Diet and Nutrition Survey

NDpE *abbreviation* net dietary protein energy ratio

neat *adjective* used for describing an alcoholic spirit served undiluted or unmixed

neck *noun* **1.** a part of the body connecting the head to the shoulders **2.** this part of an animal eaten as food

neck end *noun* a fatty cut of meat from the upper part of the neck

nectar *noun* **1.** a sweet sugary liquid produced by flowers that attracts birds or insects that in turn pollinate the flowers **2.** a thick drink made from puréed fruit

nectarine *noun* a variety of peach with a smooth shiny skin and white to red firm flesh (NOTE: It is the fruit of the deciduous tree *Prunus persica*, variety *nectarina*, grown worldwide.)

needle *noun* a thin steel rod, sharpened at one end and pierced with a flattened hole at the other, used for trussing or larding a bird or piece of meat ■ *verb* to pierce food in order to make it more absorbent, to introduce microorganisms, e.g. in making blue cheeses, or to inject fluids, as in quick curing

NEFA *abbreviation* non-esterified fatty acids

negative calorie diet *noun* a dietary plan in which negative calorie foods should be eaten as often as possible

negative calorie food *noun* a food that is claimed to provide fewer calories than are used to digest it, e.g. celery

NEL *noun* the amount of a food additive that has no discernible negative effect on the consumer. Full form **No Effect Level**

neomycin *noun* an antibiotic that is not absorbed from the digestive tract, used for treating intestinal infections

nephalism *noun* the practice of not drinking alcohol

nephrolithiasis *noun* the presence of calculi in the kidneys

N equilibrium *abbreviation* nitrogen equilibrium

nerve *noun* **1.** a bundle of fibres that can transmit electrochemical impulses and that forms part of the network that connects the brain and spinal cord to the body's organs **2.** the sensitive tissue in the root of a tooth

nerve cell *noun* same as **neuron**

nerve function *noun* the ability of a nerve to effectively transmit signals to the brain

nerve tissue *noun* tissue that forms nerves and is able to transmit nerve impulses

net dietary protein energy ratio *noun* the protein content of a food, expressed as the amount of protein contained and the quality of it. Abbreviation **NDpE**

net protein retention *noun* a measure of protein quality, comparing its protein efficiency ratio with the weight loss of a test group fed no protein. Abbreviation **NPR**

net protein utilisation *noun* a measure of protein quality, taking into account both its biological value and its digestibility. Abbreviation **NPU**

nettle tea *noun* an infusion of nettle leaves, traditionally used for cleansing and detoxifying the body

neural tube defect *noun* a congenital disorder of the spine, the risk of which is lessened if the mother takes folic acid supplements before conception

neurological function *noun* the ability of neurones to effectively send, receive and process signals

neuron, neurone *noun* a cell in the nervous system which transmits nerve impulses. Also called **nerve cell**

neuropeptide Y *noun* a neurotransmitter that has a role in controlling feeding behaviour and appetite

neurotoxicity *noun* the extent to which a substance damages, destroys or impairs the functioning of nerve tissue

neurotoxin *noun* a substance that damages, destroys or impairs the functioning of nerve tissue

neurotransmitter *noun* a chemical substance which transmits nerve impulses from one neuron to another

neurotrophic *adjective* relating to the nutrition and maintenance of tissue of the nervous system

neutral *adjective* neither acid nor alkali

neutral fat *noun* fat with no excess fatty acid

newborn *adjective* born recently ■ *noun* a recently born baby

new potatoes *plural noun* small potatoes picked at the beginning of the season

new product development *noun* the process of developing completely new products or improving existing ones. Abbreviation **NPD**

NFE *abbreviation* nitrogen-free extract

niacin *noun* a vitamin of the vitamin B complex found in milk, meat, liver, kidney, yeast, beans, peas and bread, lack of which can cause mental disorders and pellagra. Also called **nicotinic acid**

niacinamide *noun* ♦ vitamin B3

nibbed *adjective* used for describing nuts that are cut into small cubes about 2mm square

NICE *abbreviation* National Institute for Health and Clinical Excellence

nicotinamide adenine dinucleotide *noun* full form of **NAD**

nicotinamide adenine dinucleotide phosphate *noun* full form of **NADP**

nicotinic acid *noun* same as **niacin**

nigella sativa *noun* the seeds of a Southeast Asian plant, used as a spice

night blindness *noun* an inability to see in the dark, caused by vitamin A deficiency

NII *abbreviation* Nutritionists in Industry

nisin *noun* ♦ E234

nitrate *noun* a chemical compound containing the nitrate ion, e.g. sodium nitrate

nitric oxide *noun* a sports supplement that promotes vasodilation, causing an increased blood flow to the muscles. Abbreviation **NO**

nitrites *plural noun* salts of nitrous acid used for giving cured meat its pink colour

nitrofuran *noun* a drug that inhibits the growth of bacteria (NOTE: It has been banned from use in food-producing animals in many countries.)

nitrogen *noun* a gas that is the main component of air and is an essential part of protein (NOTE: The chemical symbol is **N**.)

nitrogenase *noun* an enzyme found in nitrogen-fixing bacteria that catalyses the conversion of nitrogen to ammonia (NOTE: It is a key component of the nitrogen cycle, providing nitrogen compounds for plants.)

nitrogen balance, nitrogen equilibrium *noun* the ratio between the amount of nitrogen ingested and the amount excreted. Abbreviation **N balance, N equilibrium**

nitrogen cycle *noun* the set of processes by which nitrogen is converted from a gas in the atmosphere to nitrogen-containing substances in soil and living organisms, then converted back to a gas

nitrogen fixation *noun* the process by which nitrogen in the air is converted by bacteria in some plant roots into nitrogen compounds

nitrogen-fixing bacteria *plural noun* bacteria such as *Rhizobium* in the soil which convert nitrogen in the air into nitrogen compounds by means of the process of nitrogen fixation in plants

nitrogen-free extract *noun* the portion of a foodstuff when analysed that comprises only sugars and starches. Abbreviation **NFE**

nitrosamine *noun* an organic carcinogenic compound found in various foods

nitrous acid *noun* a weak acid that can exist only in solution or as salts

nitrous oxide *noun* a gas used as a propellant in aerosols

NMES *abbreviation* non-milk extrinsic sugars

NO *abbreviation* nitric oxide

noble rot *noun* a fungus that affects grapes and concentrates the juice, allowing sweet wine to be more easily made

nocturia *noun* excessive production of urine at nighttime

No Effect Level *noun* full form of **NEL**

noisette *noun* a piece of boned and rolled meat, especially the neck or loin of lamb

noma *noun* an ulceration of the mouth, commonly found in severely malnourished children

non-alcoholic *adjective* containing no alcohol, or an extremely low amount of alcohol

non-biological *adjective* **1.** containing no enzymes **2.** not relating to biology

non-dairy *adjective* used for describing ingredients or foods that contain no dairy products

non-dairy creamer *noun* same as **creamer**

non-enzymic browning *noun* same as **Maillard reaction**

non-essential *adjective* manufactured by the body and therefore not essential in the diet

non-essential amino acids *plural noun* amino acids that can be synthesised in the body and so do not need to be obtained in the diet. ◊ **essential amino acids**

non-esterified fatty acids *noun* same as **free fatty acids**

non-fat *adjective* without fat solids, or with the fat content removed

non-fattening *adjective* not likely to cause a gain in weight

non-food *adjective* used for describing items sold in a supermarket that are not for eating or drinking

non-haem iron *noun* dietary iron found in plants. Compare **haem iron**

non-IgE mediated *adjective* used for describing an allergic reaction that is not caused by immunoglobulin E

non-insulin-dependent diabetes *noun* diabetes mellitus that does not require insulin for its treatment

non-milk extrinsic sugars *plural noun* sugars that are added to foods and drinks and are potentially causes of tooth decay

non-nutrient *adjective* used for describing a foodstuff that contains no nutrients

non-nutritive sweetener *noun* same as **low-calorie sweetener**

non-organic *adjective* used for describing crops that are not produced according to guidelines restricting the use of fertilisers and other practices, and for describing animals fed on such crops

non-perishable *adjective* used for describing food products that remain edible, without spoiling, for long periods without special storage ■ *noun* a non-perishable item of food

non-starch polysaccharides *noun* same as **dietary fibre**

non-stick *adjective* covered with a substance that prevents food from sticking when cooking

non-thermal technologies *plural noun* methods of sterilising food that do not involve heat treatment

non-wheat *adjective* not containing wheat

noodles *plural noun* long thin strips of pasta

nootropic *noun* a food supplement that is reputed to boost cognitive ability

noradrenaline *noun* a hormone secreted by the medulla of the adrenal glands that acts as a vasoconstrictor and is used for maintaining blood pressure in shock, haemorrhage or hypotension

norbixin *noun* a golden-yellow food colouring obtained from the seeds of achiote

North American Association for the Study of Obesity *noun* an organisation that promotes research into obesity. Abbreviation **NAASO**

nosocomial *adjective* referring to hospitals (*technical*)

nougat *noun* a chewy sweet made with egg whites, honey, and usually chopped nuts or dried fruit

nourish *verb* to give food or nutrients to a person

nourishing *adjective* providing the substances that people need to grow and be healthy

nourishment *noun* food or the valuable substances in food that help people to grow and be healthy

nouvelle cuisine *noun* a type of French cooking that aims at less heavy traditional dishes and attractive presentation and is often served in very small portions

novel food materials *plural noun* same as **modern food materials**

nozzle *noun* an open-ended hollow cone of varying size, used in the end of a piping bag to give a decorative effect

NPD *abbreviation* new product development

NPR *abbreviation* net protein retention

NPU *abbreviation* net protein utilisation

NSP *abbreviation* non-starch polysaccharides

nuclease *noun* an enzyme that breaks down nucleic acids

nucleoside *noun* a purine or pyrimidine base linked to a sugar, especially ribose or deoxyribose

nucleotidase *noun* any of a group of enzymes that produce nucleosides by splitting phosphoric acid from nucleotides

nucleotide *noun* a nucleoside linked to a phosphate group (NOTE: Nucleosides join together to form the polymers RNA and DNA.)

nucleus *noun* 1. the central body in a cell that contains DNA and RNA and controls the function and characteristics of the cell 2. a group of nerve cells in the brain or spinal cord (NOTE: The plural is **nuclei**.)

NuGO *abbreviation* European Nutrigenomics Organisation

nut *noun* a fruit with an edible centre inside a hard shell

nut cracker *noun* an implement used for cracking the hard outer shell of nuts using a lever or screw-thread action

nut cutlet *noun* a vegetarian cake or burger made from chopped nuts and other vegetable ingredients mixed together and sometimes formed into the shape of a meat chop or cutlet

nutmeg *noun* the seed of a tropical tree, grated and used as a spice

nutraceutical *noun* same as **functional food**

nutrient *noun* a substance in food that is necessary to provide energy or to help the body grow, e.g. a protein, a fat or a vitamin

nutrient-dense *adjective* used for describing food that is rich in vitamins and minerals and comparatively low in calories

nutrient enemata *noun* feeding using a glucose solution administered into the intestine through the anus

nutrient profile *noun* a description of the nutritional composition of a particular food

nutrient profiling *noun* a scientific method of categorising foods according to their nutritional content

nutrification *noun* the enriching of foods with added nutrients so as to make a significant difference to the diet

nutrigenomics *noun* the study of the way in which genetic and environmental influences act together on a human or an animal, and how this information can be used to boost productivity and health

nutrition *noun* **1.** the way in which food affects health **2.** the study of food

nutritional disorder *noun* any disorder or disease caused by poor nutrition

nutritional guidelines *plural noun* public advice about healthy eating given by an authority

nutritional information *noun* additional information about the nutritional value of a food product, often used on food labelling in the UK

nutritional labelling *noun* nutritional information on the label of foods and drinks, including the energy value and the amounts of protein, carbohydrate and fat contained

nutritional melagia *noun* same as **burning foot syndrome**

nutritional needs *plural noun* the amounts of the various components of food required to be eaten for health and well being. ◊ **recommended daily intake**

nutritional programme *noun* a dietary plan that is designed to achieve a particular aim, e.g. muscle building, weight loss or recovery from illness

nutritional status *noun* the balance of nutritional needs against intake and absorption

nutritional supplement *noun* ♦ **supplement**

nutritional therapist *noun* a person who works with patients to devise a dietary plan for optimum health or to identify any intolerances

nutritional therapy *noun* the alleviation of symptoms by dietary changes, sometimes using vitamin and mineral pills

nutritional value *noun* the nutrient content of a food

nutrition claim *noun* wording or a logo on food packaging that makes a claim about the nutritional content of the food inside

nutrition information *noun* same as **nutritional information**

nutrition insecurity *noun* the state of having a restricted or deficient diet that makes it difficult to get all essential nutrients

nutritionist *noun* a person who specialises in the study of nutrition and advises on diets

Nutritionists in Industry *noun* a membership organisation for nutritionists that provides a forum for the dissemination of industry information. Abbreviation **NII**

nutrition policy *noun* a government plan to inform the public about healthy eating and access to healthy foods

Nutrition Research Review *noun* the journal of the Nutrition Society

nutrition security *noun* the state of having a varied diet that will provide all essential nutrients

Nutrition Society *noun* a professional body for the nutrition industry that also runs courses and accredits courses run elsewhere

nutritious *adjective* providing a fairly high level of nourishment

nutritive *noun* a food which is necessary for growth ■ *adjective* relating to nourishment

nutritive value *noun* the degree to which a food is valuable in promoting health

nut roast *noun* a vegetarian loaf made from chopped or ground-up nuts with onions, herbs, and seasonings, bound with breadcrumbs and baked

nyctalopia *noun* same as **night blindness**

O

OAS *abbreviation* oral allergy syndrome

oatcake *noun* a dry biscuit made of oatmeal, often served with cheese

oatmeal *noun* coarse flour made from oats

oats *plural noun* a cereal food grown in northern European countries

obese *adjective* so overweight as to be at risk of several serious illnesses, including diabetes and heart disease

obesity *noun* the condition of being seriously overweight

obesity rates *plural noun* the proportion of a country's population who are more than 20% overweight

obesogenic *adjective* promoting or causing obesity

obstipation *noun* severe constipation, often caused by a blockage in the intestines

obstruent *adjective* obstructing or closing a passage in the body such as the intestinal tract ■ *noun* something that obstructs or closes a passage in the body

occupational activity levels *plural noun* the extent to which a person is active in their job, affecting their dietary energy requirements

ochratoxin *noun* a type of mycotoxin that is produced by fungus on meat products

ochratoxin A *noun* a mycotoxin that affects cereals and can cause severe kidney damage if ingested

octadecyl ammonium acetate *noun* an anticaking additive used in bread making

octopus *noun* a sea animal with a big head, a soft oval body and eight arms containing rows of suckers

octyl gallate *noun* same as **E311**

odour *noun* the property of a substance that stimulates the sense of smell. ◊ **flavour** (NOTE: The six main odour qualities are fruity, flowery, resinous, spicy, foul and burnt.)

odynophagy *noun* pain while eating or swallowing

oedema *noun* the swelling of part of the body caused by accumulation of fluid in the intercellular tissue spaces

oesophagalgia *noun* pain in the oesophagus

oesophageal *adjective* relating to the oesophagus

oesophageal motility disorder *noun* a condition in which peristalsis is abnormal due to spasms in the oesophagus

oesophagitis *noun* erosion of the lining of the oesophagus caused by acid reflux

oesophagomalacia *noun* a softening of the walls of the oesophagus

oesophagostomy *noun* a surgical operation to create an opening in the oesophagus for feeding purposes

oesophagus *noun* the tube in the body down which food passes from the pharynx to the stomach (NOTE: The plural is **oesophagi**.)

oestrogen *noun* any steroid hormone that stimulates the development of secondary sexual characteristics in females at puberty

oestrogen inhibitor *noun* a substance or drug that reduces or blocks the action of oestrogen, used as a sports supplement and in the treatment of breast cancer

offal *noun* the inside parts of an animal when used as food, e.g. the liver, kidneys and intestines (NOTE: There is no plural form. The US term is **variety meats**.)

off-the-shelf *adjective, adverb* ready-made according to a regular design

ohmic heating *noun* heating by passing an electric current through the food itself

oil *noun* a thick smooth-running liquid of various kinds used in cooking ■ *verb* to put oil on food

oil pastry *noun* shortcrust pastry made with oil instead of hard fat, rolled out between sheets of non-stick paper because of its fragility

oilseed *noun* a seed that is rich in oil, especially one grown as a crop for oil extraction, e.g. linseed, groundnut or cottonseed

oily *adjective* like oil, containing oil or covered with oil

oily fish *noun* any fish with flesh that contains more than 6% of fat by weight

OKG *abbreviation* ornithine alpha-ketoglutarate

okra *noun* a vegetable with a green pod, widely used in Mediterranean and Asian cooking. Also called **gumbo**, **lady's fingers**

oleic acid *noun* a fatty acid that is present in most oils

oleo oil *noun* a yellow fatty substance extracted from beef fat, used in the manufacture of margarine and soap

oleoresin *noun* a mixture of a resin and an essential oil, either obtained naturally from plants or produced synthetically

olestra *noun* an ester of fatty acids and sugar that behaves like oil or fat but is not absorbed by the human body, making is usefully non-fattening but nevertheless controversial in the food industry because it can sequester several vitamins and other nutrients

olfaction *noun* in sensory analysis, the sense of smell

oligoallergenic diet *noun* a restricted diet used for diagnosing the effects that particular foods have on a person

oligodipsia *noun* a reduced sense of thirst

oligopeptide *noun* a peptide consisting of fewer than ten amino acids

oligophagous *adjective* feeding on a restricted range of foodstuffs, usually a small number of different plants

oligosaccharide *noun* a carbohydrate made up of a relatively small number of linked monosaccharides

oligotrophic *adjective* used for describing foods that do not contain sufficient nutrients

olive *noun* a small black or green fruit from a Mediterranean tree, crushed to produce oil and also eaten as food

olive oil *noun* oil made from olives

omega-3 *noun* a polyunsaturated fatty acid found in fish oils, seeds and whole grains, used in the prevention of such conditions as high cholesterol, heart disease and arthritis

omega-6 oil *noun* a polyunsaturated oil deficiency of which can cause skin problems and hormonal imbalances

omelette *noun* a dish made of beaten eggs, cooked in a frying pan and folded over before serving, with any of various fillings added

omelette pan *noun* a heavy-based frying pan with rounded sloping sides, usually kept exclusively for omelettes and never washed after use but cleaned with absorbent paper

omnivore *noun* an animal that eats both plant and animal foods. ◊ **carnivore**, **herbivore** (NOTE: Humans and pigs are examples of omnivores.)

omnivorous *adjective* used for describing an animal that eats both plant and animal foods

omophagia *noun* the practice of eating uncooked or unprocessed food

oncology *noun* the scientific study of new growths, especially cancers

onion *noun* any of several varieties of strong-smelling vegetable with a round white bulb (NOTE: They belong to the genus *Allium*.)

on-pack information *noun* nutritional information that is clearly printed on food packaging

on-the-go *adjective* a term used for describing convenience food that does not need heating or other preparation and can be eaten straight from the packaging

open-cap mushroom *noun* any large flat variety of mushroom

open sandwich *noun* one slice of bread with meat, cheese or some other filling on it

open-view kitchen *noun* a kitchen that restaurant customers can see into from where they sit and can therefore watch the chefs at work

opisthorchiasis *noun* a severe infection of the biliary tract caused by a fluke found in raw fish

OPP *abbreviation* orthophenylphenol

opsomania *noun* a craving for a particular type of food

opsonic index *noun* a number that gives the strength of a person's serum reaction to bacteria

opsonin *noun* a protein that promotes the destruction of antigens by white blood cells

ORAC *abbreviation* Oxygen Radical Absorbance Capacity

oral allergy syndrome *noun* an allergic reaction to certain fresh fruits and vegetables, caused by the body mistaking the proteins in these for the proteins in pollen. Abbreviation **OAS**

oral rehydration salts *plural noun* same as **rehydration salts**

orange *noun* a sweet citrus fruit with a reddish-yellow skin

orange squash *noun* a sweet non-alcoholic drink made from oranges or with the flavour of oranges, sold in concentrated form to be diluted with water

orange yellow s *noun* ♦ **E110**

oregano *noun* a herb that is widely used in Mediterranean cooking

orexigenic *adjective* stimulating the appetite

oreximania *noun* an unusually large appetite

organic *adjective* used for describing crops that are cultivated naturally, without any chemical fertilisers or pesticides, and for describing meat from animals fed on such crops

organic food *noun* food grown or reared without synthetic or chemically produced fertilisers, pesticides and herbicides on land that itself has been organic for two years

organolepsis *noun* the study of the sensory properties of food, e.g. its appearance, smell and mouth feel

organosulphur compound *noun* a substance that contains both carbon and sulphur

organotrophic *adjective* nourishing bodily organs

Ornish diet *noun* a dietary plan for slimming originally developed to reverse heart disease, in which all cholesterol and saturated fat is prohibited

ornithine *noun* an amino acid produced by the liver

ornithine alpha-ketoglutarate *noun* a compound of ornithine and glutamine used as a sports supplement to build muscle. Abbreviation **OKG**

orotic acid *noun* a chemical produced by the body when there is a block in the flow of urea, used as a sports supplement

orthophenylphenol *noun* an antimicrobial agent used as disinfectant and to preserve fresh fruit and vegetables. Abbreviation **OPP**

orthophosphoric acid *noun* same as **phosphoric acid**

orthorexia *noun* an obsession with eating only the right things, which may lead to extreme weight loss as so many foods are rejected

osmophile *noun* bacteria that thrive under high osmotic pressure

osmosis *noun* the movement of a solvent from one part of the body through a semipermeable membrane to another part where there is a higher concentration of molecules

osmotic dehydration *noun* the dehydration of fruit using osmosis with a sugar solution

osmotic pressure *noun* the pressure required to stop the flow of a solvent through a membrane

osteoarthritis *noun* a degenerative disease of middle-aged and elderly people characterised by inflamed joints which become stiff and painful

osteocalcin *noun* a protein that helps to bind the calcium in bone

osteomalacia *noun* a softening and bending of the bones resulting from an inability to absorb calcium caused by a vitamin D deficiency

osteoporosis *noun* a condition in which the bones become thin, porous and brittle, due to low levels of oestrogen, lack of calcium and lack of physical exercise. Also called **brittle bone disease**

ostomate *noun* someone in whose body a surgical opening into the intestine has been created

ostrich *noun* a large flightless African bird bred on farms for its meat (NOTE: Its scientific name is *Struthio camelus*.)

ounce *noun* an imperial measure of weight equal to 28 g. Abbreviation **oz**

outbreak *noun* a series of cases of a disease that start suddenly

out of season *adjective* used for describing fruit and vegetables that are not available domestically because their growing season is over and that therefore have to be imported

ouzo *noun* a Greek alcoholic drink flavoured with aniseed

ovalbumin *noun* the protein that comprises about 70% of the protein in an egg white, responsible for the stability of whipped egg white

oven *noun* any enclosed box that can be heated for cooking, nowadays usually an appliance heated by gas or electricity

oven brick *noun* a terracotta container with a tightly fitting lid for slow-cooking meat in the oven

oven glove *noun* a padded hand covering used as protection when putting hot dishes into, and taking them out of, an oven

oven management *noun* the practice of using an oven correctly, including temperature settings, placement of food in the oven and oven safety

ovenproof *adjective* able to be used in an oven without being damaged by the heat

oven-ready *adjective* sold in a state ready to be put in the oven for heating or cooking, after packaging is removed

oven temperature *noun* the temperature of an oven, set according to any of four different scales, Fahrenheit, Celsius, gas mark, or the qualitative scale in which 'cool' is less than 120°C, 'slow' is around 120°C, 'moderate' is 180°C, 'hot' is 220°C and 'very hot' is 250°C. ◊ **gas mark**

overcook *verb* to cook something so long that it loses its flavour and texture

over easy *adjective* used for describing an egg that has been fried on both sides. Compare **sunny side up**

overeat *verb* to eat too much food, especially habitually

overfishing *noun* the practice of catching so many fish that the fish do not reproduce quickly enough and become rare

overnutrition *noun* the act of taking in too much of a particular nutrient, causing a condition such as obesity or hypervitaminosis

overripe *adjective* too ripe and past its best flavour and texture

overweight *adjective* having a body weight greater than that considered ideal or healthy

ovoglobulin *noun* a globulin present in egg white

ovo-lacto-vegetarian *noun* a vegetarian who eats eggs and dairy products, but no products that involve the killing of animals

own brand, own label *noun* an item for sale that has the trademark or label of the retailer, usually a large supermarket chain, instead of that of the manufacturer

own-brand, own-label *adjective* used for describing a food product that is not branded but is made for the supermarket or shop in which it is sold, usually a cheaper version of the branded product

ox *noun* a name used in the food industry to refer to meat and offal from a castrated male of any species of domestic cattle, also sometimes confusingly applied to meat and offal from either a bull or cow

oxalate *noun* a salt or ester of oxalic acid

oxalic acid *noun* a substance, found in food and also produced within the body, that can form kidney stones in large concentrations

oxidant *noun* an agent which causes oxidation

oxidase *noun* an enzyme that encourages oxidation by removing hydrogen. ◊ **monoamine oxidase**

oxidation *noun* a chemical reaction in which a substance combines with oxygen with loss of electrons (NOTE: In food, oxidation is caused by the reaction of food to the oxygen in the air. This causes the food to deteriorate.)

oxidative stress *noun* impaired performance of cells caused by the presence of too many oxygen molecules in them

oxidise *verb* to react with oxygen, or cause a chemical to react with oxygen, e.g. in forming an oxide

oxidoreductase *noun* an enzyme that catalyses the oxidation of one compound and the reduction of another

oxtail *noun* the tail of a cow or bull, used in stews or to make oxtail soup

oxycalorimeter *noun* an instrument that measures the amount of oxygen consumed and carbon dioxide produced when a food is burned

oxygen *noun* a common colourless gas that is present in the air and essential to human life (NOTE: The chemical symbol is **O**.)

oxygen absorber *noun* a sachet of iron particles inside food packaging that attracts and traps oxygen, preventing spoiling

oxygenase *noun* an enzyme that promotes the addition of oxygen to a compound

Oxygen Radical Absorbance Capacity *noun* a way of measuring the antioxidant properties of different foodstuffs. Abbreviation **ORAC**

oxygeusia *noun* a heightened or sharpened sense of taste

oxyhemoglobinometer *noun* a device for measuring the levels of oxygen in the blood

oxyntic cells *plural noun* cells that produce or secrete acid

oxyosmia *noun* a heightened or sharpened sense of smell

oxypathy *noun* a disorder in which the body cannot expel unoxidisable acids, which damage tissues

oxystearin *noun* a sequestering agent that also prevents fats from crystallising, used in salad creams and similar foodstuffs

oyster *noun* a shellfish with two rough, roundish shells

oyster knife *noun* a knife with a thin, strong, sharp-pointed blade, used for opening oysters

oyster mushroom an edible mushroom that grows on dead wood and has a soft flavourful grey cap. Latin name: *Pleurotus ostreatus*.

oyster sauce *noun* a salty bottled sauce flavoured with oysters, used in Chinese cooking

oz *abbreviation* ounce

ozone *noun* a sterilising solution used in chemical ice

P

PABA *abbreviation* para-amino benzoic acid

PAC *abbreviation* proanthocyanin

package *noun* a number of different things or operations grouped together and considered as a single item ■ *verb* to create suitable or attractive packaging in which to sell a product

packaging *noun* **1.** the wrapping or container in which an item is presented for sale, or the materials used to make it **2.** the design or style of the wrapping or container in which something is offered for sale, especially from the point of view of its appeal to buyers

packaging gas *noun* gas used in packaging, either to create a modified atmosphere or as a propellant

packaging origination *noun* the original design of food packaging

packed lunch *noun* a lunch of cold foods packed in a box or basket for eating when travelling

packing *noun* the processing and packaging of food such as meat or produce for sale

packing date *noun* the date on which a product was packaged

paddy *noun* rice after threshing, when it is still in the husk

paella *noun* a Spanish dish of cooked rice with fish, shellfish and vegetables in it

pak choi *noun* a Chinese vegetable with white stems and fleshy green leaves, used like cabbage. Also called **bok choy**

pakora *noun* a deep-fried South Asian fritter made by dipping pieces of vegetable, meat or shellfish in a chickpea-flour batter and generally eaten as a snack

PAL *abbreviation* physical activity level

palatability *noun* the extent to which something is good to eat

palatable *adjective* good to eat

palate *noun* **1.** the roof of the mouth and floor of the nasal cavity, consisting of the hard and soft palates **2.** a personal sense of taste and flavour

pale, soft, exudative *noun* ♦ **PSE meat**

palette knife *noun* a kitchen implement with a long flexible blunt-edged blade for lifting and turning food or for spreading, particularly when filling or icing cakes

pallet *noun* a standardised platform or open-ended box, usually made of wood, that allows mechanical handling of bulk goods during transport and storage

pallor *noun* the condition of being pale

palmitic acid *noun* a waxy solid derived from plant and animal fats and oils and used in making soap and candles and as a food additive

palm kernel oil *noun* oil extracted from the kernel of the oil palm, used in cooking oils and margarines

palm oil *noun* an edible oil produced from the seed or fruit of an oil palm

pan *noun* a metal cooking container with a handle

panada *noun* a very thick paste of flour and a liquid such as milk or stock, used as a base for sauces, or for binding for stuffing

panage *noun* the practice of covering food in breadcrumbs before cooking it

panary fermentation *noun* the raising action of the yeast when bread is left to rest before baking

pancake *noun* a thin soft flat cake made of flour, milk and eggs

pancetta *noun* a salt-cured and spiced form of belly of pork, used in Italian dishes

pancreas *noun* a gland on the back of the body between the kidneys that produces digestive enzymes and important hormones, including insulin

pancreatic duct *noun* a duct leading through the pancreas to the duodenum

pancreatic juice *noun* a watery alkaline secretion from the pancreas that contains digestive enzymes that break down food in the small intestine

pancreatin *noun* a solution of digestive enzymes from animals, used for replacing or supplementing pancreatic juices in humans

pandan leaf *noun* the leaf of a tropical Asian plant, used as a digestive stimulant and breath freshener and as a herb in cooking

pané *adjective* used for describing foods coated with seasoned flour, beaten egg and breadcrumbs, prior to frying

panettone *noun* a tall Italian yeast cake flavoured with vanilla and dried and candied fruits, traditionally eaten at Christmas

pan-fry *verb* to cook food in a frying pan with a small quantity of fat or oil

pangamic acid *noun* a supplement that is claimed to be an antioxidant and to ease tiredness, sometimes called vitamin B15

panini *noun* a flattish Italian white bread roll, or a sandwich or toasted sandwich made with it (NOTE: The plural is **panini**.)

panna cotta *noun* a rich dessert made from cream and milk flavoured with vanilla and set with gelatin, often served with a fruit sauce (NOTE: Literally 'cooked cream'.)

panthenol *noun* pantothenic acid in an alcohol solution

pantothenic acid *noun* a vitamin of the vitamin B complex, found in liver, yeast and eggs

PAN UK *abbreviation* Pesticide Action Network UK

panure *noun* a coating of flour, beaten egg and breadcrumbs. ◊ **pané**

papain *noun* an enzyme found in the juice of the papaya, used as a meat tenderiser

papaya *noun* a large pear- or melon-shaped tropical fruit with yellowish orange skin and juicy pinkish orange flesh with many black seeds in a central cavity. Also called **pawpaw**

papillote *noun* an oiled paper case in which meat or fish is cooked, described on a menu as 'en papillote'

pappardelle *noun* pasta in the shape of broad flat ribbons

paprika *noun* a red spice made from powdered sweet peppers (NOTE: **Paprika** is used in Central European cooking, such as goulash.)

para-amino benzoic acid *noun* part of the folic acid molecule, without which folic acid cannot be synthesised. Abbreviation **PABA**

paraben *noun* a chemical that mimics the hormone oestrogen (NOTE: Evidence suggests that parabens can play a role in the development of breast tumours.)

parageusia *noun* a distorted or impaired sense of taste

paragonimiasis *noun* a severe lung infection caused by a fluke found in raw shellfish

parakeratosis *noun* a skin disease in pigs caused by zinc deficiency

paralytic ileus *noun* an ileus caused by paralysis of the intestinal muscles

paralytic shellfish poisoning *noun* food poisoning caused by eating shellfish that are contaminated with saxitoxin. Abbreviation **PSP**

Para red dye *noun* a printing dye found to be illegally used in some food products as a colorant, sparking a product recall in 2005

parasite *noun* a plant or animal that lives on or inside a host plant or animal and derives its nourishment and other needs from it

parathyroid hormone *noun* one of four small glands which are situated in or near the wall of the thyroid gland and secrete a hormone which controls the way in which calcium and phosphorus are deposited in bones

parboil *verb* to half-cook food in boiling water

parch *verb* to dry-roast food until it is slightly brown

pare *verb* to cut the skin or peel off a fruit, vegetable, etc.

parenteral *adjective* not involving the intestinal tract

parenteral nutrition *noun* administration of nutrients directly into the veins, either as a supplement or as a complete source of nutrition for a patient

parer *noun* ♦ peeler

pareve *adjective* under Jewish dietary laws, relating to food which is made without milk or meat or derivatives of them, and which may therefore be eaten with either type. Compare **milchig, fleishig**

parfait *noun* a rich dessert consisting of frozen whipped cream or rich ice cream flavoured with fruit

parietic cells *plural noun* same as **oxyntic cells**

Parma ham *noun* dry-cured ham eaten raw, air-dried for at least 8 months, produced around the Italian town of Parma

Parmesan *noun* a very hard Italian grating cheese with a strong flavour, made from unpasteurized skimmed cows' milk, matured for well over two years

parosmia *noun* a disorder of the sense of smell

parsley *noun* a green herb with either curly or flat leaves, used in cooking as a flavouring or garnish

parsnip *noun* a plant whose long white root is eaten as a vegetable

partie *noun* a specialised section of a restaurant kitchen, making sauces, pastries, etc.

partly-milled *adjective* used for describing cereal grain that has been only partly ground in a mill, leaving whole grains and large particles

partridge *noun* a large brown and grey bird, shot for sport and food, in season between September 1st and February 1st

parts per million *noun* an expression of the proportions of active and inactive particles in a solution. Abbreviation **ppm**

part-treated *adjective* used for describing foods that are unprocessed but have flavour enhancers added

passata *noun* a thick tomato sauce with a rough texture, sometimes flavoured with herbs

PASSCLAIM *abbreviation* Process for the Assessment of Scientific Support for Claims on Foods

passion fruit *noun* a purple fruit with a hard case filled with juicy pulp and many seeds

pasta *noun* a type of food made from flour from durum wheat and shaped into forms such as lasagne, macaroni, noodles, ravioli and spaghetti (NOTE: There is no plural form.)

paste *noun* a soft food mixture produced by crushing or liquidising

pasteurisation *noun* the treatment of a liquid such as milk by heating it in order to destroy harmful bacteria

pasteurise *verb* to make a food product, especially milk, safer to drink or eat and improve its keeping qualities by heating it in order to destroy harmful bacteria

pasteurised milk *noun* milk that has been pasteurised at 72°C for 15 seconds and then rapidly cooled

pasteuriser *noun* a device for pasteurising liquids, using heated plates or pipes

pastrami *noun* smoked and strongly seasoned beef, usually prepared from a shoulder cut, that is served cold in thin slices

pastry *noun* **1.** a paste made of flour, fat and water, used for making pies **2.** a sweet cake made of pastry filled with cream or fruit

pastry bag *noun* a cloth bag with a nozzle used for piping soft foods

pastry board *noun* a square or oblong board, preferably marble but usually wood, on which pastry is rolled out

pastry brake *noun* a set of rollers with a variable gap through which pastry is prepared for commercial production (NOTE: A very small version is used domestically for pasta production.)

pastry case *noun* a piece of pastry used for lining a dish and filled either before or after baking

pastry chef *noun* a chef who specialises in preparing pastries and sweet dishes. Also called **chef pâtissier**

pastry cutter *noun* a utensil for cutting pastry into small shapes

pastry wheel *noun* a small wooden wheel with a serrated edge attached to a handle, used for crimping edges of pastry

pat *noun* a small shaped amount of a solid or semi-solid substance, especially butter ■ *verb* to shape a solid or semi-solid into a pat, traditionally by using two flat wooden paddles

pâté *noun* a paste made of cooked meat or fish finely minced

patent blue V *noun* ♦ E131

patent flour *noun* a very fine good-quality wheat flour

pathogen *noun* a microorganism that causes a disease

pathogenicity *noun* the ability of a pathogen to cause a disease

patisserie *noun* sweet pastries or cakes

patty *noun* a small flat individual cake made from minced meat, vegetables or other food

patulin *noun* a toxin in fruit juices caused by a mould affecting the unprocessed fruit

paunch *verb* to remove the internal organs from a rabbit or hare before cooking

pavlova *noun* a large circle of meringue filled with fruit and whipped cream

PBM *abbreviation* peak bone mass

PCB *abbreviation* polychlorinated biphenyl

PCT *abbreviation* primary care trust

pea *noun* a climbing plant with round green seeds that are eaten as vegetables

peach *noun* a juicy fruit with a soft hairy yellow or red-and-yellow skin and sweet yellow flesh

peak bone mass *noun* the amount of bone tissue present in the body at full maturation of the skeleton. Abbreviation **PBM**

peanut *noun* a nut that grows in the ground in pods like a pea

peanut butter *noun* a spreadable food of varying consistency made from ground peanuts, sometimes with added peanut oil, salt or sugar

pear *noun* a fruit with a greenish or yellowish skin and soft white flesh

pearl barley *noun* grains of barley used in cooking

pear shaped *adjective* used for describing a person with a body shape in which most of the subcutaneous fat deposits are carried around the hips and bottom

pecan *noun* a sweet nut from a tree that grows in the south of the USA

pecorino *noun* a hard pungent Italian cheese made from ewe's milk

pectase *noun* an enzyme in fruits involved in transforming pectin into pectic acid

pectin *noun* a mixture of polysaccharides in the cell walls of plants and fruit that helps jam to set

pectinase *noun* an enzyme used for clarifying wine and beer and for extracting juice from fruit

pectinesterase *noun* an enzyme that catalyses the breakdown of pectin

peel *noun* **1.** the outer skin of a fruit, or the skin of a potato **2.** a shovel-like tool used for lifting baked goods into and out of an oven ■ *verb* to take the skin off a fruit or vegetable

peeler *noun* a tool for taking the skins off fruit or vegetables

pelagic *adjective* used for describing fish that live in the waters of the open sea, as opposed to those living near the shore. Compare **demersal**

pellagra *noun* a disease caused by a deficiency of nicotinic acid, riboflavin and pyridoxine from the vitamin B complex, where patches of skin become inflamed and the person has anorexia, nausea and diarrhoea

PEM *abbreviation* protein energy malnutrition

pemmican *noun* compressed cooked meat and fat mixed with berries, eaten for energy

penicillin *noun* a common antibiotic originally produced from a fungus

penicillium *noun* an organism used for producing the veins in blue cheeses

penne *noun* short tube-shaped pasta cut diagonally at the ends

pentapotassium triphosphate *noun* ♦ E450(ii)

pentasodium triphosphate *noun* ♦ E450(ii)

pepper *noun* **1.** a condiment made from the crushed seeds of the pepper plant **2.** any of several varieties of flowering vine with small berries that are dried for use as a spice and seasoning ■ *verb* to sprinkle food with pepper

peppercorn *noun* a dried berry of the pepper plant

pepper mill a kitchen utensil for storing and grinding peppercorns

peppermint *noun* a flavouring prepared from the oil of a mint plant

pepsin *noun* a digestive protease that allows proteins to be converted into peptides in the stomach

pepsinogen *noun* a secretion from the gastric gland that is the inactive form of pepsin

peptic *adjective* related to or affecting the digestive system

peptic ulcer *noun* an erosion of the wall of the stomach or duodenum, caused by stomach acid

peptidase *noun* an enzyme that breaks down proteins in the intestine into amino acids

peptide *noun* a compound formed of two or more amino acids

peptide bond *noun* a linkage formed between the amino group of one amino acid and the carboxylic acid group of another

peptone *noun* a substance produced by the action of pepsins on proteins in food

peptonise *verb* to digest protein using an enzyme

PER *abbreviation* protein efficiency ratio

percentile growth chart *noun* a chart for measuring a child's development which compares them with the average development of other children and places them on a scale

perch *noun* any of various types of freshwater fish, several of which are used as food

percolator *noun* a coffeemaker in which the water boils up through a tube and filters through ground coffee

perennial *adjective* used for describing plants that grow for more than two years ■ *noun* a plant that grows for more than two years, often dying back during the winter

perennial crop *noun* a crop that lasts for more than two growing seasons, dying back after each season

performance enhancer *noun* a dietary supplement used by athletes to enhance bursts of high performance

pericarp *noun* a fibrous part of a grain, forming the major part of bran

periderm *noun* the outer layer of plant tissue in woody roots and stems

perish *verb* to deteriorate or decay, or make a material such as rubber deteriorate or decay

perishable *adjective* likely to go bad quickly

perishables *plural noun* perishable food

perishable store *noun* a storeroom for food that can go bad quickly, e.g. meat and fruit

peristalsis *noun* the movement, like waves, produced by alternate contraction and relaxation of muscles along an organ such as the intestine or oesophagus, that pushes the contents of the organ along it. Compare **antiperistalsis**

pernicious anaemia *noun* anaemia caused by a deficiency of vitamin B12

peroxisome *noun* a tiny part within a cell containing enzymes that oxidise toxic substances such as alcohol and prevent them from doing any harm

perry *noun* an alcoholic drink made from pear juice

persistent organic pollutant *noun* a compound that enters the food chain and accumulates in the human body. Abbreviation **POPs**

personalised nutrition *noun* an approach to nutrition that meets the needs of the individual, taking into account considerations such as state of health, lifestyle, age, gender, etc

pescetarian, pesco-vegetarian *noun* a person who will not eat red meat or poultry, but will eat fish

pesticide *noun* a poisonous substance used for destroying pests on crops

Pesticide Action Network UK *noun* an organisation that promotes alternatives to pesticides. Abbreviation **PAN UK**

pestle *noun* a rod-shaped object made from hard material with a rounded end that is used for crushing or grinding substances in a mortar. ◊ **pestle and mortar**

pestle and mortar *noun* a short hard crushing implement and a small hard shallow bowl, used in combination for grinding hard foods into a paste or powder

pesto *noun* a sauce or paste made by crushing together basil leaves, pine nuts, oil, Parmesan cheese, and garlic

petechiae *plural noun* small spots of bleeding under the skin, a possible indicator of nutritional deficiencies

petits fours *plural noun* very small cakes and biscuits, often containing marzipan, served with coffee after a meal

pH *noun* the concentration of hydrogen ions in a solution, which determines its acidity (NOTE: A pH less than 7 is acid, and a pH more than 7 is alkaline.)

phaeophytin *noun* a brownish derivative of chlorophyll that is formed during cooking, making vegetables lose their bright green colour

phagocyte *noun* a cell, especially a white blood cell, that can surround and destroy other cells such as bacteria cells

phagocytosis *noun* the destruction of bacteria cells and foreign bodies by phagocytes

phagodynamometer *noun* a device for measuring force used in chewing

phagology *noun* the study of eating

phagomania *noun* obsession with food or eating

phagophobia *noun* a fear of food or eating

phagosome *noun* a membranous sac formed within some types of cells that contains the microorganisms or other small particles that the cell has engulfed in order to destroy them

phagotherapy *noun* the treatment of illness by changes in diet

phagotrophy *noun* the act of obtaining nourishment by ingesting food

pharmacokinetics *noun* the study of how the body reacts to drugs over a period of time, including their absorption, metabolism and elimination ■ *plural noun* the ways in which a drug interacts with the body

pharmacological *adjective* relating to pharmacology

pharmafood *noun* same as **functional food** (*informal*)

Pharoah's curse *noun* diarrhoea associated with travel in Egypt or with eating Egyptian food (*informal*)

phase *noun* a physical form in which a substance can exist: gas, vapour, liquid or solid (NOTE: Two or more phases are common in many foods. For example, milk and cream contain two liquid phases, water and butterfat.)

phaseolamin *noun* a substance that inhibits alpha amylase, allowing less sugar to be absorbed by the digestive tract, sold as a diet aid

pheasant *noun* a large bird with a long tail, shot for sport and food and in season from October 1st to February 1st

phenolic acid *noun* a plant metabolite with antioxidant properties

phenolic compound *noun* a compound of phenolic acids derived from plants, added to food as an antioxidant

phenol oxidase *noun* the enzyme that causes the cut surfaces of foods such as apples and potatoes to brown in air

phenylalanine *noun* an essential amino acid found in many proteins and converted to a non-essential amino acid by the body

phenyl benzene *noun* ♦ **E230, diphenyl**

phenylketonuria *noun* a genetic disease that affects the metabolisation of phenylalanine and can have severe effects on the brain of a developing child

pheromone *noun* a chemical produced by an animal that sends a message to others of the same species, some of which are used in agriculture to interrupt insect breeding cycles and control pests

PHF *abbreviation* potentially hazardous food

phlegm *noun* same as **sputum**

phosphatase *noun* an enzyme in milk, the presence of which indicates inadequate pasteurisation

phosphate *noun* a salt of phosphoric acid, used for flavouring and as a stabiliser. ◊ **polyphosphate** (NOTE: The important ones used in the food industry are disodium dihydrogen, tetrasodium, tetrapotassium and trisodium diphosphate, all classified as E450(a), and pentasodium triphosphate and pentapotassium triphosphate, classified as E450(b).)

phosphaturia *noun* cloudy urine caused by a high concentration of phosphate salts, indicating possible formation of kidney stones

phosphofructokinase *noun* an enzyme that catalyses the transfer of phosphate to a fructose compound during the metabolism of glucose

phosphoglucomutase *noun* an enzyme that catalyses the breakdown and synthesis of glycogen, providing energy that can be used or stored

phosphoglyceraldehyde *noun* an intermediate product in carbohydrate metabolism

phospholipase *noun* an enzyme that catalyses the hydrolysis of phospholipids in cell membranes. Also called **lecithinase**

phospholipid *noun* a compound with fatty acids, which is one of the main components of membranous tissue

phosphomonesterase *noun* an enzyme promoting the breakdown of phosphoric acid esters that have only one ester group

phosphoprotein *noun* a protein that contains an enzymatically bound phosphate group

phosphoric acid *noun* an acid that is very soluble in water and gives rise to acid, neutral and alkali salts

phosphorus *noun* a toxic chemical element that is present in very small quantities in bones and nerve tissue (NOTE: The chemical symbol is **P**.)

phosphorylase *noun* an enzyme that aids the process of carbohydrate metabolism

photosensitivity *noun* the fact of being sensitive to light

photosynthesis *noun* the process by which green plants convert carbon dioxide and water into sugar and oxygen using sunlight as energy

phrynoderma *noun* a disease of the skin caused by vitamin A deficiency

phycotoxin *noun* a toxin that is eaten by fish and shellfish and accumulates in their bodies

physical activity *noun* exercise and general movement which a person carries out as part of their day

physical activity level *noun* the amount of physical activity that a person undertakes each day, which is used in calculating their daily calorie requirements. Abbreviation **PAL**

physical treatment *noun* physical processes such as heating and cooling that food undergoes

physico-chemical *adjective* involving both physical and chemical changes

physiological *adjective* referring to physiology and the regular functions of the body

physiological availability *noun* same as **bioavailability**

physiology *noun* the study of regular body functions

phytate *noun* a component of plant fibres that has antioxidant properties

phytic acid *noun* a plant acid that binds iron and zinc in vegetable foods and carries them through the human gut, with the result that they are not absorbed by the body

phytochemical *noun* any naturally occurring plant substance, some of which have been shown in research to protect against disease

phytoestrogen *noun* same as **isoflavone**

phytonutrient *noun* same as **phytochemical**

phytosterol *noun* a group of phytochemicals that are used as food additives and may have cholesterol-lowering properties

phytotoxin *noun* a poisonous substance produced by a plant

pica *noun* same as **allotriophagy**

pickle *noun* a mixture of chopped vegetables preserved in a spicy vinegar- or brine-based liquid, served as a condiment ■ *verb* to preserve food in a vinegar- or brine-based liquid

pickling *noun* a way of preserving food by keeping it in a liquid that inhibits microbiological activity, usually vinegar or brine

pick-up station *noun* the place in a kitchen where the prepared meals are left ready for the waiters to collect and deliver them

picowave *verb* to expose food to radiation in order to kill insects, worms or bacteria

pie *noun* a cooked dish of pastry with a filling of meat or fruit, eaten hot or cold

pie marker *noun* an implement used for accurately cutting pies and cakes, consisting of a frame with a wheel-shaped cutting blade

pie tin *noun* a round shallow baking dish with sloping walls

pig *noun* an animal of the *Suidae* family kept exclusively for meat production (NOTE: The males are called **boars**, the females are **sows**, the young are **piglets**. Pigs reared for pork meat are called **porkers** and those reared for bacon are **baconers**.)

pigmeat *noun* a term used in the EU for meat from pigs

pigment *noun* a substance that gives colour to parts of the body such as blood, the skin and hair

pigment rubine *noun* ♦ E180

pilaff *noun* a name given to various rice-based dishes cooked in an oven, strictly one that contains finely chopped onions sweated in butter, with rice then added and cooked in white stock or fish stock, with butter stirred in at the end

pilchard *noun* a small fish similar to a herring, sold in tins

piles *plural noun* same as **haemorrhoids**

pilot production *noun* a stage of product development that is a test run for mass production, carried out in order to find any flaws with the process

pimento *noun* a large heart-shaped variety of chilli

pinch *noun* an amount of powder held between the thumb and forefinger, roughly equal to one quarter of a gram

pineapple *noun* a tropical fruit with a tough knobbly skin, pale yellow flesh and leaves sprouting from the top

pine nut *noun* a small sweet seed of some pine trees, especially the piñon pine. Also called **pine kernel**

pinholing *noun* the formation of small holes in food packaging as it flexes during handling, breaking the hermetic seal

pinotherapy *noun* the act of treating a disease by starving the body of the nutrients that are causing it

pint *noun* an imperial fluid measure equal to 20 fluid ounces or 567.5 ml in the UK, and 16 fluid ounces or 473 ml in the US. ◊ **gallon**

pinto bean *noun* a mottled brown and pink kidney-shaped bean, cooked and eaten as a vegetable or used as fodder

pinworm *noun* same as **threadworm**

pip *noun* a small seed found in fruits such as apples, citrus fruits, grapes and melons ■ *verb* to remove pips from fruit or vegetables

pipe *verb* to squeeze soft food mixture through a small tube, so as to make decorative shapes

piping *noun* the decorative lines of icing piped onto a cake

piping bag *noun* an implement used for applying a soft food in a decorative way, consisting of a triangular-shaped bag with a cone fitted at the pointed end. Also called **forcing bag**, **icing bag**

piping hot *adjective* extremely hot

piquant *adjective* having a flavour, taste or smell that is spicy or savoury, often with a slightly tart or bitter edge to it

piri piri *noun* a meat or fish dish served with piri piri sauce

piri piri sauce *noun* a spicy sauce made with chillies

pistachio *noun* a nut of a small tree native to central Asia and now cultivated in Mediterranean regions, eaten salted or in confectionery

pit *noun* the stone in some fruit such as cherries, plums, peaches, or dried fruit such as prunes and dates

pith *noun* the soft white material under the skin of a lemon, orange or other citrus fruit

pitta bread *noun* flat white unleavened bread, served with Greek and Turkish food

pitting *noun* the act of removing the pits from fruit

pituitary gland *noun* the main endocrine gland in the body that secretes hormones that stimulate other glands

pizza *noun* an Italian savoury dish consisting of a flat round piece of dough cooked with tomatoes, onions, cheese and often sliced meat or vegetables on top

pizza dough *noun* dough made of strong flour, tepid water, yeast, salt and olive oil, proved, knocked back and proved again

pizza oven *noun* a traditional brick oven with a stone floor and a wood fire to one side, radiating heat from the brick roof onto the pizza, or a modern oven that mimics these characteristics by having a large hot mass of metal

pizza stone *noun* a piece of bakeware, usually made of terracotta, that is used to brown and crisp a pizza base

pizza wheel *noun* a utensil with a small, sharp rotating disc on a handle, used for cutting pizza

placebo *noun* a tablet that appears to be a drug but has no medicinal substance in it, used in tests and trials

place of origin *noun* the place in which a food product was manufactured, a required element in food labelling in the UK

plaice *noun* any of three varieties of flat white sea fish (NOTE: The plural form is **plaice**.)

plain chocolate *noun* dark, bitter chocolate

plain flour *noun* flour that has had no baking powder added to it

plain yoghurt *noun* same as **natural yoghurt**

plank *verb* to cook meat or fish on an oiled wooden board

plansifter *noun* a series of sieves mounted together that sort a material by particle size

plant *noun* **1.** a vegetable organism that does not have a permanent woody stem, e.g. a flower or herb rather than a bush or tree **2.** a factory, power station, or other large industrial complex where something is manufactured or produced

plantago *noun* same as **psyllium**

plantain *noun* the name given to various types of large banana used for cooking

plant extract *noun* a preparation of plant chemicals used in foods, cosmetics and toiletries

plant exudate *noun* any substance that seeps from a plant, e.g. a gum or resin

plant senescence *noun* the final stage in the life cycle of a plant, leading to the death of part or all of the plant (NOTE: Knowledge of plant senescence is important for farmers as it determines when they should harvest a crop in order to ensure it is of the highest possible quality.)

plant sterol *noun* same as **phytosterol**

plaque *noun* a film of saliva, mucus, bacteria and food residues that builds up on the surface of teeth and can cause gum damage

plasticity *noun* variability in the growth of a plant in response to differences in the supply of resources

plastic wrap *noun* a clear plastic film that sticks to itself and to surfaces, used for wrapping food for storage

plate *verb* to place food and garnishes on a plate ready for serving it to a customer

plateau *noun* a large dish with a display of food on it (NOTE: The plural form is **plateaux**.)

plate count *noun* an estimate of the number of bacteria in a sample, carried out by treating them so that they become visible to the naked eye

plate heat-exchanger *noun* a piece of machinery used in food manufacture that transfers heat to and from liquids using metal plates

plate ring *noun* a metal ring used for stacking plated food in such a way that the food is not spoiled

plate waste *noun* food left on the plate by customers in a restaurant, the amount of which is monitored by a good restaurant so that adjustments can be made to quality or portion size

platter *noun* a large plate generally used for serving food to several people or for serving several foods on the same plate

ploughman's lunch *noun* a cold lunch, typically served in a pub, consisting of a plate of bread, cheese, pickle or chutney, and a pickled onion

pluck *verb* to remove some or all of the feathers or hair from a bird or other animal ■ *noun* the liver, lungs and heart of an animal

plucking *noun* the act of removing the feathers from a bird before butchering

plum *noun* a gold, red or purple fruit with a smooth skin and a large stone

plumpy *noun* an enriched peanut paste bar that is highly nutritious, distributed by humanitarian agencies during times of famine

plum tomato *noun* a variety of tomato that is egg-shaped and is the variety most usually used for canning

pneumatic conveying *noun* the transport of powder materials from one place to another using air currents, used in the food processing industry

pneumophagy *noun* same as **aerophagy**

poach *verb* to cook something, e.g. eggs without their shells, or fish, in gently boiling liquid

poached egg *noun* a shelled egg, yolk intact, placed in acidulated water just below simmering point for about three minutes until set then carefully removed

pod *noun* a container for several seeds, e.g. a pea pod or bean pod

point-of-sale *noun* a shop or other place where a food product is sold. Abbreviation **POS**

polenta *noun* in Italian cooking, fine yellow maize meal cooked to a mush with water or stock, sometimes set, sliced and served baked or fried

poliomyelitis, polio *noun* a severe infectious viral disease, usually affecting children or young adults, that inflames the brain stem and spinal cord, sometimes leading to loss of voluntary movement and muscular wasting

pollo-vegetarian *noun* a person who will not eat red meat but will eat poultry and fish

poly- *prefix* more than one, or more than normal

polyalcohol *noun* same as **polyol**

polyavitaminosis *noun* an illness caused by a deficiency of more than one vitamin

polychlorinated biphenyl *noun* a contaminant in fish. Abbreviation **PCB**

polycosanol *noun* a supplement extract of plant waxes that is reputed to reduce levels of LDL cholesterol

polydextrose *noun* a bulking agent used in reduced-calorie and low-calorie foods

polydipsia *noun* an unusually intense thirst

polymixin *noun* a type of antibiotic that is active against coliform bacteria

polyneuropathy *noun* serious nerve damage caused by dietary deficiencies or alcoholism

polyol *noun* an alcohol that contains more than two hydroxyl groups, e.g. glycerol. Also called **polyalcohol**

polyoxyethylene sorbitan monolaurate *noun* ♦ E432

polyoxyethylene sorbitan monooleate *noun* ♦ E433

polyoxyethylene sorbitan monopalmitate *noun* ♦ E434

polyoxyethylene sorbitan monostearate *noun* ♦ E435

polyoxyethylene sorbitan tristearate *noun* ♦ E436

polypeptide *noun* a type of protein formed of linked amino acids

polyphagia *noun* constant eating, or obsessive interest in food

polyphenol oxidase *noun* an enzyme that oxidises food and increases its activities when subjected to high pressure

polyphosphate *noun* any of various complex phosphates of sodium and potassium used mainly to retain added water in frozen chickens, ham, bacon and other similar meat products, and also as stabilisers and emulsifiers

polysaccharide *noun* a long chain or branched chain of simple sugars that makes up starch, dextrins, cellulose and other carbohydrates of natural origin

polysorbate *noun* an emulsifier used in preparing some foods and drugs

polytetrafluoroethylene *noun* full form of **PTFE**

polyunsaturated fat *noun* a type of fat with more than one double atom bond, typical of vegetable and fish oils. Compare **saturated fat, unsaturated fat**

polyuria *noun* excessive production of urine

pomace *noun* the dry remains of something such as fruit or fish after the juice or oil has been extracted

pomegranate *noun* a fruit with yellowish pink or red skin, masses of seeds and sweet red flesh

ponceau 4R *noun* ♦ E124

ponderal index *noun* the cube root of a person's body weight divided by height, a measure of how fat a person is

ponderocrescive *adjective* used for describing foods that stimulate weight gain

ponderoperditive *adjective* used for describing foods that stimulate weight loss

POP *abbreviation* persistent organic pollutant

poppadom *noun* a thin round crisp Indian pancake, fried or grilled

porcini *noun* an Italian name for the cep mushroom, often sold sliced and dried

pore *noun* a tiny hole in an egg's shell that allows carbon dioxide to seep out

pork *noun* fresh meat from pigs, as opposed to cured meat, which is bacon or ham (NOTE: There is no plural form.)

pork belly *noun* meat from the underside of the abdominal and chest cavity of a pig, consisting of alternating layers of fat and lean muscle. Also called **belly pork**

pork pie *noun* minced pork in a pastry case, usually eaten cold

pork scratchings *plural noun* ♦ **scratchings**

porous *adjective* used for describing a substance that allows fluids to pass through it

porphyria *noun* a hereditary disease affecting the metabolism of porphyrin pigments

porphyrin *noun* a substance that develops into haem when acted upon by enzymes, necessary for the health of the blood and bone marrow

porridge *noun* a soft food consisting of oatmeal cooked in water, often eaten as a breakfast food

porridge oats *plural noun* oats that have been crushed ready to be made into porridge

port *noun* a dessert wine from Portugal, usually served after a meal

porterhouse steak *noun* a very large boneless beef steak from the short loin, possibly including some of the sirloin and including the fillet

portion *noun* a small quantity, especially enough food for one person ■ *verb* to divide something into portions

portion control *noun* the process of keeping a check on the amount of food served by splitting it up into individual portions, e.g. by serving butter in small individual packets or pots

portion size *noun* the weight or number of each item in one serving

portobello mushroom *noun* a very large dark mushroom known for its meaty texture

POS *abbreviation* point-of-sale

pot *noun* **1.** a deep cylindrical metal or ceramic container with a lid and two handles, used on the stove for stews and other foods to be cooked slowly **2.** a cylindrical ceramic or glass container in which food is placed for serving or storage ■ *verb* to put food into a jar or ramekin and seal it, either for presentation at the table or for preserving

potable *adjective* clean and safe to drink

potage *noun* thick soup, especially one made from vegetables

potassium *noun* a metallic element that exists naturally in seawater and in several minerals (NOTE: The chemical symbol is **K**.)

potassium acetate *noun* ♦ **E261**

potassium alginate *noun* ♦ **E402**

potassium benzoate *noun* ♦ **E212**

potassium bicarbonate *noun* a raising agent

potassium bitartrate *noun* a white powder or crystalline compound used as a raising agent in baking

potassium carbonate *noun* a white salt used in brewing and in the manufacture of ceramics, explosives, fertilisers, glass and soap

potassium chloride *noun* a colourless crystalline salt used as a fertiliser and in photography and medicine

potassium dihydrogen citrate *noun* a potassium salt of citric acid. ◊ **E332**

potassium dihydrogen orthophosphate *noun* a chemical treatment used for making water safe for human consumption

potassium ferrocyanide *noun* a yellow crystalline compound used in medicines and explosives

potassium gluconate *noun* ♦ **E577**

potassium hydrogen carbonate *noun* a white powder or granular compound used in baking powder and as an antacid

potassium hydrogen tartrate *noun* ♦ **cream of tartare**

potassium hydroxide *noun* a caustic and poisonous white solid, used in making soap, detergents, liquid shampoos and matches

potassium lactate *noun* ♦ **E326**

potassium malate *noun* ♦ **E351**

potassium metabisulphite *noun* ♦ **E224**

potassium nitrite *noun* ♦ **E249**

potassium polyphosphate *noun* ♦ **E452**

potassium proprionate *noun* ♦ **E283**

potassium salt *noun* a crystalline compound formed from the neutralisation of an acid solution containing potassium

potassium sodium tartrate *noun* a colourless crystalline salt used as a mild laxative and food preservative

potassium sorbate *noun* ♦ E202

potassium sulphate *noun* ♦ E515

potassium tartrate *noun* ♦ **cream of tartar**

potato *noun* a vegetable that grows from the roots of a plant, has a brown skin and white flesh, and can be eaten boiled, roasted, fried or baked

potato croquette *noun* a deep-fried cylinder of mashed potato with butter, milk, seasoning and possibly eggs

potato masher *noun* an implement for mashing boiled or steamed potatoes, consisting of a flat perforated metal or plastic disc with an upright handle, pressed onto the potatoes with an up and down movement

potato ricer *noun* an implement, rather like a large garlic press, for mashing potatoes

potato starch *noun* powdered starch used as a stabilising agent

poteen *noun* in Ireland, a spirit that has been distilled illegally, especially from potatoes

potency *noun* the strength of something such as a drug, medicine or alcoholic drink

potentially hazardous food *noun* food that needs to be carefully stored to keep it safe for human consumption. Abbreviation **PHF**

pot liquor *noun* the liquid left in a pan after cooking something

potomania *noun* an unusually strong desire to drink alcohol

potophobia *noun* an unusually strong aversion to drinking alcohol

pot-roast *verb* to cook meat in a covered pan or casserole with a little fat and a small amount of liquid or vegetables over a low heat for a considerable time

pottage *noun* a thick soup made with vegetables, or meat and vegetables

potted *adjective* cooked or preserved in a pot or jar

potted shrimps *plural noun* shrimps that have been cooked and put in a small pot with melted butter, served with lemon and brown bread and butter

poulet *noun* a chicken between three and eight months old

poultry *noun* a general term for domestic birds kept for meat and egg production, e.g. chickens, turkeys and ducks (NOTE: The word is mainly used in butchers' shops and recipe books.)

poultry lacer *noun* a device for holding a chicken together during roasting to prevent the stuffing spilling out

poultry needle *noun* a large curved needle used for sewing up the abdominal cavity of poultry and game birds

poultry shears *plural noun* heavy scissors or secateurs with a serrated edge and a good hand grip, used for cutting through the bones of poultry

pound[1] *noun* an imperial unit of weight equal to 453.6 g, divided into 16 ounces

pound[2] *verb* **1.** to bruise, break up and crush any hard food item to reduce it to a smooth consistency or a fine powder **2.** to beat meat in order to tenderise it or flatten it into, e.g., an escalope

poussin *noun* a chicken reared to be eaten when very young and tender

powdered cellulose *noun* ♦ E460(ii)

powdered milk *noun* a powder made from dried milk solids, used as a substitute for fresh milk or as a protein supplement

ppm *abbreviation* parts per million

practitioner *noun* a qualified person who works in the medical profession

Prader-Willi syndrome *noun* a condition in which the hypothalamus is non-functioning, meaning that the person has a constant urge to overeat without ever feeling satisfied

praline *noun* a sweet made of crushed nuts and caramelised sugar

prawn *noun* a type of shellfish, like a large shrimp

prawn cocktail *noun* a starter consisting of shelled prawns in mayonnaise and tomato dressing, served in a glass

PRE *abbreviation* protein retention efficiency

prebiotic *noun* a dietary supplement in the form of non-digestible carbohydrate that promotes the growth of desirable microflora in the large bowel. ◊ **probiotic**

precipitate *verb* to make a substance separate from a chemical compound and fall to the bottom of a liquid during a chemical reaction ■ *noun* a substance that is precipitated during a chemical reaction

precook *verb* to cook food completely or partially in advance, especially before it is sold, so that it only need minimal cooking or reheating before it is eaten

precursor *noun* a substance or cell from which another substance or cell is developed

predigest *verb* to treat food with chemicals or enzymes so that it is more easily digested by people with digestion problems

preference test *noun* a consumer taste test in which the testers decide which product they prefer from a choice of two or more

pregnancy *noun* **1.** the time between conception and childbirth when a woman is carrying the unborn child in her uterus **2.** the condition of being pregnant

pregnant *adjective* with an unborn child in the uterus

preheat *verb* to heat an oven, dish or other item before using it

premium brand *noun* a brand that is perceived as better quality than its competitors and charges above average for its products

pre-packaged, **pre-packed** *adjective* already packaged before being sold

prepare *verb* **1.** to get food ready to be cooked, e.g. by washing, chopping or boning it **2.** to make something

prep counter *noun* a metal counter on which food is prepared

presbyoesophagus *noun* a slowing down of swallowing ability caused by advancing age

preservation *noun* the process or practice of treating of food in order to slow down natural decay caused by bacteria (NOTE: Traditional methods of food preservation include pickling, curing, freezing and drying. Modern techniques include the use of modified atmosphere packaging and irradiation.)

preservative *noun* a substance, e.g. a sugar or salt, added to food to preserve it by slowing natural decay caused by bacteria

preserve *noun* a food consisting of fruit or vegetables cooked and kept in jars or cans for future use, e.g. jam or chutney ■ *verb* to treat something such as food so that it keeps for a long time

preserving pan *noun* a very large pan for making jam or chutney

preserving sugar *noun* a refined white sugar in the form of large crystals, used for jam-making because it minimises scum formation and reduces caramelisation when it is being dissolved

press *noun* a device or machine for crushing fruit or vegetables to extract the juice ■ *verb* to crush fruit or seeds to extract juice or oil

pressure-cook *verb* to cook food in a pressure cooker, very quickly and at a temperature above the normal boiling point of water

pressure cooker *noun* a type of pan with a tight-fitting lid that cooks food rapidly under pressure

pressure frying *noun* a method of frying in that keeps meat under enough pressure to prevent any water from boiling away, leaving it juicy

pressure preservation *noun* a method of food preservation in which it is treated in a high-pressure vessel, which restricts microorganism activity

pressure steaming *noun* a method of cooking vegetables or meat in which a purpose-built steamer is used to create steam under high pressure so that the food cooks rapidly

pressure steam oven *noun* a special oven where food can be steamed under pressure

pressure-temperature relationship *noun* the fact that the boiling point of water depends on the pressure exerted on its surface, so that it is 100°C at sea level in an open container but it rises to 120.5°C at a pressure of 15 pounds per square inch above atmospheric pressure and decreases by approximately 2.7°C for every 1000 m above sea level

preventive *adjective* used for describing an action taken to stop something happening, especially to stop a disease or infection from spreading

primary care *noun* in the UK, health services offered directly to individuals by GPs, dentists, opticians and other health professionals who may also refer a patient on to specialists for further treatment

primary care trust *noun* in the UK, the top level of the primary care group with extra responsibilities such as direct employment of community staff. Abbreviation **PCT**

primary processing *noun* the part of a food processing plant that receives raw materials and prepares them for further processing, e.g. by cleaning, milling or separating

primary protein energy malnutrition *noun* malnutrition caused by a severe lack of protein and energy in the diet

primavera *adjective* made with an assortment of fresh spring vegetables, especially sliced as an accompaniment to pasta, meat or seafood

prion *noun* a variant form of a protein found in the brains of mammals and causing diseases such as scrapie in sheep, BSE in cattle and variant CJD in humans

Pritikin diet *noun* a dietary plan for slimming that advises eating high-bulk, low-calorie foods such as vegetables to reduce hunger

proanthocyanidin *noun* any one of a class of flavonoids found in many plants that can be used as a dietary supplement to enhance immunity and to strengthen connective tissue

proanthocyanin *noun* a flavonoid that is found in berries and is a powerful antioxidant. Abbreviation **PAC**

probiotic *noun* a substance containing live microorganisms that claims to be beneficial to humans and animals, e.g. by restoring the balance of microflora in the digestive tract. ◊ **prebiotic**

procarcinogen *noun* a substance that is not carcinogenic but may be metabolised or form a compound with another substance to become one

process *noun* a technical or scientific action ■ *verb* to treat food in a way so that it will keep longer or become more palatable

process control *noun* the monitoring and standardising of food production processes

processed cheese *noun* a product made by beating and mixing one or more types of cheese and adding colouring, flavouring and emulsifiers

processed food *noun* food that is specially treated to preserve it, improve its appearance or make it more convenient to use

processed meats *plural noun* products made from meat that has been treated in some way, e.g. bacon or sausages

Process for the Assessment of Scientific Support for Claims on Foods *noun* a programme developed by the European Commission for evaluating the various schemes that assess claims that producers make about their food. Abbreviation **PASSCLAIM**

process industry *noun* any industry in which raw materials are treated or prepared in a series of stages, e.g. oil refining, water and sewage treatment and food production

processing aid *noun* any substance that is used during the processing of food, traces of which may end up in the finished product as long as they pose no risk to human health

processing plant *noun* a factory that receives raw materials and processes them into consumer products

proctology *noun* the scientific study of the rectum and anus and their associated diseases

procyanidin *noun* a polyphenol extracted from apples that stimulates human hair growth

product analysis *noun* an examination of each separate product in a company's range to find out information such as why it sells and who buys it

production line *noun* a system of manufacturing a food product in which the item moves through a factory from one process to another until the product is finished (NOTE: Each stage of the production line is carefully checked to ensure that hygiene standards are met.)

product launch *noun* the act of putting a new product on the market

product name *noun* the name and explanation of what a food product is, a required element in food labelling in the UK

product recall *noun* an occasion on which a particular batch of a food product is recalled by the manufacturer because it has been found to pose a health risk, e.g. because of contamination with bacteria

product safety device *noun* a piece of machinery on a food production line that routinely checks for contamination of products and equipment

product specification *noun* in product design, an outline of what a product is intended to achieve, used later in the evaluation of its success

product storage *noun* methods of storing foods that are designed to maximise its keeping time, e.g. refrigeration

proenzyme *noun* a biologically inactive substance that is the precursor of an enzyme

profiterole *noun* a small ball of choux pastry filled with cream and usually served with chocolate sauce

progoitrin *noun* a proenzyme of goitrogens, found in plants

pro-hormone *noun* a substance that is the precursor of a hormone, used as a bodybuilding supplement as an attempt to boost the body's natural supply of that hormone

proof *noun* the relative strength of an alcoholic drink expressed by a number that is twice the percentage of the alcohol present in the liquid

propane-1, 2-diol alginate *noun* ♦ E405

propeller mixer *noun* a food mixer consisting of a rotating column with propeller blades attached

propionate *noun* a chemical compound that is a salt or ester of propionic acid

propionibacteria *plural noun* bacteria in starter cultures, used for Swiss cheese, that convert the lactic acid to carbon dioxide, causing holes to form

proprionic acid *noun* ♦ E280

propyl 4-hydroxybenzoate *noun* ♦ E216

propyl gallate *noun* an ester of gallic acid used as a powerful antioxidant

prosciutto *noun* Italian cured ham, usually served cold and uncooked in thin slices

prostaglandin *noun* any of a class of unsaturated fatty acids found in all mammals that control smooth muscle contraction, inflammation and body temperature, are associated with the sensation of pain and have an effect on the nervous system, blood pressure and in particular the uterus at menstruation

prostate cancer *noun* a malignant tumour of the prostate gland, found especially in men over 55

prosthetic group *noun* the non-protein part of a conjugated protein, e.g. the lipid group in a lipoprotein

protean *noun* a slightly denatured, insoluble protein

protease *noun* an enzyme that hydrolyses proteins. Also called **proteolytic enzyme**

protease inhibitor *noun* a compound that breaks down protease, inhibiting the replication of viruses and development of some cancers

protein *noun* a compound that is an essential part of living cells and is one of the elements in food that is necessary to keep the human body working properly

proteinase *noun* an enzyme that splits the peptide bonds of proteins

protein bodies *plural noun* roughly spherical structures consisting of protein encapsulated in a membrane, present in all seeds, including cereals. ◊ **gluten, glutenin, gliadin** (NOTE: They cannot be broken mechanically but water causes them to swell and break open, which is what happens in germination and in dough production.)

protein efficiency ratio *noun* a measure of protein quality, expressed as the amount of weight gained by an animal per gram of protein ingested. Abbreviation **PER**

protein energy malnutrition *noun* a severe lack of protein and calories in a person's diet, or their inability to absorb them from food, leading to wasting and general deterioration of health. Abbreviation **PEM**

protein intolerance *noun* an allergic reaction to a particular protein

protein powder *noun* a bodybuilding supplement of concentrated egg or milk proteins, made into a drink

protein quality *noun* a measure of how effective a particular protein is at nourishing the body

protein retention *noun* the percentage of dietary protein that is absorbed and used by the body

protein retention efficiency *noun* net protein retention shown on a percentage scale. Abbreviation **PRE**

protein score *noun* a measure of protein quality, expressed as its content of certain amino acids as compared to egg protein

protein shake *noun* a drink made with protein powder, used as a bodybuilding aid

proteolysis *noun* the breaking down of proteins in food by digestive enzymes

proteolytic enzyme *noun* same as **protease**

proteose *noun* a water-soluble compound formed during hydrolytic processes such as digestion

prove *verb* to leave dough to rest before baking so that the yeast can ferment

Provençale *adjective* used for describing a dish prepared with olive oil, garlic, herbs and tomatoes

provitamin *noun* a substance that can be metabolised into a vitamin

Provolone *noun* a semisoft Italian cheese originally made from water buffalo's milk and now from cow's milk, often smoked and used widely in cooking

prune *noun* a dried plum ■ *verb* to remove pieces of a plant, in order to keep it in shape, to promote growth in spring, or to reduce its size in autumn

PSE meat *noun* meat from stressed animals in which the pH decreases too fast after slaughter. Full form **pale, soft, exudative**

PSP *abbreviation* paralytic shellfish poisoning

psychrophilic *adjective* used for describing microorganisms that tolerate or prefer low temperatures

psyllium *noun* small seeds used as a laxative when mixed with water

pteroylglutamic acid *noun* same as **folic acid**

PTFE *noun* a non-stick coating used for cooking utensils, marketed under the tradename Teflon. Full form **polytetrafluoroethylene**

ptomaine *noun* a nitrogenous compound produced when protein is broken down by bacteria

ptomaine poisoning *noun* food poisoning caused by bacteria, but formerly believed to be caused by ptomaines

ptyalin *noun* an enzyme in saliva that cleanses the mouth and converts starch into sugar

ptyalism *noun* the excessive production of saliva

ptyalolithiasis *noun* same as **sialolithiasis**

puberty *noun* the physical and psychological changes that take place when childhood ends and adolescence and sexual maturity begin and the sex glands become active

public health *noun* the study of illness, health and disease in the community. ◊ **community medicine**

public health intervention *noun* action taken by authorities in response to a risk to public health

public health nutritionist *noun* a professional who works to educate others in the community about eating for health. Also called **community dietitian**

pudding *noun* **1.** same as **dessert 2.** any food made with flour and suet, cooked by boiling or steaming

pudding basin *noun* a bowl used for cooking steamed puddings

pudding mould *noun* a rounded bowl used for shaping puddings

pudding rice *noun* a type of short-grain rice that is chalky when raw and sticky when cooked

PUFA *abbreviation* polyunsaturated fatty acid

puff pastry *noun* a type of soft pastry made from flour and butter, in which air is trapped by repeated folding and rolling of the dough

pulp *noun* a soft mass that results when something with liquid in it is crushed ■ *verb* **1.** to crush something into pulp **2.** to remove the soft fleshy tissue from fruit or vegetables

pulse *noun* a general term for a certain type of seed that grows in pods, and which is often applied to an edible seed of a leguminous plant used for human or animal consumption, e.g. a lentil, bean or pea

pumping *noun* the transfer of food by mechanised means from one part of the production line to the next

pumpkin *noun* a large round orange-coloured vegetable

pumpkin seeds *plural noun* large flat green seeds from pumpkins and squashes eaten raw or cooked, in sweet or savoury dishes or as a snack food

punch *verb* to fold dough and beat it with your fist to expel air

punctured can *noun* a can with a hole in it that breaks the hermetic seal

purée *noun* **1.** a type of soup in which fresh vegetables and pulses are simmered in stock with flavouring then forced through a sieve or liquidised to give a smooth consistency **2.** a food that has been made into a thick moist paste by rubbing it through a sieve, mashing it or blending it

purgative *adjective, noun* same as **laxative**

purge *verb* to induce evacuation of the bowels

purine *noun* a chemical compound which is metabolised into uric acid, excessive quantities of which can cause gout

purslane *noun* a trailing wild plant sometimes used in salad or cooked and served as a vegetable (NOTE: There are several varieties, belonging to the genus *Portulaca*.)

putrefaction *noun* the decomposition of dead organic substances by bacteria

putrescine *noun* an amine produced in cheese while it is ripening, with an aroma like rotting meat

puy lentil *noun* a small dark blue-green lentil with a distinctive flavour

pyloric sphincter *noun* a ring of muscle that separates the stomach from the duodenum and relaxes to let food pass

pylorus *noun* an opening at the bottom of the stomach leading into the duodenum (NOTE: The plural is **pylori**.)

pyrazine *noun* a ring compound produced during Maillard browning that supplies a nutty flavour

Pyrex a trade name for borosilicate glass, used for making oven-safe cooking pots

pyridoxal *noun* ♦ vitamin B6

pyridoxamine *noun* ♦ vitamin B6

pyridoxine *noun* ♦ vitamin B6

pyrimidine *noun* **1.** a nitrogenous based compound with a six-sided ring structure that is the parent compound of several biologically important substances **2.** a biologically significant derivative of pyrimidine, especially the bases cytosine, thymine and uracil found in RNA and DNA

pyruvate *noun* a sports supplement that increases metabolism

pyruvic acid *noun* a chemical formed in living cells when carbohydrates and proteins are metabolised

Q

QA *abbreviation* quality assurance

QC *abbreviation* quality control

QDA *abbreviation* quantitative descriptive analysis

QMS *abbreviation* Quality Meat Scotland

quail *noun* any of various small to medium-sized birds, often eaten roasted or stuffed

quality assurance *noun* a set of criteria that are designed to check that people in an organisation maintain a high standard in the products or services they supply. Abbreviation **QA**

quality control *noun* the work of checking that the quality of a product is good. Abbreviation **QC**

Quality Meat Scotland *noun* the marketing board for red meat in Scotland. Abbreviation **QMS**

quantitative descriptive analysis *noun* a method of sensory testing in which a food product is rated and placed on a scale for different qualities alongside its competitors. Abbreviation **QDA**

quantitative ingredient declaration *noun* the requirement for the amount of a particular ingredient used in a foodstuff to be included on its labelling, in cases where this may be misleading or confusing, e.g. the actual amount of juice used in a 'juice drink'. Abbreviation **QUID**

queen scallop *noun* a small variety of scallop with an almost circular shell and a vivid red roe, found in deeper waters than the great scallop (NOTE: Two species exist: *Pecten opercularis* and *Chlamys opercularis*.)

queen substance *noun* same as **royal jelly**

quenelle *noun* 1. a small dumpling consisting of fish, meat or poultry meat bound with eggs or fat poached in a cooking liquor 2. any soft food substance which is formed into an oval shape, e.g. quenelles of mousse

quiche *noun* a savoury tart made of a pastry case filled with a mixture of eggs and milk, with other ingredients such as onion, bacon, vegetables or cheese added

quiche Lorraine *noun* a quiche with a filling of small pieces of bacon and sometimes cheese

quick-freeze *verb* to preserve food by cooling it quickly to 0°C or less

QUID *abbreviation* quantitative ingredient declaration

quiescent cooling, quiescent freezing *noun* slow cooling and freezing of a food mixture without stirring, leading to the formation of ice crystals

quince *noun* a hard yellow or orange fruit, shaped like an apple or pear and used for making jelly

quinoa *noun* a tiny golden seed from South America that is similar to rice but has a higher protein content

quinoline yellow *noun* ♦ E104

Quorn *noun* a trade name for a vegetable protein used in cooking as a meat substitute

R

rabbit *noun* a common wild animal with grey fur, long ears and a short white tail, used as food

rachitis *noun* same as **rickets**

rack of lamb *noun* best end of neck of lamb, a joint for roasting

raclette *noun* a Swiss dish consisting of slices of melted cheese served on boiled potatoes or bread

radappertisation *noun* the use of ionising radiation in food production to remove micro-organisms that cause spoilage

radiation *noun* electromagnetic waves given off by some substances, especially radioactive substances. ◊ **ionising radiation**

radicchio *noun* a variety of chicory with reddish-purple and white leaves, usually eaten raw in salads

radicidation *noun* the elimination of pathogens in food using ionising radiation

radioallergosorbent test *noun* an allergy test carried out by treating a person's blood sample with known allergens and monitoring rises in immunoglobulin E. Abbreviation **RAST**

radio frequency heating *noun* same as **microwave cooking**

radionuclide *noun* any element that gives out radiation

radish *noun* a small red root vegetable with a pungent flavour, eaten raw in salads

radurisation *noun* the process of reducing the level of spoilage organisms in perishable food using ionising radiation

ragout *noun* a rich slow-cooked stew of meat and vegetables

rainbow trout *noun* a freshwater trout with a silvery green back banded with pink (NOTE: Its scientific name is *Salmo gairdneri*.)

raise *verb* to lighten baked doughs and cake mixtures by adding raising agents or by fermenting with yeast prior to cooking

raised pie *noun* a pie made with a very stiff pastry that is self supporting, e.g. a pork pie

raisin *noun* a dried grape

raising agent *noun* any chemical mixture, e.g. bicarbonate of soda or baking powder, that releases carbon dioxide on heating and hence lightens the mixture it is in

Ramadan *noun* in the Islamic calendar, the ninth month of the year, during whch Muslims fast between dawn and dusk as a religious observance

ramekin *noun* a small dish for baking food in an oven, or food cooked in this type of dish

ramen *noun* a Japanese dish of thin white noodles served in a thin well-flavoured soup or stock

rancid *adjective* used for describing butter that tastes bad because it is stale

rancidity *noun* the state of being rancid

rapeseed oil *noun* oil from the seed of the rape plant, a yellow-flowering plant of the cabbage family, used as a cooking oil and for margarine manufacture

rare *adjective* used for describing steak that is very lightly cooked

rasp *verb* to grate or break bread up into raspings

raspberry *noun* a small red soft fruit shaped like a tiny cup (NOTE: The plant's botanical name is is *Rubus idaeus.*)

raspberry leaf *noun* a food supplement taken during pregnancy to prepare the smooth muscles of the uterus and ease morning sickness

raspings *plural noun* very fine breadcrumbs used for coating foods before cooking

RAST *abbreviation* radioallergosorbent test

rastrello *noun* a sharp-edged spoon used for removing the pulp from a halved citrus fruit

ratafia *noun* a sweet biscuit or drink flavoured with almonds

ratatouille *noun* a Mediterranean vegetable stew of onions, tomatoes, aubergines, peppers and courgettes cooked in olive oil

ration *noun* an amount of food given to an animal or person ■ *verb* to allow someone only a certain amount of food

ravioli *noun* a dish made from small squares of pasta sealed around a meat, cheese or vegetable filling

raw *adjective* in its original uncooked state

raw food diet *noun* a diet in which only raw, unprocessed foods may be consumed

raw material *noun* a substance that is used to manufacture something, e.g. the eggs and flour that might be used to produce cakes (NOTE: The raw materials that are used in commercial food production are subject to strict hygiene and quality controls, to ensure that they do not cause any contamination in the finished product.)

raw milk *noun* milk that has not been pasteurised

raw sugar *noun* unrefined sugar imported for treatment

RDA *abbreviation* recommended daily amount

RDI *abbreviation* recommended daily intake

reactive arthritis *noun* arthritis caused by a reaction to something such as a virus

ready-cooked meal *noun* same as **ready meal**

ready-made food *noun* food that has been processed so that it requires no extra preparation at home

ready meal *noun* any convenience food that consists of an entire precooked meal, designed to be quickly reheated. Also called **ready-cooked meal**

ready-to-eat *adjective* used for describing any convenience food that does not require reheating. Abbreviation **RTE**

reamer *noun* same as **lemon squeezer**

réchaud *noun* a small heater, usually with a spirit lamp under it, used for keeping food hot on the table or for cooking dishes rapidly next to the guest's table

rechauffé *noun* leftover food that is reheated

recipe *noun* written details of how to cook a dish

recipe development *noun* the act of creating and publicly disseminating a new recipe to promote the use of a particular food product

recipe engineering *noun* the design, development and testing of a commercial recipe

recommended daily intake *noun* the amounts of vitamins, minerals and other nutrients that the government recommends people take in their food or otherwise every day to avoid ill health. Abbreviation **RDI**

recommended retail price *noun* the price at which a manufacturer recommends their product should be sold on the retail market, although this may be reduced by the retailer. Abbreviation **RRP**

reconstitute *verb* to add water or other liquid to dried foods so as to restore them to some semblance of their original state

recontamination *noun* contamination of a foodstuff after it has been effectively sterilised, caused by poor storage

recovery *noun* the process of returning to health after being ill or injured

recovery time *noun* the time it takes for a cooking appliance to return to the required temperature for another batch of food after a batch of cooked food has been removed from it

rectal feeding *noun* same as **nutrient enemata**

rectoscopy *noun* an internal examination of the lower colon and rectum

rectum *noun* the end part of the large intestine leading from the sigmoid colon to the anus

red 2G *noun* ♦ E128

red blood cell *noun* any red-coloured cell in blood that contains haemoglobin and carries oxygen to the tissues

red cabbage *noun* a variety of cabbage with red to purple leaves and a round firm head, generally available in autumn and winter, often casseroled with sugar, sultanas and vinegar, or pickled (NOTE: Its botanical name is *Brassica oleracea*, variety *capitata*.)

redcurrant *noun* a red soft fruit growing in small clusters, mainly used to make jam and jelly, or used as decoration on cold dishes such as pâté

red grouse *noun* the finest flavoured of the grouse family, found only in the UK and Ireland (NOTE: Its scientific name is *Lagopus lagopus scoticus*.)

red meat *noun* meat that is relatively dark red in colour when raw, e.g. beef or lamb

red mullet *noun* a small red sea-fish, used in Mediterranean cooking

red snapper *noun* a large reddish-coloured fish. ◊ **snapper**

reduce *verb* to boil sauce so as to make it smaller in quantity and more concentrated

reduced-fat *adjective* containing less than 25% of the fat normally found in the product

reductase *noun* an enzyme that catalyses the chemical reduction of an organic compound

reduction *noun* a chemical reaction in a molecule in which it takes on electrons from another molecule

reduction milling *noun* the stage in the conversion of grain to flour in which the endosperm is ground from semolina size particles to flour after the preceding bran separation

reduction sauce *noun* any sauce based on vinegar, wine or stock concentrated by boiling to give an intense flavour and sometimes a pouring consistency

red wine *noun* wine that becomes red because the grape skins are left for a time in the fermenting mixture

reference nutrient intake *noun* ◆ **dietary reference value**

reference protein *noun* a standard or test protein against which the quality of others is measured, commonly egg protein

refine *verb* to process something to remove impurities

refined sugar *noun* sugar that has been processed to remove all but the simple carbohydrate content

refinery *noun* a processing facility where impurities are removed from raw materials such as oil or sugar

reflux *noun* a situation in which a fluid flows in the opposite direction to its usual flow

reformed meat *noun* meat that has not been cut from a joint but is made from compressed meat fibres pressed into shape

refractive index *noun* a measure of how light is refracted when passing through a medium, used for measuring the purity of substances such as oil or sugar

refractory rickets *noun* rickets that responds only to very large doses of vitamin D, owing to a deficiency in its reception or metabolisation

refresh *verb* **1.** to immerse blanched vegetables in fast running cold water so as to cool them quickly and prevent further cooking **2.** to make slightly wilted herbs, leaves and vegetables crisp again by immersing them in cold water

refried beans *plural noun* in Mexican and TexMex cuisine, beans cooked with spices, mashed, then fried

refrigerate *verb* to keep food cold so that it will not go bad

refrigerator *noun* a large appliance in which food is kept cold

regeneration *noun* the task of preparing food from frozen, e.g. by putting it in a microwave

regimen *noun* a fixed course of treatment, e.g. a course of drugs or a special diet

regional enteritis *noun* same as **Crohn's disease**

regional food *noun* same as **local food**

Registered Nutritionist *noun* a nutritionist on the Nutrition Society's register. Abbreviation **RNutr**

Regulation (EC) 178/2002 *noun* a legal rule establishing the European Food Safety Authority, and also setting out basic principles and procedures for food safety

Regulation (EC) 258/97 *noun* a legal rule relating to modern food materials

Regulation (EC) 1829/2003 *noun* a legal rule that standardises national laws on the labelling and marketing of GM food products

Regulation (EC) 1830/2003 *noun* a legal rule that sets out requirements for the satisfactory traceability of GM organisms in food

Regulation (EEC) 2081/92 *noun* a legal rule that protects the naming rights of food and drink products originating from a specified geographical area, e.g. Champagne

Regulation (EC) No 1760/2000 *noun* a legal rule providing for the marking of cattle with details of their farm of origin, as a disease control measure

Regulation (EC) No 1935/2004 *noun* a legal rule that specifies the types of substances that may be used in food preparation equipment to prevent contamination of food

regulatory body *noun* an independent organisation, usually established by a government, that makes rules and sets standards for an industry and oversees the activities of companies within it

regulatory system *noun* a system of laws, procedures and supervisory bodies governing the production and sale of something

reheat *verb* to heat food again

rehydrate *verb* to restore body fluids to a healthy level, or to cause this to occur

rehydration salts *plural noun* minerals mixed with water to make a rehydration solution

rehydration solution *noun* a drink that contains substances such as minerals and electrolytes, used for treatment when a person is dehydrated, e.g. because of illness or strenuous exercise

reinforcement feature *noun* a measure such as beading that protects a food tin against deformation during cooking and handling

reject *verb* to vomit food or drink

relative density *noun* same as **specific gravity**

relative protein value *noun* a measure of protein quality, expressed as its ability to support nitrogen balance in the body. Abbreviation **RPV**

release agent *noun* a substance such as silicone that prevents food products from sticking to packaging

releasing oil *noun* an oil used to grease bakeware to prevent the food sticking during cooking

relief cook *noun* a cook who takes the place of a cook who is absent

religious food law *noun* a requirement to avoid certain foods, to avoid combining certain foods, or to prepare certain foods or slaughter certain animals in particular ways, many of which exist in the major religions (NOTE: For example, Buddhists are usually vegetarian; Hindus have complex food laws depending on caste, but generally avoid beef; Jews avoid meat from pigs and horses, eat only seafood with fins and scales, avoid mixing dairy products and meat, and eat meat from animals slaughtered and prepared by licensed persons; Muslims avoid pork and alcohol, eat meat slaughtered in a special way, and avoid gold and silver plate on cooking and serving implements; and Jainists are strict vegetarians who avoid eggs but allow themselves other dairy products.)

relish *noun* a sharp or spicy sauce made with vegetables or fruit which adds extra flavour when eaten with other food

rémoulade *noun* mayonnaise with herbs, mustard, capers and gherkins added, and sometimes chopped hard-boiled egg

renal calculus *noun* same as **kidney stone**

renal colic *noun* strong pain experienced when passing kidney stones

renal failure *noun* a medical condition in which the kidneys stop working efficiently, resulting in infections and the formation of kidney stones

renal threshold *noun* the concentration of a particular nutrient in the blood at which the kidney begins to excrete any excess

render *verb* to melt something in order to purify or extract substances from it, especially to heat solid fat slowly until as much liquid fat as possible has been extracted from it

renin *noun* an enzyme secreted by the kidney to prevent loss of sodium, and which also affects blood pressure

rennet *noun* a substance made from the lining of calves' stomachs that is used in cheese making

rennin *noun* same as **chymosin**

research dietitian, research nutritionist *noun* a professional who is sponsored to undertake a specific area of nutritional research for a company or institution

resistant starch *noun* starch that is not broken down in the digestive tract and counts as a component of dietary fibre

resource management *noun* a system of controlling the use of resources in such a way as to avoid waste and to use them in the most effective way

respiratory paralysis *noun* an inability to breathe sometimes caused by severe food toxins such as botulinum

respiratory tract *noun* the parts of the body that are responsible for breathing, including the lungs, trachea, mouth and nose

rest *verb* **1.** to leave pastry or dough for a while after it has been kneaded to allow the gluten in the flour to relax **2.** to leave a piece of meat for a while after cooking to allow some of the juices to be reabsorbed into the fibre of the meat, making the meat more tender

resting energy expenditure *noun* the number of calories needed to maintain the body's normal function while at rest

restoration *noun* the addition of nutrients to a food stuff to replace those lost in processing

resveratrol *noun* an antioxidant present in many plants and plant products, especially in red grape skins

retail multiple *noun* a retail company with two or more outlets

retention of moisture *noun* the degree to which a substance keeps its water content without evaporation

retentiveness *noun* the degree to which a substance can retain something such as water or nutritional content on time

reticulin *noun* a fibrous protein that is one of the most important components of reticular fibres

retinoic *adjective* relating to retinol

retinoic acid *noun* same as **tretinoin**

retinol *noun* a vitamin found in liver, vegetables, eggs and cod liver oil that is essential for good vision

retort *noun* same as **autoclave**

retort pouch *noun* a flexible sealed pouch or package in which food can be stored for long periods without spoiling

retrogradation *noun* the change over time in the composition of starch, caused by the action of amylopectin and amylose, which contributes to food spoilage

retrograde *adjective* returning to an earlier worse or less developed state

RF heating *abbreviation* radio frequency heating

rheology *noun* the study of how materials flow, used in scientifically analysing the texture and behaviour of non-solid foods

rheumatoid arthritis *noun* a general painful disabling collagen disease affecting any joint, but especially the hands, feet and hips, making them swollen and inflamed. ◊ **osteoarthritis**

Rhodotorula *noun* a family of yeasts that cause discoloration in foods

rhodoxanthin *noun* ♦ E161(f)

rhubarb *noun* a plant with long red leaf stalks that are cooked and eaten as dessert

rib *noun* **1.** any of a set of bones that form a protective cage across the chest **2.** a piece of meat with the rib bone attached to it. Also called **chop**

ribbon blender *noun* a piece of machinery in a food processing plant that mixes powders, pastes and liquids

ribbon stage *noun* the stage at which whipped eggs or cream become just stiff enough to form ribbons when dropped from a spoon

riboflavin *noun* vitamin B2, the yellow component of the B complex group, an important coenzyme in many biochemical processes, found in foods such as spinach, eggs, milk and liver

ribonucleic acid *noun* full form of **RNA**

ribose *noun* a type of sugar found in RNA

rice *noun* a cereal grass that produces edible grains, or these grains used as food

Rice Association *noun* an organisation that promotes the interests of those working in the rice production, import, packaging and marketing industries

rice ball *noun* a metal utensil for steaming rice, in which the rice is placed and suspended over a pan of boiling water

rice cooker *noun* a special electric pan for boiling rice

rice flour *noun* ground polished rice that is mainly starch with very little gluten, used in the same way as corn flour and for noodles, sweets and short pastry

rice noodles *plural noun* noodles made with rice flour in very long strands and of varying thicknesses and widths, very common in Vietnam

rice paper *noun* very thin paper that you can eat, used in cooking

ricer *noun* a kitchen utensil consisting of a perforated plate in one end of an open cylinder through which foods can be pressed to form long strings

rice vinegar *noun* vinegar made by oxidising beer or wine made from fermented rice starch, uses in Asia

rice wine *noun* an alcoholic liquid with a sherry-like taste, made by fermenting a cooked ground rice mash and used both as a drink and as a cooking liquid. ◊ **sake**

rich *adjective* used for describing food that has a high calorific value

ricin *noun* a highly toxic albumin found in the seeds of the castor oil plant

ricing *noun* the process of pressing food into long thin pieces

rickets *noun* a disease of children in which the bones are soft and do not develop properly, owing to a lack of Vitamin D. Also called **rachitis**

ricotta *noun* a soft white mild-tasting Italian cheese made from whey and used mostly in cooking

rigatoni *plural noun* short rounded tubes of pasta with narrow ridges running along them

rigor mortis *noun* the stiffening of the muscles of recently dead animals due to production of lactic acid, which can be reversed by conditioning the meat

rillettes *plural noun* seasoned pork or goose cooked in its own fat until very tender and potted as a type of soft spreadable pâté

rind *noun* the skin on fruit or meat or cheese

ring mould *noun* a round mould used for cakes, desserts and jellies

ring-pull *noun* a ring or tab of metal on the top of a drinks can that is pulled in order to open it

ripe *adjective* **1.** mature and ready to be picked and eaten **2.** matured or aged enough to have developed the best flavour

ripen *verb* to become ready for eating, or to make something, especially a fruit, ready for eating

ripple ribbon tube *noun* a nozzle for a piping bag that produces a ribbed ribbon shape

rise *verb* (*of a yeast dough*) to increase in size by the production of bubbles of carbon dioxide within it. ◊ **prove, lift**

risk assessment *noun* a process used for determining the risk from a substance, technology or activity

risotto *noun* an Italian dish of cooked rice with meat, fish, or vegetables in it

rissole *noun* a fried ball of minced meat, fish, etc.

rissolé *adjective* used for describing cooked food that is well-browned

RNA *noun* a nucleic acid chain that takes coded information from DNA and translates it into specific proteins. Full form **ribonucleic acid**

RNI *abbreviation* reference nutrient intake

RNutr *abbreviation* Registered Nutritionist

roast *noun* **1.** a joint of meat that will be cooked in an oven **2.** a dish of meat that has been cooked in an oven ■ *verb* to cook food over a fire or in an open pan in an oven ■ *adjective* cooked over a fire or in an oven

roast chef *noun* the chef in charge of roast meats. Also called **chef rôtisseur**

roaster *noun* **1.** a pan, dish or oven for roasting food in **2.** an item of food, especially a chicken, that is suitable for roasting

roasting pan *noun* a large rectangular metal pan about 8 cm deep

roasting tin *noun* a large low-sided metal dish in which meat is roasted in the oven

roast joint *noun* a joint of meat such as lamb or beef that has been roasted

roast potatoes *plural noun* parboiled potatoes roasted in the oven in a tray containing hot fat that is used to baste the potatoes until the surface is crisp and brown

rocket *noun* a green salad plant with a peppery flavour

rock salt *noun* edible salt obtained from rock deposits, as distinct from sea salt

roe *noun* a solid mass of fish eggs used as a cooking ingredient or eaten raw

roll *noun* a tube of something that has been turned over and over on itself ■ *verb* to turn something over and over

rolled joint *noun* a joint of meat made from a flat piece of meat turned over and over to make a roll and then tied with string

rolled oats *plural noun* ♦ **porridge oats**

roller drying *noun* the act of drying food by passing it over pre-heated rollers, which then transfer it to storage

roller mill *noun* a piece of equipment used in the preparation of flour and animal feed, with two smooth steel rollers which crush the grain

roller milled flour *noun* flour produced from cereal grains by passing the larger pieces or whole grains though rollers that are set close together and rotate at slightly different speeds so as to shear the grain

rolling pin *noun* a cylinder, sometimes with small handles at either end, used for rolling out and flattening dough, pastry, or other uncooked food

rollmop *noun* a fillet of raw herring wrapped around a slice of onion or a pickle and left to marinate in spiced vinegar, usually served as an hors d'oeuvre

roll out *verb* to make a ball of pastry or dough flat using a rolling pin

romaine *noun* same as **cos**

rooibos tea *noun* tea made from the leaves of a southern African plant called the rooibos, drunk for its healthful properties

room temperature *noun* the temperature in an ordinary room, usually around 20°C, at which most red wines should be served

root *noun* an underground plant part that is used as a vegetable, e.g. a carrot or turnip ■ *verb* to produce roots

root ginger *noun* the solid root form of ginger, either fresh or dried

root vegetable *noun* a vegetable such as a carrot, turnip or beet that is grown for its fleshy edible underground parts

rope *noun* a type of bacteria that infects bread and milk, giving them a ropy consistency

ropiness *noun* a defect of wine in which it tastes greasy, caused by lactic acid bacteria

Roquefort *noun* a moist, strongly flavoured, blue-veined cheese made from ewes' milk and matured in caves

rosé *noun* a pink-coloured wine, especially one made by fermenting red grapes and removing the skins from the juice before all the colour has been extracted

rose hip *noun* the small orange to dark red fruit of some species of rose, usually used to make syrups and jams and valued for its high vitamin C content

rosemary *noun* a pungent herb with spiky green leaves, used in cooking

rose water *noun* diluted essence of rose petals used as a flavouring in confectionery and desserts especially in Middle Eastern, Indian and Southeast Asian cooking

rösti *noun* a Swiss fried potato cake made from thinly sliced or grated potatoes, sometimes with added onions and bacon

rotary beater *noun* a hand-held and hand-operated mechanical whisk or beater consisting of two counter rotating intermeshed metal loops

rotary moulding *noun* a piece of machinery, used in bakery production lines, that cuts and shapes dough into biscuits or rolls and transports them to an oven

roti *noun* an unleavened bread made from wheat flour and cooked on a griddle, originally from northern South Asia but also eaten in the Caribbean

rotisserie *noun* 1. a cooking appliance for roasting meat using a rotating spit 2. a shop or restaurant where meat is roasted and sold

roughage *noun* same as **dietary fibre**

rough puff pastry *noun* puff pastry with a heavy texture achieved by mixing solid cubes of fat with the flour

rough rice *noun* same as **paddy**

rouille *noun* a sauce made from chillies, garlic, and olive oil served as an accompaniment to Provençal foods such as bouillabaisse

roulade *noun* a dish in which a piece of food is coated with a sauce or filling and rolled up before being cooked, so that each slice has a spiral appearance

roundworm *noun* any of several common types of parasitic worms with round bodies, e.g. hookworms. Compare **flatworm**

roux *noun* a mixture of fat and flour cooked to make a base for a sauce

royal jelly *noun* a protein-rich substance that worker bees secrete and feed to larvae in the early stages of their development and to the larvae of queen bees in all stages of their development. Also called **queen substance**

RPV *abbreviation* relative protein value

RRP *abbreviation* recommended retail price

RTE *abbreviation* ready-to-eat

rubber spatula *noun* a spatula with a flexible head used for mixing and folding batters and doughs

rubbery *adjective* having the elastic or tough texture of rubber, usually unpleasantly so

rub in *verb* to combine hard fat with flour and other dry ingredients using the tips of the fingers or a food processor so as to produce a dry mixture resembling breadcrumbs

rubixanthin *noun* ♦ E161(d)

ruminant *noun* an animal that has a stomach with several chambers, e.g. a cow

rumination *noun* an eating disorder in which food is regurgitated and re-swallowed

rump *noun* a cut of beef that is tender and contains some fat, taken from the animal's hindquarters

runny *adjective* in a form that flows easily, perhaps too easily

runs *noun* diarrhoea (*informal*)

rutin *noun* one of the bioflavonoids found in high concentration in buckwheat

rye *noun* **1.** a hardy cereal crop grown in temperate areas **2.** same as **rye bread**

rye bread *noun* bread made from rye, usually very dark in colour

S

sabayon *noun* a mixture of egg yolk and a little water whisked to the ribbon stage over gentle heat

sac *noun* any part of the body shaped like a bag

saccharase *noun* same as **invertase**

saccharin *noun* a substance used as a substitute for sugar

saccharo- *prefix* sugar

saccharometer *noun* a hydrometer used for measuring the percentage of sugar in a sugar and water solution

SACN *abbreviation* Scientific Advisory Committee on Nutrition

saddle *noun* a very large cut of meat that is the unseparated loin from both sides of the animal

safflower *noun* an oilseed crop grown mainly in India, the oil from which is used in the manufacture of margarine (NOTE: The plant's botanical name is *Carthamus tinctorius*.)

saffron *noun* an orange-coloured powder made from crocus flowers, from which colouring and flavouring are obtained

sage *noun* an aromatic plant with silvery-green leaves used as a herb in cookery (NOTE: Its botanical name is *Salvia officinalis*.)

sago *noun* a white powder made from the sago palm, used as food and as a thickening agent

St Anthony's fire *noun* same as **ergotism**

St John's Wort *noun* an extract from the yellow-flowering St John's wort, used as a herbal remedy for mild depression, anxiety, insomnia and seasonal affective disorder

sake *noun* a Japanese alcoholic beverage made from fermented rice, traditionally served warm

salad *noun* a cold dish of various raw or cooked vegetables, often served with cold meat, fish or cheese

salad cream *noun* a commercially-prepared sauce made of eggs, oil and vinegar, used on salad and usually available in bottles or sachets

salad dressing *noun* a liquid sauce put on lettuce and other cold raw or cooked vegetables to give them additional flavour

salade niçoise *noun* a French salad made with lettuce, hard-boiled eggs, cold boiled potatoes, anchovy fillets, black olives and tomatoes, with garlic in the dressing

salamander *noun* a cooking utensil heated in a fire then used to heat or brown food

salami *noun* a dry spicy pork sausage, originally from Italy

salicylic acid *noun* a white antiseptic substance that destroys bacteria and fungi and is used as a food preservative

salifiable *adjective* used for describing a chemical base that is capable of forming a salt when combined with an acid

salination, salinisation *noun* a process by which the salt concentration of soil or water increases, especially as a result of irrigation in hot climates

saline laxative *noun* a substance that draws water into the contents of the bowel through the intestinal wall, moistening it

salinity *noun* the concentration of salt in an amount of water or soil

salinometer *noun* an instrument that measures the salinity of a solution

saliva *noun* a fluid in the mouth, secreted by the salivary glands, that starts the process of digesting food

salivant *noun* a substance that promotes or increases the production of saliva

salivate *verb* to produce saliva, especially in response to a stimulant such as an aroma

salmon *noun* any of various large fish that are typically born in fresh water, migrate to the sea, and return to fresh water to breed (NOTE: They belong to the family *Salmonidae*.)

salmonella *noun* a rod-shaped bacterium found in the intestine that can cause food poisoning, gastroenteritis and typhoid fever

salmonellosis *noun* food poisoning caused by salmonella in the digestive system

salmon trout *noun* a large sea trout with pink flesh like that of a salmon

salsa *noun* a pungent sauce made of tomatoes, onions and chillies

salsify *noun* a plant with a long, white root and green leaves, all of which are eaten as vegetables

salt *noun* **1.** a substance consisting of small white tangy-tasting crystals, consisting mainly of sodium chloride, used for flavouring and preserving food **2.** any crystalline compound formed from the neutralisation of an acid by a base containing a metal ∎ *adjective* **1.** containing common salt **2.** cured or preserved or seasoned with salt ∎ *verb* **1.** to add salt to food **2.** to preserve food by keeping it in salt or in salt water

salt beef *noun* beef that has been preserved in brine, then cooked and usually served cold in thin slices, in rye bread sandwiches

salt cellar *noun* a small pot containing salt usually with a hole in the top so that it can be sprinkled on food

salt cod *noun* filleted cod layered in coarse salt and allowed to dry out, used throughout southern Europe and the Caribbean as a cheap source of fish protein

salted butter *noun* butter with a small amount of salt added, for use as a spread

salt-free *adjective* containing no salt

saltimbocca *noun* a dish consisting of thin slices of veal rolled up with prosciutto ham and fresh sage leaves, lightly fried and braised in white wine

salting *noun* a way of preserving meat or fish by covering them with salt

saltpetre *noun* potassium nitrate, when used commercially

salt shaker *noun* same as **salt cellar**

salty *adjective* containing or tasting strongly of salt

samosa *noun* an Indian dish consisting of a small triangular pastry containing spiced meat or vegetables, usually deep-fried and served as a starter or snack

samphire *noun* an annual plant of salt marshes with fleshy stems that are cooked like asparagus and succulent young leaves and shoots that can be used in salads (NOTE: Its botanical name is *Salicornia europaea.*)

sandwich *noun* **1.** a dish of two slices of bread with a filling between them, eaten as a light meal or snack **2.** a type of cake formed of two pieces of sponge cake, one on top of the other, with a cream or jam filling in between

sandwich tray *noun* a large serving tray with a selection of small sandwiches, part of a buffet selection

sanitation *noun* the practice of maintaining public hygiene by the effective removal and processing of human waste

sanitiser *noun* same as **hand sanitiser**

sap *noun* a liquid inside plants that carries nutrients around it

SAPP *noun* sodium acid pyrophosphate, used for preventing blackening in potatoes

saprophyte *noun* an organism that feeds on decaying plant materials and may infect humans if ingested in raw fruit or vegetables

sardine *noun* a small oily fish of the herring family, often sold tinned

sarsparilla *noun* a flavouring made from the dried roots of a tropical climbing plant, used mainly for soft drinks (NOTE: The plant's botanical name is *Smilax officinalis.*)

sashimi *noun* a Japanese dish consisting of slices of raw fish, usually served with a dipping sauce, e.g. a seasoned soy sauce

sassafras *noun* a flavouring used in root beer

satay *noun* an appetiser served in South-East Asian cooking, made of marinated meat cooked on a little skewer, and served with peanut sauce

satiating *adjective* used for describing food that is satisfyingly filling

satiety *noun* the state of having eaten enough

satsuma *noun* a type of small sweet orange that peels easily

saturated fat *noun* a type of fat that is typical of animal-derived fats, is not essential in the diet and is thought to increase blood cholesterol. Compare **unsaturated fat, polyunsaturated fat**

saturated solution *noun* a solution containing the maximum amount of solid that can be dissolved in a liquid solvent and still remain in solution at a particular temperature

sauce *noun* liquid with a particular taste poured over food to give it an extra flavour

sauce boat *noun* an oval shallow wide-mouthed jug on an oval plate, used for serving sauces

sauce chef *noun* the chef in charge of preparing sauces. Also called **chef saucier**

saucepan *noun* a deep metal cooking pot with a long handle

sauce tartare *noun* same as **tartare sauce**

saucisson *noun* a dry spicy pork sausage from France

sauerkraut *noun* a German dish of pickled cabbage, often served with sausages

sausage *noun* a tube of edible skin filled with minced and seasoned pork or other meat

sausage maker *noun* a long hollow cylinder that fits over the outlet of a mincing machine, over which a sausage casing is placed to be filled with the mixture extruded from the machine

sausagemeat *noun* a mixture of meat, bread and flavourings for making sausages, sold separately, and used in pies and sausage rolls

sauté *adjective* fried quickly in a little fat ■ *verb* to fry in a little fat

sauté pan *noun* a cooking pan with a wide flat bottom, straight sides, a lid and a long handle

savarin *noun* a rich yeast mixture similar to a baba, baked in a ring mould, sometimes soaked in spirit or liqueur-flavoured sugar syrup and filled or decorated

savory *noun* any of various herbs of the genus *Satureja*, used traditionally for flavouring beans

savoury *adjective* with a salty flavour or another flavour that is not sweet ■ *noun* a snack, served at the end of a large meal, that is salty or made of cheese

Savoy cabbage *noun* a winter cabbage with crinkled leaves

saxitoxin *noun* a naturally-occurring toxin in marine algae that can cause paralysis and failure of the respiratory system

scald *noun* an injury to the skin caused by touching a very hot liquid or steam ■ *verb* to plunge a fruit or vegetable into boiling water for a short time in order to loosen the skin or to prepare it for freezing

scalded mouth syndrome *noun* same as **burning mouth syndrome**

scale *noun* any of the small flat bony or horny overlapping plates that cover the bodies of fish ■ *verb* to remove the scales from fish

scales *noun* a machine for weighing

scallion *noun* same as **spring onion**

scallop *noun* a type of shellfish with a semi-circular ridged shell

scalloped potatoes *plural noun* potatoes that are sliced and cooked in a shallow dish in the oven

scampi *noun* large prawns usually served fried in batter (NOTE: The plural form is **scampi**.)

Scarsdale diet *noun* a dietary plan that drastically reduces calorie intake for a period of between 7 and 14 days

SCDP *abbreviation* Scottish Community Diet Project

Schilling test *noun* a test for vitamin B12 deficiency

schnitzel *noun* a thin flat piece of veal or pork dipped in egg and breadcrumbs and fried. ◊ **Wiener schnitzel**

School Food Trust *noun* a national project set up in 2005 in the UK, funded by the Department of Education and Skills, whihc aims to improve nutritional education in schools

school meal *noun* a meal, typically lunch, that is processed on school premises and given to schoolchildren

Scientific Advisory Committee on Nutrition *noun* an advisory committee of independent experts that provides advice to the Food Standards Agency and Department of Health as well as other Government Agencies and Departments, with a remit including the nutrient content of individual foods and advice on diet. Abbreviation **SACN**

scombroid poisoning *noun* a type of food poisoning caused by eating seafood that has not been stored properly (NOTE: Unlike many types of food poisoning, this form is not produced by an organism or virus.)

scone *noun* a type of small crusty bread, sometimes with dried fruit in it, eaten with butter and jam or with cream

scoop *noun* a type of spoon with a hemispherical bowl, used for serving ice cream and for dispensing powders

score *verb* to make notches, cuts or lines in the surface of a food, e.g. so that herbs or seasoning can be pressed into the food

scoreline *noun* a fine embossed line on a can along which the metal tears when opened with a ring-pull or key

Scotch broth *noun* a thick soup with barley, vegetables and lamb

Scotch egg *noun* a hard-boiled egg, covered in sausage meat and fried and usually eaten cold

Scottish Community Diet Project *noun* an initiative to improve health and nutritional education in Scottish communities, funded by the Scottish Executive. Abbreviation **SCDP**

Scottish Executive Environment and Rural Affairs Department *noun* the department of the Scottish Executive that deals with farming, the environment, animal welfare and rural development in Scotland. Abbreviation **SEERAD**

Scottish Food and Drink Federation *noun* an organisation that represents the interests of the Scottish food and drink industries. Abbreviation **SFDF**

Scoville heat unit *noun* the unit of measurement used in the Scoville scale. Abbreviation **SHU**

Scoville Organoleptic Test *noun* a way of measuring the hotness of a spice or chilli pepper, describing at what solution in sugar water it is detectable to a panel of testers

Scoville scale *noun* a scale of hotness used for measuring spices, ranging from 0 up to 900,000 for the hottest edible peppers

scrag, scrag end *noun* same as **neck end**

scramble *verb* to stir beaten eggs continuously over heat, scraping solid egg off the base of the pan until all is set to the required consistency

scrambled eggs *plural noun* eggs mixed together and stirred as they are cooked in butter

scrape *verb* to remove only the outermost layer of the skin of a vegetable or fruit by scraping it with a knife

scraped surface heat exchange *noun* a piece of machinery for rapidly warming and cooling food without affecting its texture. Abbreviation **SSHE**

scraper *noun* same as **peeler**

scratchings *plural noun* small pieces of fried pork rind and fat that are eaten as a snack

screw cap *noun* a lid or cap that screws onto a container

scurvy *noun* a disease caused by lack of vitamin C

scutellum *noun* **1.** a hard plate or scale, e.g. on the thorax of an insect or a toe of a bird **2.** the shield-shaped embryonic leaf of a grass seed

scybala *noun* a hardened mass of faeces in the bowel caused by long-term constipation

sea bass *noun* a bony sea fish that has a long body, large mouth, and spiny dorsal fin and is a popular game fish (NOTE: Its scientific name is *Centropristis striata*.)

sea bream *noun* any of various blunt-nosed medium-sized oily seawater fish of the *Pagellus* and *Spondyliosoma* families, with deep, red to pink bodies and pink or white flesh. ◊ **bream**

seafood *noun* fish and shellfish that can be eaten (NOTE: There is no plural form.)

sealing compound *noun* a substance used for hermetically sealing a can end

seam defect *noun* an improper seal where a can is moulded together, causing the contents to leak or become adulterated

sear *verb* to cook meat or fish in a pan at a very high temperature for a short time, before grilling or roasting

sea salt *noun* crystals of sodium chloride extracted from sea water, as distinct from rock salt

season *noun* 1. one of the four parts into which a year is divided, namely spring, summer, autumn or winter 2. a period of time when a particular food is available or a particular game bird may be legally shot ■ *verb* to add flavouring to a dish

seasonal *adjective* available to eat at the present time of year

seasonality *noun* the fact of being available only at certain times of the year, not all year round

seasoning *noun* salt, pepper, herbs or spices used to give flavour to food

sea water fish *noun* any fish that lives in the sea, e.g. halibut, haddock and cod

seaweed *noun* any of various species of large marine algae, some of which are edible (NOTE: There is no plural form.)

seaweed gelatine *noun* same as **agar-agar**

secondary processing *noun* the part of a food processing plant that receives processed materials from primary processing and makes them into a finished food product ready for retail

secondary protein energy malnutrition *noun* malnutrition caused by the body's inability to absorb protein and energy from dietary sources, caused by serious illness such as cancer

second chef *noun* a deputy for a chef, who replaces the chef when he or she is away

secretagogue *noun* an agent that stimulates the pituitary gland to release more growth hormone, used by athletes

secretin *noun* a hormone secreted by the duodenum that encourages the production of pancreatic juice

section *verb* to divide an animal into cuts of meat during butchering

sediment *noun* unwanted solid particles that settle at the bottom of liquids

seed *noun* part of a plant that germinates and grows to produce a new plant ■ *verb* 1. to produce new plants by dropping seed that germinates and grows into plants in following seasons 2. to sow seeds in an area

SEERAD *abbreviation* Scottish Executive Environment and Rural Affairs Department

seethe *verb* to simmer something

segmentation *noun* the state of being divided into separate parts

segregation *noun* the act of keeping raw materials or ingredients away from each other, in order to avoid contamination

seitan *noun* wheat gluten obtained by washing the starch out of flour dough, marinated in soy sauce with various flavourings and used in vegetarian meals as a protein source and flavouring agent

selenium *noun* a non-metallic trace element (NOTE: The chemical symbol is **Se**.)

self-basting *adjective* used for describing a meat joint or a bird that is commercially prepared with added fat to prevent drying out when it is cooked in an oven

self-heating can *noun* a can containing two separated chemicals in its outer layer that produce heat when the barrier between them is removed, warming the food inside

self-raising flour *noun* a type of flour with baking powder added to it

self-service *noun* a type of service of food where the customers go to a counter where food is laid out and usually help themselves, especially to cold items

sell-by date *noun* a date stamped on the label of a food product that is the last date on which the product should be sold to guarantee good quality. Compare **best-before date, use-by date**

seltzer *noun* water that has been carbonated by adding sodium bicarbonate

semi-hard *adjective* used for describing cheese that has a consistency firm enough to slice but that is moist and pliable

semi-skimmed *adjective* used for describing milk from which some of the fat has been removed

semi-soft *adjective* used for describing a food that holds its shape but is easily cut with a knife

semi-sweet *adjective* lightly sweetened

semi-vegetarian *noun* a person who does not eat all meats, but will eat particular types, typically fish or poultry

semolina *noun* hard grains of wheat left when flour is sifted, used in puddings, and stews

senescence *noun* the ageing process. ◊ **plant senescence**

senna *noun* a herb that has a laxative effect

sensitise *verb* to produce in someone an unusual sensitivity to a substance such as a food ingredient or drug so that subsequent exposure to the substance triggers an allergic reaction

sensitive *adjective* having an unexpected reaction to an allergen or to a drug, caused by the presence of antibodies which were created when the person was exposed to the drug or allergen in the past

sensory analysis, sensory evaluation *noun* the application of design and statistical analysis to the use of the senses in order to evaluate consumer products such as food

sensory property *noun* a quality of something that can be noticed using the senses, e.g. smell, taste or appearance

sensory science *noun* the application of scientific principles to the evaluation of the human senses and interpretation of the signals that they pick up

separate *verb* to take one part of a substance away from the whole, e.g. to take the yolk from a whole egg or cream from whole milk

sepsis *noun* the presence of bacteria and their toxins in the body, which kills tissue and produce pus, usually following the infection of a wound

sequestrant *noun* a chemical that in effect removes ions from a solution, used as a food additive

serine *noun* an amino acid produced in the hydrolysis of protein

serotonin *noun* a compound that is a neurotransmitter and exists mainly in blood platelets, released after tissue is injured

serotype *noun* **1.** a category of microorganisms or bacteria that have some antigens in common **2.** a series of common antigens that exist in microorganisms and bacteria ▶ also called **serological type** ■ *verb* to group microorganisms and bacteria according to their antigens

serrated knife *noun* a knife with a toothed blade, especially a bread knife

serve *verb* **1.** to bring food or drink to a customer **2.** to deal with a customer in a shop or bar **3.** to be enough food for a particular number of people

service *noun* **1.** a full set of crockery for a specific meal for several people **2.** the attendance given to customers in a restaurant by waiters and staff

service charge *noun* a sum of money, usually calculated as a percentage of a customer's bill, added to the bill in a restaurant or hotel to pay the staff for their service

services *noun* an area next to a motorway with a service station, restaurants and sometimes a hotel

serving *noun* 1. the amount of food served to one person 2. the act of serving a customer

serving spoon *noun* a large spoon used for serving food, especially liquids such as gravy, and vegetables

serving suggestion *noun* the way a manufacturer suggests that you serve the product

sesame oil *noun* a strongly flavoured oil from sesame seeds, widely used in East and Southeast Asian cooking

sesame seeds *plural noun* cream to black oval seeds from the seed pods of an annual plant, given a pleasant nutty taste by dry-roasting, used in bread and cakes, to make tahini and to add texture to other foods. ◊ **tahini** (NOTE: The plant's botanical name is *Sesamum indicum* and it is mainly grown in China, Central America and the southwestern USA.)

sesamin *noun* a supplement that improves liver function, releasing thermogenic enzymes, used as a sports supplement

set *verb* to become solid

set point *noun* the body weight at which a person's metabolism is naturally constant and balanced

Seville orange *noun* an orange that is rather bitter, used for making marmalade. Also called **bitter orange**

sew *verb* to close a pocket of meat or the abdominal cavity of a bird or fish by sewing it with thick thread so as to prevent a stuffing from leaking out during cooking

SFDF *abbreviation* Scottish Food and Drink Federation

sfumatrice *noun* a device for extracting the oil from citrus peel

shallot *noun* a small variety of onion

shallow-fry *verb* to cook food in a small amount of hot oil or fat in a frying pan with the aim of completing the cooking of the middle of the food at the same time as the outside is brown and crisp

shandy *noun* a drink made by mixing beer and lemonade

shank *noun* the lower part of an animal's leg between the knee and the foot

sharp *adjective* 1. with a pungent, tart or acid flavour 2. used for describing a knife that has a finely ground and honed edge

shechita *noun* the ritual slaughter of animals using methods stated in Jewish dietary laws

shelf display technology *noun* the way in which a food product is packaged and presented at the point of sale

shelf efficiency *noun* the extent to which an item of food packaging can be stacked neatly, safely and attractively in the minimum amount of shelf space

shelf life *noun* the length of time food can be kept in a shop before it goes bad

shelf-ready packaging *noun* containers for storing and transporting food that also function as display boxes for the supermarket shelf

shelf-stable *adjective* capable of being stored for long periods at room temperature without spoiling

shell *noun* 1. the hard outside part of an egg or a nut 2. the hard outside part that covers some animals such as crabs and lobsters ■ *verb* to take something out of a shell, or be taken out of a shell

shellac *noun* a strained resin exuded by various insects, used for coating apples to give them a glossy appearance

shellfish *plural noun* edible water animals such as mussels, oysters, lobsters and prawns that have shells and live in them

shellfish poisoning *noun* same as **paralytic shellfish poisoning**

shepherd's pie *noun* a dish of minced lamb with a layer of mashed potatoes on top. Compare **cottage pie**

sherry *noun* a fortified wine from Spain

sherry vinegar *noun* fine matured vinegar made from a blend of wines

Shigatoxic E coli *noun* same as **enterohaemorrhagic E coli**

Shiga toxins *plural noun* same as **verotoxins**

shigella *noun* a type of bacteria that causes dysentery, found especially in milk

shiitake mushroom *noun* a variety of mushroom with a white stem, a brown flattish cap and white ruffled gills, often used in Southeast Asian cooking (NOTE: Literally 'tree mushroom'.)

shin *noun* the front part of the lower leg

shirr *verb* to bake food, especially eggs, in small shallow containers or dishes in the oven

shirred eggs *plural noun* shelled eggs baked in a shallow tray in the oven

short bowel syndrome *noun* malnutrition caused by the reduced absorption of nutrients from the small intestine

shortbread *noun* a thick sweet crumbly biscuit

short chain fatty acids *plural noun* fatty acids with fewer than 6 carbon bonds

shortcrust pastry *noun* a widely used type of pastry made with fat and flour

shorten *verb* to make pastry more crumbly by adding more fat

shortening *noun* a fat used in pastry, cakes and bread

shortening power *noun* the ability of a fat to allow air bubbles to become trapped in a mixture and therefore lighten the texture of the resulting baked item

short-grain rice *noun* rice with short grains, used in rice pudding

short-life products *plural noun* products that have a short shelf life, especially fruit, vegetables, fish and meat

short order *noun* a restaurant order for something that can be cooked quickly to order, e.g. bacon and eggs

short-order chef, cook *noun* a cook who specialises in short orders

shoulder *noun* a joint where the top of the arm joins the main part of the body

shred *verb* to cut food into very thin strips

shredder *noun* a device for cutting vegetables into very thin strips

shrimp *noun* a small shellfish with a long tail

shrimp paste *noun* a paste of ground, salted and partially fermented shrimps, dried and compressed into blocks

shrinkage *noun* the reduction in size of baked items or roast meat and poultry due to loss of water, which is generally less when the item is cooked at a low temperature

shrink-wrap *noun* a clear thermoplastic film that is wrapped around a product and shrunk to its original smaller size using heat, thereby forming a tightly sealed package ■ *verb* to wrap goods in shrink-wrap

SHU *abbreviation* Scoville heat unit

shuck *verb* to remove the outer casing or shell of something

sialoaerophagy *noun* excessive swallowing of saliva and air

sialogastrone *noun* a protein in saliva that is thought to inhibit gastric secretions

sialogogue *noun* a substance that promotes the flow of saliva

sialolithiasis *noun* the formation of a salivary calculus in the body

sialorrhoea *noun* an excessive production of saliva

Siberian ginseng *noun* same as **eleuthero**

sida cordifolia *noun* a supplement for athletes containing ephedrine, extracted from an Indian plant

side dish *noun* a small plate or bowl of food eaten to accompany a main course

side effect *noun* an undesirable secondary effect of a drug or other form of medical treatment

siderosis *noun* an accumulation of iron in the bone marrow, caused by iron leaching from cooking utensils into food over a period of time

side stripe *noun* a stripe of lacquer inside a tin that protects the weld from corrosion

sieve *noun* a kitchen utensil made of metal or plastic net, used for straining liquids or powders to remove lumps ■ *verb* to pass something such as flour or liquid through a sieve to remove lumps

sift *verb* same as **sieve**

sifter *noun* a closed cylindrical container with a sieve or perforated top at one end for sprinkling flour, sugar or other powders over food items

sigmoid colon *noun* the fourth section of the colon, which continues as the rectum

sigmoidoscope *noun* a surgical instrument with a light at the end that can be passed into the rectum so that the sigmoid colon can be examined

signature dish *noun* a special dish for which a particular chef or restaurant is well known

signposting *noun* same as **traffic-light labelling**

silica gel *noun* silicon dioxide in a form that absorbs water from the air, used as a drying agent and anticaking agent

silicone *noun* a heat-resistant synthetic substance in the form of a grease, oil or plastic, used in lubricants and water-repellent substances

silicone paper *noun* paper with a built-in release agent, used in baking and food packaging so that food does not stick

silverside *noun* a cut of beef taken from behind and below the rump and topside, usually used for roasting or pot-roasting

simmer *verb* to boil something gently

simple carbohydrates *plural noun* carbohydrates with simple molecules containing few linked glucose units, broken down very quickly by the body

singe *verb* to use a flame to burn the last bits of down from a plucked bird

single-acting baking powder *noun* a chemical raising agent that releases carbon dioxide only on contact with water. Compare **double-acting baking powder**

single-blind testing *noun* a form of blind testing in which the researchers are aware from the beginning which subjects are receiving the supplement and which are receiving a placebo. Compare **double-blind testing**

single cream *noun* liquid cream with a relatively low fat content

single-crust *adjective* used for describing a pie or food dish with a single layer of pastry below the filling, and none above

single-malt *noun* a whisky that is the product of a single distillery

single-serve *adjective* packaged in small amounts intended for one person

sirloin *noun* the best cut of beef from the back of the animal

sitiomania *noun* a craving for particular types of food

sitiophobia *noun* hatred of food and eating

sitology *noun* the scientific study of food, diet and nutrition as they relate to health

sitomania *noun* a desire to eat particular types and quantities of foods

sitotherapy *noun* the use of food as a therapeutic treatment

sitotoxin *noun* any toxin developed in food by mould or bacteria, e.g. aflatoxin

sitotoxism *noun* food poisoning caused by a sitotoxin

size reduction *noun* the reduction of food particles to smaller particles, e.g. by crushing or grinding

skate *noun* a large flat sea fish with white flesh (NOTE: The plural form is **skate**.)

skeleton *noun* the set of bones that make up the framework of the body

skewer *noun* a long thin metal rod for putting through pieces of meat when cooking ■ *verb* to stick a long metal rod through something

skillet *noun* a frying pan

skim *verb* to remove fat or scum from the surface of boiling liquids

skimmed *adjective* used for describing milk that has had most of its fat content removed

skimmed milk powder *noun* dried milk powder from skimmed milk, containing relatively little fat. Abbreviation **SMP**

skin *noun* **1.** the outer covering of the body **2.** the outer surface of fruit, vegetable or meat

skinless *adjective* **1.** used for describing meat such as chicken which is sold without the skin, often as a healthier option **2.** used for describing sausages prepared using a casing that is removed before the product is packaged and sold

skinning *noun* the process of removing the hide from a carcass

skinning knife *noun* a sharp knife used for skinning animal carcasses

skinny *adjective* used for describing a latte made with skimmed milk

skipjack reaction *noun* same as **scombroid poisoning**

skipjack tuna *noun* a cheap species of tuna fish that is often substituted for the more expensive yellow fin or the rare blue fin (NOTE: Its scientific name is *Katsuwonus pelamis*.)

skirt *noun* a stewing cut of beef taken from the flank, below the sirloin and rump

slake *verb* to satisfy a desire for something, especially a drink

slaughter *noun* the killing of animals for food (NOTE: Animal welfare codes lay down rules for how animals should be slaughtered to ensure that they are not caused any avoidable and unnecessary pain or distress.) ■ *verb* to kill animals for food

slice *noun* a thin piece cut off something ■ *verb* to cut something into slices

sliced bread *noun* a loaf of bread that has been sliced mechanically before it is sold

sliced meat *noun* meat that has been pre-sliced from the joint and packaged

slicing knife *noun* a knife with a long thin blade with a rounded end, used for slicing

slicing machine *noun* a machine for slicing a solid food item, e.g. a joint of ham, with a motor-driven circular knife blade together with a tray, moved by hand or mechanically so as to cut the food in slices of a predetermined thickness. Also called **food slicer**

slim *verb* to try to become thinner or try to lose weight

slimline *adjective* designed to help with a weight-reducing diet

slimming *noun* the use of a special diet or special food that is low in calories and is supposed to help a person lose weight

slimming pill *noun* a pill that supposedly helps to reduce weight, whether by increasing the metabolism, suppressing hunger or blocking the absorption of fats

slimming product *noun* a food product that is low-calorie and designed especially for people on a weight-reducing diet

slippery elm *noun* **1.** the moist sticky inner bark of an elm, used as a natural remedy in alternative medicine to relieve inflammation in the digestive tract **2.** a deciduous hardwood tree from which slippery elm is obtained, native to North America (NOTE: Its botanical name is *Ulmus rubra*.)

slotted spoon *noun* a large long-handled spoon with holes in the bowl end, used for removing large solids from a liquid

slow cook *verb* to cook food at a low temperature in the range 80°C to 95°C

slow cooker *noun* a thermostatically controlled metal container into which a lidded earthenware or glass pot is placed, used for slow cooking

Slow Food *noun* a movement that advises taking time over food preparation and eating, and avoiding processed convenience food

sludge *noun* ♦ gallbladder sludge

small intestine *noun* a section of the intestine from the stomach to the caecum, consisting of the duodenum, the jejunum and the ileum

smart food *noun* nutritious foods eaten for health and fitness

smart materials *plural noun* materials which can adapt to their surroundings, with a range of potential applications in food packaging technology

smelt *noun* a small sea fish often fried and eaten whole (NOTE: The plural form is **smelt**.)

smetana *noun* a soured low-fat cream, originally from Eastern Europe

smoke *noun* vapour and gas given off when something burns ■ *verb* to preserve food such as meat, fish, bacon or cheese by hanging it in the smoke from a fire

smoked haddock *noun* a common smoked fish, often yellow in colour

smoked salmon *noun* salmon that has been cured by smoking, served in very thin slices, often as an hors d'oeuvre

smoke point *noun* the temperature at which a cooking oil begins to break down and smoke

smoking *noun* the act of hanging meat or fish in hot smoke to flavour and preserve it

smoothie *noun* a drink made from puréed fruit, sometimes with milk, yoghurt or ice cream

smorgasbord *noun* a Swedish-style buffet of many cold dishes

SMP *abbreviation* skimmed milk powder

snack *noun* a light meal, or a small amount of food eaten ■ *verb* to eat between the times that meals are usually served, or eat a snack instead of a main meal

snacking market *noun* the potential consumer audience for convenience snack foods, typically children and busy professionals

snack pack *noun* a small pack of food intended to be eaten as a snack

snapper *noun* a name given to numerous perch-like fishes that live in tropical and subtropical waters, the **red snapper** being among the most common varieties used as food

sneeze guard *noun* same as **counter guard**

soak *verb* to put something in liquid so that it absorbs some of it

soba noodles *plural noun* thin brown noodles with a square cross section made from buckwheat flour or a mixture of buckwheat and wheat flour, popular in Japanese cooking

sober *adjective* not drunk

social marketing *noun* the idea of 'selling' a lifestyle choice to a community for the long-term benefit of that community, such as with anti-smoking campaigns

social responsibility *noun* the duty of food producers and suppliers to behave in an ethical way, e.g. without wasting resources or causing damage such as pollution

Society of Food Hygiene Technology *noun* an independent body which represents the interests of those involved in food hygiene. Abbreviation **SOFHT**

soda *noun* a general name for alkaline sodium compounds such as caustic soda, bicarbonate of soda, washing soda and soda ash

soda water *noun* water made fizzy by putting gas into it, drunk with alcohol or fruit juice

sodium *noun* a chemical element that is the basic substance in salt (NOTE: The chemical symbol is **Na**.)

sodium 5'-ribonucleotide *noun* ♦ E635

sodium acetate *noun* ♦ E262

sodium alginate *noun* ♦ E401

sodium aluminium phosphate *noun* ♦ E541

sodium ascorbate *noun* ♦ E301

sodium benzoate *noun* ♦ E211

sodium bicarbonate *noun* a chemical compound used as a raising agent in baked goods and to make fizzy drinks fizzy

sodium carboxymethyl cellulose *noun* ♦ E466

sodium caseinate *noun* a food additive made from milk protein, used for maintaining colour in sausages and other processed meats

sodium chloride *noun* common salt

sodium citrate *noun* a white crystalline salt used as a buffer in foods and an anticoagulant in stored blood

sodium dihydrogen citrate *noun* same as **E331**

sodium dihydrogen orthophosphate *noun* a chemical used for purifying water for human consumption

sodium ethyl 4-hydroxybenzoate *noun* ♦ E215

sodium ferrocyanide *noun* ♦ E535

sodium ferulate *noun* a compound used in Chinese medicine to treat vascular diseases such as thrombosis

sodium formate *noun* ♦ E237

sodium gluconate *noun* ♦ E576

sodium guanylate *noun* ↓ E627

sodium hydrogen carbonate *noun* same as **sodium bicarbonate**

sodium hydrogen diacetate *noun* a sodium salt of acetic acid used as a preservative and firming agent

sodium hydrogen L-glutamate *noun* same as **monosodium glutamate**

sodium hydrogen malate *noun* ↓ E350

sodium hydrogen sulphite *noun* ↓ E222

sodium hydroxide *noun* same as **caustic soda**

sodium inosinate *noun* same as E631

sodium lactate *noun* ↓ E325

sodium L-ascorbate *noun* ↓ E301

sodium metabisulphite *noun* ↓ E223

sodium methyl 4-hydroxybenzoate *noun* ↓ E219

sodium nitrate *noun* a white crystalline salt, used as a fertiliser and in curing meat

sodium nitrite *noun* ↓ E250

sodium orthophenylphenate *noun* same as E232

sodium phosphate *noun* an emulsifier used in various processed foods for helping to incorporate water

sodium polyphosphate *noun* a chemical used for increasing the water uptake of poultry and other meats so as to increase their weight

sodium propionate *noun* a colourless crystalline powder used for slowing spoilage in packaged foods

sodium propyl 4-hydroxybenzoate *noun* ↓ E217

sodium saccharin *noun* a sodium salt of saccharin used in the same way as saccharin

sodium salt *noun* a crystalline compound formed from the neutralisation of an acid solution containing sodium

sodium sesquicarbonate *noun* same as E501

sodium sorbate *noun* ↓ E201

sodium stearoyl-2-lactylate *noun* ↓ E481

sodium sulphate *noun* ↓ E514

sodium sulphite *noun* a white crystalline compound used in medicine, as a food preservative, and in making paper

SOFHT *abbreviation* Society of Food Hygiene Technology

soft-boiled *adjective* used for describing an egg that has been cooked in boiling water for a short time so that the yolk is hot, but still liquid

soft brown sugar *noun* refined white sugar coated with a layer of molasses to make it soft and sticky

soft cheese *noun* any cheese that is soft, or soft in the middle, e.g. Camembert or Brie

soft drink *noun* a drink that is not alcoholic, sold either ready prepared in a bottle or can or in concentrated form to be mixed with water

soften *verb* **1.** to allow hard fats or frozen foods to become soft by raising their temperature **2.** to sweat chopped vegetables in a little oil or fat to make them soft

soft flour *noun* flour made from soft wheat consisting of unbroken starch granules, mostly used for cakes, biscuits and general thickening

soft fruit *noun* a general term for all fruits and berries that have a relatively soft flesh, and so cannot be kept, except in some cases by freezing, e.g. raspberries, strawberries, blueberries and blackberries

soft-scoop ice cream *noun* ice cream containing additives that make it easy to serve, a food that should be avoided by pregnant women as it carries the risk of listeria contamination

soft swell *noun* a can that cannot be forced back into shape by hand but has ends that yield slightly to pressure. ◊ **swell**

soft water *noun* water that does not contain calcium and other minerals that are found in hard water and is easily able to make soap lather

soft wheat *noun* wheat in which the starch granules are loosely bound with spaces between, a structure thought to be caused by the protein triabolin which is only found in soft wheats

soggy *adjective* used for describing a cake that is damp and heavy in the centre due to excess moisture, lack of raising agent or incorrect baking temperature

soil *noun* the earth in which plants grow ■ *verb* to make something dirty

Soil Association *noun* a UK organisation that certifies organically grown food

sol *noun* a liquid colloidal solution

solanine *noun* a toxic compound found in potatoes that have sprouted or turned green with age

solar drying *noun* same as **sun-drying**

sole *noun* a type of flat sea fish with delicate white flesh

solid diet *noun* a normal diet for a healthy adult, consisting of both solid and liquid food

solidify *verb* to become solid, or cause something to become solid

solids *plural noun* food that has to be chewed

solubility *noun* the ability of a substance to dissolve in another substance or solvent at a given temperature and pressure

soluble *adjective* able to dissolve

soluble fibre *noun* a type of fibre in vegetables, fruit, pulses and porridge oats that is partly digested in the intestine and reduces the absorption of fats and sugar into the body, so lowering the level of cholesterol

solution *noun* a mixture of a solid substance dissolved in a liquid

solvent *noun* a liquid in which a solid substance can be dissolved

somatotrophin *noun* a hormone secreted by the pituitary gland that controls bone and tissue development

somen *noun* fine wheat noodles

sommelier *noun* the person in charge of ordering, storing and serving the wines in a restaurant

Sonoma diet *noun* a dietary plan based on the Mediterranean diet that also advocates portion size control

sorbet *noun* sweet flavoured ice made with water and flavouring and sometimes cream

sorbic acid *noun* a white crystalline solid acid found in the berries of the mountain ash tree, synthetically manufactured for use as a food preservative and fungicide

sorbitan monolaurate *noun* ♦ E493

sorbitan mono-oleate *noun* ♦ E494

sorbitan monopalmitate *noun* ♦ E495

sorbitan monostearate *noun* ♦ E491

sorbitan tristearate *noun* ♦ E492

sorbitol *noun* a white crystalline sweet alcohol used as a sweetener and a moisturiser, and in the manufacture of vitamin C

sorbitol syrup *noun* ♦ E420(ii)

sorghum *noun* a drought-resistant cereal plant grown in semi-arid tropical regions such as Mexico, Nigeria and Sudan

sorrel *noun* a plant with a sour juice sometimes eaten as a salad

sorting and grading *noun* the process of organising products that are of differing types, sizes or qualities into groups

soufflé *noun* a light cooked dish made from beaten egg whites and cream or custard, with sweet or savoury flavouring, eaten hot

soufflé dish *noun* a straight sided ovenproof dish in which soufflés are baked

soufflé omelette *noun* whisked sweetened or seasoned egg whites, folded into slightly stirred egg yolks, a little water added, rewhisked then cooked as an omelette, often with a sweet filling

soul food *noun* the traditional foods of African Americans of the American South, with typical dishes including yams, chitterlings, black-eyed peas and collard greens

soup *noun* a liquid dish usually eaten at the beginning of a meal

soup chef *noun* the chef in charge of making soups. Also called **chef potager**

soup spoon *noun* a flattish spoon used for eating soup

sour *adjective* **1.** with a sharp taste that is not sweet **2.** used for describing food that has gone bad

source *noun* **1.** the substance from which something is obtained **2.** the place where something comes from ■ *verb* to get materials or products from a particular place or supplier

sour cream *noun* smooth thick cream that has been soured artificially, used in cooking and baking and as a topping

sourdough bread *noun* bread in which a little fermented dough from a previous batch is used as the raising agent, in place of yeast, thought by some to have a superior taste

soured cream *noun* same as **sour cream**

souring agent *noun* any edible substance containing a reasonable concentration of acid, e.g. vinegar or lemon juice

sour milk *noun* milk that has curdled naturally or has been deliberately exposed to some acid-producing organism and has thus curdled at around 30°C to 35°C

sous-chef *noun* a chef who is the assistant to the main chef in a restaurant kitchen (NOTE: **sous-chef** comes from the French noun meaning 'under-chef'.)

souse *verb* to marinate or cook food in vinegar

soused herring *noun* herring that has been pickled in vinegar and herbs

sous vide *noun* a method of preparing ready-cooked food for resale, in which the food is heat-sealed in plastic trays or in plastic bags with some of the air removed from the container

South Beach diet *noun* a dietary plan that draws a distinction between different types of carbohydrates and fats and uses this to determine which foods should be eaten

soya *noun* a plant that produces edible beans with a high protein and fat content and very little starch

soya bean *noun* a bean from a plant used for food and oil

soya flour *noun* flour produced from soya beans, with a high fat and protein content, used together with wheat flour in baking and in ice creams and other manufactured foods

soya lecithin *noun* lecithin from soya beans, used as an emulsifier in chocolate

soya milk *noun* a substitute for cows' milk, used by vegetarians and vegans, made by boiling ground soya beans with water for long periods of time and filtering off the sediment

soya oil *noun* oil extracted from soya beans, used as a cooking oil, for salad dressings and for the manufacture of margarine (NOTE: It is said to have protective effects against breast cancer.)

soya protein, soy protein *noun* protein found in soya beans, low in fat and cholesterol

soy sauce, soya sauce *noun* a strong-tasting liquid available in light and dark varieties, obtained by fermenting soya beans and various cereal grains, widely used in Southeast Asian cooking

spaghetti *plural noun* pasta in the form of long thin strips

spaghetti bolognese *noun* spaghetti with a meat and tomato sauce

spaghetti carbonara *noun* spaghetti with an egg and bacon sauce

Spanish omelette *noun* same as **tortilla 2**

spare ribs *plural noun* pork ribs cooked in a savoury sauce

sparkling *adjective* used for describing wine or water with bubbles in it

spastic colon *noun* same as **irritable bowel syndrome**

spatchcock *noun* a chicken or other fowl that is split, dressed and grilled

spatula *noun* a flat flexible tool with a handle, used for scooping, lifting, spreading or mixing things

spear *noun* a young pointed sprout of a plant, especially asparagus

spearmint *noun* a type of mint with closely set toothed leaves and a clean flavour, used for drinks and for flavouring

special dietary requirements *plural noun* the requirements of someone who has a restricted diet, e.g. who is vegetarian, vegan, eats only kosher or halal food, is pregnant or breastfeeding or has wheat, gluten or nut allergies

species *noun* a group of living things that have the same characteristics and can interbreed (NOTE: The plural is **species**.)

specific gravity *noun* the ratio of the density of a substance to the density of water at the same temperature. Abbreviation **SG**. Also called **relative density**

spelt flour *noun* flour made from an ancient variety of wheat with a high gluten content and a hard husk that makes it difficult to mill

sphygmomanometer *noun* a device for measuring blood pressure

spice *noun* a substance made from the roots, flowers, seeds or leaves of plants, used for flavouring food ■ *verb* to add spice to a dish

spicy *adjective* tasting of spices

spinach *noun* a common green-leaved vegetable

spirit *noun* any liquid produced by distillation, especially a distilled solution of ethanol and water

spirit burner, spirit lamp *noun* apparatus in which methylated spirits is burned, used for keeping food hot on the table, or for cooking food rapidly next to the table

spirometer *noun* a device used for measuring oxygen consumption by an organism

Spirulina *noun* a nutrient-rich algae used as a food supplement

spit *noun* a long metal rod that is passed through meat and turned so the meat is evenly cooked

spit-roast *verb* to roast meat whilst it is being turned on a spit

splanchnic *adjective* used for referring to the internal organs (*technical*)

spleen *noun* an organ in the top part of the abdominal cavity behind the stomach and below the diaphragm, which helps to destroy old red blood cells, form lymphocytes and store blood

split *verb* if something such as a sauce splits, the ingredients do not mix together as they should

split pea *noun* dehusked dried peas split into two equal hemispheres along the natural dividing line

spoilage *noun* decay in food

spoilage retardant *noun* any substance that prevents food from decaying or slows down decay. ◊ **preservative**

sponge cake *noun* a light open-textured cake made of flour, eggs, sugar, flavouring and traditionally no fat

sponge fingers *plural noun* thin fingers of sponge made from creamed egg yolks and caster sugar

sponge flan *noun* a circular flan case made with a sponge cake mixture in place of pastry

spoon *noun* **1.** an eating utensil with a bowl and a long handle **2.** the amount that a spoon can hold. Also called **spoonful**

spore *noun* a reproductive body of particular bacteria and fungi that can survive in extremely hot or cold conditions for a long time

sports drink *noun* a soft drink that is intended to quench thirst faster than water and replenish the sugar and minerals lost from the body during physical exercise

sports gel *noun* a concentrated carbohydrate gel that is easy to metabolise during exercise

sports nutrition *noun* specialised nutrition for a professional sportsperson, designed to provide enough energy to sustain a very active lifestyle as well as providing nutrients that support tissue growth and repair

sports nutritionist *noun* a professional who looks after the specialised dietary needs of athletes

sports supplement *noun* a dietary supplement used by athletes to enhance performance

sprat *noun* a very small herring-like fish

spray-drying *noun* a method of drying solutions of foods by spraying the liquid solution into a warm atmosphere and collecting the solid powder

spread *noun* a soft food consisting of meat, fish or cheese that you can spread on something such as bread ■ *verb* to cover food with a layer of something

spreadable butter *noun* butter with added oil or margarine that allows it to stay soft and spreadable even when refrigerated

springer *noun* a can that appears normal until it is sharply tapped, causing one end to bulge. ◊ **swell**

spring-form cake tin *noun* a cake tin with a flexible side that can be tightened around or loosened from the circular base by means of a latch mechanism, making it easy to remove the cooked cake

spring onion *noun* a very small onion with long green leaves, used in salads and in cooking

spring roll *noun* a hot snack or starter of mixed savoury ingredients formed into a slightly flattened cylindrical shape, wrapped in thin dough and fried until crisp and golden

sprinkle *verb* to scatter a substance such as water or sugar onto something

spritzer *noun* a drink of white wine and soda water

sprout *noun* 1. a young shoot of a plant 2. same as **Brussels sprout** ■ *verb* to send out new growth

sprue *noun* malnutrition caused by underdevelopment or wasting of the villi, causing incomplete absorption of nutrients from the intestine

sputum *noun* mucus that is formed in an inflamed nose, throat or lungs and is coughed up. Also called **phlegm**

squash *noun* 1. concentrated juice of a fruit to which water is added to make a long drink 2. a name given to several varieties of plant of the marrow family

squeezer *noun* a device for pressing fruit such as lemons and oranges to let the juice run out

squid *noun* a sea animal with a longish body and octopus-like tentacles around its head (NOTE: The plural form is **squid**.)

SRD *abbreviation* State Registered dietitian

SSHE *abbreviation* scraped surface heat exchange

stabilisation *noun* the action of making a foodstuff stable, or the action of becoming stable

stabilise *verb* to make a foodstuff stable, or to become stable

stabiliser *noun* a substance added to food to keep it stable

stable emulsion *noun* an emulsion that will not separate into its components under the conditions for which it was made

stachyose *noun* a sugar, present in legumes, that is fermented in the intestine, causing the flatulence commonly associated with these

stackability *noun* the ability of food packaging to be stored and transported in the minimum amount of space, without damage

stack beading *noun* same as **beading**

stackburn *noun* deterioration in the quality of canned food, caused by heat retention when cans are stacked before they have cooled

stainless steel *noun* a chromium and nickel iron alloy that is corrosion-proof and does not tarnish, used for basins and cooking utensils

stainless steel soap *noun* a solid block of stainless steel used by chefs to remove food odours from the hands

stale *adjective* no longer fresh

standing time *noun* the time for which a dish should be left in the microwave oven after cooking and before serving

stanol *noun* a chemical compound that is proven to have an LDL-reducing effect, often added to margarine spreads

staphylococcal poisoning *noun* short-term food poisoning by staphylococcus, causing vomiting and diarrhoea

staphylococcus *noun* a bacterium that causes boils and food poisoning (NOTE: The plural is **staphylococci**.)

Staphylococcus aureus *noun* a pathogen found in salad vegetables

staple crop *noun* a food plant that provides a major source of energy or protein for a population, the five most important staple crops being rice, wheat, maize, cassava and beans

staple food *noun* a food that forms the basis of the diet of the people of a region or of an animal

star anise *noun* a star-shaped with an aniseed flavour, widely used in Chinese cooking and medicine

starch *noun* the usual form in which carbohydrates exist in food, especially in bread, rice and potatoes

starch granule *noun* a small cluster of starch arranged in concentric rings

starch-reduced *adjective* used for describing bread products with a lower proportion of carbohydrates than usual

starchy *adjective* containing a lot of starch

starflower oil *noun* oil that is extracted from borage and is rich in gamma-linolenic acid, used in the same way as evening primrose oil

starter *noun* the first course of a meal

starter culture, starter *noun* any bacterial or fungal culture used for causing fermentation to begin

starve *verb* to become unwell because of having very little or nothing to eat

State Registered dietitian *noun* a dietitian registered with the Health Professions Council in the UK, after completing a degree or postgraduate qualification in Dietetics. Abbreviation **SRD**

station head waiter *noun* same as **maître d'hôtel de carré**

station waiter *noun* a waiter who serves a particular group of four or five tables in a restaurant. Also called **chef de rang**

stay-on tab *noun* a type of ring-pull that does not separate from the can when pulled

steak *noun* **1.** a thick slice of beef cut from the best part of the animal **2.** a thick slice cut across the body of an animal or fish

steak and kidney *noun* a typically English combination of cubes of beef and kidney, cooked together with onions in a thick sauce in a pie or pudding

steak au poivre *noun* a steak that has been grilled and has a sauce made with pepper and peppercorns poured over it

steak knife *noun* a very sharp knife or a knife with a serrated edge, used when eating meat

steak tartare *noun* a dish of raw minced steak, served mixed with raw eggs, raw onion and herbs

steam *noun* vapour that comes off hot water or other hot liquids ■ *verb* to cook something using the steam from boiling water

steamed pudding *noun* a pudding based on sweetened suet pastry or a cake sponge mixture with additions and flavourings, cooked in a pudding basin, in a cloth or in a special hinged closed container using either steam or boiling water

steamer *noun* a type of pan with holes in the bottom that is placed over boiling water for steaming food

steaming *noun* a way of cooking food using the steam from boiled water

steaming oven, steaming cabinet *noun* an oven in a restaurant kitchen used for steaming large quantities of food at the same time

steam stripping *noun* a method of disinfecting and deodorisation food production machinery using pressurised steam

steam table *noun* a stainless steel table or counter with openings to take food containers heated by steam or hot water, used for keeping food hot prior to its being served. ◊ **bain-marie**

stearic acid *noun* a saturated acid in many vegetable and animal fats, used for making candles, soaps and various plastics

stearyl tartrate *noun* an ester of stearyl alcohol and tartaric acid with the same uses as E481

steatorrhoea *noun* the passage of large amounts of dietary fat through the digestive tract without it being absorbed

steatosis *noun* the accumulation of fat in an internal organ such as the liver, caused by diseases and exposure to toxins

STEC *abbreviation* Shigatoxic E. coli.

steel *noun* a steel rod, often with a handle, that knives are drawn back and forward along in order to sharpen them

steep *verb* to soak a food in water or another liquid to extract its flavour

stem ginger *noun* round portions of the underground stem of a ginger plant, cooked until tender and preserved in syrup

stem vegetable *noun* a vegetable in which the stem of the plant is the part eaten, e.g. celery, kohlrabi or asparagus

stenophagy *noun* the practice of eating a small or restricted diet

sterigmatocystin *noun* a type of mycotoxin that is produced by fungus on grain, coffee beans and cheese

sterile *adjective* **1.** with no harmful microorganisms present **2.** not able to produce children

sterilisation *noun* the destruction of living microorganisms to prevent infection

sterilise *verb* to heat food to between 115°C and 140°C in order to kill all pathogenic organisms and most microorganisms and spores

sterilised milk *noun* milk heated to 120°C for a few minutes or to just over 100°C for 20 to 30 minutes in order to kill all pathogenic and most other microorganisms and spores

sterol *noun* any insoluble substance that belongs to the steroid alcohols, e.g. cholesterol

stew *noun* a dish of meat and vegetables cooked together for a long time ■ *verb* to cook food for a long time in liquid

stewing steak *noun* pieces of beef used for making stews

stickwater *noun* the moisture extracted from pressed fish when making fishmeal, rich in nutrients

stiffen *verb* to briefly cook meat of fish in water or fat until it stiffens but is not coloured

Stilton *noun* either of two strong-flavoured British white cheeses made from whole milk, one veined with blue mould, the other plain

stimulant *noun* something such as a drug that produces a temporary increase in the activity of a body organ or part

stimulant drink *noun* a drink that contains stimulants, typically caffeine

stimulant laxative *noun* a substance that promotes bowel movement by stimulating the muscles of the intestine

stiparogenic *adjective* used for describing food that tends to relieve constipation

stiparolytic *adjective* used for describing food that tends to cause constipation

stir *verb* to move a liquid or semiliquid food around so as to mix it or keep it mixed

stir-fry *verb* to cook small thin pieces of meat or vegetables very rapidly using hot oil in a wok by continuously moving them and turning them over, a method widely used in Southeast Asian cooking

stock *noun* **1.** the quantity of goods or raw materials kept by a business **2.** the goods in a warehouse or shop **3.** liquid made from boiling meat, vegetables or bones in water, used as a base for soups and sauces ▪ *verb* to hold goods for sale in a warehouse or store

stock cube *noun* a small cube of dried and concentrated food extracts that, when added to hot water, makes a stock for use in soups, stews and sauces. Also called **bouillon cube**

stockpot *noun* a large pot for cooking soups and stock

stock syrup *noun* a basic sugar solution with many uses

stodgy *adjective* used for describing food which is heavy and filling to eat and usually fairly tasteless

stoma *noun* an opening created surgically, especially in the abdomen to allow a feeding tube to be inserted

stomach *noun* **1.** the part of the body shaped like a bag, into which food passes after being swallowed and where the process of digestion continues **2.** the abdomen

stomach pump *noun* same as **gastric lavage**

stomach ulcer *noun* erosion of the stomach lining by excessive gastric acid

stomatodynia *noun* same as **burning mouth syndrome**

stomatodysodia *noun* same as **halitosis**

stomatology *noun* the medical study of the mouth and diseases that affect it

stomatonecrosis *noun* same as **noma**

stone *noun* the hard central seed of fruits such as the cherry, peach, mango and olive, usually with a hard woody shell enclosing a soft kernel. Also called **pit** ▪ *verb* to remove the central stone from a fruit

stone fruit *noun* same as **drupe**

stoneground flour *noun* flour that has been ground between a stationary and a rotating stone, not between rollers like most flour

stool *noun* a piece of solid matter passed from the bowels

storage *noun* the act of keeping goods in store or in a warehouse

storage conditions *plural noun* the way in which a food product should be stored, a required element in food labelling in the UK

storage requirements *plural noun* same as **product storage**

stored food *noun* food that is not eaten fresh and that is kept either in a dry store, vegetable store, refrigerator or freezer

stork process *noun* UHT sterilisation of milk, followed by resterilisation inside the bottle

stove *noun* same as **cooker**

straight *adjective* used for describing an alcoholic spirit served undiluted or unmixed

strain *verb* to pour liquid through a sieve in order to separate out solids

strainer *noun* a utensil made with metal or nylon mesh, used for separating solids from a liquid

straining bag *noun* a cloth bag used for filtering liquids

strawberry *noun* a common red heart-shaped soft summer fruit, used in desserts and also preserved as jam

straw potatoes *plural noun* deep-fried and lightly salted julienne potatoes, often used as a garnish for grilled meat

street vendor *noun* a person who sells food or small items in the street

string *verb* **1.** to remove the stringy fibres from fruit or vegetables before cooking or eating **2.** to remove currants from their stalks by sliding them off between the prongs of a fork

string beans *plural noun* same as **green beans**

stroke *noun* a sudden blockage or breaking of a blood vessel in the brain that can result in loss of consciousness, partial loss of movement or loss of speech

strong flour *noun* flour of any type made from a hard wheat, usually containing between 11% and 12% protein that is mostly gluten, used mainly for bread and puff and choux pastry

strongyle *noun* a parasitic nematode worm related to the hookworms that infests the intestinal tract of mammals

strongyloidiasis *noun* the fact of being infested with strongyles

strudel *noun* a pastry made with very thin pastry rolled and baked with a filling, usually of chopped apples, raisins and sugar

struvite *noun* crystals of magnesium ammonium phosphate that sometimes form in tinned fish

stud *verb* to insert small items such as cloves, sprigs of herbs or slivers of garlic at intervals over the surface of a food item such as an onion or a joint of meat

stuff *verb* to put stuffing inside meat, fish or vegetables and cook and serve them together as a special dish

stuffing *noun* a mixture of chopped meat or vegetables with breadcrumbs or rice and herbs and spices, usually put inside meat or vegetables

stunted growth *noun* a condition in which a child does not develop to their full physical potential because of early malnutrition

sturgeon *noun* a large edible fish whose eggs are caviar (NOTE: The plural form is **sturgeon**.)

subcutaneous *adjective* under the skin. Abbreviation **s.c.**

subsidy *noun* **1.** money given to help something that is not profitable **2.** money given by a government to make something cheaper

substrate *noun* a substance that is acted on by a catalyst such as an enzyme

subtilin *noun* an antibiotic used as a food preservative outside the EU

succinic acid *noun* a colourless water-soluble acid used in the manufacture of lacquers, perfumes and pharmaceuticals (NOTE: It is derived from amber and from plant and animal tissues or is artificially synthesised.)

succulent *adjective* tender and juicy

succus entericus *noun* intestinal juices (*technical*)

sucralose *noun* an artificial non-caloric sweetener created from sugar by replacing three hydroxyl groups with three chlorine atoms

sucrase *noun* an enzyme in the intestine that breaks down sucrose into glucose and fructose

sucroglyceride *noun* a glyceride of a sucrose ester, used as a food additive

sucrose *noun* a sugar, formed of glucose and fructose, found in plants, especially in sugar cane, beet and maple syrup

Sudan dye *noun* a solvent dye found to be illegally used in some food products as a colorant, sparking a product recall in 2005

suet *noun* hard fat from an animal, used in cooking

suet pastry, suet crust pastry *noun* a mixture of self-raising flour and shredded beef suet with a little salt, brought together with water, kneaded slightly and rested

suet pudding *noun* a dish made with flour and suet, cooked by steaming or boiling, with a sweet or savoury filling

sugar *noun* any of several sweet carbohydrate substances that occur naturally, the types used for cooking being refined from sugar cane and sugar beet

sugar beet *noun* a type of beet grown for the high sugar content of its roots, cultivated in temperate regions

sugar cane *noun* a large perennial grass with stems that contain a sweet sap from which sugar is refined

sugarcraft *noun* the art of decorating cakes with icing sugar, and making designs out of sugar

sugar cube *noun* a small cube of grains of sugar, used for sweetening a hot drink

sugar doctor *noun* an additive such as cream of tartar that prevents sugar from crystallising when boiled

sugar-free *adjective* not containing sugar

sugar lump *noun* a small, usually cube-shaped block of sugar, used especially for sweetening a hot drink

sugar pan *noun* a pan for boiling sugar, traditionally made from copper

sugar sifter *noun* a tall container for powdered sugar, with a perforated top through which the sugar can be sprinkled over food

sugarsnap *noun* a variety of garden pea with an edible flattish pod

sugar thermometer *noun* a thermometer used for measuring the temperature of boiling sugar syrups

sulphite *noun* any of various salts of sulphurous acid used as food preservatives. ◊ **E221**, **E226**

sulphorophane *noun* a component of cruciferous vegetables that neutralises free radicals

sulphur *noun* a yellow non-metallic chemical element that is contained in some amino acids and is used in creams to treat some skin disorders (NOTE: The chemical symbol is **S**.)

sulphur dioxide *noun* ✦ **E220**

sulphuric acid *noun* a strong colourless oily corrosive acid that has many uses

sulphuring *noun* the preservation of food using sulphur dioxide

sulphurous acid *noun* a weak colourless acid made by dissolving sulphur dioxide in water, used as a disinfectant, food preservative and bleaching agent

sultana *noun* a type of large seedless raisin. Compare **currant**, **raisin**

sun-dried *adjective* dried out naturally by the sun, not by applying artificial heat

sun-drying *noun* the process of naturally drying fruits and vegetables by laying them out in strong sun

sunflower oil *noun* an edible oil made from the seeds of the sunflower

sunflower seeds *plural noun* the large seeds of the sunflower, eaten raw, roasted as a snack and used in salads

sunlight flavour *noun* an undesirable change in the flavour of foods as a result of exposure to sunlight

sunny side up *adjective* used for describing eggs fried without being turned over

sunset yellow FCF *noun* ♦ E110

superchill *verb* to chill food to a temperature of –1°C to –4°C

superfood *noun* a nutritionally rich food that is eaten for health

supermarket *noun* a large store, usually selling food, where customers serve themselves and pay at a checkout

superweed *noun* a weed resistant to herbicides that might develop in future as hybrid of a weed and a genetically modified plant

supplement *noun* **1.** a substance with a specific nutritional value taken to make up for a real or supposed deficiency in diet **2.** a substance added to improve the nutritional content of a diet or foodstuff

supplementation *noun* the act of enriching a diet or a foodstuff with nutritional supplements

supplement drink *noun* an enriched drink which contains high levels of particular nutrients such as vitamins

supply chain *noun* all the manufacturers and suppliers who provide the parts that make up a particular product

sur commande *adverb* cooked to order, not pre-prepared and kept warm

surface-ripened cheese *noun* a type of cheese that is ripened by the growth of moulds on the surface, as are Camembert and Brie, or by bacteria, as are Pont l'Evêque and Munster

surf and turf *noun* a meal, menu or dish including both seafood and meat, especially steak and lobster

surfeit *noun* an excessive number or quantity of a foodstuff, especially so much of it that people become sickened, repelled or bored by it

susceptor plates *plural noun* thin metallic filmed plates used in microwave food packaging to concentrate the energy in a particular area, e.g. to brown the outside

sushi *noun* a dish consisting of rice, various pickles and, typically, raw fish, made into little rolls and eaten cold

Sustain *noun* an alliance campaigning for sustainable practices in food production and farming

sustainability *noun* the ability of a process or human activity to meet present needs but maintain natural resources and leave the environment in good order for future generations

sustainable farming *noun* environmentally friendly methods of farming that allow the production of crops or livestock without damage to the ecosystem

sustainable sourcing *noun* the sourcing of ingredients produced by sustainable farming practices

swallow *verb* to make liquid, food and sometimes air go down from the mouth to the stomach

sweat *noun* a salty liquid produced by the sweat glands to cool the body as the liquid evaporates from the skin ■ *verb* to cook food in a pan in its own juices with a small amount of fat or oil until tender

swede *noun* a common vegetable with a round root and yellow flesh, used mainly in soups and stews

sweet *adjective* tasting like sugar, and therefore not sour or bitter ■ *noun* **1.** a small piece of food made of sugar, eaten as a snack **2.** same as **dessert**

sweet almond *noun* ♦ **almond**

sweet-and-sour *adjective* cooked in or served with a sauce that has sugar and vinegar among the ingredients

sweet basil *noun* ♦ **basil**

sweetbread *noun* the pancreas or thymus of a calf, lamb or other young animal soaked, fried and eaten as food

sweet chestnut *noun* an edible chestnut

sweetcorn *noun* the large yellow seeds of a type of maize, eaten cooked

sweeten *verb* to make something taste sweet or sweeter by adding sugar or another natural or artificial substance

sweetener *noun* an artificial substance added to food to make it sweet, e.g. saccharin

sweetness *noun* a state of being sweet

sweet pepper *noun* a pepper that can be green, red or yellow and is eaten cooked or raw in salads

sweet potato *noun* a starchy root vegetable grown in tropical and subtropical regions

swell *noun* a can that is bulging at one or both ends because of gases produced by spoilage of the food inside

swirl *verb* to mix one liquid with another or a soluble solid in a liquid by a gentle circular, figure-of-eight or to-and-fro motion

Swiss roll *noun* a cake made by rolling up a thin sheet of sponge cake covered with jam or cream

swizzle stick *noun* a small thin plastic rod used for stirring a drink to mix the ingredients, make it frothy, or reduce its effervescence

swordfish *noun* a large fish with an upper jaw that extends into a long point, caught for food and sport (NOTE: Its scientific name is *Xiphias gladius*.)

syllabub *noun* a sweet food made of cream whipped with wine

synbiotic *noun* a supplement consisting of both a probiotic and a prebiotic

Syndrome X *noun* same as **metabolic syndrome**

synergistic effect *noun* a reaction that needs two or more substances in combination to take place

synthesis *noun* **1.** the process of combining different ideas or objects into a new whole **2.** a new unified whole resulting from the combination of different ideas or objects **3.** the formation of compounds through chemical reactions involving simpler compounds or elements

synthesisation *noun* same as **synthesis**

synthesise *verb* to produce a substance or material by chemical or biological synthesis

synthetic *adjective* artificial, not natural

synthetic fat *noun* any of various esters of fatty acids all derived from natural products for use in place of natural fats and oils, to improve the keeping qualities of foods and to soften and stabilise them

syringe *noun* a piston and cylinder to which a piping nozzle can be attached, used in cake decorating where the paste or cream is too thick for a piping bag

syrup *noun* a thick sweet liquid

systolic blood pressure *noun* the pressure of blood in a person's artery when the heart rests between beats, shown written under the diastolic blood pressure reading. Compare **diastolic blood pressure**

T

tabbouleh *noun* a Middle Eastern dish consisting of bulgur wheat, mint, tomato, spring onions and other herbs, with lemon juice and various seasonings

table knife *noun* a knife used at table with a fork for cutting food, especially the food of a main course

table salt *noun* fine salt suitable for use on food that has been served out

tablespoon *noun* a large spoon for serving food at table

tablespoonful *noun* the amount contained in a tablespoon

table sugar *noun* sugar suitable for use at table

tachycardia *noun* a rapid heartbeat, sometimes linked to anaemia and vitamin B1 deficiency

tachyphagy *noun* extremely fast eating

taco *noun* in Mexican cooking, a dish consisting of a maize tortilla with a filling

tactile *adjective* relating to the sense of touch

tagine *noun* **1.** a Moroccan stew cooked very slowly in a tagine and consisting usually of meat or poultry combined with fruit **2.** a cooking pot with a high cone-shaped earthenware lid and a cast-iron or earthenware base, used especially for stews in Moroccan cookery and requiring little liquid

tagliatelle *noun* pasta in the form of long narrow ribbons

tahini *noun* an oily paste made from crushed sesame seeds

tailing *noun* the continued presence of bacteria at low concentrations in food even after sterilising treatment

takeaway *noun* **1.** a shop or small restaurant where you can buy cooked food to eat somewhere else **2.** a hot meal that you buy at a takeaway

tamarind *noun* a pod from the tropical tamarind tree that contains many seeds in an acid-tasting pulp, used in preserves, drinks and medicines

tamper evident packaging *noun* packaging that changes when its hermetic seal is broken, so that consumers can check for this before buying

tandoor *noun* a clay oven used especially in the cuisine of northern South Asia for cooking food quickly at high temperature, traditionally fuelled by charcoal or wood to give the food a distinctive smoky flavour

tangerine *noun* a small orange with soft skin that peels easily

tannic acid *noun* one of the acids in tannin, used for flavouring and as a clarifying agent in beer, wine and cider and other natural brewed drinks

tannin *noun* a brownish or yellowish compound found in plants, used in tanning, in dyes, and as an astringent

tapas *noun* small plates of snacks, typically fried squid, olives and cheese, served with beer or wine

tapenade *noun* a paste made from puréed black olives, capers and anchovies

tapioca *noun* the cassava plant, or the processed starch produced from cassava by cooking, drying and then flaking the starch, used as a thickener

taramasalata *noun* a creamy pink or beige paste made from smoked fish roe, usually served in the form of a pâté or dip as an appetiser or snack

tarragon *noun* a herb with a slight aniseed flavour, often used for flavouring chicken

tart *noun* a pastry case usually filled with sweet food, but sometimes also savoury ■ *adjective* bitter in flavour

tartare sauce *noun* a sauce made of mayonnaise and chopped pickles, served with fish. Also called **sauce tartare**

tartaric acid *noun* a white crystalline organic acid found in fruit, used as baking powder and in photographic processes and tanning leather

tarte tatin *noun* an apple tart, cooked upside down, made of sliced apples cooked in butter with the pastry on top, then reversed in the serving dish

tartrate *noun* any of various salts of tartaric acid used as stabilisers, the principal ones being sodium, potassium and the potassium sodium mixed salt E337

tartrazine *noun* a yellow substance added to food to give it an attractive colour

taste *noun* **1.** the sense by which you can tell differences of flavour between things you eat, using the tongue **2.** the flavour of a food or drink ■ *verb* **1.** to sense the flavour of something **2.** to have a flavour

taste buds *plural noun* cells on the tongue that enable you to tell differences in flavour

taurine *noun* an amino acid that forms bile salts

tawa *noun* a circular steel or iron griddle with a handle, used for making Indian breads or, when placed below another dish, to reduce the heat especially on a heat source that is difficult to control

T-bone *noun* a cut of beef with a T-shaped bone, from the back of the animal

T-bone steak *noun* a large thick sirloin steak containing a T-shaped bone

TD *abbreviation* traveller's diarrhoea

TE *abbreviation* Trolox equivalent

tea *noun* **1.** a hot drink made by pouring boiling water onto the dried leaves of an Asian plant **2.** the dried leaves of an Asian plant used for making a hot drink **3.** the dried leaves or flowers of other plants, used for making a drink **4.** a meal taken in the afternoon, usually between 4 and 5 o'clock

teacake *noun* a type of bun with raisins in it, usually eaten toasted with butter

teaspoon *noun* **1.** a small spoon for stirring tea or other liquid **2.** the amount that a teaspoon holds. Also called **teaspoonful**

teetotal *adjective* used for describing someone who never drinks alcohol

Teflon the trademark for PTFE

tempeh *noun* a solid food made from fermented soya beans, similar to tofu but with a higher content of dietary fibre and vitamins, as well as firmer texture and stronger flavour

temper *verb* to bring a food to the desired consistency, texture or temperature

temperature probe *noun* a small pointed rod inserted into food to measure its internal temperature and therefore the degree to which it is cooked

tempura *noun* a Japanese dish of vegetables or seafood coated in light batter and deep-fried

tender *adjective* easy to cut or chew, not tough

tenderise *verb* to soften meat in any of various ways, e.g. by beating it with a spiked mallet, by treating it with chemicals or by hanging it

tenderiser *noun* an enzyme or weak acid used for tenderising meat

tenderloin *noun* a fillet of pork cut from the backbone

tenderness *noun* the degree to which a piece of meat is soft and easy to cut or chew

tendon *noun* a sinew or strand of strong connective tissue that attaches a muscle to bone, usually cut out and discarded

tenesmus *noun* spasms of the bladder or rectum, a feature of irritable bowel syndrome

teniasis *noun* the presence of a parasitic worm in the intestine

tepid *adjective* used for describing water at a temperature of about 50°C to 60°C

teratogen *noun* a substance which causes the usual development of an embryo or foetus to be disrupted

teriyaki *noun* a Japanese dish consisting of grilled shellfish or meat brushed with a marinade of soy sauce, sugar and rice wine

terrine *noun* a coarse pâté or similar cold food cooked and sometimes served in a small dish with a tight-fitting lid

tertiary processed food *noun* same as **processed food**

tertiary processing *noun* the part of a food processing plant that receives some cooked food products and subjects them to further processing

test kitchen *noun* a kitchen used for recipe development and testing of kitchen equipment

tetany *noun* an extreme sensitivity of the motor nerves, associated with calcium deficiency

tetracycline *noun* an antibiotic of a group used for treating a wide range of bacterial diseases such as chlamydia

Tetrapak a trade name for various types of carton used for packaging drinks and liquid foods

tetrasodium diphosphate *noun* ♦ E450(iii)

tetrodotoxin *noun* the toxic substance found in fugu

TexMex *adjective* used for describing the Texan and Mexican style of American cooking, based on steaks, barbecued meat and Mexican dishes such as chilli and tortillas

texture *noun* the quality in the structure of a food that makes it firm or soft or rough or smooth

textured vegetable protein *noun* a substance made from processed soya beans or other vegetables, used as a substitute for meat. Abbreviation **TVP**

texture profile *noun* a sensory description of the texture of a foodstuff

texture profile method *noun* a method of sensory testing in which the testers choose from a single lexicon of texture descriptors for all competing products, making the similarities and differences clear

texturise *verb* to give food a particular texture

texturiser *noun* a food additive used for changing or improving the texture of food

TFS *abbreviation* tin-free steel

thaw *verb* to melt something that is frozen

The Obesity Awareness and Solutions Trust *noun* a national association dedicated to the study of obesity and public education about the issues surrounding it. Abbreviation **TOAST**

therapeutic *adjective* given in order to cure or ease a disorder or disease

therapeutic food *noun* an enriched food product that is used as a nutritional supplement for elderly people or people who are ill

therapist *noun* a person specially trained to give therapy

thermal effect of food *noun* same as **diet-induced thermogenesis**

thermal technologies *plural noun* methods of sterilising food that involve heat treatment

thermisation *noun* the process of heating food to reduce the number of microorganisms, although not as severely as in pasteurisation

thermoduric *adjective* used for describing bacteria that are not killed by pasteurisation

thermogenesis *noun* the process in which food or fat deposits in the body are burned to produce heat

thermogenic *adjective* used for describing a food supplement that raises the metabolic rate and causing thermogenesis

thermolabile *adjective* used for describing substances such as some enzymes that are easily destroyed or altered by heat

thermometer *noun* an instrument for measuring temperature, used for determining when meat is cooked, for oven, freezer, refrigerator, fat and sugar temperatures and for ensuring adequate defrosting and cooking in microwave ovens

thermopeeling *noun* a way of peeling fruit by superheating it briefly and then spraying the skins with water

thermophile *noun* a bacterium that thrives in high temperatures

thermophilic *adjective* used for describing microorganisms that tolerate or prefer high temperatures

thermostat *noun* an instrument that monitors and regulates the temperature in an enclosure, commonly used in ovens, refrigerators and freezers, deep fat fryers, slow cookers and similar appliances

thiamin *noun* ♦ vitamin B1

thiazole *noun* a ring compound produced during Maillard browning that produces a meaty flavour

thicken *verb* to become more dense and viscid and flow less easily

thickener *noun* any substance used for increasing the viscosity or consistency of liquids

thigh *noun* the part of an animal's leg that corresponds to a human thigh

thiobendazole *noun* an antifungal agent used for treating bananas

thirst *noun* a feeling of wanting to drink

thirsty *adjective* wanting to drink

Thousand Island dressing *noun* a type of salad dressing made with mayonnaise and chopped pimento, with chilli sauce, ketchup and paprika

threadworm *noun* a thin parasitic worm that infests the large intestine and causes itching round the anus. Also called **pinworm**

threadworm disease *noun* infestation of the rectum with threadworms

three-piece can *noun* a can consisting of three pieces, the body and both ends, welded together, vulnerable to defects along the seams

threonine *noun* an essential amino acid

threpsis *noun* nutrition (*technical*)

threpsology *noun* the science of proper nutrition

thrombosis *noun* the blocking of an artery or vein by a mass of coagulated blood

thuricide *noun* a bacterial treatment that kills insects on crops but is harmless to humans

thyme *noun* any of numerous varieties of low-growing plants with small leaves used as a herb, especially common thyme, a Mediterranean variety

thyroid *adjective* relating to the thyroid gland

thyroid gland *noun* an endocrine gland in the neck that secretes a hormone that regulates the body's metabolism

thyroid hormone *noun* a hormone produced by the thyroid gland

tiger prawn *noun* a very large type of prawn

tikka *noun* a type of Indian cooking done in a hot clay oven with red curry sauce

tilapia *noun* a perch-like fish that is now the most widely farmed fish in the tropics

timbale *noun* 1. a dish consisting of a mixture of ingredients, often set with eggs, made in a mould and served hot or cold 2. a small deep or tall mould in which a timbale is cooked

tin *noun* 1. any metal container used for baking or for storing or preserving food 2. a relatively inert metal used for coating the inside of copper cooking utensils to prevent corrosion in acid solutions

tinfoil *noun* same as **aluminium foil**

tin-free steel *noun* corrosion-resistant metal used to make cans. Abbreviation **TFS**

tinned food *noun* food preserved in tins

tin opener *noun* same as **can opener**

tiramisu *noun* an Italian dessert of sponge cake soaked in marsala wine and topped with cream

tisane *noun* a drink made by pouring boiling water on dried or fresh leaves or flowers

tissue *noun* a type of substance that the body is made up of, e.g. skin, muscle or nerves

tissue culture *noun* tissue grown in a culture medium in a laboratory

tissue repair *noun* the rebuilding of damaged body tissues using dietary nutrients to synthesise new tissue

titanium oxide *noun* a white pigment used in foods and cosmetics

toad-in-the-hole *noun* an English dish of sausages cooked in batter

toast *noun* 1. a slice of bread that has been grilled 2. the act of drinking to someone's health or success ■ *verb* 1. to grill bread or other food until it is brown 2. to drink to wish someone health or success

TOAST *abbreviation* The Obesity Awareness and Solutions Trust

toaster *noun* an appliance that toasts bread, especially an electrical appliance with vertical slots for slices of bread and a spring-loaded carrier that ejects the bread when it is toasted

toastie *noun* a sandwich that has been fried or toasted between two electrically heated grill plates pressed together

TOBEC *noun* a way of measuring the amount of fat in the body using the difference in electrical conductivity between fat and lean tissue. Full form **total body electrical conductivity**

tocopherol *noun* one of a group of fat-soluble compounds that make up vitamin E, found in vegetable oils and leafy green vegetables

toffee *noun* a sweet that can be soft and chewy or hard and brittle, made by boiling brown sugar or treacle with butter and sometimes flavourings or nuts

tofu *noun* a soft white paste made from soya beans, also available in blocks for use as a meat substitute

tolerance *noun* the ability of the body to tolerate a substance or an action

tomato *noun* a common red vegetable that is the fruit of a climbing plant of the potato family, widely used in salads and sauces

tomato purée, tomato paste *noun* partially dehydrated sieved tomato pulp with a deep red colour and spreadable consistency, sold in collapsible tubes, tins and jars

tongs *plural noun* a utensil used for handling things such as hot food and consisting of two hinged or sprung arms that press together in a pinching movement around the object to be lifted

tonic water *noun* a fizzy drink of water and sugar, containing quinine

tooth decay *noun* the wearing away of tooth enamel caused by attack by acids

tooth-friendly *adjective* used for describing a sweetener that does not cause tooth decay

top and tail *verb* to remove either end of a fruit or vegetable prior to cooking or eating

topping *noun* any covering, e.g. breadcrumbs or grated cheese, placed on the surface of a prepared dish as a garnish or decoration or as an integral part of the dish

topside *noun* a lean boneless cut of beef from the outer thigh

toque *noun* a tall white hat worn by chefs

tortellini *plural noun* pasta in the form of small filled rings

tortilla *noun* **1.** a thin flat Mexican bread, cooked on a hot griddle and eaten folded, with a filling **2.** an omelette filled with a selection of vegetables, usually including tomatoes and cooked potato. Also called **Spanish omelette**

tortilla chip *noun* a thin crunchy crisp made of maize meal, often served with dips such as salsa and guacamole

torula *noun* an edible yeast that is cultivated for use as a medicine and food additive

TOS *abbreviation* toxic oil syndrome

toss *verb* **1.** to turn food over, usually with two spoons, so that it becomes coated with a dressing, e.g. melted butter on vegetables or vinaigrette dressing on salads **2.** to coat pieces of food with a powder such as flour by shaking them together in a bag **3.** to turn over something being cooked in a frying pan by throwing it into the air with a flicking motion of the pan and catching it

total body electrical conductivity *noun* full form of **TOBEC**

total energy expenditure *noun* the number of calories needed to maintain the body's normal function during all normal activities over the course of a day

total fat *noun* the total amount of fat consumed by a person in a day, including both saturated and unsaturated fats

total parenteral nutrition *noun* administration of nutrients through a catheter, as a complete source of nutrition for a patient. Abbreviation **TPN**

tottie pad *noun* a heat-resistant pad for resting pans on

tough *adjective* difficult to chew or to cut

tournedos *noun* a thick round piece of fillet steak

toxaemia *noun* the presence of poisonous substances in the blood

toxic *adjective* poisonous

toxic oil syndrome *noun* a disease outbreak in Spain in which denatured industrial oil was sold commercially as rapeseed oil, causing disabilities and hundreds of deaths. Abbreviation **TOS**

toxin *noun* a poisonous substance produced in the body by microorganisms

toxoplasmosis *noun* a potentially fatal disease caused by the parasite toxoplasma that is carried by animals, capable of causing encephalitis and hydrocephalus

TPN *abbreviation* total parenteral nutrition

traceability *noun* the concept that each stage in the supply chain from farm to consumer can be traced so that the quality of the food can be guaranteed

trace chemical *noun* a chemical found in very small quantities in a foodstuff

trace element *noun* a substance that is essential to the human body but only in very small quantities

trace mineral *noun* a mineral found in very small quantities in a foodstuff

trachea *noun* the main air passage that runs from the larynx to the lungs, where it divides into the two main bronchi

tract *noun* **1.** a series of organs or tubes that allow something to pass from one part of the body to another **2.** a series or bundle of nerve fibres connecting two areas of the nervous system and transmitting nervous impulses in one or in both directions

trade tariff *noun* a duty payable on imported or exported goods

Trading Standards Institute *noun* an association representing trading standards professionals at a national level. Abbreviation **TSI**

traditional biotechnology *noun* traditional methods of food preparation using the action of microorganisms, e.g. brewing and breadmaking

traffic-light labelling *noun* nutritional information on food packaging that is presented with a green, amber or red symbol, for 'eat freely' 'eat in moderation' and 'eat only occasionally'

traife *adjective* used for describing food that is not kosher

trail mix *noun* a snack containing nuts, dried fruit and seeds

trancheur *noun* the person in the kitchen who cuts meat (NOTE: From French, meaning 'carver'.)

transamination *noun* the process by which amino acids are metabolised in the liver

transdermal *adjective* used for describing nutrients that are able to be absorbed through the skin

trans-fatty acid *noun* an unsaturated fat formed during the hydrogenation of vegetable oils to produce margarine, viewed as a health risk because they raise cholesterol levels

transgenic *adjective* **1.** used for describing an organism into which genetic material from a different species has been transferred using the techniques of genetic modification **2.** used for describing the techniques of transferring genetic material from one organism to another ■ *noun* an organism produced by genetic modification

trans isomer *noun* an isomer in which the atom groups are positioned on opposite sides of the central bond

transverse colon *noun* the second section of the colon, which crosses the body below the stomach

traveller's diarrhoea *noun* diarrhoea caused by exposure to unfamiliar bacteria or unsanitary conditions while travelling. Abbreviation **TD**

tray service *noun* a way of serving food in which the complete meal is assembled on a tray and taken or given to the consumer, as in hospitals or prisons

treacle *noun* a thick dark-brown syrup produced when sugar is refined, used for making treacle toffee

tree nut *noun* a nut from a tree, e.g. an almond, pecan or walnut

trematode *noun* same as **fluke**

tretinoin *noun* a drug related chemically to vitamin A and used in the treatment of acne and other skin disorders. Also called **retinoic acid**

tri- *prefix* containing three atoms, radicals or groups

triabolin *noun* a protein that is found only on the starch granules of soft wheats and may be responsible for reducing the adhesion between them

triammonium citrate *noun* ♦ **E380**

tricalcium citrate *noun* same as **E333**

tricalcium orthophosphate *noun* ♦ **E341(c)**

trichina *noun* a small slender nematode worm that infests the intestines of meat-eating mammals and whose larvae form cysts in skeletal muscle, with symptoms including diarrhoea, nausea, and fever

trichinosis, thichinellosis *noun* an infestation of the intestine with trichina worms, caused by eating undercooked infected pork or game

trichodystrophy *noun* inadequate nutrition of the hair that may cause it to thin or fall out

trichomonad *noun* a flagellated protozoan that lives as a parasite in the digestive and reproductive tracts of humans and animals

trichopoliodystrophy *noun* same as **Menkes' syndrome**

trichuriasis *noun* an infestation of the intestine with whipworms

triethylamine *noun* a fishy-tasting molecule in eggs produced when the hen has indigestible choline in their diet

triglyceride *noun* a substance such as fat that contains three fatty acids

trim *verb* **1.** to cut off parts of meat or fish because they are not needed **2.** to cut small amounts off something **3.** to decorate something

trimethylamine *noun* an amine produced in cheese that is ripening

trimmings *plural noun* **1.** pieces cut off when preparing meat or fish **2.** sauces and garnishes that are usually served with a dish

tripe *noun* part of a cow's stomach used as food

tripotassium citrate *noun* same as **E332**

trisodium citrate *noun* same as **E331**

trisodium diphosphate *noun* same as **E450(ii)**

triticale *noun* a new high-protein hybrid of wheat and rye

trivet *noun* a small metal stand on which hot dishes are kept off the table surface or on which delicate food items may be held in a pan so that they can be removed without damage

Trolox *noun* a derivative of vitamin E that functions as an antioxidant

Trolox equivalent *noun* vitamin E derivatives with the same antioxidant properties as Trolox, measured in Oxygen Radical Absorbance Capacity tests. Abbreviation **TE**

trophic *adjective* relating to nutrition, digestion and growth

trophology *noun* the study of dietary requirements in humans and animals

trophoneurosis *noun* a disorder of the nerves caused by their being inadequately nourished

trophonosis *noun* any disease or disorder caused by nutritional deficiencies

trophotherapy *noun* treatment of a condition using appropriate foodstuffs

tropical fruit *noun* fruits that grow in hot countries, e.g. the pineapple, mango, pomegranate and banana

tropical sprue *noun* a tropical disease characterised by oily, loose stools and sores in the mouth, thought to be caused by a nutrient deficiency

trots *noun* diarrhoea (*informal*)

trotters *noun* pig's feet cooked for food

trout *noun* any of various edible freshwater fish of the salmon family

truffle *noun* **1.** an edible underground fungus that is regarded as a delicacy **2.** a rich ball-shaped chocolate with a centre of soft chocolate

truss *verb* to tie or skewer a bird or a boned joint of meat into shape before cooking it

trypsin *noun* a protein-digesting enzyme secreted by the pancreas

trypsin inhibitor *noun* a substance found in some beans that inhibits the action of trypsins

trypsinogen *noun* an enzyme secreted by the pancreas into the duodenum

tryptophan *noun* an essential amino acid

tsatsiki *noun* a Greek dish of cucumber, mint and yoghurt

TSI *abbreviation* Trading Standards Institute

tube feeding *noun* same as **enteral nutrition**

tuber *noun* the swollen root of any plant used as a vegetable, e.g. a potato

tumbler *noun* a short glass with a flat base and straight sides

tumbler mixer *noun* a piece of machinery in a food processing plant that mixes powders, pastes and liquids

tuna *noun* a very large edible sea fish with dark pink flesh (NOTE: The plural form is **tuna**.)

turbinado *noun* raw, unprocessed sugar

turbot *noun* a large flat edible white sea fish (NOTE: The plural form is **turbot**.)

tureen *noun* a large serving dish for soup

turista *noun* same as **traveller's diarrhoea**

turkey *noun* a large poultry bird raised for meat

turmeric *noun* a yellow spice obtained by grinding the underground stem of the turmeric plant of the ginger family, used especially in pickles and curries

turn *verb* **1.** to become sour or start to ferment, usually undesirably **2.** to rotate a piece of food so that it cooks or browns evenly **3.** to shape vegetables for decoration

turnip *noun* a common vegetable with a round white root, used mainly in soups and stews

turnover *noun* a pastry with a sweet filling, baked or fried

turntable *noun* **1.** a rotating circular platform on a stand, on which a cake is placed for icing and decoration **2.** a rotating circular platform on the base of a microwave oven, on which the dish of food being cooked is placed to ensure even penetration of microwaves

TVP *abbreviation* textured vegetable protein

2–(thiazol-4-yl) benzimidazole *noun* ♦ E233

2-hydroxy diphenyl *noun* a compound that inhibits the metabolism of arachidonic acid

tying off *noun* the practice of sealing either end of a butchered animal's digestive tract when it is removed, to stop the contents contaminating the meat

tympanites *noun* the expansion of the stomach with gas. Also called **meteorism**

Type I diabetes *noun* the type of diabetes mellitus in which the beta cells of the pancreas produce little or no insulin, and the person is completely dependent on injections of insulin for survival

Type II diabetes *noun* the type of diabetes mellitus in which cells throughout the body lose some or most of their ability to use insulin

typhlitis *noun* inflammation of the large intestine

typhoid *noun* a serious and sometimes fatal bacterial infection of the digestive system, caused by ingesting food or water contaminated with the bacillus *Salmonella typhi*, with symptoms of fever, severe abdominal pain and sometimes intestinal bleeding. Also called **typhoid fever** ■ *adjective* relating to typhoid

tyramine *noun* an enzyme found in cheese, beans, tinned fish, red wine and yeast extract that can cause high blood pressure if found in excessive quantities in the brain. ◊ **monoamine oxidase**

tyrosinase *noun* an enzyme that oxidises tyrosine, responsible for the browning of some fruit and vegetables when they are cut

tyrosine *noun* an amino acid in protein that is a component of thyroxine and is a precursor to the catecholamines dopamine, noradrenaline and adrenaline

U

ugli fruit *noun* a naturally occurring hybrid of the grapefruit and mandarin with a very rough blemished peel and soft juicy orange flesh, found growing wild in Jamaica in 1914

UHT *abbreviation* ultra high temperature

UL *noun* the maximum daily intake of a particular nutrient that poses no risk to health. Full form **upper level**

ulcer *noun* an open sore in the skin or in a mucous membrane that is inflamed and difficult to heal

ulceration *noun* lesions formed inside the gastrointestinal tract, causing pain and bleeding present in blood and stools

ulcerative colitis *noun* inflammation of the rectum and colon with ulcers

ulcerative gingivitis *noun* painful inflammation of the gums accompanied by the formation of ulcers, a condition associated with bacterial infection and malnutrition

ultra high temperature, ultra heat treated *adjective* used for describing something such as milk that has undergone a process of sterilisation at very high temperatures. Abbreviation **UHT**

ultrapasteurised *adjective* used for describing milk that has undergone UHT pasteurisation

ultraviolet *adjective* used for describing the range of invisible radiation wavelengths just greater than those of the visible spectrum. Abbreviation **UV**

umami *noun* a Japanese word for a savoury flavour

unbleached flour *noun* flour which has not been whitened using a bleaching agent such as chlorine

uncinariasis *noun* infestation of the intestines with hookworms

unclean meats *plural noun* meats that are not fit to eat according to religious dietary laws, e.g. non-kosher meats in Judaism

uncured *adjective* not preserved by smoking, salting, pickling or drying

undercook *verb* to cook something for too short a time or at too low a heat, so that it is less well done that it should be

undercooked *adjective* not thoroughly cooked and therefore still slightly cold, hard or raw

underdish *noun* a flat dish on which another deeper dish is placed before serving

underdone *adjective* same as **undercooked**

undereat *verb* to eat an insufficient amount of food

undernourish *verb* to fail to supply someone with enough food or other resources to provide for proper development

undernutrition *noun* the fact of not receiving enough nutrients in the diet

underplate *noun* same as **underdish**

underweight *adjective* used for describing someone whose body weight is less than is medically advisable

undigested *adjective* used for describing food that is not digested in the body

UNDP *abbreviation* United Nations Development Programme

undressed *adjective* **1.** not fully prepared for cooking or eating **2.** not covered with a dressing or sauce

unhygienic *adjective* not clean or good for health

unique selling point *noun* a characteristic of a product that makes it different from all similar products. Abbreviation **USP**

unit *noun* a single part of a larger whole, or a single item of several

United Nations Development Programme *noun* the global development arm of the UN, which has eradicating poverty-related hunger as one of its central aims. Abbreviation **UNDP**

unitise *verb* to form into a single unit, or make something into a single unit

unitising *noun* the process of packaging items together into a single load for transport purposes

unit operation *noun* an operation that is common to the food processing industries, e.g. drying, mixing or sterilisation

Universal Product Code *noun* a bar code containing a unique 12-digit number that identifies a commercial product. Abbreviation **UPC**

unleavened *adjective* made without yeast or any other raising agent

unmatured *adjective* used for describing food or drink that has not yet matured to acquire the maximum flavour

unmilled *adjective* used for describing a grain that is whole, not ground in a mill

unmould *verb* to remove a food from a mould

unpasteurised *adjective* not treated with heat so as to remove harmful bacteria

unrefined *adjective* not processed to remove impurities or unwanted substances

unsalted *adjective* containing no added salt

unsaturated fat *noun* a type of fat that does not contain a large amount of hydrogen and so can be broken down more easily. Compare **saturated fat**, **polyunsaturated fat**

unstrained *adjective* used for describing something from which lumps have not yet been removed using a strainer

unsweetened *adjective* served, cooked, or manufactured with no added sugar or other natural or artificial sweetening agent

untreated milk *noun* milk that has not been processed in any way

UPC *abbreviation* Universal Product Code

uperisation *noun* the sterilisation of milk using pressurised steam

upper level *noun* full form of **UL**

urbanisation *noun* the process of migration from the countryside to the towns by which modern societies came to have more people living in cities and towns than in the country

urea *noun* a substance produced in the liver from excess amino acids, excreted by the kidneys into the urine

uric acid *noun* a chemical compound that is formed from nitrogen in waste products from the body and that also forms crystals in the joints of people who have gout

uridine *noun* a nucleoside, consisting of uracil and ribose, that plays a role in the metabolism of carbohydrates

urine *noun* a yellowish liquid, containing water and waste products, mainly salt and urea, that is excreted by the kidneys and passed out of the body through the ureters, bladder and urethra

urokinase *noun* an enzyme formed in the kidneys that begins the process of breaking down blood clots

urolithiasis *noun* the presence of calculi in the urinary system

use-by date *noun* an indication of when a perishable food product will not longer be edible, a required element in food labelling in the UK

USP *abbreviation* unique selling point

UV *abbreviation* ultraviolet

uvula *noun* a piece of soft tissue that hangs down from the back of the soft palate

V

vaccine *noun* a substance used to inoculate or vaccinate

vac-pac *noun* a vacuum pack (*informal*)

vacreation *noun* a way of removing an unpleasant smell from cream using steam distillation

vacuole *noun* a space in a fold of a cell membrane

vacuum contact drying *noun* a way of drying food using hot plates that maintain contact with the food as it shrinks

vacuum cooling *noun* a method of chilling food in a vacuum

vacuum drying *noun* a method of drying foods by subjecting them to a vacuum so that the water evaporates at ambient temperatures, used with frozen food

vacuum pack *noun* a long-life pack in which food is sealed under vacuum in polythene or other clear plastic pouches

vacuum-packed *adjective* packed in a special plastic pack from which all air has been excluded, and then chilled or frozen

valine *noun* an essential amino acid

vanadium *noun* an essential mineral that activates enzymes in the body

vanilla *noun* a flavouring made from the seed pods of a tropical plant

vanillin *noun* a white aldehyde obtained from vanilla or prepared synthetically, used as a flavouring

variant CJD *noun* a form of Creutzfeldt-Jakob disease that was observed first in the 1980s, especially affecting younger people. Abbreviation **vCJD**

varied diet *noun* a diet that includes a range of different foods

variegate porphyria *noun* a type of porphyria that causes skin sensitivity to sunlight. Abbreviation **VP**

variety meats *plural noun* the US word for offal

vasoamine *noun* substances such as histamine that are naturally present in some foods and can trigger an allergic reaction in large quantities

vasodilatation *noun* the relaxation of blood vessels, especially the arteries, making them wider and leading to increased blood flow or reduced blood pressure

vasodilator *noun* a chemical substance which makes blood vessels become wider, so that blood flows more easily and blood pressure falls

vat *noun* a large tub used for fermenting and ageing wine, also used for large-scale processing of some foods, e.g. cheese and pickles

vCJD *abbreviation* variant CJD

VDLD *abbreviation* very low density lipoprotein

veal *noun* meat from a calf

VEGA *abbreviation* Vegetarian Economy and Green Agriculture

vegan *noun* someone who does not eat meat, dairy produce, eggs or fish and eats only vegetables and fruit. Compare **vegetarian** ■ *adjective* involving a diet of only vegetables and fruit

Vegan Society *noun* an association that provides information on living a vegan lifestyle

vegetable *noun* a savoury plant part used as food, e.g. a potato, carrot, onion, cabbage, cauliflower, pea or bean

vegetable black *noun* ♦ E153

vegetable chef *noun* the chef in charge of preparing vegetables and pasta. Also called **chef entremétier**

vegetable knife *noun* a small sharp knife used for chopping vegetables

vegetable oil *noun* an oil that has been extracted from a plant or the seeds of a plant, e.g. olive oil, sunflower oil or sesame oil

vegetable parer *noun* same as **peeler**

vegetable pepsin *noun* same as **papain**

vegetable rennet *noun* plant enzymes that perform the same function as rennet, used in making vegetarian cheeses

vegetable shortening *noun* shortening made from hydrogenated vegetable oil, with a bland flavour

vegetarian *noun* someone who does not eat meat or fish, only vegetables, fruit and dairy produce. Compare **vegan** ■ *adjective* involving a diet without meat

vegetarian cheese *noun* cheese that has been made with vegetable rennet

Vegetarian Economy and Green Agriculture *noun* a research, information and campaigning organisation that focuses on farming, food, health and the land. Abbreviation **VEGA**

Vegetarian Society *noun* an association that provides information on living a vegetarian lifestyle

veggieburger *noun* a flat cake made from vegetables, grains or legumes, often served in the same way as a burger

vein *noun* a blood vessel that takes deoxygenated blood containing waste carbon dioxide from the tissues back to the heart

velouté *noun* any soup with a creamy texture

vending machine *noun* a machine from which you can buy something, such as sweets, chocolate, cigarettes or drinks, by putting coins into a slot

venison *noun* meat from a deer

ventilation hood, ventilation canopy *noun* a device placed over an oven or other cooking surface to remove smells and steam

verbascose *noun* a sugar present in legumes that is fermented in the intestine, causing the flatulence commonly associated with these

verjuice *noun* a very acidic juice made by pressing unripe grapes or crab apples, used as a flavouring

vermicelli *plural noun* pasta in the form of very thin strands, like very thin spaghetti

vermicide *noun* a substance that kills worms in the intestine

vermiculation *noun* decorative wavy lines, patterns or carvings

vermifuge *noun* a substance that removes worms from the intestine

verotoxic E coli *noun* same as **enterohaemorrhagic E coli**

verotoxins *plural noun* toxins produced by enterohaemorrhagic E coli bacteria

very low density lipoprotein *noun* a form of lipoprotein produced by the liver which transports lipids around the bloodstream. Abbreviation **VDLD**

veterinary drug residues *plural noun* traces of medicines used for treating livestock that are still present when the animal is slaughtered for food

Vibrio parahaemolyticus *noun* an infective food poisoning bacterium found in shellfish and other seafood, producing symptoms of diarrhoea that often lead to dehydration, abdominal pain and fever

Vibrio vulnificus *noun* a marine bacterium that can be ingested in seafood and causes severe symptoms in patients with existing liver disease

vichyssoise *noun* a creamy soup made from leeks, potatoes, and onions, often served chilled

vicine *noun* the toxin in broad beans that causes favism

Vietnamese coriander, Vietnamese mint *noun* a herb used in Vietnamese cuisine

villi *plural noun* the small hair-like projections of the mucous membrane in the small intestine, which serve to increase its surface area and therefore its ability to absorb nutrients

vinaigrette *noun* a salad dressing made with oil, vinegar, salt and other flavourings. Also called **French dressing**

Vincent's angina *noun* a painful mouth inflammation with ulcers and gum damage

vindaloo *noun* a very hot curry sauce made with coriander, red chilli, ginger and other spices, or a dish cooked in this sauce

vinegar *noun* liquid made from sour wine or cider, used in cooking and for preserving food

vintage *noun* **1.** the work of collecting grapes to make wine, or the grapes that are collected **2.** a fine wine made in a particular year

violaxanthin *noun* ♦ E161(e)

viosterol *noun* same as **vitamin D2**

virgin oil *noun* oil that has not been treated after being pressed from the fruit or seed, giving it a more distinctive flavour and a higher vitamin content

virgin olive oil *noun* olive oil produced by the pressing of heated olive pulp after fine olive oil has been removed

virgin pastry *noun* puff pastry after it is first made, not after rerolling, used for vol-au-vents and other items that require an even rise or lift

virus *noun* a parasite consisting of a nucleic acid surrounded by a protein coat that can only develop in other cells

viscogen *noun* a thickening agent used especially in whipping cream

viscosity *noun* the state of a liquid that moves slowly

viscous *adjective* used for describing a liquid that is thick and slow-moving

vision *noun* the sense of sight

vitafoods *plural noun* food products that are designed for health-conscious consumers

vitamin *noun* any of various substances that are not synthesised in the body but are found in most foods, essential for good health

vitamin A *noun* a vitamin that is soluble in fat and can be synthesised in the body from precursors, but is mainly found in food such as liver, vegetables, eggs and cod liver oil. Also called **retinol** (NOTE: Lack of vitamin A affects the body's growth and resistance to disease.)

vitamin A2 *noun* a form of vitamin A obtained from fish liver

vitamin B1 *noun* a water-soluble vitamin that maintains normal carbohydrate metabolism and nervous system function and is found in high concentration in yeast, in the outer layers and germ of cereals, in beef, in pork and in pulses. Also called **aneurin, thiamin**

vitamin B2 *noun* a water-soluble vitamin that is essential for metabolic processes and for cell maintenance and repair, present in all leafy vegetables, in eggs, milk and the flesh of warm blooded animals. Also called **riboflavin**

vitamin B3 *noun* a water-soluble vitamin that occurs in the form of niacin, nicotinic acid and nicotinamide and is widely distributed in foodstuffs, with meat, fish, wholemeal flour and peanuts being major sources

vitamin B5 *noun* a water-soluble vitamin that is destroyed by boiling, found in all animal and plant tissues, especially poultry, liver, fish, eggs, potatoes and whole grains. Also called **pantothenic acid**

vitamin B6 *noun* a water-soluble vitamin that consists of the compounds pyridoxal, pyridoxol and pyridoxamine, found in low concentration in all animal and plant tissues, especially in fish, eggs and wholemeal flour

vitamin B12 *noun* a cobalt-containing water-soluble vitamin that, together with folic acid, has a vital role in metabolic processes and in the formation of red blood cells and is responsible for the general feeling of well-being in healthy individuals (NOTE: It is normally found only in animal products, particularly ox kidney and liver and oily fish.)

vitamin B13 *noun* same as **pangamic acid**

vitamin B15 *noun* same as **orotic acid**

vitamin B complex *noun* a group of vitamins such as folic acid, riboflavine and thiamine

vitamin C *noun* a vitamin that is soluble in water and is found in fresh fruit, especially oranges and lemons, raw vegetables and liver. Also called **ascorbic acid** (NOTE: Lack of vitamin C can cause anaemia and scurvy.)

vitamin D *noun* a vitamin which is soluble in fat, and is found in butter, eggs and fish (NOTE: It is also produced by the skin when exposed to sunlight. Vitamin D helps in the formation of bones, and lack of it causes rickets in children.)

vitamin D1 *noun* a form of vitamin D obtained through ultraviolet irradiation of a type of alcohol called ergosterol

vitamin D2 *noun* a precursor of vitamin D. Also called **viosterol**

vitamin D3 *noun* a precursor of vitamin D. Also called **cholecalciferol**

vitamin E *noun* a vitamin found in vegetables, vegetable oils, eggs and wholemeal bread

vitamin H *noun* ♦ **biotin**

vitamin K *noun* a vitamin, found in green vegetables such as spinach and cabbage, that helps the clotting of blood and is needed to activate prothrombin

vitamin pill, vitamin supplement *noun* a pill containing one or several vitamins or minerals, taken as a food supplement

vitamin-rich *adjective* containing high levels of vitamins

vitellin *noun* the protein found in egg yolk

viticulture *noun* the cultivation of grapes

vodka *noun* **1.** a strong colourless alcohol distilled from grain or potatoes, made originally in Russia and Poland **2.** a glass of this alcohol

vol-au-vent *noun* a small round case of pastry, usually filled with a savoury mixture, eaten hot or cold

volume *noun* an amount of a substance

voluntary fortification *noun* enrichment of food products that is not required by government policy but is carried out at the discretion of the manufacturer, e.g. the enrichment of some breakfast cereals with folic acid

votator *noun* a machine used in the manufacture of margarine

VP *abbreviation* variegate porphyria

VTEC *abbreviation* verotoxic E coli

VTEC 0157 *noun* same as **E coli 0157**

W

wafer *noun* a thin sweet biscuit eaten with ice cream

waffle *noun* a type of thick crisp pancake cooked in an iron mould and eaten with syrup

waffle-iron *noun* an iron mould used for making waffles

waist-to-hip ratio *noun* a way of describing the distribution of adipose tissue in the body

Waldorf salad *noun* a salad made of diced raw apples, celery and walnuts with a mayonnaise dressing

walnut *noun* a hard round nut with a wrinkled shell

walnut oil *noun* oil produced by crushing walnuts

warm *verb* to heat food until it is quite hot

warming cupboard *noun* a specially heated cupboard in a kitchen, where food can be kept warm

wasabi *noun* a strong-tasting green powder or paste obtained from a plant root, used as a condiment in Japanese cooking

waste *noun* material that is useless, especially material that is left over after all the useful parts or substances have been used up ■ *verb* to use more of something than is needed ■ *adjective* used for describing material that is useless

wasted *adjective* of bodily tissues, shrunken and weakened as a result of illness or poor nutrition

water *noun* the liquid that is essential to life and makes up a large part of the body

water balance *noun* a state in which the water lost by the body, e.g. in urine or sweat, is made up by water absorbed from food and drink

water-binding agent *noun* salt or sugar used for preserving foods by reducing their water activity

water biscuit *noun* a thin unsweetened hard biscuit made of flour and water, eaten with cheese

water brash *noun* the sudden filling of the mouth with acidic juices from the stomach, usually accompanied by heartburn and often resulting from indigestion, a condition that is common in pregnancy but may also be an indication of a disorder of the digestive tract

water chestnut *noun* a round white crunchy stem base of a Chinese water plant, often used in Asian cooking

watercress *noun* a creeping plant grown in water and eaten in salads and soup. ◊ **cress**

water filter *noun* an appliance or fitting for removing unwanted matter from water, especially bacteria or harmful chemicals from drinking water

water glass *noun* a glass on a table for drinking water, placed next to a wine glass in a table setting

water icing *noun* same as **glacé icing**

Waterlow classification *noun* categories of malnutrition in children, based on the ratio of actual weight to expected weight and on the ratio of actual height to expected height

watermelon *noun* a large, very juicy green fruit with red flesh and black seeds

water retention *noun* the build-up of fluid in bodily tissues, causing swelling

water-soluble vitamins *plural noun* vitamins B and C, which can form a solution in water

watery *adjective* liquid, like water

waxed paper *noun* same as **greaseproof paper**

waxing *noun* the practice of coating fruit and vegetables in wax to improve the appearance and prevent moisture loss

waxy *adjective* **1.** smooth and shiny **2.** covered with wax

weak flour *noun* flour of any type with a lower protein content than strong flour, used for making biscuits and cakes but not suitable for bread-making

wean *verb* to make a baby stop breastfeeding and take other liquid or solid food, or to make a baby start to eat solid food after having only had liquids to drink

weep *verb* to ooze fluid

weight bearing activity *noun* resistance exercise that strengthens the bones and prevents osteoporosis

weighted dietary survey *noun* a dietary survey of a group, e.g. a family, that gives both individual and average results

weight-for-age *noun* an index of a child's weight against the average weight for a child of that age, showing whether they are being adequately nourished for growth

weight-for-height *noun* an index of a child's weight against the average weight for a child of that height, showing whether they are being adequately nourished for growth

weight loss *noun* the fact of losing weight or of becoming thinner

weld *noun* the seam along the length of a can that is vulnerable to corrosion

Wellcome classification *noun* categories of malnutrition in children, based on the ratio of actual weight to expected weight and on the presence or absence of oedema

well done *adjective* completely cooked

well-hung *adjective* used for describing meat that has been hung up long enough to mature and be good to eat

wellness *noun* physical wellbeing, especially when maintained or achieved through good diet and regular exercise

wellness foods *plural noun* nutritionally rich foods eaten for health

Wernicke-Korsakoff syndrome *noun* a form of brain damage caused by severe nutritional deficiencies in people with long-term alcoholism

WFP *abbreviation* World Food Programme

wheat *noun* a grain harvested in temperate regions from a widely cultivated cereal plant, used for making flour for bread, pasta, and other foods

wheat flakes *plural noun* partially boiled cracked wheat crushed between rollers then dried, lightly toasted and used in muesli and as a breakfast cereal

wheat germ *noun* the centre of the wheat grain that is milled finely and sometimes toasted, used for sprinkling over cereals and in cooking

wheat germ flour *noun* the pulverised germ of wheat usually dry-fried or roasted before use

wheat grain *noun* a single kernel of unprocessed wheat ready for milling

wheatgrass *noun* wheat grains sprouted to a height of around 7 inches or 17 cm, cut and pulped to produce a highly nutritious juice that is drunk in very small quantities

wheat hardness *noun* a measure of the ease with which wheat is ground into flour

wheat intolerance *noun* an inability to digest wheat

wheat protein *noun* ♦ seitan

wheat starch *noun* a gluten-free wheat flour consisting mainly of starch, used as a thickener and mixed with tapioca starch to make a boiling water dough suitable, after kneading and rolling or flattening, for wrapping small parcels of food such as dim sum

whelk *noun* a type of edible sea snail

whey *noun* the watery liquid that separates from the solid part of milk when it turns sour or when enzymes are added in cheese making. Compare **curd**

whey protein concentrate *noun* a high-protein supplement used by bodybuilders, containing bioavailable milk proteins. Abbreviation **WPC**

whey protein isolate *noun* a sports supplement that is more purified than whey protein concentrate. Abbreviation **WPI**

whip *verb* to make food such as batter or cream stiff and creamy by adding air to it with short quick movements, using a fork, whisk or electric beater

whipped cream *noun* cream that is beaten until it is stiff, flavoured with sugar and vanilla

whipping cream *noun* a heavy cream containing a high proportion of butterfat that causes it to stiffen when whipped

whipworm *noun* the worm that causes the condition trichuriasis

whisk *noun* a kitchen tool made of curved or coiled wires attached to a handle, used for whipping soft or liquid foods ■ *verb* to whip a soft or liquid substance with a fork, whisk or other utensil

white *adjective* of a colour like snow or milk ■ *noun* an egg white

white adipose tissue *noun* fat stored in the body that is not metabolically active and is hard to burn. Compare **brown adipose tissue**

whitebait *noun* a small young fish fried and eaten whole (NOTE: The plural form is **whitebait**.)

white bread *noun* bread made from refined white flour

white chocolate *noun* a cream-coloured confection containing the same ingredients as chocolate but lacking cocoa powder

white fat *noun* same as **white adipose tissue**

white fish *noun* **1.** any edible sea fish with whitish flesh, e.g. the cod, hake or whiting, as distinct from a flat fish such as the plaice and an oily fish such as the mackerel **2.** a small freshwater fish related to the salmon and trout, often smoked

white flour *noun* wheat flour from which the bran and wheat germ have been removed, leaving between 72% and 74% of the original dehusked grain, sometimes bleached chemically to enhance the white colour

white meat *noun* light-coloured meat, such as the breast meat on a chicken

white pepper *noun* a light-coloured pepper made from peppercorns that have had their dark husk removed

white pudding *noun* a food that consists of pork meat and fat, suet, bread, and oatmeal, formed into the shape of a large sausage, similar to black pudding but without the blood

white roux *noun* a roux that contains equal quantities of plain soft flour and butter, cooked without being coloured, used for béchamel sauce

white sauce *noun* a basic sauce made from fat, flour and liquid usually milk or stock

white sugar *noun* same as **granulated sugar**

white wine *noun* wine made without leaving the grape skins in the fermenting mixture, making the wine pale yellow or green instead of deep red

whiting *noun* a type of small sea fish (NOTE: The plural form is **whiting**.)

WHO *abbreviation* World Health Organisation

wholefood *noun* food that has been grown without the use of artificial fertilisers and has not been processed

wholegrain *noun* food such as rice of which the whole of the seed is eaten

wholemeal *noun* flour that contains a large proportion of the original wheat seed, including the bran ■ *adjective* containing wheat germ and bran

whole milk *noun* cows' milk with a least 3.25% butterfat and 8.25% non-fat solids

whole school approach *noun* healthy eating education combined with the provision of nutritious meals and snacks at school, reinforcing the message

wholewheat *noun* same as **wholemeal**

Wiener schnitzel *noun* a slice of veal covered in breadcrumbs and fried

wild mushroom *noun* any of various types of edible mushroom found in the countryside and now also cultivated (NOTE: Ceps and chanterelles are the best-known wild mushrooms.)

wild rice *noun* a species of grass that is found naturally in North America and is similar to rice

wilted *adjective* **1.** used for describing a crisp leaf vegetable that has been lightly cooked so that it is no longer crunchy **2.** used for describing a plant or vegetable that has drooped or shrivelled through lack of water or too much heat

wine *noun* **1.** an alcoholic drink made from the juice of grapes **2.** an alcoholic drink made from the juice of fruit or flowers

wine glass *noun* a glass for serving wine

wine vinegar *noun* vinegar made from wine, as distinct from cider vinegar or malt vinegar

winkle *noun* a type of small edible sea-snail

winterise *verb* to remove saturated glycerides from oil so that it does not become cloudy at low temperatures

wire rack *noun* a raised tray made of wire for cooling hot food such as cakes on

wishbone *noun* the V-shaped bone found between the breasts of a chicken or other bird

withdrawal *noun* a period during which a person who has been addicted to a drug stops taking it and experiences unpleasant symptoms

wok *noun* a Chinese round-bottomed frying pan

wolf *verb* to eat food quickly and greedily or in gulps

wolfberry *noun* a nutritionally rich berry with high concentrations of antioxidants, considered a superfood

won ton *noun* in Chinese cookery, a small dumpling made from a square of noodle dough with a little filling in the middle, boiled in soup or deep-fried

wood pigeon *noun* a wild pigeon that is used as food

woodruff *noun* a perennial plant with leaves that are used, mainly in Germany, to flavour wine, beer, brandy, sausages and jam, and to make a herbal tea with gentle sedative properties

Worcestershire sauce, Worcester sauce *noun* a thin pungent table sauce flavoured with soy, tamarind and spices, originally made in Worcestershire

work surface *noun* a rigid flat area on which work is done, e.g., a tabletop or kitchen counter

World Food Programme *noun* a part of the Food and Agriculture Organization of the United Nations intended to give international aid in the form of food from countries with food surpluses. Abbreviation **WFP**

World Health Assembly *noun* an annual meeting of delegates from all member states of the WHO, at which major policy decisions are made

World Health Organisation *noun* the United Nation's agency for health, promoting global health education and provision of healthcare facilities. Abbreviation **WHO**

worms *plural noun* a condition in which a human or animal is infested with parasitic worms that can cause disease

WPC *abbreviation* whey protein concentrate

WPI *abbreviation* whey protein isolate

wrap *noun* a soft bread, like a tortilla, wrapped round a filling to make a snack

XYZ

xanthan gum *noun* gum produced from a bacterium by commercial fermentation, used as a thickener or gelling agent. Also called **E415**

xanthelasma *noun* yellow deposits on the eyelids caused by high levels of cholesterol in the blood

xanthoma *noun* a yellow fatty mass, often on the eyelids and hands, found in people with a high level of cholesterol in the blood (NOTE: The plural is **xanthomata**.)

xanthophyll *noun* a yellow pigment, found in the leaves of most plants, that gives egg yolks their yellow colour

xanthosis *noun* high blood concentrations of betacarotene creating a yellow tinge in the skin

xenobiotic *adjective* used for describing a substance found in the body that is not normally expected to be there

xerophagia *noun* the practice of eating only dry food

xerophonia *noun* a dry-sounding voice caused by diabetes medication

xerophthalmia *noun* severe vitamin A deficiency leading to ulceration of the cornea

xerosis *noun* abnormal dryness of an organ or tissue

xerostomia *noun* dryness of the mouth caused by medication that arrests the salivary glands

xylitol *noun* a type of alcohol somewhat sweeter than sugar, used in sugar-free chewing gum

yakitori *noun* a dish of Japanese origin consisting of small pieces of grilled chicken that are basted on skewers with a sauce of soya, stock, sugar and mirin

yam *noun* **1.** the thick starchy tuber of a tropical plant, used like a potato **2.** same as **sweet potato**

yarrow *noun* a flowering plant of northern countries with leaves that are taken as a digestive stimulant and anti-inflammatory

yeast *noun* a living fungus used for making bread and beer

yeast extract *noun* a thick sticky brown food obtained from yeast and eaten as a spread or used in cooking

yeast infection *noun* an overgrowth of a fungus in the vagina, intestines, skin or mouth, causing irritation and swelling

Yersinia enterocolitica *noun* a strain of bacteria that causes yersiniosis, found in raw pork products

yersiniosis *noun* a condition, mainly found in children and young adults, caused by a bacterium and characterised by intestinal pain and symptoms that resemble appendicitis

yield *noun* the number of servings or portions obtained from a given recipe or amount of food

yoghurt *noun* milk fermented by bacteria to give a tangy or slightly sour flavour and a lightly set or thick and creamy consistency

yolk *noun* the yellow central part of an egg

yolk greening *noun* the formation of a greenish-grey film on the outside of a hard-boiled egg yolk, caused by the deposition of ferrous sulphur

Yorkshire pudding *noun* a mixture of eggs, flour and milk, cooked in the oven, the traditional accompaniment to roast beef

yo-yo dieting *noun* a situation in which a person repeatedly loses weight through dieting and then regains the weight that he or she has lost

zabaglione *noun* a dessert made of egg yolks, sugar and marsala wine beaten over hot water until pale and foamy and served hot with sponge finger biscuits

zander *noun* a freshwater fish of the perch family, native to central Europe (NOTE: Its scientific name is *Stizostedion lucioperca*.)

Z blade mixer *noun* a food mixer with a rotating zig-zag blade

zearalenone *noun* a type of mycotoxin that is produced by fungus on cereals in storage

zeaxanthin *noun* a type of carotenoid found in eggs and citrus fruit that contributes to eye health

zen macrobiotics *noun* a very strict form of macrobiotic diet that avoids, e.g., eating foods that are out of season or foods that have been transported a long distance

zest *noun* the thin outer rind of the peel of a citrus fruit that is cut, scraped or grated to yield a sharp fruity flavouring for foods and drinks

zester *noun* a small utensil with a row of tiny sharpened holes or edges at its tip for cutting strips of zest from oranges, lemons and other citrus fruits

zinc *noun* a white metallic trace element (NOTE: The chemical symbol is **Zn**.)

zinc deficiency *noun* a condition that can cause tissue wasting and delayed puberty in boys

zinc monomethionine aspartate and magnesium aspartate *noun* full form of **ZMA**

ZMA *noun* a supplement for athletes containing zinc and magnesium, reputed to increase testosterone. Full form **zinc monomethionine aspartate and magnesium aspartate**

Zone diet *noun* a dietary plan in which 40% of daily calories should come from carbohydrates, 30% from proteins and 30% from fats

zucchini *noun* same as **courgette**

zygosaccharomyces *plural noun* types of yeast that prefer sugary atmospheres

zymase *noun* the enzyme mixture found in yeast

zymochemistry *noun* the chemical reactions involved in fermentation

zymogen *noun* same as **proenzyme**

zymogene *noun* a microbe that causes fermentation

zymogenesis *noun* the transformation of a zymogen into an enzyme

zymogenic *adjective* causing or promoting fermentation

zymology *noun* the branch of chemistry concerned with the action of enzymes

zymolysis *noun* the action of enzymes in the process of fermentation. Also called **zymosis**

zymoprotein *noun* a protein that also functions as an enzyme

zymosthenic *noun* an agent that amplifies the effect of an enzyme

zymurgy *noun* the branch of chemistry concerned with brewing and distilling

SUPPLEMENTS

Weights and Measures
Micronutrient Sources and Deficiencies
Recommended Daily Amounts (RDAs):
Vitamins
Minerals
Energy
Protein
Saturated and Unsaturated Fats
Body Mass Index Calculator
HACCP Procedure for Food Hygiene
Nutrition Contacts
Food Industry Contacts
Health Contacts

Weights and Measures

Imperial - Metric

1 dash	=	4 ml.
1 teaspoon	=	5 ml.
1 dessert spoon	=	10 ml.
1 tablespoon	=	15 ml.
1 fluid ounce	=	28.4 ml.
1 pint	=	568 ml.
1 quart	=	1.1 l.
1 gallon	=	4.5 l.
1 ounce	=	28.4g.
1 pound	=	454g.

Metric - Imperial

10 millilitres	=	2.5 dash
10 millilitres	=	2 tsp.
10 millilitres	=	1 dsp.
10 millilitres	=	0.5 tbsp.
10 millilitres	=	0.35 fl. oz.
1 litre	=	1.75 pints
1 litre	=	0.9 quarts
1 litre	=	0.22 gallons
10 grams	=	0.35 oz.
1 kilogram	=	2.2 lb.

Temperature conversions

Fahrenheit	Celsius	Gas Mark
225°F	110°C	¼
250°	130°	½
275°	140°	1
300°	150°	2
325°	170°	3
350°	180°	4
375°	190°	5
400°	200°	6
425°	220°	7
450°	230°	8
475°	240°	9

(All measurements are approximate)

Micronutrient Sources and Deficiencies

Vitamins:

	Dietary sources	*Deficiency symptoms*	*Overdose symptoms*
Vitamin A	Liver, dairy products, spinach, oily fish, carrots	Night blindness, anaemia, weakened immune system, dry skin	Bone defects, liver damage. Can cause harm to unborn babies.
Thiamine	Pork, fruit, eggs, grains, fortified breakfast cereals	Headache, tiredness, anorexia, muscle wasting	None known
Riboflavin	Milk, eggs, fortified breakfast cereals, rice	Weakened nervous system, cracks in mouth and lips	None known
Niacin	Beef, pork, chicken, eggs, milk	Weakened digestive and nervous systems	Skin flushing, liver damage, digestive dysfunction
Pantothenate	Chicken, kidney, broccoli, tomatoes	Impaired absorption of energy from food	Fatigue, nausea, cold hands and feet
Vitamin B6	Pork, cod, eggs, whole grains, milk	Anaemia, nausea, confusion	Temporary nerve damage
Vitamin B12	Meat, fish, yeast, dairy products	Anaemia, fatigue, impaired absorption of folic acid	None known
Biotin	Kidney, eggs, dried fruit	Fatigue, hair loss, depression, weight loss	None known
Vitamin C	Citrus fruit, vegetables	Loose teeth, joint pain, hair loss, anaemia	Diarrhoea, stomach pain, flatulence
Vitamin D	Oily fish, eggs, liver, sunlight	Bone softening, loose teeth	Kidney damage, calcium deposits in soft tissues

Micronutrient Sources and Deficiencies *cont.*

Vitamins cont.

	Dietary sources	*Deficiency symptoms*	*Overdose symptoms*
Vitamin E	Seeds, nuts, vegetable oils, whole grains	Cell damage, anaemia, weakness	None known
Vitamin K	Green leafy vegetables, cereals, oils,	Impaired healing of wounds, haemorrage	None known
Folic Acid	Brussels sprouts, broccoli, peas, yeast	Anaemia, fatigue, swollen tongue. Can cause damage to unborn babies.	Covers up Vitamin B12 deficiency

Minerals:

	Dietary sources	*Deficiency symptoms*	*Overdose symptoms*
Calcium	Green leafy vegetables, dairy products	Impaired blood clotting, weak bones, irregular heartbeat	Stomach pain, diarrhoea
Magnesium	Nuts, bread, spinach	Impaired bone health, fatigue	Diarrhoea
Selenium	Nuts, bread, fish, meat, eggs	Damage to cells and tissues, weakened immune system	Loss of hair and nails, skin damage, chronic illness
Zinc	Shellfish, meat, dairy products	Bone damage, decreased sexual function	Amaemia, bone weakening, eye damage
Iron	Liver, red meat, pulses, dried fruit	Anaemia	Stomach pain, nausea, constipation
Iodine	Sea fish, shell fish, milk	Decreased thyroid function	Thyroid damage

Data from Food Standards Agency: *www.eatwell.gov.uk*

RDAs: Water-Soluble Vitamins

Water-soluble vitamins

Group	Vitamin C (mg/day)	Thiamine (mg/day)	Riboflavin (mg/day)	Niacin* (mg/day)	Vitamin B6 (mg/day)	Pantothenate (mg/day)	Biotin (/day)	Vitamin B12 (/day)	Folate (/day)
Infant (0-12 months)	27.5	0.25	0.35	3	0.2	1.75	5.5	0.5	80
Child (1-9 years)	32	0.7	0.7	9	0.8	3	14	1.3	225
Adolescent (10-18 years)	40	1.2	1.2	16	1.3	5	25	2.4	400
Adult female (19-65 years)	45	1.1	1.1	14	1.4	5	30	2.4	400
Adult male (19-65 years)	45	1.2	1.3	16	1.5	5	30	2.4	400
Elderly (65+ years)	45	1.2	1.2	15	1.6	5	**	2.4	400
Pregnant	55	1.4	1.4	18	1.9	6	30	2.6	600
Lactating	70	1.5	1.6	17	2	7	35	2.8	500

* or dietary equivalents   ** no figures available

All data derived from *Vitamin and mineral requirements in human nutrition: Report of a Joint FAO/WHO Expert Consultation. Geneva, WHO* (2005)

RDAs: Fat-Soluble Vitamins and Minerals

Group	Fat-soluble vitamins				Minerals					
	Vitamin A (/day)	Vitamin D (mg/day)	Vitamin E (mg/day)	Vitamin K (/day)	Calcium (mg/day)	Magnesium (mg/day)	Selenium (/day)	Zinc* (mg/day)	Iron ** (mg/day)	Iodine (/day)
Infant (0-12 months)	380	5	2.7	7.5	350	40	8	3	9.3	90
Child (1-9 years)	450	5	6	20	600	30	20	4.8	15	100
Adolescent (10-18 years)	600	5	8	45	1300	225	29	7.9	24	150
Adult female (19-65 years)	500	7.5	7.5	55	1150	220	26	4.9	50	150
Adult male (19-65 years)	600	7	10	65	1300	260	34	7	28	150
Elderly (65+ years)	600	15	9	60	1300	210	29	5.5	25	150
Pregnant	300	5	7.5	55	1200	220	29	7.5	100	200
Lactating	850	55	7.5	55	1000	270	37	8.5	30	200

* moderate bioavailability   ** 10% bioavailability

All data derived from *Vitamin and mineral requirements in human nutrition: Report of a Joint FAO/WHO Expert Consultation*. Geneva, WHO (2005)

RDAs: Energy

Age	Male		Female		Male + female	
	% of total population	Energy requirement (kcal/day)	% of total population	Energy requirement (kcal/day)	% of total population	Energy requirement (kcal/day)
0	0.62	800	0.59	740	1.22	820
1	0.62	1200	0.60	1140	1.22	1220
2	0.63	1410	0.60	1310	1.22	1380
3	0.63	1560	0.60	1440	1.23	1500
4	0.63	1690	0.62	1540	1.27	1620
0-4	3.16	1330	3.0	1240	6.16	1290
5-9	3.42	1980	3.26	1760	6.67	1860
10-14	3.48	2390	3.33	2050	6.81	2210
15-19	3.49	2780	3.34	2160	6.83	2420
20-59	27.56	2590	27.68	2090	55.24	2230
60+	7.44	2160	10.84	1880	18.28	1890
Pregnant	n/a	n/a	1.2	200 extra	1.2	200 extra
Lactating	n/a	n/a	0.3	500 extra	0.3	500 extra
Whole population	48.55	2400	51.45	1980	**100%**	**2180**

All data derived from *Energy and protein requirements: Report of a Joint FAO/WHO Expert Consultation*. Geneva, WHO (1985)

RDAs: Protein

Age	Male % of total population	Male Energy requirement (kcal/day)	Female % of total population	Female Energy requirement (kcal/day)	Male + female % of total population	Male + female Energy requirement (kcal/day)
0	0.62	12.9	0.59	11.9	1.22	12.3
1	0.62	14.1	0.60	13.3	1.22	14.0
2	0.63	15.5	0.60	15.0	1.22	15.5
3	0.63	16.9	0.60	16.5	1.23	16.7
4	0.63	18.5	0.62	17.3	1.27	17.9
0-4	3.16	15.7	3.0	14.9	6.16	15.3
5-9	3.42	24.4	3.26	24.1	6.67	24.3
10-14	3.48	42.1	3.33	41.5	6.81	41.8
15-19	3.49	54.4	3.34	44.7	6.83	49.7
20-59	27.56	50.2	27.68	41.2	55.24	45.9
60+	7.44	50.2	10.84	41.2	18.28	44.9
Pregnant	n/a	n/a	1.2	200 extra	1.2	200 extra
Lactating	n/a	n/a	0.3	500 extra	0.3	500 extra
Whole population	48.55	45.9	51.45	39.5	**100%**	**42.4**

All data derived from *Energy and protein requirements: Report of a Joint FAO/WHO Expert Consultation*. Geneva, WHO (1985)

Saturated and Unsaturated Fats

Food product	Saturated (% of total fats)	Monounsaturated (% of total fats)	Polyunsaturated (% of total fats)
Beef	50	42	4
Butter	62	29	4
Canola oil	7	55	33
Chicken	30	45	21
Cocoa butter	60	35	2
Coconut oil	86	6	2
Corn oil	13	24	59
Cottonseed oil	26	18	50
Hard margarine	18	59	18
Lamb	47	42	4
Olive oil	13	74	8
Palm kernel oil	81	11	2
Palm oil	49	37	9
Peanut oil	17	46	32
Pork	40	45	11
Safflower oil	9	12	75
Soft margarine	17	47	31
Soybean oil	4	23	58
Sunflower oil	13	24	59
Vegetable shortening	31	51	14
Walnut oil	9	16	70

All figures represent the percentage of total fats in the food or oil. Total fat content of foods may vary.

Data from *Food and Cooking: and Encyclopedia of Kitchen Science, History and Culture* (McGee, Hodder and Stoughton, 2004)

Body Mass Index Calculator

Height (cm)	Body Weight (kg)																
150cm	43	45	47	49	52	54	56	58	60	63	65	67	69	72	74	76	78
152cm	44	46	49	51	54	56	58	60	63	65	67	69	72	74	76	79	81
155cm	45	48	50	53	55	57	60	63	65	67	69	72	74	77	79	82	84
157cm	47	49	52	54	57	59	62	64	67	69	72	74	77	79	82	84	87
160cm	49	51	54	56	59	61	64	66	69	72	74	77	79	82	84	87	89
163cm	50	53	55	58	61	64	66	68	71	74	77	79	82	84	87	89	93
165cm	52	54	57	60	63	65	68	71	73	76	79	82	84	87	90	93	95
168cm	54	56	59	62	64	67	70	73	76	78	81	84	87	90	93	95	98
170cm	55	57	61	64	66	69	72	75	78	81	84	87	90	93	96	98	101
172cm	57	59	63	65	68	72	74	78	80	83	86	89	92	95	98	101	104
175cm	58	61	64	68	70	73	77	80	83	86	89	92	95	98	101	104	107
178cm	60	63	66	69	73	76	79	82	85	88	91	95	98	104	104	107	110
180cm	62	65	68	71	75	78	81	84	88	91	94	98	101	104	107	110	113
183cm	64	67	70	73	77	80	83	87	90	93	97	100	103	107	110	113	117
185cm	65	68	72	75	79	83	86	89	93	96	99	103	107	110	113	117	120
188cm	67	70	74	78	81	84	88	92	95	99	102	106	110	113	116	120	123
191cm	69	73	76	80	83	87	91	94	98	102	105	109	113	116	120	123	127
BMI	19	20	21	22	23	24	25	26	27	28	29	30	31	32	33	34	35

Find your height in the left-hand column, then move along the row to find your weight. The number at the bottom of that column is your BMI.
Less than 20 = underweight. 20–25 = desirable weight. 25–30 = overweight. More than 30 = obese.

HACCP Procedure for Food Hygiene

Step	Potential Hazard	Measures to take	CP/CCP
Sourcing	Contaminated food from poor-quality source	Ensure source is trusted and has appropriate qualifications	CP
Food Transport	Bacterial growth and contamination	Store food at appropriate temperature during transport. Ensure food is effectively sealed	CP
Storage	Spoilage	Store food at appropriate temperature, no longer than recommended time	CP
Thawing	Bacterial growth, cross-contamination	Do not thaw in same area as other foods, use promptly after thawing	CP
Cooking	Survival of bacteria	Cook to appropriately high internal temperature, monitoring with thermometer	CCP
Hot holding	Bacterial growth	Hold at appropriately high temperature, check often	CCP
Serving	Bacterial contamination	Serve within short time of preparation. Do not allow personal contact with food	CCP
Keeping leftovers	Bacterial growth, spoilage	Cool food rapidly, do not keep for longer than appropriate. Do not allow personal contact with food.	CCP
Serving leftovers	Bacterial growth	Reheat quickly and thoroughly, serve promptly	CCP

CP = Control Point Step
(failing to observe this poses a general risk to the safety and quality of food)

CCP = Critical Control Point Step
(failing to observe this poses a serious risk to human health)

Nutrition contacts

American Society for Nutrition
9650 Rockville Pike, Suite L-4500, Bethesda, MD 20814
Website: *www.nutrition.org*

British Association for Nutritional Therapy
27 Old Gloucester Street, London WC1N 3XX
Website: *www.bant.org*

British Dietetic Association
Charles House, 148/9 Great Charles Street, Queensway, Birmingham B3 3HT
Website: *www.bda.org.uk*

British Nutrition Foundation
High Holborn House, 52-54 High Holborn, London WC1V 6RQ
Website: *www.nutrition.org.uk*

Department for Education and Skills
Sanctuary Buildings, Great Smith Street, London SW1P 3BT
Website: *www.dfes.gov.uk*

Department for Environment, Food and Rural Affairs (DEFRA)
Nobel House, 17 Smith House, London SW1P 3JR
Website: *www.defra.gov.uk*

Department for Health
Richmond House, 79 Whitehall, London SW1A 2NS Tel: 020 7210 4850
Website: *www.doh.gov.uk*

European Food Information Council
Rue Guimard, 19, 1040-Brussels, Belgium
Website: *www.eufic.org*

Food and Agriculture Organization of the United Nations
Viale delle Terme di Caracalla, 00100 Rome, Italy
Website: *www.fao.org*

Food and Drug Administration
5600 Fishers Lane, Rockville MD 20857-0001
Website: *www.fda.gov*

Food and Nutrition Information Center
Online service provided by the US National Agricultural Library
Website: *www.nal.usda.gov*

Food Commission
94 White Lion Street, London N1 9PF
Website: *www.foodcomm.org.uk*

Nutrition contacts *cont.*

Food Ethics Council
39-41 Surrey Street, Brighton BN1 3PB
Website: *http://foodethicscouncil.org*

Food Standards Agency
UK Headquarters: Aviation House, 125 Kingsway, London WC2B 6NH
Website: *www.food.gov.uk* OR *www.eatwell.gov.uk*

Institute for Optimum Nutrition
Avalon House, 72 Lower Mortlake Road, Richmond, Surrey TW9 2JY
Website: *www.ion.ac.uk*

Institute of Food Research
Norwich Research Park, Colney, Norwich NR4 7UA
Website: *www.ifr.ac.uk*

Institute of Food Science and Technology
5 Cambridge Court, 210 Shepherds Bush Road, London W6 7NJ
Website: *www.ifst.org*

International Association for Food Protection
6200 Aurora Avenue, Suite 200W, Des Moines, Iowa 50322-2864, USA
Website: *www.foodprotection.org*

International Food Information Council
1100 Connecticut Avenue, NW, Suite 430, Washington, DC 20036
Website: *www.ific.org*

International Life Sciences Institute
One Thomas Circle, NW, 9th Floor, Washington, DC 20005-5802
Website: *www.ilsi.org*

International Union of Food Science and Technology
No. 19, 511 Maplegrove Road, Oakville, Ontario, Canada L6J 6X0
Website: *www.iufost.com*

Joint Health Claims Initiative
Devonshire House, 66 Church Street, Leatherhead, Surrey KT22 8DP
Website: *www.jhci.co.uk*

McCarrison Society
London Metropolitan University, 166-222 Holloway Rd, London N7 8DB
Website: w*ww.mccarrisonsociety.org.uk*

Nutrition Society
10 Cambridge Court, 210 Shepherds Bush Road, London W6 7NJ
Website: *www.nutritionsociety.org.uk*

Nutrition contacts *cont.*

Scientific Advisory Committee on Nutrition
Food Standards Agency, Aviation House, 125 Kingsway, London WC2B 6NH
Website: *www.sacn.gov.uk*

Society of Food Hygiene Technology
PO Box 37, Lymington, Hampshire SO41 9WL
Website: *www.sohft.co.uk*

UK Food Group
PO Box 100, London, SE1 7RT
Website: *www.ukfg.org.uk*

United Nations Development Programme
One United Nations Plaza, New York, NY 10017
Website: *www.undp.org*

World Health Organization
Avenue Appia 20, 1211 Geneva 27, Switzerland
Website: *www.who.int*

Nutrition projects and campaigns:

5-A-Day Campaign   *www.5aday.nhs.uk*

Better Hospital Food Programme   *www.betterhospitalfood.com*

Healthy Lifestyle Advice for Schools *www.wiredforhealth.gov.uk*

Healthy Living Scotland   *www.healthyliving.gov.uk*

Healthy Schools Programme   *www.lhsp.org*

National Food Safety Week   *www.foodlink.org.uk*

National Salt Awareness Week   *www.actiononsalt.org.uk*

Scottish Community Diet Project   *www.dietproject.org.uk*

World Food Programme   *www.wfp.org*

World Health Day   *www.who.int/world-health-day.*

Food Industry contacts

Association of Bakery Ingredients Manufacturers
4a Torphichen Street, Edinburgh EH3 8JQ
Website: *www.abim.org.uk*

Association of Cereal Food Manufacturers
Federation House, 6 Catherine Street, London WC2B 5JJ
Website: *www.breakfastcereal.org*

Biscuit, Cake, Chocolate and Confectionary Alliance
37-41 Bedford Row, London WC1R 4JH
Website: *www.bccca.org.uk*

British Cheese Board
Dragon Court, 27 Macklin Street, London WC2B 5LX
Website: *www.cheeseboard.co.uk*

British Egg Information Service
1 Chelsea Manor Gardens, London SW3 5PN
Website: *www.britegg.co.uk*

British Frozen Food Federation
Springfield House, Springfield Business Park, Grantham, Lincs NG31 7BG
Website: *www.bfff.co.uk*

British Meat Nutrition Education Service
Holborn Gate, 26 Southampton Buildings, London WC2A 1PQ
Website: *www.meatandhealth.co.uk*

British Potato Council
4300 Nash Court, John Smith Drive, Oxford Business Park, Oxford OX4 2RT
Website: *www.potato.org.uk*

British Poultry Council
Europoint House, 5 Lavington Street, London SE1 0NZ
Website: *www.poultry.uk.com*

British Soft Drinks Association
20 Stukeley Street, London WC2B 5LR
Website: *www.britishsoftdrinks.com*

Campden and Chorleywood Food Research Association
Chipping Campden, Gloucestershire GL55 6LD
Website: *www.campden.co.uk*

Canned Food UK
1st Floor, Griffin House, 18 Ludgate Hill, Birmingham B3 1DW
Website: *www.cannedfood.co.uk*

Food Industry contacts *cont.*

Chilled Food Association
PO Box 6434, Kettering NN15 5XT
Website: *www.chilledfood.org*

Coffee Science Information Centre
12 Market Street, Chipping Norton, Oxon OX7 5NQ
Website: *www.cosic.org*

Dairy Council
Henrietta House, 17/18 Henrietta Street, London WC2E 8QH
Website: *www.milk.co.uk*

European Food Safety Authority
Largo N. Palli 5/A, I-43100 Parma, Italy
Website: *www.efsa.europa.eu*

European Snacks Association
6 Catherine Street London WC2B 5JJ
Website: *www.esa.org.uk*

Fairtrade Foundation
Room 204, 16 Baldwin's Gardens, London EC1N 7RJ
Website: *www.fairtrade.org.uk*

Flour Advisory Bureau
21 Arlington Street, London SW1A 1RN
Website: *www.fabflour.co.uk*

Food and Drink Federation
6 Catherine Street, London WC2B 5JJ
Website: *www.fdf.org.uk*

Freedom Food
RSPCA, Wilberforce Way, Southwater, Horsham, West Sussex RH13 9RS
Website: *www.freedomfood.co.uk*

Fresh Fruit and Vegetable Information Bureau
Lockwood Press, 1 Nine Elms Lane, London SW8 5NN
Website: *www.freshinfo.com*

Grain Information Service
21 Arlington Street, London SW1A 1RN
Website: *www.wheatintolerance.co.uk*

Health Food Manufacturers' Association
63 Hampton Court Way, Thames Ditton, Surrey KT7 0LT
Website: *www.hfma.co.uk*

Food Industry contacts *cont.*

International Dairy Federation
Diamant Building, Boulevard Auguste Reyers 80, 1030 Brussels, Belgium
Website: *www.fil-idf.co.uk*

London Food Centre
London South Bank University, 103 Borough Road, London SE1 0AA
Website: *www.londonfood.org.uk*

Margarine and Spreads Association
Federation House, 6 Catherine Street, London WC2B 5JJ
Website: *www.margarine.org.uk*

Meat and Livestock Commission
PO Box 44, Winterhill House, Snowdon Drive, Milton Keynes MK6 1AX
Website: *www.mlc.org.uk*

Out of Home Group
Federation House, 6 Catherine Street, London WC2B 5JJ
Website: *www.outofhome.org*

Provision Trade Federation
17 Clerkenwell Green, London EC1R 0DP
Website: *www.provtrade.co.uk*

Red Meat Industry Forum
PO Box 44, Winterhill House, Snowdon Drive, Milton Keynes MK6 1AX
Website: *www.redmeatindustryforum.org.uk*

Rice Association
Federation House, 6 Catherine Street, London WC2B 5JJ
Website: *www.riceassociation.org.uk*

Salt Manufacturers' Association
PO Box 125, Kendal, Cumbria LA8 8XA
Website: *www.saltsense.co.uk*

Society of Independent Brewers
The Old Sawmill, Nyewood, Rogate, Petersfield, Hampshire GU31 5HA
Website: *www.siba.co.uk*

Sugar Bureau
Duncan House, Dolphin Square, London SW1V 3PW
Website: *www.sugar-bureau.co.uk*

UK Tea Council
9 The Courtyard, Gowan Avenue, London SW6 6RH
Website: *www.tea.co.uk*

Health contacts

Alcoholics Anonymous
PO Box 1, Stonebow House, Stonebow, York YO1 7NJ
Website: *www.alcoholics-anonymous.org.uk*

Allergy UK
Deepdene House, 30 Bellegrove Road, Welling, Kent DA16 3PY
Website: *www.allergyfoundation.com*

Anaphylaxis Campaign
PO Box 275, Farnborough GU14 6SX
Website: *www.anaphylaxis.org.uk*

British Diabetic Association
10 Queen Anne Street, London W1M 0BM
Website: *www.diabetes.org.uk*

British Heart Foundation
14 Fitzhardinge Street, London W1H 6DH
Website: *www.bhf.org.uk*

Caroline Walker Trust
22 Kindersley Way, Abbots Langley, Herts WD5 0DQ
Website: *www.cwt.org.uk*

Coeliac Disease Resource Centre
Nutricia Dietary Care, Newmarket Avenue, White Horse Business Park,
Trowbridge, Wiltshire BA14 0XQ
Website: *www.cdrc.org.uk*

Consensus Action on Salt and Health
Blood Pressure Unit, St George's Hospital, Cranmer Terrace, London
SW17 ORE
Website: *www.actiononsalt.org.uk*

Core
3 St Andrews Place, London NW1 4LB
Website: *www.digestivedisorders.org.uk*

Diabetes UK
Macleod House, 10 Parkway, London NW1 7AA
Website: *www.diabetes.org.uk*

Drinkaware Trust
7-10 Chandos Street, London W1G 9DQ
Website: *www.portmangrouptrust.org.uk*

Health contacts *cont.*

Eating Disorders Association
103 Prince of Wales Road, Norwich NR1 1DW
Website: *www.edauk.com*

General Medical Council
Regent's Place, 350 Euston Road, London NW1 3JN
Website: *www.gmc-uk.org*

Health Education Trust
18 High Street, Broom, Alcester, Warwickshire B50 4HJ
Website: *www.healthedtrust.com*

Health Professions Council
Park House, 184 Kennington Park Road, London SE11 4BU
Website: *www.hpc-uk.org*

Infant and Dietetic Foods Association
Federation House, 6 Catherine Street, London WC2B 5JJ
Website: *www.idfa.org.uk*

International Association for Food Protection
6200 Aurora Avenue, Suite 200W, Des Moines, IA 50322-2864 USA
Website: *www.foodprotection.org*

International Association for the Study of Obesity
231 North Gower Street, London NW1 2NR
Website: *www.iaso.org*

National Association for Colitis and Crohns Disease
4 Beaumont House, Sutton Road, St Albans, Herts AL1 5HH
Website: *www.nacc.org.uk*

The Obesity Awareness and Solutions Trust
The Latton Bush Centre, Southern Way, Harlow, Essex CM18 7BL
Website: *www.toast-uk.org.uk*

Rowett Research Institute
Greenburn Road, Bucksburn, Aberdeen, AB21 9SB
Website: *www.rowett.ac.uk*

Vegan Society
D Watson House, 7 Battle Road, St-Leonards-on-sea, East Sussex TN37 7AA
Website: *www.vegansociety.com*

Vegetarian Society
Parkdale, Dunham Road, Altrincham, Cheshire WA14 4QG
Website: *www.vegsoc.org*